Science Teachers' Knowledge Development

Cultural and Historical Perspectives on Science Education

DISTINGUISHED CONTRIBUTORS

Series Editors

Catherine Milne (*New York University, USA*)
Kathryn Scantlebury (*University of Delaware, USA*)

VOLUME 8

The titles published in this series are listed at *brill.com/psec*

Science Teachers' Knowledge Development

By

Jan van Driel

BRILL

LEIDEN | BOSTON

All chapters in this book have undergone peer review.

The Library of Congress Cataloging-in-Publication Data is available online at https://catalog.loc.gov

Typeface for the Latin, Greek, and Cyrillic scripts: "Brill". See and download: brill.com/brill-typeface.

ISSN 2589-6202
ISBN 978-90-04-50544-5 (paperback)
ISBN 978-90-04-39368-4 (hardback)
ISBN 978-90-04-50545-2 (e-book)

Copyright 2022 by Koninklijke Brill NV, Leiden, The Netherlands, except where stated otherwise.
Koninklijke Brill NV incorporates the imprints Brill, Brill Nijhoff, Brill Hotei, Brill Schöningh, Brill Fink, Brill mentis, Vandenhoeck & Ruprecht, Böhlau Verlag and V&R Unipress.
All rights reserved. No part of this publication may be reproduced, translated, stored in a retrieval system, or transmitted in any form or by any means, electronic, mechanical, photocopying, recording or otherwise, without prior written permission from the publisher. Requests for re-use and/or translations must be addressed to Koninklijke Brill NV via brill.com or copyright.com.

This book is printed on acid-free paper and produced in a sustainable manner.

Contents

Preface IX
List of Figures and Tables XII
About the Author XIV

1 **Developing Science Teachers' Pedagogical Content Knowledge** 1
  1 Why I Conducted the Study 1
  2 Context 2
  3 Impact and Follow Up 5
  Developing Science Teachers' Pedagogical Content Knowledge, by Jan H. van Driel, Nico Verloop and Wobbe de Vos (reprinted article) 7

2 **Professional Development and Reform in Science Education: The Role of Teachers' Practical Knowledge** 38
  1 How This Article Came About 38
  2 Content and Context 39
  3 Impact and Follow Up 41
  Professional Development and Reform in Science Education: The Role of Teachers' Practical Knowledge, by Jan H. van Driel, Douwe Beijaard and Nico Verloop (reprinted article) 44

3 **Teacher Knowledge and the Knowledge Base of Teaching** 73
  1 How This Article Came About 73
  2 What the Article Is About 73
  3 Impact and Follow Up 75
  Teacher Knowledge and the Knowledge Base of Teaching, by Nico Verloop, Jan van Driel and Paulien Meijer (reprinted article) 78

4 **Teachers' Knowledge of Models and Modelling in Science** 102
  1 Why I Conducted the Study 102
  2 Context 103
  3 Reflection and Follow Up 105
  Teachers' Knowledge of Models and Modelling in Science, by Jan H. van Driel and Nico Verloop (reprinted article) 109

5 Development of Experienced Science Teachers' Pedagogical Content Knowledge of Models of the Solar System and the Universe   125
  1 How the Study Came About   125
  2 How the Study Was Conducted …   126
  3 … And What Was Found   127
  4 Reflection and Follow Up   129
     Development of Experienced Science Teachers' Pedagogical Content Knowledge of Models of the Solar System and the Universe, by Ineke Henze, Jan H. van Driel and Nico Verloop (reprinted article)   132

6 The Development of Preservice Chemistry Teachers' Pedagogical Content Knowledge   157
  1 How the Study Came About   157
  2 Reflection and Follow Up   159
  3 Next Steps   162
     The Development of Preservice Chemistry Teachers' Pedagogical Content Knowledge, by Jan H. van Driel, Onno De Jong and Nico Verloop (reprinted article)   165

7 The Conceptions of Chemistry Teachers about Teaching and Learning in the Context of a Curriculum Innovation   192
  1 How the Study Came About   192
  2 Impact and Follow Up   195
     The Conceptions of Chemistry Teachers about Teaching and Learning in the Context of a Curriculum Innovation, by Jan H. van Driel, Astrid M. W. Bulte and Nico Verloop (reprinted article)   199

8 Taking a Closer Look at Science Teaching Orientations   226
  1 How the Article Came About   226
  2 What the Article Is About   227
  3 Impact and Follow Up   229
     Taking a Closer Look at Science Teaching Orientations, by Patrica Friedrichsen, Jan H. van Driel and Sandra K. Abell (reprinted article)   233

9 Professional Learning of Science Teachers   260
  1 How the Chapter Came About   260
  2 Follow Up   262
     Professional Learning of Science Teachers, by Jan H. van Driel (reprinted article)   265

10 **Attention to Intentions: How to Stimulate Strong Intentions to Change** 288
    1   How the Article Came About 288
    2   What Is the Article About 291
    3   Follow Up 292
        Attention to Intentions – How to Stimulate Strong Intentions to Change, by M. Dam, F. J. J. M. Janssen and J. H. van Driel (reprinted article) 294

Reflection 320

Index 327

Preface

> Educational change depends on what teachers do and think – it's as simple and as complex as that.
> FULLAN (2007, p. 129)

∴

In this volume, I focus on the academic work that I am best known for, that is, research on science teachers' knowledge and its development. Starting during my PhD in the late 1980s, I have conducted and supervised a number of studies on the knowledge and beliefs of in-service science teachers in the context of curriculum reform or innovation. Related to this, I have studied the pedagogical content knowledge (PCK) of pre-service science teachers and how it develops in the context of initial teacher education. The outcomes of these studies have been published in international journals since the late 1990s and many of these articles have resonated strongly with the international research community, which is reflected in high numbers of citations.

This volume is based on previously published work. Each of the following chapters has a similar structure. Preceding the reprint of a full article or chapter, I provide a commentary, consisting of (i) an explanation of why the research was conducted, or how the article came about, (ii) a sketch of the background to the study, such as the context in which it was done or the methodological issues underpinning it, and (iii) the impact of the article and what happened next. Typically, the commentary allows a view behind the curtain. Journal articles tend to follow a rather strict format, which suggests that research is a more or less linear and straightforward process. The commentary reveals some of the messiness, or how accidental, unplanned events sometimes influenced the course of a project.

Ten papers have been selected for this volume. The first three articles address some of the main conceptual ideas that informed most of my research. These articles review the literature on teacher practical knowledge and PCK and include examples from empirical studies. The next three papers focus on empirical studies on in-service and pre-service teachers' knowledge of models and modelling in science, including specific models of the universe and of the particulate nature of matter. These papers show how my research in this area evolved through multiple collaborations over a decade, starting in the late

1990s. The next paper describes a study of the beliefs of in-service chemistry teachers in the context of a national curriculum reform in the early 2000s. The following paper focuses on orientations to teaching science. It is the product of an international collaboration which significantly influenced my thinking about teachers' beliefs in relation to PCK. The last two papers discuss several more recent studies, conducted with postdocs and PhD candidates and focusing on professional learning of pre-service and in-service teachers of science in a variety of contexts. The research in these chapters contributed to broadening my views about studying teacher learning. In the final chapter, I reflect on my research and briefly review plans for future research.

I am the first author of six of the papers in this selection. Of only one of these, I am the sole author. Of the remaining papers, I am second or third author. First of all, this reflects my personal view that educational research requires multidisciplinary teamwork. All my studies and papers have benefited enormously from the input of different scholars, whether they were colleagues or students. Each one of the collaborators and co-authors brought their specific expertise to the project, either disciplinary knowledge or particular project or research skills. I enjoy working with and learning from people with backgrounds in different educational sectors and disciplines including biology, physics, mathematics, psychology, sociology and medical science. Second, there is an evolution in my research output, where I have become a second, third or fourth author more in the last decade than in the period before 2010. This is related to the progression in my career: as a full professor (or institute director) my role has increasingly shifted to mentoring colleagues and PhD candidates and writing together with them about research projects in which they did most of the work.

The narrative that connects these articles details my own development, from school teacher to PhD student into an academic career and becoming an international research leader. I will highlight how the ideas and collaborations with colleagues and students have shaped and continue to shape the course of my research trajectory. The selection of articles and chapters in this volume doesn't capture all my research interests and endeavours. Over the past 25 years, I have been involved in and have published about studies in a wide range of areas, including student learning and motivation, the nexus between teaching and research in higher education, peer feedback and self-regulated learning, language teaching and, more recently, science and gender and informal science learning. In particular, I have been and still am interested in research in higher education. I have supervised seven PhD candidates to completion in this area and published with all of them and their co-supervisors in international journals in that field. Across all these areas, the focus in the large majority of my research projects is on the role of teachers: their knowledge, beliefs and practices, and how these change in a specific context.

Underpinning my research in all these years has been my view that teachers should be seen as professionals, who are strongly committed to their students. I have always argued that each teacher should be considered as an individual who brings specific strengths and qualities to education and whose ideas and expectations regarding teaching and learning need to be recognised as a starting point for change. This contrasts with the deficit-driven approaches to teacher development which are common in many countries, aimed to 'fix' or 'upskill' teacher, preferably as quick and cheap as possible. Similarly, I prefer to see each student as an individual with capabilities, rather than as a member of a specific subgroup with particular deficits.

From a methodological perspective, I don't have a particular stance, other than that the design of a study should be fit for purpose. If you are interested in the beliefs of a large population of teachers, a survey design incorporating a questionnaire is probably appropriate and a sophisticated statistical approach to data analysis may be necessary to answer your research questions. However, if your main interest is the process of knowledge construction or development, you might need to apply a combination of instruments (such as interviews, (video) observations, thinking aloud) to follow a small group of people over a certain period of time. In my research, I have applied all the above techniques, and more, as is evident from the selection of papers in this volume. I am not an expert in a particular approach to data collection or analysis, and I enjoy continuing to learn from each new study and from my collaborators.

Over the course of my career, I have been incredibly fortunate to meet and work with fantastic colleagues and students. With many of them I have co-authored publications and quite a few became good friends. Some have passed away and some have retired, while others are thriving. In particular, I'd like to thank Wobbe de Vos, Nico Verloop, Douwe Beijaard, Onno de Jong, Rosária Justi, John Gilbert, Sandra Abell, Pat Friedrichsen, William Veal, Amanda Berry, John Loughran, David Clarke, Pernilla Nilsson, Ineke Henze, and Fred Janssen for their inspiration, guidance, wisdom and friendship over many years.

Reference

Fullan, M. (2007). *The new meaning of educational change* (4th ed.). Teachers College Press.

Figures and Tables

Figures

5.1   Type A of PCK.   150
5.2   Type B of PCK.   152
8.1   PCK model for science teaching (simplified version) (from Magnusson et al., 1999, p. 99; adapted with permission).   236
9.1   A model of teacher change (Guskey, 1986).   266
9.2   The interconnected model of teacher professional growth (Clarke & Hollingsworth, 2002, p. 951).   268
9.3   The development of T1's PCK about the production of teaching models.   273
9.4   The development of T3's PCK about the use of teaching models.   274
9.5   Pictorial representations of development of knowledge of instructional strategies.   280
10.1 Graphical representation of the theory of planned behavior. Behavior is influenced by intentions, which in turn are underpinned by three categories of beliefs (Fishbein & Ajzen, 2010).   298

Tables

1.1   Knowledge components in different conceptualizations of pedagogical content knowledge.   11
3.1   Clusters of teachers with different practical knowledge about teaching reading comprehension.   87
4.1   Scales within the Likert-type scale questionnaire on models and modelling, and sample items.   118
4.2   Scores of clusters 1 and 2 on the three scales: means (M), standard deviations (SD) and differences between the means (Diff. means).   120
5.1   PUSC as a framework to improve students' understanding of science.   135
5.2   General phrasings of the interview questions.   138
5.3   Codes applied to the teachers' interview responses (2002).   141
5.4   PCK Types A and B (2002).   143
6.1   Differences in the answers of the preservice teachers to the two questionnaires.   174
6.2   Growth of the preservice teachers' PCK inferred from interview data.   177
7.1   Examples of items in Part 2 of the questionnaire.   207
7.2   Scales and examples of items in Part 3 of the questionnaire.   208

7.3	General characteristics of the respondents.	212
7.4	Mean score, standard deviations, and values of Cronbach's alpha for the scales in Part 2.	212
7.5	Pearson correlations between the scales in Part 2 and Part 3.	214
7.6	Mean score, standard deviations, and values of Cronbach's alpha for the scales in Part 3.	215
7.7	Rotated component matrix.	216
7.8	Mean scores of the clusters on the scales in Part 2 and Part 3.	217
9.1	Identification of the types of teachers' change for each of the aspects (CS change sequence, GN growth network).	272
9.2	Demographics of the in-service teachers participating in the study.	278
10.1	Details of participants.	303
10.2	Survey of lesson segments used in this research.	304
10.3	Survey of intentions in the baseline test and the MECI.	307

About the Author

Jan van Driel was born in 1959. He is a Professor of Science Education and leader of the Mathematics, Science & Technology Education Group in the Melbourne Graduate School of Education (MGSE) at the University of Melbourne. His research interests include science teacher knowledge, teacher education and professional learning, science and gender, and interdisciplinary science and STEM education. Currently, he is co-Editor-in-Chief of the *International Journal of Science Education* and a member of the executive board of the Australasian Science Education Research Association (ASERA) and the Education Committee of Council of the Australian Academy of Science (AAS). In addition, he has been and is a member of the editorial boards of a range of international journals including *Journal of Teacher Education*, *Review of Educational Research*, *Science Education*, *Journal of Research in Science Teaching*. He has served on the boards of a number of associations for educational research in the Netherlands and the USA. In 2018, he was identified as national field leader in Education by *The Australian*. In 2021, he received the MGSE Research Excellence Award.

After obtaining a Master's degree in chemistry (1984), Jan worked as a teacher of chemistry in a secondary school. He did a PhD at Utrecht University, the Netherlands, which focused on the teaching and learning of chemical equilibrium (1990). From 1995–2016, he worked at ICLON – Leiden University Graduate School of Teaching. In 2006 he was appointed full professor of science education. From 2010–2016, he was the director of ICLON, until moving to the University of Melbourne in September 2016. From 2017–2020, he was Associate Dean-Research of the Melbourne Graduate School of Education (MGSE).

Jan has developed international profiles in three different areas of educational research: science education, teaching & teacher education, and higher education. In all of these three domains, he supervised PhD students, and published in the respective top journals. He is regarded as one of the leading scholars in the world in research on teachers' pedagogical content knowledge (PCK). He published several highly cited articles about this topic and has been invited to give talks and workshops about this topic all over the world. As a former schoolteacher, he holds the view that an educational researcher should be engaged in issues of practice and policy. Therefore, he published since 1987 in professional journals for teachers and continues to give lectures and workshops at conferences for teachers, teacher educators, and at schools. To date, Jan's research output includes 111 international and 24 national refereed journal articles, two co-edited books, 38 book chapters, and 53 professional publications (teacher journals, reports). Taken together, these outputs have attracted nearly 15,000 citations, resulting in a Google scholar h-index of 55 (September 2021).

CHAPTER 1

Developing Science Teachers' Pedagogical Content Knowledge

1 Why I Conducted the Study

This article originates from the research that I conducted for my PhD thesis. When I started to work as a chemistry teacher in grades 9–12 in the Netherlands in the early 1980s, I was driven by the ambition to teach chemistry in ways that would engage my students. I didn't expect all of them to share my fascination for chemistry, but I wanted them to understand the meaning of basic chemical ideas and the relevance of this understanding for their personal lives. However, despite my efforts and enthusiasm, many students did not seem convinced. Even if their achievements on tests were good or excellent, they would raise questions about why they had to learn certain topics, or what the purpose of doing chemical experiments was.

These experiences inspired me to embark on a PhD at Utrecht University. I wanted to understand the chemistry learning experiences of students, especially in grades 9 and 10, and use this understanding to develop and trial an alternative approach to teaching chemistry and investigate the student experiences related to this approach. The study was set up as what was labelled 'developmental research' (Lijnse, 1995), that is, it consisted of cycles of designing, implementing and researching a unit on a particular topic from the curriculum. For a number of reasons, chemical equilibrium in grade 10 was chosen as the focus of this unit. I conducted a pilot study focusing on student conceptions of relevant topics and a literature study on the teaching and learning of chemical equilibrium, and working with my main supervisor Wobbe De Vos, I developed a first version of a unit of about 10 to 12 lessons. The pedagogical approach was based on constructivist theory and included conceptual change strategies. Each section of the unit consisted of a number of tasks, including chemical experiments, and students worked in groups of three or four on these tasks. The teacher's role was to provide just-in-time support to the groups through hints, suggestions or asking questions, rather than giving explanations or solutions.

The first cycle was conducted in the school where I still worked part-time and one other school. My colleagues were willing to implement the first version of the unit in their grade 10 classes. I sat in many lessons, observed and recorded the discussions that took place in some of the student groups, including the occasional interactions with their teacher, and collected the written work (i.e., their consensual responses to the tasks) of as many student groups as possible. I fondly remember the enthusiasm of some of the students, trying to explain the unexpected outcomes of the chemical experiments in the unit. For the second and third cycle, the number of participating schools expanded to 11 and 25, respectively. The idea behind this was that as the study progressed, a better understanding of teaching and learning processes would help to improve the unit through each cycle. Implementing the next version among a larger number of schools added rigour to the study. A detailed account of the study and its outcomes was published in the *International Journal of Science Education* (Van Driel, De Vos, Verloop, & Dekkers, 1998).

Inherent to this approach was that with each cycle more teachers implemented the unit in their classrooms. To support them, I wrote a teacher guide to accompany the unit. Also, De Vos and I set up a professional development program which consisted of four meetings: two preceding, one during and one after the implementation of the unit. Although my study was mostly focused on the student experience, I decided – with consent of the participating teachers – to audio record these meetings. In hindsight, this was a crucial decision! The discussions with and between the teachers would reveal many aspects of their professional expertise, such as their chemical content knowledge, their pedagogical beliefs and values about teaching and learning in general, or specific to chemistry, and their often very specific ideas and experiences related to the teaching and learning of chemical equilibrium.

During the meetings, usually attended by ten to twenty teachers, we would encourage them to talk about their past experiences of teaching chemical equilibrium and compare these with their experiences with 'my' unit. The most fascinating moments occurred when a teacher gave a detailed account of a classroom event, including observations of students and strategies they had applied to support student learning. Often this would inspire others to tell their stories about similar events and explain their interventions. Since discussions like this were relevant to the focus of my study, I decided to transcribe and analyse those parts of the recordings. Some of these data were included in my thesis, typically in combination with data from students related to the same aspect of chemical equilibrium, such as the concept of reversible chemical reactions.

2   Context

It must be noted that this work took place between 1986 and 1990, when I completed my thesis. As I was focused on the teaching and learning of specific chemistry content, my reading of the research literature was concentrated on studies with this focus. The bibliography in my thesis is dominated by publications in chemistry and chemistry education and only included a handful of references to literature on constructivism, educational psychology and methodology. At the time, I wasn't aware of the emerging literature on teacher thinking and teacher knowledge, nor was any of my supervisors.

After finishing my PhD, I accepted a position at Delft University of Technology. My job concentrated on developing and providing training and advice to university lecturers, mostly engineers who were teaching large classes in undergraduate programs without a degree or background in education. Through this work, I became more sensitised to and interested in understanding teachers' experiences, views and values. The job included a small time fraction to do research, which enabled me to conduct a few short studies on professional development of university teachers. These studies were published in local journals.

It was not until I obtained a position at the Leiden University Graduate School of Teaching in 1995 that research on teachers and teacher education became a major focus in my work. The graduate school had recently been established to boost teacher education and professional development for in-service teachers at Leiden University. The director of the school, Professor Nico Verloop, had set up a new research program called *The knowledge base of teaching* alongside these activities and my role in this program was to do research in the domain of science education. As part of my induction in the program, I read a large number of seminal papers and handbook chapters on teacher knowledge and beliefs, teacher thinking and teacher learning or development. Among these were the papers by Lee Shulman (1986, 1987) in which he introduced the concept pedagogical content knowledge (PCK).

Reading these papers reminded me of the conversations I'd had with a senior colleague, Tom van Eck, during my first year as a teacher in the early 1980s. Tom was an experienced chemistry teacher who volunteered to mentor me. We met about once per week and often our conversations focused on my recent or upcoming classes. Tom impressed me with his detailed knowledge of student learning of chemistry: he could explain how students might respond to specific tasks, or questions they might ask related to an experiment. He would emphasise the differences between students and explain how his strategies to support student learning would work well in some situations and for some students, but not all that well for others or in other situations. He would give me advice, but never in a prescriptive manner. It was now, more than a decade after these conversations took place, that I realised Tom had very rich pedagogical content knowledge.

Around the same time, I was discussing research plans and publishing opportunities with Nico Verloop, who was my supervisor and an international expert in research on teacher knowledge. Given its focus on the teaching and learning of specific content, pedagogical content knowledge came up as a central concept to frame future studies. Also, looking at research I had done in the past, I realised that PCK offered an interesting perspective to the data I had collected in the context of the teacher professional development meetings during my PhD study. We decided to work together with Wobbe De Vos on a paper that would provide an overview of PCK research to date, focusing on studies in the domain of science education. It quickly appeared that PCK had been conceptualised by scholars in ways that differed from the original ideas of Shulman. Specifically, authors extended the scope of PCK by adding knowledge components to those proposed as the core of PCK by Shulman, that is, "the ways of representing and formulating the subject that make it comprehensible to others" and "an understanding of what makes the learning of specific topics easy or difficult" (Shulman, 1986, p. 9). Our review of published PCK research, as it turned out, demonstrated that many studies did not really focus on the teaching and learning of specific content but had a much broader orientation. Referring to Shulman's ideas, we argued that this undermined the essence of the construct.

To address this issue, we decided to present an example of an empirical study of teachers' PCK of a specific topic, that is chemical equilibrium, and included some of the unpublished data from my PhD thesis for this purpose. The gist of the study was to demonstrate how the combination of implementing the unit in their classes and discussing their experiences with other teachers had contributed to teachers explicating and developing their PCK. Specifically related to Shulman's core components, they expressed an increased awareness of student learning of chemical equilibrium and specific difficulties and misconceptions related to this topic. Also, they spoke about specific teaching strategies or interventions that contributed to student understanding. Obviously, the outcomes were different for individual teachers.

We decided to submit the manuscript to the *Journal of Research in Science Teaching*, in the first place because no less than 18 out of the 68 references in the manuscript were published in this journal. Related to this, we were aware that PCK was a trending topic in research on science education in the USA more than elsewhere, and we recognised that the *Journal of Research in Science Teaching* was the most prestigious American journal in the field. Being aware that this status implied a high rejection rate, we certainly did not expect our manuscript to be accepted. I remember it took forever before we heard from the editor (note that in those days all correspondence still occurred via regular mail), but when the reviews finally arrived, we were excited to be given a chance to revise the manuscript. There were 14 months between the submission of the initial and the revised manuscript, which was accepted promptly. It was one of the first articles I published in an international journal.

3 Impact and Follow Up

The impact of this article has been massive in ways that I could never have anticipated. It is not an exaggeration to state that it established my international reputation as a science education researcher. To date, the article has been cited over 1,800 times (Google Scholar). It is listed as #19 of most cited papers published in the *Journal of Research in Science Teaching* (since 1963). Citations grew steadily and didn't peak until 2016 (159 citations), down to 105 in 2020. For many years, it featured among the journal's most downloaded papers.

More important than these numbers, scholars began to contact me after the publication of this article. This resulted in meetings at international conferences, such as NARST ('A global organization for improving science education through research') and ESERA (European Science Education Research Association), with colleagues who were doing research on science teacher knowledge and development. Some of these meetings subsequently led to international collaborations and invitations to give keynotes and, over time, to several professional friendships. To name just two of these, Professors Sandra Abell (University of Missouri-Columbia, USA) and John Loughran (Monash University, Australia) have been very important to me. Their research on science teacher knowledge, and their views and ideas on science education more broadly, influenced me and my future work significantly. Moreover, both of them introduced me to colleagues and research students, which led to further collaborations, including a Special Issue on science teachers' PCK for the *International Journal of Science Education* (Berry, Loughran, & Van Driel, 2008). Both Sandra and John visited my institute in Leiden and invited me to visit theirs. These visits, again, inspired new collaborative projects and outputs (e.g., Friedrichsen, Van Driel, & Abell, 2011, see Chapter 8; Berry & Van Driel, 2013).

It is not easy to understand why this particular article has attracted so much attention. Reading it today, it seems a bit dated and the writing, certainly, is a bit naïve. I think the paper carried an important message regarding research on PCK. It reminded the readers that the essence of the construct – according to Shulman – was its focus on the teaching and learning of specific content and it showed that research on PCK in the decade that had passed since Shulman's seminal papers had more or less lost that focus. The empirical study, based on my PhD thesis, probably presented an example of what research on PCK could look like if it did focus on a specific topic.

The article has shaped several of my later research projects and those of my PhD students. For instance, the studies I conducted in collaboration with Onno De Jong and Rosária Justi among cohorts of pre-service science teachers built on the ideas laid out in this article (see Chapter 6). The PhD studies from Ineke Henze, Pernilla Nilsson and Dirk Wongsopawiro investigated PCK development and were strongly related to the conceptual and methodological perspectives in the article, that is, the focus on teaching and learning of specific subject matter and the importance to capture teachers' voices.

It is worth noting that my research, starting with my PhD, is firmly rooted in the European 'Didaktik' tradition of education research in which the reciprocal interactions between teachers, learners and content are front and central (see, for instance, Meyer & Rakhkochkine, 2018). Being aware that the term 'didactic' has specific connotations in the English-speaking world, we decided not to refer to this tradition explicitly in the article. However, there are certain parallels between PCK and what would be called 'vakdidactische kennis' in Dutch ('content didactical knowledge'). This is not the place to elaborate on those parallels; the interested reader is referred to Kansanen (2009). As a footnote, it may be interesting to mention that *not* referring to 'Didaktik' led me to being heavily criticised by some of the professors in the group where I did my PhD. They argued that I should have written the article from a 'Didaktik' perspective and discuss PCK in relation to that tradition; by not mentioning 'Didaktik' at all, I had 'betrayed my roots'. I may have been the first European scholar who applied their Didaktik background – implicitly – to PCK and used PCK as a lens to portray the expertise of science teachers related to teaching particular content. Apparently, I did it at the right time and I chose the right outlet. To me, the article is a gift that never stopped giving.

Developing Science Teachers' Pedagogical Content Knowledge[1]

Jan H. van Driel, Nico Verloop and Wobbe de Vos

Abstract

This article discusses the concept of pedagogical content knowledge (PCK) within the context of science teaching. First, an attempt is made to define this concept within the tradition of research on teachers' craft knowledge and to identify possible purposes of research on PCK. From this point of view, recent research on science teaching is investigated. This investigation identifies teaching experience as the major source of PCK, whereas adequate subject-matter knowledge appears to be a prerequisite. Finally, an empirical study is presented which focuses on PCK with respect to a specific topic – that is, chemical equilibrium. The effects on teachers' PCK of participation in an in-service workshop and conducting an experimental course in classroom practice are reported. This leads to the identification of elements of PCK teachers can use to promote student understanding. It is concluded that research on topic-related PCK may complement research on student learning of specific topics.

The concept of pedagogical content knowledge (PCK) was introduced by Shulman in a paper in which he argued that research on teaching and teacher education has undeservedly ignored research questions dealing with the content of the lessons taught (Shulman, 1986). The concept of PCK refers to teachers' interpretations and transformations of subject-matter knowledge in the context of facilitating student learning. Notably, PCK encompasses understanding of common learning difficulties and preconceptions of students. As many of the latter have been revealed by research on student learning, submitting PCK to scientific inquiry offers an opportunity to link research on teaching with research on learning.

This article revolves around the question of to what extent PCK has become or may become a valuable concept within the field of research on science teaching. The article consists of three main sections. First, we will concisely review the literature on teachers' craft knowledge and PCK with respect to teaching in general. This section mainly serves to clarify the concept of PCK and to identify possible purposes of research on PCK. The second section discusses the literature on teachers' craft knowledge and PCK within the domain of science education. Finally, in the third section, an example of an empirical study is presented. This study focuses on the development of teachers' PCK with respect to a specific topic (i.e., chemical equilibrium) within the context of an in-service program.

Background

Teachers' Craft Knowledge

In the past decade, attention in research on teaching and teacher education has shifted from observable behaviors or teaching skills to teachers' knowledge and beliefs. This shift was influenced by a growing dissatisfaction with the results of process-product research. Doyle (1990) argued that the focus in process-product research on indicators of effectiveness has led to a fragmented and mechanistic view of teaching in which the complexity of the teaching enterprise is not acknowledged. To understand why teachers behave as they do, it is necessary to investigate how teachers construct meaning in classroom settings (Doyle, 1990). Initially, research on teachers' knowledge and beliefs focused on teachers' thought processes (Clark & Peterson, 1986). More recently, the interest in teachers' practical knowledge (Carter, 1990) or craft knowledge (Grimmett & MacKinnon, 1992) has increased. Although researchers differ in their research purposes and definitions, craft knowledge broadly refers to the knowledge teachers have with respect to their teaching practice. For some, research on craft knowledge implies the acknowledgment of the complex and the context specific nature of teaching, and may therefore contribute to the empowerment of teachers and to an enhancement of the status of teaching as a profession (Doyle, 1990).

The concept of craft knowledge has been the subject of controversy. Tom and Valli (1990) reviewed some major criticisms, such as the supposedly non-scientific nature of craft knowledge and the conservatism inherent in teaching practice. They suggested that the codification of craft knowledge, sensitive as it is to various contexts and contrasting conceptions of good teaching, might turn out to be "a contradiction in terms" (Tom & Valli, 1990, p. 390). Grimmett and MacKinnon (1992) tried to solve this dilemma by defining craft knowledge *not* as "a knowledge base as such, but as a framework for helping prospective and experienced teachers develop their repertoire of responses, understandings, and magical tricks" (p. 441). According to Grimmett and MacKinnon, the essence of craft knowledge pertains to a "teaching sensibility" rather than to "a knowledge of propositions" (p. 393).

In this article, we define craft knowledge as integrated knowledge which represents teachers' accumulated wisdom with respect to their teaching practice. As this knowledge guides the teachers' actions in practice, it encompasses teachers' knowledge and beliefs with respect to various aspects such as pedagogy, students, subject matter, and the curriculum. Although deeply rooted in teachers' practical work, craft knowledge is, in our view, not opposite theoretical or scientific knowledge. Instead, craft knowledge encompasses knowledge derived from prior education as well as from ongoing schooling activities (cf. Beijaard & Verloop, 1996). Moreover, craft knowledge is supposedly influenced by factors related to teachers' personal backgrounds and by the context in which they work (cf. Hoyle & John, 1995). As a consequence of this definition, research on craft knowledge cannot lead to the establishment of a knowledge base with a prescriptive nature. However, research on craft knowledge should attempt to surpass the idiosyncratic level of individual narratives. As for us, we are looking for common patterns in craft knowledge and in the development of this knowledge to develop "frameworks" in the sense of Grimmett and MacKinnon (1992). Moreover, we believe that research on craft knowledge can lead to the formation of a knowledge base which, although different in nature and content, may prove to be a vital addition to existing educational knowledge bases (cf. Verloop, 1992).

Shulman introduced PCK as a specific category of knowledge "which goes beyond knowledge of subject matter per se to the dimension of subject matter knowledge *for teaching*" (Shulman, 1986, p. 9). The key elements in Shulman's conception of PCK are knowledge of representations of subject matter on the one hand and understanding of specific learning difficulties and student conceptions on the other. Obviously, these elements are intertwined and should be used in a flexible manner: The more representations teachers have at their disposal and the better they recognize learning difficulties, the more effectively they can deploy their PCK.

In a later article, Shulman included PCK in what he called "the knowledge base for teaching". This knowledge base consists of seven categories, three of which are content related (i.e., content knowledge, PCK, and curriculum knowledge). The other four categories refer to general pedagogy, learners and their characteristics, educational contexts, and educational purposes (Shulman, 1987). Whereas Shulman's knowledge base encompasses every category of knowledge which may be relevant for teaching, our definition of craft knowledge is restricted to types of knowledge which actually guide the teachers' behavior during classroom practice. Within our own definition of craft knowledge (cf. previous section), we consider PCK to be a specific form of this craft knowledge. This is explained as follows. PCK implies a transformation of subject-matter knowledge, so that it can be used effectively and flexibly in the communication process between teachers and learners during classroom practice. Thus, teachers may derive PCK from their own teaching practice (e.g., analyzing specific learning difficulties) as well as from schooling activities (e.g., an in-service course on student conceptions). More important, when dealing with subject matter, teachers' actions will be determined to a large extent by their PCK, making PCK an essential component of craft knowledge.

Elaborating on Shulman's work, other scholars have adopted the two key elements of PCK mentioned above (i.e., knowledge of comprehensible representations of subject matter and understanding of content-related learning difficulties). Moreover, each of them has extended the concept by including in PCK some of the categories of knowledge distinct in Shulman's knowledge base for teaching. Table 1.1 summarizes the conceptualizations of PCK of various authors. For example, Grossman (1990) perceived PCK as consisting of knowledge of strategies and representations for teaching particular topics and knowledge of students' understanding, conceptions, and misconceptions of these topics (i.e., Shulman's two key elements). In addition, PCK is composed of knowledge and beliefs about the purposes for teaching particular topics and knowledge of curriculum materials available for teaching. In Grossman's model of teacher knowledge, PCK is at the heart surrounded by three related categories: namely, knowledge of subject matter, general pedagogical knowledge and contextual knowledge. Grossman identified the following sources from which PCK is generated and developed: (a) observation of classes, both as a student and as a student teacher, often leading to tacit and conservative PCK; (b) disciplinary education, which may lead to personal preferences for specific purposes or topics; (c) specific courses during teacher education, of which the impact is normally unknown; and (d)classroom teaching experience.

Marks (1990) also broadened Shulman's model by including in PCK knowledge of subject matter per se as well as knowledge of media for instruction. In a discussion of sources of PCK, however, Marks perceived the development of PCK as an integrative process revolving around the interpretation of subject-matter knowledge and the specification of general pedagogical knowledge, thereby focusing on Shulman's two key elements. Marks also discussed some ambiguities in PCK by presenting examples in which it is impossible to distinguish PCK from either subject-matter knowledge or general pedagogical knowledge.

Based on an explicit constructivist view of teaching, Cochran, DeRuiter, and King (1993) renamed PCK as pedagogical content *knowing* (PCKg) to acknowledge the dynamic nature of knowledge development. In their model, PCKg is conceptualized much broader than in Shulman's view. PCKg is defined as "a teacher's integrated understanding of four components of pedagogy, subject matter content, student characteristics, and the environmental context of learning" (Cochran et al., 1993, p. 266). Ideally, PCKg is generated as a synthesis from the simultaneous development of these four components.

The idea of integration of knowledge components is also central in the conceptualization of PCK by Fernandez-Balboa and Stiehl (1995). These authors

TABLE 1.1 Knowledge components in different conceptualizations of pedagogical content knowledge

Knowledge of:

Scholars	Subject matter	Representations and strategies	Student Learning and conceptions	General pedagogy	Curriculum and media	Context	Purposes
Shulman (1987)	a	PCK	PCK	a	a	a	a
Grossman (1990)	a	PCK	PCK	a	PCK	a	PCK
Marks (1990)	PCK	PCK	PCK	b	PCK	b	b
Cochran, et al. (1993)	PCKg	b	PCKg	PCKg	b	PCKg	b
Fernandez-Balboa & Stiehl (1995)	PCK	PCK	PCK	b	b	PCK	PCK

a Distinct category in the knowledge base for teaching.
b Not discussed explicitly.

identified five knowledge components of PCK: subject matter, the students, instructional strategies, the teaching context, and one's teaching purposes.

The preceding discussion was not meant to be exhaustive. Instead, we have tried to demonstrate that there is no universally accepted conceptualization of PCK. Between scholars, differences occur with respect to the elements they include or integrate in PCK, and to specific labels or descriptions of these elements. Yet, we suggest that all scholars agree on Shulman's two key elements – that is, knowledge of representations of subject matter and understanding of specific learning difficulties and student conceptions. In addition, there appears to be agreement on the nature of PCK. First, as PCK refers to *particular topics*, it is to be discerned from knowledge of pedagogy, of educational purposes, and of learner characteristics in a general sense. Second, because PCK concerns the *teaching* of particular topics, it may turn out to differ considerably from subject-matter knowledge per se. Finally, all scholars suggest that PCK is developed through an integrative process rooted in classroom practice, implying that prospective or beginning teachers usually have little or no PCK at their disposal. This supports our view described above, that PCK is indeed a specific type of teachers' craft knowledge.

Purposes for Research on PCK
Concluding the discussion in this section Pedagogical Content Knowledge, we propose two main purposes for research on teachers' PCK:

1. As little is yet known about the ways teachers transform subject-matter knowledge, how they relate their transformations to student understanding, and how they develop these abilities, research on these themes is part of a "missing paradigm" (Shulman, 1986, p. 7).
2. To facilitate the development of prospective teachers' PCK and to prevent every teacher from reinventing the wheel, research on PCK may resolve a blind spot in both preservice and in-service teacher education (Verloop, 1992).

Research on Science Teachers' Craft Knowledge and Pedogical Content Knowledge

In this section, the focus of attention is shifted toward research in science teaching. Our aim is to determine to what extent research on science teaching has paid attention to science teachers' craft knowledge in the last decade. Rather than presenting an exhaustive review, it is our purpose to identify specific lines of research in the domain of science teaching *from a craft knowledge perspective*. This implies that studies which do not explicitly relate teachers' knowledge and beliefs to classroom practice are either omitted or not commented upon (however, see Anderson & Mitchener, 1994). Analogous to the previous section, we will start with a brief summary of recent research on science teachers' craft knowledge from a generic point of view. This summary revolves around studies on knowledge and beliefs about the nature of science, and about the teaching and learning of science. Next, we will discuss in more detail studies on science teachers' pedagogical content knowledge (cf. Tobin, Tippins, & Gallard, 1994). Included are some studies on science teachers' subject-matter knowledge in relation to teaching practice which do not explicitly refer to PCK. However, these studies are interpreted from a PCK perspective.

Science Teachers' Craft Knowledge
The Nature of Science

Research on science teachers' conceptions of the nature of science appears to have a long tradition (Lederman, 1992). In general, these studies amount to the conclusion that irrespective of their academic background, science teachers possess limited knowledge of the history and philosophy of science (King, 1991; Gallagher, 1991) and as a consequence, hold inadequate or naive conceptions of the nature of science (Abd-El-Khalick & BouJaoude, 1997). For example, many teachers appear to hold positivist views, believing that the substantive content of science is fixed and unchangeable rather than tentative. Pomeroy (1993), however, reported relatively many "nontraditional views" of science among science teachers as compared to scientists. She suggested that such views may result from both teachers' "actual practice with children" as well as from "a growing awareness of and commitment to constructivism among educators" (Pomeroy, 1993, p. 272). Yet, the influence of teachers' conceptions of the nature of science on classroom practice is not unambiguously ascertained, owing to "the strong influence of curriculum constraints, administrative policies, and teaching context on the translation of teachers' conceptions into classroom practice" (Lederman, 1992, p. 348).

The Teaching and Learning of Science

Many studies on teachers' conceptions of the teaching and learning of science have been conducted in the context of the implementation of a conceptual change approach. As constructivist epistemology is based upon specific assumptions regarding the nature of knowledge and knowledge acquisition, the implementation of a conceptual change approach may have far-reaching consequences for teachers (Prawat, 1992). In this context, teachers' beliefs about teaching and learning appear to have a pervasive influence on classroom practice (Appleton & Asoko, 1996). Studies focus either on the effects of in-service (Constable & Long, 1991; Porlan Ariza & Garda Gomez, 1992; Hand & Treagust, 1994) or preservice programs (Hewson & Hewson, 1987, 1989; Stofflett, 1994) or on the actual implementation in classroom practice (Johnston, 1991; Briscoe, 1991; Cronin-Jones, 1991; Glasson & Lalik, 1993; Tobin, 1993). Both in-service and preservice training programs are reported to result in changes in the participants' conceptions of teaching and learning science. Specifically, conceptual change strategies are adopted as they are found to be intelligible or attractive. When it comes to the implementation of such strategies in classroom practice, however, problems are reported. Teachers' existing belief structures (Cronin-Jones, 1991) or their commitment to the existing curriculum (Johnston, 1991) or their colleagues (Tobin, 1993) are among the factors that can hinder the implementation. Discrepancies between conceptions teachers express and their actual classroom behavior are observed (Briscoe, 1991; Johnston, 1991). However, some case studies claim distinct, although subtle changes in both teachers' conceptions and their classroom practice toward constructivist ideas. These changes seem to take place on the conditions that sufficient time and professional support are available (Glasson & Lalik, 1993; Tobin, 1993; Appleton & Asoko, 1996). For that matter, these results themselves seem congruent with the basics of constructivist epistemology.

Relations between the Nature of Science and the Teaching and Learning of Science

Another group of studies investigated relations between science teachers' conceptions of the nature of science and their knowledge and beliefs about the teaching and learning of science. Studies in which teachers' conceptions are explicitly connected with their actual teaching practice reveal an apparent distinction between experienced teachers and prospective or beginning teachers. Experienced teachers appear to have developed a conceptual framework in which knowledge and beliefs about science, subject matter, teaching and learning, and students are interrelated in a coherent manner, while their teaching behavior seems consistent with this framework (Brickhouse, 1990). However, individual teachers may have developed quite different frameworks or "functional paradigms", even when they teach the same curriculum (Lantz & Kass, 1987). Tobin and McRobbie (1996) described four "cultural myths" that determine an experienced science teacher's classroom practice. Among others, these myths refer to the transmission of knowledge and the maintenance of the rigor of the curriculum. From an innovative point of view, these myths are perceived as conservative forces.

For beginning and prospective science teachers, a different picture emerges. These teachers often seem to experience conflicts between their personal views of science and science teaching on the one hand and their own actual classroom practice on the other (Brickhouse & Bodner, 1992). Moreover, their personal views sometimes show internal conflicts and their classroom practice may be variable. Powell (1994) identified some constraints in this respect, such as an influential and conservative cooperating teacher, unrealistic expectations about students' motivation, and insufficient laboratory facilities. Roberts and Chastko (1990) studied beginning science teacher thinking in relation to reflective capability. The latter seemed to vary considerably. Moreover, the authors were hardly successful in developing this capability.

Summary. Summarizing the above, it appears that within research on science teachers' craft knowledge so far, many studies focus on teachers' conceptions of the teaching and learning of science. In some studies, these conceptions are related to conceptions about the nature of science. The latter studies reveal a significant distinction between experienced teachers and prospective or beginning teachers.

Science Teachers' Pedagogical Content Knowledge

In a number of studies, teaching practice was investigated as a function of familiarity with a specific domain. These studies lead to similar results, indicating that teachers, when teaching unfamiliar topics, have little knowledge of potential student problems and specific preconceptions, and have difficulties selecting appropriate representations of subject matter. Moreover, when teaching unfamiliar topics, teachers express more misconceptions (Hashweh, 1987) and they talk longer and more often, and mainly pose questions of low cognitive level (Carlsen, 1993). In only one of these studies (Sanders, Borko, & Lockard, 1993), these results are interpreted in terms of PCK rather than subject-matter knowledge. It is stated that experienced science teachers, when teaching a topic out of their area of certification, seem to be sustained by their wealth of general pedagogical knowledge, while their PCK is limited. The authors also noticed that experienced teachers quickly learn the new content as well as adequate content-specific instructional strategies, while relying on their knowledge of general pedagogy. The latter helps them to maintain the flow in their classes. The authors concluded that pedagogical knowledge provides a framework for teaching that is "filled in by content knowledge and pedagogical content knowledge ... when teachers taught within and outside their science area" (Sanders et al., 1993, p. 733).

Smith and Neale (1989) studied the effects of an in-service workshop – that is, a summer program for elementary teachers – that focused upon the implementation of conceptual change strategies in science teaching. The program offered opportunities to practice these strategies in a science summer camp. The authors conclude that the program was particularly successful in promoting teachers' knowledge of specific contents. Also, beliefs about the nature of science changed toward constructivist views. However, Smith and Neale reported only marginal success with respect to the development of PCK. This is explained by the fact that participants were still constructing a "deeply principled conceptual knowledge of the content" (Smith & Neale, 1989, p. 17), the latter apparently being perceived as a prerequisite for the development of PCK.

Leinhardt and Smith (1985) investigated the subject-matter knowledge of expert teachers in elementary mathematics. They chose a difficult topic – fractions – and investigated teachers' subject-matter knowledge of this topic by means of interviews and card-sorting tasks as well as observations of lessons. The authors reported that although expert teachers may seem quite similar in their knowledge of subject matter per se, their classroom presentations of it may differ substantially. The identification of these differences is considered to be a potential source for "in-service support that is tied to lesson presentation rather than to independent thematic issues" (Leinhardt & Smith, 1985, p. 269). As the results of this study, which predated Shulman's introduction of the concept of PCK, refer to differences in the ways teachers transform and present subject matter in relation to student difficulties, they can be interpreted in terms of differences in PCK.

In two partially overlapping studies, Clermont, Krajcik, and Borko (1993, 1994) investigated chemistry teachers' PCK with respect to chemical demonstrations as an instructional strategy. The second study compared PCK of experienced and novice demonstrators, concluding that experienced teachers possess a greater repertoire of representations and strategies when demonstrating a particular topic. Moreover, they are able to use certain demonstrations more flexibly for various purposes, and they can relate their demonstrations more effectively to student learning than novices. In the first study, the effects on PCK of an in-service workshop for novice demonstrators were investigated. As growth of novices' PCK toward that of experienced demonstrators was observed the authors concluded that PCK "can be enhanced through intensive, short-term, skills-oriented workshops" (Clermont et al., 1993, p. 41).

Adams and Krockover (1997), who studied the development of beginning science teachers' PCK, found that knowledge of instructional strategies was derived both from experiences as a learner and as a teacher or teaching assistent. Knowledge development appeared to be dominated by individual and contextual factors. This resulted, however, among others, in the adoption of conventional instructional strategies, stressing procedures instead of student understanding.

Geddis (1993) studied the transformation of preservice science teachers' subject-matter knowledge into "teachable content knowledge". According to Geddis, PCK plays a critical role in this transformation process. This conclusion was based on a vignette in which a discussion among preservice teachers about students' misconceptions (viz. about electrical current) in comparison to their own views appeared to promote the development of subject-matter representations and instructional strategies.

The transformation of subject-matter knowledge in the context of preservice science teacher education was also studied by Lederman and coworkers. In one of their studies, the subject-matter structures of preservice biology teachers were investigated during a year of professional teacher education (Gess-Newsome & Lederman, 1993). These knowledge structures appeared to be mainly derived from college science coursework. While these structures were often vague and fragmented on entering teacher education, they developed toward more coherent and integrated views of biology during teacher education. Most important, however, was the observation that the translation of these subject-matter structures into classroom practice appeared to be complicated by classroom complexity. The authors suggested that until a teacher has gained experience and masters basic classroom skills, it may be unrealistic to expect a readily accessible and useful translation of subject-matter knowledge into classroom practice. In another study of knowledge development during teacher education, Lederman, Gess-Newsome, and Latz (1994) investigated the self-reported changes in preservice science teachers' conceptions of subject matter and pedagogy. Although distinct changes in both knowledge domains seem to take place mainly as a result of teaching experiences, preservice teachers appear not to integrate these domains. Again, the authors explained that this results from a lack of teaching experience, suggesting that "with the benefit of experience and continual use of one's subject matter structure for purposes of teaching, the division between pedagogical knowledge and subject matter knowledge may become blurred" (Lederman et al., 1994, p. 143). Thus, the development of PCK may be postponed until teachers reach this stage.

Summary. Summarizing the research on science teachers' PCK, it appears that familiarity with a specific topic in combination with teaching experience positively contributes to PCK. Moreover, general pedagogical knowledge may constitute a supporting framework for the development of PCK. Experienced science teachers' PCK may differ considerably, even when their subject-matter knowledge is similar and when they teach the same curriculum. These differences appear from the use of different representations and instructional strategies during classroom practice.

Conclusions from the Literature

We explained in the introduction to this section that we would review the literature on science teaching, looking for studies which contribute to an understanding of science teachers' craft knowledge. Specifically, our interest concerns the application of the concept of pedagogical content knowledge in this domain. We observed numerous studies in which science teachers' knowledge and beliefs are explicitly related to teachers' classroom practice. The impact of constructivist epistemology seems to be important in this respect. As constructivism emphasizes the role of previous experience in knowledge construction processes, it is not surprising that teachers' knowledge is studied in relation to their practice in research from this point of view.

From the literature discussed above, we can draw the following conclusions:

1. It appears that the craft knowledge guiding experienced science teachers' classroom practice is constituted by a framework, integrating knowledge and beliefs about the teaching and learning of science, the nature of science, subject matter, and students. In particular, conceptions about the teaching and learning of science seem to exert a major influence on teaching practice. As these conceptions appear to be rather stable, the innovation of science education may be seriously complicated by science teachers' craft knowledge. Specific programs for teacher education, inspired by constructivist innovations, may result in distinct changes in teachers' conceptions about the teaching and learning of science. There is no clear picture as yet, however, whether these changes are lasting and whether they consistently influence classroom practice.

2. Although the possibility to distinguish PCK from subject-matter knowledge has been the subject of controversy (Marks, 1990; Tobin et al., 1994), studies on science teachers' PCK indicate that a thorough and coherent understanding of subject matter acts as a prerequisite, preceding the development of PCK. This conclusion applies both to studies on the effect of the teaching of unfamiliar topics (e.g., Sanders et al., 1993) and to studies in the context of teacher education (e.g., Smith & Neale, 1989). The other crucial factor in this development is, obviously, teaching experience. This explains why prospective or novice science teachers usually express little to no PCK (e.g., Lederman et al., 1994). Teacher training programs usually do not exert a major influence on science teachers' PCK (for example, Smith & Neale, 1989), although Clermont et al. (1993) claimed a significant improvement as a result of a specific workshop. These conclusions correspond with the findings of Grossman (1990), cited earlier. Grossman identified four sources of PCK, attributing a positive influence to both classroom teaching experience and disciplinary education (i.e.,

knowledge of subject matter). Either a negative or conservative influence (i.e., observation of classes) or an unknown impact (i.e., specific courses for teacher education) is attributed to the other two sources.

3. Another conclusion from the studies on science teachers' PCK is that most scholars focus on the nature and the development of PCK in relation to other types of knowledge. For example, Sanders et al. (1993) stressed the supporting function of general pedagogical knowledge, whereas others (Clermont et al., 1993, 1994; Adams & Krockover,1997) applied the concept of PCK to an instructional strategy (e.g., chemical demonstrations), thus interpreting PCK as a specification of pedagogical knowledge rather than a blend of subject-matter knowledge of specific topics and general pedagogical knowledge. Lederman and Gess-Newsome (1992), reacting to Shulman's work cited above (Shulman, 1986, 1987), even questioned the relevance of the concept of PCK altogether. Although the authors acknowledged the importance of "the interaction between subject matter knowledge and pedagogical knowledge as a function of experience" (p. 19), they considered the question of whether pedagogical content knowledge is an important separate domain of knowledge "more of a theoretical argument than a practical one" (p. 19).

As a consequence of this emphasis on general aspects of PCK, the explicit attention for science teachers' knowledge and beliefs with respect to the teaching of specific topics is still marginal. This observation is remarkable given the fact that more than 10 years have passed since Shulman urged researchers of teacher thinking and teacher knowledge to put the content of education high on their agendas, and introduced the concept of PCK particularly for this purpose. The absence of studies on specific topics implies that we cannot yet formulate conclusions with respect to the purposes for research on science teachers' PCK mentioned earlier: At the level of specific topics, research does not inform us about the way science teachers transform subject-matter knowledge and how they relate their transformations to student understanding. Neither have we found specific input for teacher education in this respect. It is important to note that this conclusion applies to *research* on teachers' PCK. Journals focusing on the teaching of specific subjects often contain articles in which a teacher explains his or her successful ways of dealing with specific topics (e.g., *Journal of Chemical Education*). Although these articles are valuable, as the authors have succeeded in making their PCK explicit, we do not consider such articles to be research reports.

As an example of a study which aims at contributing to the purposes mentioned above, we will next present an empirical study on teachers' PCK of a specific topic, that is, chemical equilibrium. This study was conducted in the context of an educational innovation aimed at promoting conceptual change among students when they were introduced to the concept of chemical equilibrium.

Empirical

Context

The present study was conducted within a long-term research project in the Netherlands on chemical education, in which the concept of chemical reaction was central (De Vos & Verdonk, 1985). The concept of chemical equilibrium was chosen because the introduction of this concept challenges the conceptions about chemical reactions students have derived from previous education. Therefore, the introduction of chemical equilibrium offers an opportunity to study processes of conceptual change with respect to chemical reaction among students. A specific research purpose concerned the identification of factors either promoting or hindering such processes. Research results focusing on student learning are described by Van Driel, De Vos, Verloop and Dekkers (1998).

To achieve this purpose, both (a) an experimental course on chemical equilibrium for students of upper-secondary education, and (b) an in-service workshop for chemistry teachers using the experimental course in their own classes were designed. We applied a qualitative research design (see below) in which three cycles of designing, implementing, evaluating, and reflecting on the experimental course were conducted. In the course of the second and third cycles, two consecutive versions of the in-service workshop were designed, implemented, and evaluated. In what follows, we will focus on the third cycle. After elaborating on the design of the workshop and the experimental course, we will present information about the participants and about the way the study was designed. Next, effects of the workshop and the experimental course on participants' PCK of chemical equilibrium will be described. Finally, we will discuss these results.

Design of Workshop and Experimental Course

The workshop's overall purpose was to enhance chemistry teachers' PCK of chemical equilibrium. Specifically, the aims were to improve chemistry teachers' abilities to recognize specific preconceptions and conceptual difficulties related to chemical equilibrium, and to promote their use of interventions and strategies promoting conceptual change during classroom practice. These goals were to be realized by a combination of teachers' use of our experimental course in their own classes and their participation in the workshop. Therefore, workshop meetings were organized before, during, and after the period in which the experimental course was used.

As most of the workshop's participants were chemistry teachers who had been teaching chemical equilibrium for several years, we expected all of them already to possess PCK about this topic to some degree. On the other hand, we assumed that these teachers could benefit from the results of research on student learning of chemical equilibrium and of our educational analyses of chemical literature and curriculum materials dealing with chemical equilibrium. Combining these assumptions, we designed the workshop meetings as follows:

1. The first meeting focused on the PCK of chemical equilibrium participants held on entering the workshop. Therefore, participants performed and discussed chemical experiments and assignments from current chemistry textbooks. Moreover, they were asked to react to authentic student responses. For this purpose, research results with respect to student learning of chemical equilibrium were used as input in the workshop. (A similar design was applied by Shymansky, Woodworth, Norman, Dunkhase, Matthews, & Liu, 1993.)
2. The following two or three meetings coincided with the implementation of the experimental course. These meetings were used both to discuss recent practical experiences as well as to prepare participants for topics following shortly after the meeting, in the way described above.
3. A final meeting was organized to reflect on experiences with the experimental course. In this meeting, teachers not only exchanged and discussed their personal experiences, but were also presented with specific results of our research. The latter was meant to facilitate reflection on a theoretical level. Also, this meeting served to evaluate the experimental course. Therefore, participants were asked to fill in an evaluative questionnaire.

As one can see, the workshop was not designed to provide participants with checklists or recipes for the effective teaching of chemical equilibrium. Instead, adopting constructivist views, we tried to support and facilitate participants' construction of PCK by providing them with both practical experiences and results of research, and by organizing interactions between these two possible sources of knowledge construction.

The experimental course aimed at fostering conceptual change among students by (a) including assignments designed to challenge students' existing conceptions, and (b) stimulating active student engagement through small-group discussions and the execution of chemical experiments by students. This course design was based upon the assumption that for conceptions to be changed, dissatisfaction with existing conceptions is a prerequisite (Posner, Strike, Hewson, & Gertzog, 1982). Through small-group discussions facilitated by questions in the course material, students should try to explain phenomena conflicting with their initially held conceptions. Together, they should be able to solve the anomalies and reconstruct their conceptions. Obviously, the teacher has a crucial role in this design in helping students to overcome preconceptions and in guiding them toward conceptions that are chemically more valid.

From the teachers' perspective, this design also aims at developing their PCK. As teachers spend most of their time in classroom listening to and participating in student discussions, they are presented with opportunities to gain understanding of student reasoning, of their preconceptions and possible misconceptions, and of factors either promoting or hindering conceptual change. While taking part in student discussions, teachers can explore ways of explaining or representing subject matter. Reacting to student responses, they can expand their repertoire of approaches that may be effective for certain students in specific situations.

Research Method
Applying a grounded theory approach (Strauss, 1987), our research project consisted of three consecutive research cycles. In this article, we focus on the in-service workshop that was part of the third and last cycle of our research. The workshop sessions were attended by 12 participants. All of them had an academic background in chemistry and more than 5 years of experience in teaching chemistry in upper-secondary education. As the topic of chemical equilibrium is a key subject in the national curriculum, all participants were familiar with this topic, both as a learner and as a teacher. All participants had chosen to attend to the workshop on a voluntary basis. Mostly, their choice was inspired either by interest in the topic or by the wish to innovate their educational practice. Most of the participants had previously taken part in similar workshops, for example, on the chemical reaction, electrochemistry, stoichiometric calculations, and the like. Some of them had previously been subjected voluntarily to research describing this as "an instructive experience".

All workshop sessions were recorded on audiotape. Additional data consisted of participants' written responses to assignments carried out during the sessions, and to the evaluative questionnaire. Moreover, during the implementation stage, audio recordings were made of classroom lessons of two of the participants. Finally, all participants collected and corrected the written responses of their students to the assignments in the experimental course. These written responses were handed over to the researchers.

The analysis of both types of audio recording was performed following a stepwise procedure. This involved the selection of fragments relevant with respect to teachers' subject-matter knowledge or PCK. These fragments were transcribed verbatim and analyzed by the first and the third author. Researcher triangulation was aimed at by comparing and discussing interpretations of individual researchers until agreement occurred (Janesick, 1994). The validation of these interpretations was promoted by applying the constant comparative method (Denzin, 1994). This involved the comparison of the analyses of the transcripts with other sources, such as (a) chemistry schoolbooks, to trace the possible origins of teachers' representations of subject-matter, and (b) additional data, especially the written responses of both teachers and students that had been collected. In the first place, the analyses were aimed at constructing a picture of each teachers' conceptions and of possible changes in these conceptions. At a general level, the analyses resulted in theoretical notions with respect to the teaching and learning of chemical equilibrium.

Research Results

This article is limited to research results concerning chemistry teachers' PCK of certain aspects of chemical equilibrium. Specifically, we will review the PCK participants held about the dynamic nature of chemical equilibrium on entering the in-service workshop, followed by a description of changes in some participants' PCK that were observed during the process of attending the workshop and implementing the experimental course. In relation to this, some relevant aspects of students' conceptual change processes will be described. Where appropriate, we will illustrate our results with fragments from the transcripts mentioned above. First, however, we will briefly sketch the educational context in which chemical equilibrium is being taught.

In the Netherlands, the introduction of the concept of chemical equilibrium usually takes place during the second year of chemistry education (cf. grade 10). Previously, chemical reactions have been introduced as events in which the original substances disappear, while other, new substances are being formed. These conversions are accompanied by observable effects such as color changes or energy effects. Initially, chemical reactions are supposed to take place in one direction only and to proceed to completion as well. On the molecular level, substances are represented by molecular species. Molecules of the same species are considered identical; that is, they do not differ from each other in any way except position and motion (De Vos & Verdonk, 1987).

Some of these notions are challenged when the concept of chemical equilibrium is introduced. In the case of chemical equilibrium, the reaction under consideration does not proceed to completion, and appears to be reversible as well. Moreover, it is supposed that in a state of equilibrium, two opposite reactions take place at the same rate, although this cannot be deduced from direct observations. This so-called dynamic nature of chemical equilibrium is associated with many student problems and misconceptions (see e.g., Gussarsky & Gorodetsky, 1990; Camacho & Good, 1989; Banerjee, 1991; Quílez-Pardo & Solaz-Portolés, 1995).

The participants in our workshop appeared to consider this dynamic nature as a key element of chemical equilibrium. They reported that this aspect in particular was problematic for many students. Some participants described specific misconceptions similar to the ones described in the literature, although they were ignorant of this body of research. Moreover, most teachers themselves struggled with the abstract nature of the dynamic conception of chemical equilibrium, and its relation to observations during chemical experiments. This is illustrated in the following fragment of a discussion of five teachers with the first author during the first workshop session. The participants had been asked to react to the question of whether they think a forward and a backward reaction are taking place in a specific chemical system at equilibrium conditions.

Transcript 1.
Teacher 1: I don't see it. I don't see a forward and backward reaction.
Researcher 1: No, and you don't think a forward and a backward reaction are taking place in this situation as well?
Teacher 1: Well, not necessarily.
Teacher 2: Well, I do think so.
Teacher 3: From my chemical knowledge and experience, I have no reason *not* to assume ...
Teacher 1: No, but can you see it?
Teacher 2: No.
Teacher 1: No, okay, then we agree about that.
Teacher 4: I don't think it's logical from the experiments we've performed that under equilibrium conditions, a forward and a backward reaction are taking place.
Teacher 3: It doesn't show from this experiment, but it simply follows from one's chemical experience.
Researcher 1: You mean, during other experiments you've experienced that this is actually so?

Teacher 3:	During formal education, one is so much indoctrinated with this thesis; one is so used to speak in these terms and images, it became a fairly consistent story.
Teacher 4:	But then there is a big gap between you and your students, as they don't have that background. So, you fail good arguments from which follows: for this or that reason it is so ....
Teacher 2:	I could tell them a story about the energy distribution of molecules, but I cannot observe it. It doesn't show from anything, but it's logical.
Teacher 5:	I can explain it by assuming a dynamic equilibrium. That's the only thing.

As one can see from this fragment, these teachers lacked theoretical arguments to promote student understanding. They admitted that their usual arguments are weak and not very convincing for most of their students. The best they felt they could do was to demonstrate the dynamic equilibrium conception with the help of metaphors or analogies. In this respect, almost every participant appeared to have developed his or her own repertoire. Some of them used the analogies included in chemistry schoolbooks. Others had worked out their own analogies (cf. Thiele & Treagust, 1994). During the first session of the workshop, participants discussed the strengths and weaknesses of each other's favorite analogies. Common in these analogies was the representation of molecules by people or students or the attribution of human characteristics to molecules (e.g., "molecules don't fancy changing"). Remarkable in their discussion was that chemical validity seemed to prevail. Arguments from the students' perspective were barely noticed.

Following the first workshop session, participants implemented the experimental course in their chemistry classes. Clearly, the implementation process had a large impact on the teachers. Examples of this impact can most directly be observed in the transcripts of discussions of two of the participants with their respective students during the lesson series. In one of these discussions, Teacher 6 tried to clarify the dynamic nature of chemical equilibrium by comparing the equilibrium system with a classroom with two doors, through which students continuously move in and out. His explanation was interrupted by one of the students, who stated, "But that is not a chemical reaction!" Teacher 6 responded as follows: "No, you are right. But as this is about the disappearance and the appearance of particles, I can, of course, use people as well".

However, the students persisted in rejecting the teacher's analogy. During a discussion with the first author after this particular lesson, Teacher 6 asserted that the "incident" described above had made him realize the uselessness of his analogy, which had been an element of his PCK with respect to chemical equilibrium for some time. However, the incident had not provided him a new, more successful representation or strategy. Thus, in terms of conceptual change theory (Posner et al., 1982), although he had become dissatisfied with his present conception, he had not yet reached the stage of a new fruitful and plausible conception.

In another discussion, Teacher 7 initially did not recognize the arguments of his students. The students focused on the anomaly between a chemical system that does not seem to change and the idea that two opposite reactions are taking place continuously. Some of the students (Students 1 and 2; see Transcript 2) reasoned that they would expect the system to change from one state to another and back. However, these changes would then have to be accompanied by color changes corresponding to the students' observations during previous experiments, so that the system would resemble a traffic light. Teacher 7 presented several lengthy explanations to the students, but these apparently did not contribute to their understanding. The problem was eventually solved in the following fragment:

Transcript 2.
Student 1: So it becomes blue, and then pink, blue, and pink again, all the time, doesn't it?
Student 2: That would be fun. So it continues to react spontaneously?
Student 3: Yes, but you cannot see it!
Student 4: So the color stays the same, but there are a whole lot of wild events going on inside ...
Student 2: Oh! Now I see ...
Teacher 7: Exactly, on the inside. You got it! On the inside, the backward and the forward reaction keep taking place. But as they proceed at the same rate, you do not observe changes in the color.

After this lesson, Teacher 7 told the first author that it was only through the argumentation of Students 3 and 4 that he had eventually recognized the problem of Students 1 and 2. Until then, he had not explicitly discussed the idea that in this case the chemical reactions are taking place both simultaneously and unobservably, thus failing to address the students' problem. Through reflection on this discussion, this teacher's PCK was not only extended with knowledge of specific learning difficulties, but also with strategical knowledge of how to deal with these difficulties effectively.

The impact of experiences with the experimental course also emerged from teachers' reports during consecutive workshop sessions. As an example, the following transcript contains a fragment of a discussion recorded during the final workshop session. It illustrates how teachers can benefit from participating in small-group discussions with students.

> *Transcript 3.*
> Teacher 8: For many students, the reaction is still one thing, not two.
> Teacher 9: It can either proceed forward or backward, but not in both directions at the same time.
> Researcher 1: It's hard to talk in terms of coinciding events, anyway.
> Teacher 10: One of my students had problems with the idea of reversibility. Sounding very surprised, she said: "But I don't see it becoming pink, and then back to blue, and then pink again and back to blue again". She really missed the traffic light.
> Researcher 3: The term "reversible" itself implies forward and backward.
> Teacher 10: Forward and backward are separated in time. You can't be on your way to an island with a boat and at the same time go back, or something like that.
> Researcher 3: You only go back after you've arrived.
> Teacher 11: Still, it makes sense to discuss these ideas with students. That it would be like a traffic light if you could observe individual molecules. Such discussions may turn out to be very productive. At least, that's my experience ....
> Teacher 12: For me, it was very instructive when a student reasoned that color of constant intensity was caused by different molecules all the time. His idea was that new molecules were continuously formed, but as the color remained unchanged, they had to be different molecules all the time.
> Researcher 1: So he could relate the apparent static outside with the conception of reactions still taking place.
> Teacher 12: Thus, he overcame the idea of forward and backward. But this was only in one group. But I could use this argument in other groups as well!

The last phrase in particular demonstrates an explicit extension of a teacher's PCK: An argumentation is added to his repertoire that has proved to be effective to promote conceptual change (cf. Teacher 7 in Transcript 2).

Transcript 3 also illustrates that the participants of the workshop, reflecting on their experiences with the experimental course, have recognized student problems similar to the ones mentioned earlier (e.g., Teacher 10). In fact, on the questionnaire evaluating the in-service workshop, many of them indicated that by listening carefully to students' reasoning their understanding of specific student conceptions had improved. Nevertheless, the participants reported both successes and failures with respect to the introduction of the dynamic equilibrium conception. About half of the participants indicated that this conception offered serious difficulties to their students. Some of them argued that their students refused to accept the possibility of unobservable reactions. Other teachers described students who persisted to reason in terms of only "one reaction" (cf. Teachers 8 and 9 in Transcript 3). On the other hand, however, participants claiming a successful introduction of the dynamic equilibrium conception often cited examples of productive student reasoning. They had discovered, for example, that students would reason that it was logical for both reactions to proceed, because all conditions for these reactions to take place were satisfied. Students used both macroscopic terms (e.g., "When all substances are present together, they will always react") as well as molecular terms (e.g., "Whenever molecules are present, they will collide, thus leading to reactions") in this respect.

From analyzing their answers to the evaluative questionnaire, it appeared that in particular, the participants' understanding of students' conceptions of molecules had deepened. When students discussed their ideas of molecules in relation to their observations of reversible and incomplete chemical conversions, the teachers had observed two types of reasoning. The first type of reasoning was described by one of the participants in terms of "students who put themselves in the position of one particle". Such students could not understand why some molecules may change whereas others remain intact. This type of reasoning hindered the acceptance of the dynamic equilibrium conception. In the second type of reasoning, however, students had introduced statistical notions in their molecular ideas. To illustrate this type of reasoning, one participant cited a typical student answer: "All particles will eventually change, but not at the same time".

The teachers' responses during the workshop sessions indicated that they had gained knowledge of specific types of students' reasoning and learning difficulties in the context of the introduction of chemical equilibrium. In addition, some reported to have extended their repertoire of successful strategies and representations with respect to this topic.

Discussion and Conclusions from the Empirical Study
The results of the empirical study have contributed to our understanding of chemistry teachers' PCK with respect to chemical equilibrium. Specifically,

elements of PCK were identified which differ considerably from the representations of chemical equilibrium commonly found in chemistry schoolbooks. Teachers succeeded in promoting conceptual change by discussing the anomalous results of certain chemical experiments with students. They challenged students' conceptions about chemical reactions by urging students to explain phenomena which indicate the reversibility and the incomplete conversion of chemical reactions. Thus, they provided students with a basis for the dynamic equilibrium conception to become an acceptable explanation of the anomalous experimental results. Many students indicated difficulties in accepting the idea of opposite reactions taking place simultaneously. Teachers could facilitate the process of overcoming this barrier by applying two different strategies:

1. They can discuss the possibility of continuous changes taking place at the molecular level. This implies an introduction of the element of time in the notion that molecules of the same species are identical. At a specific moment a molecule of Type X may be formed, while at the same time another molecule X at another place is converted. Thus, a statistical molecular image emerges in which the total amount of molecules X remains constant, but the collection consists of different molecules.
2. Because all conditions are satisfied for both the forward and the backward reaction to proceed, teachers can discuss the possibility of these reactions taking place observably, one after the other (traffic light reaction). As this possibility obviously conflicts with observations of the chemical system, one can proceed to assume that both reactions do proceed at the same rate, thereby canceling each other's observable effects.

Obviously, not every individual participant in our workshop reconstructed his or her PCK in the way described above. Instead, this description is constructed by the researchers through a synthesis of the research results with respect to individual teachers and students. In this way, we contributed to the first purpose for research on teachers' PCK mentioned earlier in this article: the increase of knowledge about the way teachers transform subject-matter knowledge and how they can relate their transformations to student understanding. Notably, this contribution is limited to the introduction of chemical equilibrium.

We have also added to the second purpose – that is, resolving a blind spot in preservice and in-service teacher education. The strategies we identified to successfully facilitate the introduction of chemical equilibrium are to be included in both types of teacher education. As the PCK teachers initially hold about chemical equilibrium appears to be inspired by current chemistry schoolbooks, fragments from these schoolbooks may be used to challenge teachers' conceptions. In particular, we suggest a critical discussion concerning the use of analogies and metaphors during the introduction of dynamic equilibrium. Contrary to Treagust, Duit, Joslin, and Lindauer (1992), we would hesitate to recommend the use of analogies to promote conceptual change. Next, teachers may be invited to perform and discuss chemical experiments commonly used in schoolbooks to introduce the idea of reversible reactions. Through these discussions, teachers' attention may be drawn to the occurrence of specific learning difficulties and misconceptions.

These can then be studied by providing both literature on specific research and authentic student responses. Preferably, examples must be included that illustrate typical ways of student reasoning: for example, the traffic light conception of a reversible reaction and the static conception of molecules, emerging from student questions such as "Why do some molecules react while others don't?" To simulate classroom practice, teachers may be asked to react to this type of student reasoning and to discuss their reactions mutually. Finally, the strategies described may be offered as possible approaches to stimulate students' conceptual change. Ideally, teachers should then be provided with opportunities to use these strategies in classroom practice and to reflect on their experiences.

Concluding Remarks

In this final section, we return to the central topic of this article. Relating the results of our empirical study to the literature discussed earlier, we will discuss possible purposes for research on science teachers' PCK from a craft knowledge point of view.

As stated before, the literature discussed indicated that experienced science teachers' classroom practice is guided by a coherent and integrated set of knowledge and beliefs, within which conceptions about the teaching and learning of science play an important role. The content of teachers' conceptions appears to be rather traditional, particularly in terms of instructional strategies and goals. Therefore, science teachers' craft knowledge is often reported to hinder the innovation of science education. How do these findings relate to our introduction of the concept of craft knowledge in the beginning of this article? First, as the craft knowledge of science teachers actually differs from recent academic conceptions of teaching and learning, research on science teachers' craft knowledge may indeed lead to the establishment of an alternative knowledge base in addition to codified educational knowledge bases. Second, the understanding of science teachers' craft knowledge appears to be a vital source for in-service and preservice teacher education, especially when teacher education aims at improving science teaching practice. From the literature, it appears that specific workshops building on science teachers' craft knowledge actually succeed in promoting conceptual change among science teachers' knowledge and beliefs (e.g., Stofflett, 1994). Moreover, specific designs in which science teachers receive support or supervision may lead to gradual changes in classroom practice (e.g., Glasson & Lalik, 1993).

Shifting the focus of our discussion to PCK, we would like to call to mind a conclusion we drew from reviewing the literature on science teachers' PCK. So far, research on science teachers' PCK has focused on the nature and the development of PCK, rather than investigating science teachers' PCK with respect to specific topics. This research identified the importance of a thorough and coherent knowledge of subject matter and the necessity of teaching experience. Therefore, this research offers general guidelines for the design of teacher training programs aiming at the development of PCK. In particular, such programs should enable teachers to study the subject matter of specific topics from a teaching perspective. In this respect, teachers' subject-matter knowledge may be improved by studying the structure and evolution of students' ideas about particular topics (Shymansky et al., 1993). Furthermore, teacher training programs should provide opportunities to use PCK in teaching situations and to reflect on these practical experiences (Clermont et al., 1993).

Earlier, PCK was perceived as encompassing knowledge of representations of subject matter and understanding of specific learning difficulties and student conceptions with respect to specific topics (Shulman, 1986). From this conceptualization, we derived two main purposes for research on teachers' PCK, referring to the improvement of our understanding of the way teachers transform subject-matter knowledge in relation to student learning and to the application of this understanding in the context of in-service and preservice teacher education. As stated above, we observed the absence of studies on science teachers' PCK with respect to specific topics. Our empirical study was presented as an example of such research. We argue that this type of study may significantly add to the value of the concept of PCK within the domain of research on science teaching. In our view, the value of PCK lies essentially in its relation with specific topics. Therefore, PCK is to be discerned from general pedagogical knowledge on the one hand, and from subject-matter knowledge per se on the other. As the results from our case study show, we have gained insight into the ways chemistry teachers transform their knowledge of chemical equilibrium to stimulate student understanding of this topic. The teaching strategies we identified are not useful in a universal sense, but refer exclusively to this topic. Still, as teachers teach specific topics, these strategies add a unique and valuable element to the educational knowledge base. Moreover, other teachers may benefit from this type of topic-related PCK as it can be used as input in preservice or in-service teacher education. In addition to the general guidelines identified above and analogous to the in-service workshop we conducted, we suggest that a course on topic-related PCK includes activities which invite teachers to (a) critically review schoolbooks, (b) perform scientific experiments, and (c) study authentic student responses. Through specific assignments and discussions, participants may be stimulated to integrate these activities and to reflect on both academic subject matter and on classroom practice. In this way, participants' PCK may be improved.

In the introduction to this article, we suggested that research on PCK can potentially be related to research on student learning. Studies of specific learning difficulties and student conceptions with respect to specific topics are of particular interest, since PCK encompasses understanding of these difficulties of conceptions. In our empirical study, we could indeed benefit from incorporating research on student learning of chemical equilibrium. In view of the vast amount of research on student conceptions and conceptual change with respect to specific science topics that has become available since the 1970s (e.g., Driver & Easley, 1978; Dykstra, Boyle, & Monarch, 1992; Vosniadou, 1994), we would welcome studies on the same topics from the teachers' perspective. Specifically, studies focusing on teachers' representations and instructional strategies to overcome student misconceptions and to promote conceptual change would add to the knowledge base of science teachers' PCK.

Finally, we remind the reader of the controversy concerning the question whether research on teachers' craft knowledge, including PCK, would have to be limited to idiosyncratic descriptions (Tom & Valli, 1990). We think that both the discussion of the literature and the empirical study demonstrate that research on science teachers' craft knowledge or PCK may indeed surpass the individual level and generate knowledge of a more general nature instead. For example, through generalization from the results of the empirical study, patterns of instructional strategies with respect to chemical equilibrium were deduced. This does not imply, however, that every teacher participating in the study has incorporated these strategies in his or her PCK. Consistent with some findings in the literature (Lantz & Kass, 1987; Leinhardt & Smith, 1985), considerable differences between teachers' craft knowledge may occur at the individual level even if their academic knowledge and their educational contexts are similar. Besides, teachers develop their craft knowledge in different ways. For example, participation in our workshop has had serious impact for some teachers, while others' PCK apparently was hardly affected. As for us, this is an essential implication from the adoption of a craft knowledge perspective. Instead of generating checklists with indicators of effective instruction, we aim at providing teachers with a knowledge base which enables them to teach specific topics effectively and flexibly in situations that are subjected to different contextual, situational, and personal influences. We think that PCK with respect to various specific topics constitutes a vital element of this knowledge base.

Note

1   Originally published as Van Driel, J. H., Verloop, N., & de Vos, W. (1998). Developing science teachers' pedagogical content knowledge. *Journal of Research in Science Teaching*, 35(6), 673–695. Reprinted, with minor edits, with permission from the publisher.

References

Abd-El-Khalick, F., & BouJaoude, S. (1997). An exploratory study of the knowledge base for science teaching. *Journal of Research in Science Teaching*, 34, 673–699.

Adams, P. E., & Krockover, G. H. (1997). Beginning science teacher cognition and its origins in the preservice secondary science teacher program. *Journal of Research in Science Teaching*, 34, 633–653.

Anderson, R. D., & Mitchener, C. P. (1994). Research on science teacher education. In D. L. Gabel (Ed.), *Handbook of research on science teaching and learning* (pp. 3–44). Macmillan.

Appleton, K., & Asoko, H. (1996). A case study of a teacher's progress toward using a constructivist view of learning to inform teaching in elementary science. *Science Education*, 80, 165–180.

Banerjee, A. C. (1991). Misconceptions of students and teachers in chemical equilibrium. *International Journal of Science Education*, 13, 487–494.

Beijaard, D., & Verloop, N. (1996). Assessing teachers' practical knowledge. *Studies in Educational Evaluation*, 22, 275–286.

Berry, A., Loughran, J. J., & Van Driel, J. H. (2008). Revisiting the roots of Pedagogical Content Knowledge. *International Journal of Science Education*, 30(10), 1271–1279.

Berry, A., & Van Driel, J. H. (2013). Teaching about teaching science: Aims, strategies and backgrounds of science teacher educators. *Journal of Teacher Education*, 64(2), 117–128.

Brickhouse, N. W. (1990). Teachers' beliefs about the nature of science and their relationships to classroom practice. *Journal of Teacher Education*, 41, 53–62.

Brickhouse, N. W., & Bodner, G. M. (1992). The beginning science teacher: Classroom narratives of convictions and constraints. *Journal of Research in Science Teaching*, 29, 471–485.

Briscoe, C. (1991). The dynamic interactions among beliefs, role metaphors, and teaching practices: A case study of teacher change. *Science Education, 75*, 185–199.

Camacho, M., & Good, R. (1989). Problem solving and chemical equilibrium: Successful versus unsuccessful performance. *Journal of Research in Science Teaching, 26*, 251–272.

Carlsen, W. S. (1993). Teacher knowledge and discourse control: Quantitative evidence from novice biology teachers' classrooms. *Journal of Research in Science Teaching, 30*, 471–481.

Carter, K. (1990). Teachers' knowledge and learning to teach. In W. R. Houston (Ed.), *Handbook of research on teacher education* (pp. 291–310). Macmillan.

Clark, C. M., & Peterson, P. L. (1986). Teachers' thought processes. In M. C. Wittrock (Ed.), *Handbook of research on teaching* (3rd ed., pp. 255–296). Macmillan.

Clermont, C. P., Borko, H., & Krajcik, J. S. (1994). Comparative study of the pedagogical content knowledge of experienced and novice chemical demonstrators. *Journal of Research in Science Teaching, 31*, 419–441.

Clermont, C. P., Krajcik, J. S., & Borko, H. (1993). The influence of an intensive in-service workshop on pedagogical content knowledge growth among novice chemical demonstrators. *Journal of Research in Science Teaching, 30*, 21–43.

Cochran, K. F., DeRuiter, J. A., & King, R. A. (1993). Pedagogical content knowing: An integrative model for teacher preparation. *Journal of Teacher Education, 44*, 263–272.

Constable, H., & Long, A. (1991). Changing science teaching: Lessons from a long-term evaluation of a short in-service course. *International Journal of Science Education, 13*, 405–419.

Cronin-Jones, L. L. (1991). Science teacher beliefs and their influence on curriculum implementation: Two case studies. *Journal of Research in Science Teaching, 28*, 235–250.

De Vos, W., & Verdonk, A. H. (1985). A new road to reactions, part 1. *Journal of Chemical Education, 62*, 238–240.

De Vos, W., & Verdonk, A. H. (1987). A new road to reactions, part 4: The substance and its molecules. *Journal of Chemical Education, 64*, 692–694.

Denzin, N. K. (1994). The art and politics of interpretation. In N. K. Denzin & Y. S. Lincoln (Eds.), *Handbook of qualitative research design* (pp. 500–515). Sage.

Doyle, W. (1990). Themes in teacher education research. In W. R. Houston (Ed.), *Handbook of research on teacher education* (pp. 3–24). Macmillan.

Driver, R., & Easley, J. (1978). Pupils and paradigms: A review of literature related to concept development in adolescent science students. *Studies in Science Education, 5*, 61–84.

Dykstra, D. I., Jr., Boyle, C. F., & Monarch, I. A. (1992). Studying conceptual change in learning physics. *Science Education, 76*, 615–652.

Fernandez-Balboa, J.-M., & Stiehl, J. (1995). The generic nature of pedagogical content knowledge among college professors. *Teaching & Teacher Education, 11*, 293–306.

Friedrichsen, P., Van Driel, J. H., & Abell, S. K. (2011). Taking a closer look at science teaching orientations. *Science Education, 95*(2), 358–376.

Gallagher, J. J. (1991). Prospective and practicing secondary school science teachers' knowledge and beliefs about the philosophy of science. *Science Education, 75,* 121–133.

Geddis, A. N. (1993). Transforming subject-matter knowledge: The role of pedagogical content knowledge in learning to reflect on teaching. *International Journal of Science Education, 15,* 673–683.

Gess-Newsome, J., & Lederman, N. G. (1993). Preservice biology teachers' knowledge structures as a function of professional teacher education: A year-long assessment. *Science Education, 77,* 25–45.

Glasson, G. E., & Lalik, R. V. (1993). Reinterpreting the learning cycle from a social constructivist perspective: A qualitative study of teachers' beliefs and practices. *Journal of Research in Science Teaching, 30,* 187–207.

Grimmett, P. P., & MacKinnon, A. M. (1992). Craft knowledge and the education of teachers. In G. Grant (Ed.), *Review of research in education* (Vol. 18, pp. 385–456). AERA.

Grossman, P. L. (1990). *The making of a teacher: Teacher knowledge and teacher education.* Teachers College Press.

Gussarsky, E., & Gorodetsky, M. (1990). On the concept "chemical equilibrium": The associative framework. *Journal of Research in Science Teaching, 27,* 197–204.

Hand, B., & Treagust, D. F. (1994). Teachers' thought about changing to constructivist teaching/learning approaches within junior secondary science classrooms. *Journal of Education for Teaching, 20,* 97–112.

Hashweh, M. Z. (1987). Effects of subject-matter knowledge in the teaching of biology and physics. *Teaching & Teacher Education, 3,* 109–120.

Hewson, P. W., & Hewson, M. G. A'B. (1987). Science teachers' conceptions of teaching: Implications for teacher education. *International Journal of Science Education, 9,* 425–440.

Hewson, P. W., & Hewson, M. G. A'B. (1989). Analysis and use of a task for identifying conceptions of teaching science. *Journal of Education for Teaching, 15,* 191–209.

Hoyle, E., & John, P. D. (1995). *Professional knowledge and professional practice.* Cassell.

Janesick, V. J. (1994). The dance of qualitative research design. In N. K. Denzin & Y. S. Lincoln (Eds.), *Handbook of qualitative research design* (pp. 209–219). Sage.

Johnston, K. (1991). High school science teachers' conceptualisations of teaching and learning: Theory and practice. *European Journal of Teacher Education, 14,* 65–78.

Kansanen, P. (2009). Subject-matter didactics as a central knowledge base for teachers, or should it be called pedagogical content knowledge? *Pedagogy, Culture & Society, 17,* 29–39.

King, B. B. (1991). Beginning teachers' knowledge of and attitudes toward history and philosophy of science. *Science Education, 75,* 135–141.

Lantz, O., & Kass, H. (1987). Chemistry teachers' functional paradigms. *Science Education, 71*, 117–134.

Lederman, N. G. (1992). Students' and teachers' conceptions of the nature of science: A review of the research. *Journal of Research in Science Teaching, 29*, 331–359.

Lederman, N. G., & Gess-Newsome, J. (1992). Do subject matter knowledge, pedagogical knowledge, and pedagogical content knowledge constitute the ideal gas law of science teaching? *Journal of Science Teacher Education, 3*, 16–20.

Lederman, N. G., Gess-Newsome, J., & Latz, M. S. (1994). The nature and development of preservice science teachers' conceptions of subject matter and pedagogy. *Journal of Research in Science Teaching, 31*, 129–146.

Leinhardt, G., & Smith, D. A. (1985). Expertise in mathematics instruction: Subject matter knowledge. *Journal of Educational Psychology, 77*, 247–271.

Lijnse, P. L. (1995). 'Developmental research' as a way to an empirically based 'didactical structure' of science. *Science Education, 79*, 189–199.

Marks, R. (1990). Pedagogical content knowledge: From a mathematical case to a modified conception. *Journal of Teacher Education, 41*, 3–11.

Meyer, M. A., & Rakhkochkine, A. (2018). Wolfgang Klafki's concept of 'Didaktik' and its reception in Russia. *European Educational Research Journal, 17*, 17–36.

Pomeroy, D. (1993). Implications of teachers' beliefs about the nature of science: Comparison of the beliefs of scientists, secondary science teachers, and elementary teachers. *Science Education, 77*, 261–278.

Porlan Ariza, A., & Garda Gomez, M. S. (1992). The change of teachers' conceptions: A strategy for in-service science teachers' education. *Teaching & Teacher Education, 8*, 537–548.

Posner, G. J., Strike, K. A., Hewson, P. W., & Gertzog, W. A. (1982). Accomodation of a scientific conception: Toward a theory of conceptual change. *Science Education, 66*, 211–227.

Powell, R. (1994). From field science to classroom science: A case study of constrained emergence in a second-career science teacher. *Journal of Research in Science Teaching, 31*, 273–291.

Prawat, R. S. (1992). Teachers' beliefs about teaching and learning: A constructivist perspective. *American Journal of Education, 32*, 354–395.

Quílez-Pardo, J., & Solaz-Portolés, J. J. (1995). Students' and teachers' misapplication of Le Chatelier's principle: Implications for the teaching of chemical equilibrium. *Journal of Research in Science Teaching, 32*, 939–957.

Roberts, D. A., & Chastko, A. M. (1990). Absorption, refraction, reflection: An exploration of beginning science teacher thinking. *Science Education, 74*, 197–224.

Sanders, L. R., Borko, H., & Lockard, J. D. (1993). Secondary science teachers' knowledge base when teaching science courses in and out of their area of certification. *Journal of Research in Science Teaching, 3*, 723–736.

Shulman, L. S. (1986). Those who understand: Knowledge growth in teaching. *Educational Researcher, 15,* 4–14.

Shulman, L. S. (1987). Knowledge and teaching: Foundations of the new reform. *Harvard Educational Review, 57,* 1–22.

Shymansky, J. A., Woodworth, G., Norman, O., Dunkhase, J., Matthews, C., & Liu, C.-T. (1993). A study of changes in middle school teachers' understanding of selected ideas in science as a function of an in-service program focusing on student preconceptions. *Journal of Research in Science Teaching, 30,* 737–755.

Smith, D. C., & Neale, D. C. (1989). The construction of subject matter knowledge in primary science teaching. *Teaching & Teacher Education, 5,* 1–20.

Stofflett, R. T. (1994). The accomodation of science pedagogical knowledge: The application of conceptual change constructs to teacher education. *Journal of Research in Science Teaching, 31,* 787–810.

Strauss, A. L. (1987). *Qualitative analysis for social scientists.* Cambridge University Press.

Thiele, R. B., & Treagust, D. F. (1994). An interpretive examination of high school chemistry teachers' analogical explanations. *Journal of Research in Science Teaching, 31,* 227–242.

Tobin, K. (1993). Referents for making sense of science teaching. *International Journal of Science Education, 15,* 241–254.

Tobin, K., & McRobbie, C. J. (1996). Cultural myths as constraints to the enacted science curriculum. *Science Education, 80,* 223–241.

Tobin, K., Tippins, D. J., & Gallard, A. J. (1994). Research on instructional strategies for teaching science. In D. L. Gabel (Ed.), *Handbook of research on science teaching and learning* (pp. 45–93). Macmillan.

Tom, A. R., & Valli, L. (1990). Professional knowledge for teachers. In W. R. Houston (Ed.), *Handbook of research on teacher education* (pp. 372–392). Macmillan.

Treagust, D. F., Duit, R., Joslin, P., & Lindauer, I. (1992). Science teachers' use of analogies: Observations from classroom practice. *International Journal of Science Education, 14,* 413–422.

Van Driel, J. H., De Vos, W., Verloop, N., & Dekkers, H. (1998). Developing secondary students' conceptions of chemical reactions: The introduction of chemical equilibrium. *International Journal of Science Education, 20*(4), 379–392.

Verloop, N. (1992). Praktijkkennis van docenten: Een blinde vlek van de onderwijskunde [Craft knowledge of teachers: A blind spot in educational research]. *Pedagogische Studien, 69,* 410–423.

Vosniadou, S. (Ed.). (1994). Conceptual change in the physical sciences [Special issue]. *Learning and Instruction, 4*(1).

CHAPTER 2

Professional Development and Reform in Science Education

The Role of Teachers' Practical Knowledge

1 How This Article Came About

After the PCK article discussed in the previous chapter was published, I was invited to become a member of the editorial board of the *Journal of Research in Science Teaching*. During a meeting of the board, the editors, Jim Gallagher and Andy Anderson, introduced the idea to publish a series of articles on reform in science education. After the meeting, I talked with one of them (Jim Gallagher) about certain recent innovations of science education and how these had failed to realise their ambitions. We spoke about the crucial role of teachers in the implementation of reforms. In the end, I indicated that I was interested in writing a paper for the new series on the role of teachers' knowledge and beliefs in the context of science education reform. Jim encouraged me to do this, of course reminding me that the paper had to go through the usual rigorous peer review process.

Back at Leiden University, I interested my colleagues Douwe Beijaard and Nico Verloop to work with me on the paper. Douwe and Nico were experts in research on teacher education and teacher knowledge but didn't have a background in science education. According to Google Scholar, Douwe is currently the world's most cited author on teachers' professional identity and teacher knowledge. Both Douwe and Nico had published about methodologies to capture and assess teacher knowledge. The three of us shared an interest in what we initially called teachers' craft knowledge and later referred to as teachers' practical knowledge. In the 1998 PCK article (Chapter 1), we argued that PCK should be considered as a specific form of craft knowledge, which was defined as:

> integrated knowledge which represents teachers' accumulated wisdom with respect to their teaching practice. As this knowledge guides the teachers' actions in practice, it encompasses teachers' knowledge and beliefs with respect to various aspects such as pedagogy, students, subject matter, and the curriculum. (Van Driel et al., 1998, p. 674)

For the new article, we decided to review research on science education reform through the lens of teachers' practical knowledge, which in this article would be described as "the integrated set of knowledge, conceptions, beliefs, and values teachers develop in the context of the teaching situation" (Van Driel et al., 2001, p. 141). Furthermore, practical knowledge is action-oriented, person and context specific, and to a large extent implicit or tacit. We demonstrated how a practical knowledge perspective acknowledged the status of teaching as a profession and how it opposed the depersonalized, context-free, and mechanistic view of teaching that had emerged from the process-product research tradition that was dominant in research on teaching in the 1970s and 80s.

Some of my PhD experiences had contributed to adopting this practical knowledge perspective. As explained in Chapter 1, the number of participating teachers increased in each cycle. During meetings of the professional development program, teachers expressed rather different views of teaching chemistry, both generally and specifically related to chemical equilibrium. This sparked a concern in me that implementation of the carefully designed teaching unit could vary considerably from teacher to teacher, and sometimes quite different from my intentions. The data collected from different schools indeed showed a lot of variation. For instance, some teachers would explain theoretical concepts prior to the students' empirical explorations thus changing the nature of the learning process. Gradually, however, I came to accept that teachers tailored the unit to their context (students, resources), aligned with their beliefs, values, and experiences. Of course, I did not always agree with or approve their approaches, but who was I to mandate or restrict teachers' practice? Moreover, the insights that some teachers expressed in the teaching and learning of chemical equilibrium surpassed my expectation. Some of their ideas were actually helpful in the process of analysing data. These teachers surely had "accumulated wisdom with respect to their teaching practice" and were able to share it.

2 Content and Context

Our practical knowledge stance determined how we approached the published research on reform in science education. First, we showed how reforms in education, generally and commonly, had typically followed a similar pattern. This consisted of a design phase, led by policy makers and curriculum developers, including an analysis of teaching skills that were deemed necessary to implement the innovation, which then formed the basis for training sessions and workshops for teachers, often supplemented with curricular materials. We argued that more often than not, this approach resulted in the reform being implemented in ways that differed from the intentions thus not realising its objectives. Typically, teachers would be blamed for incompetency or lack of loyalty or fidelity.

Around this time, I was involved in an innovation of science education in the Netherlands which followed the above pattern almost painfully accurate. The innovation concerned the introduction of a new subject *Algemene Natuurwetenschappen* (ANW; General Science) in the national curriculum for secondary education. The subject aimed to provide all students, especially those who would opt out of science after grade 10, with a meaningful science learning experience. In Chapters 4 and 5, the subject will be discussed in more detail. The new subject was part of a broader innovation of secondary education that was mandated by the Dutch government at the end of the 1990s. The content of ANW was designed by educational researchers and curriculum developers. Teachers and schools were not included in this process and, with some exceptions, were not particularly enthusiastic when it was launched. A national program for teacher professional development was organised to provide teachers with a qualification which was required to teach ANW. When it was offered, it turned out that obtaining this qualification was the main motivation for teachers, many of whom had been selected by their school rather than out of interest in ANW. Obviously, this compromised the impact of the program upfront. This lack of motivation on the side of teachers and schools was of course reflected in the way ANW was received by students. Complaints about the new subject quickly reached politicians, and within a few years after it was introduced the government decided to change the status of ANW from a mandatory to an elective subject, leaving it up to schools whether to offer it or not.

In the article, we reviewed research on science teachers' practical knowledge, which included pedagogical content knowledge, beliefs about the teaching of science, the nature of science, and views about specific reforms of science education. This review led us to conclude that reforms require "teachers to restructure their knowledge and beliefs, and, on the basis of teaching experiences, integrate the new information in their practical knowledge" (p. 148). We proceeded to review studies with a focus on professional development related to reform in science education. From our perspective on practical knowledge, we identified approaches that productively contribute to teacher learning in support of the innovation. These included collegial networks, peer coaching and collaborative action research. What these approaches shared was the premise that teachers need to be involved in all phases of the reform and not just in the implementation. Also common was the importance of collaboration or partnerships between teachers, educators, researchers, and administrators. All these stakeholders play a role in the process and need each other. Finally, of course, time is needed to enable and support authentic and sustained change.

We concluded that to increase the likelihood of successful reform, the practical knowledge of teachers involved in a reform should be investigated at the start of the process and monitored throughout the planning, implementation and evaluation of the reform. In case a large gap emerges between the innovative ideas and the practical knowledge of a vast number of teachers, it may be wise or even necessary to adjust the goals of the reform.

The manuscript turned out to be a kind of position paper, based on a review of the research literature through a specific lens (i.e., teachers' practical knowledge). There are more than 100 items in the list of references, which take up more than five out of the 21 pages of the published article. We received reviews that were thorough but favourable and this time it took just over 10 months between initial submission and acceptance of the final version of the manuscript.

3 Impact and Follow Up

Similar to the article in Chapter 1, this article has gained a lot of traction in terms of citations and downloads. It started to pick up citations quickly and the number of citations continued to grow until 2016 (121), down to 101 in 2020. To date, this article has been cited nearly 1,600 times (Google Scholar). It is listed as #23 of most cited papers in the *Journal of Research in Science Teaching* (since 1963). I assume that, again, the timing was right.

The article was published in 2001, the year in which the No Child Left Behind Act was passed in the USA. This law supported education reform based on the premise that setting high standards and establishing measurable goals would improve student outcomes in education. The law put pressure on schools and teachers to implement 'scientifically based research' practices in the classroom including the use of technology to enhance student learning achievements. Large amounts of funding were reserved for teacher professional development. Similar trends were visible in other countries, such as the Netherlands where a complete overhaul of secondary education was implemented by the government (including the introduction of new subjects such as Algemene Natuurwetenschappen). The Dutch reform was accompanied by large scale professional development initiatives. The increased attention for teacher professional development is reflected in trends in educational research. Science teacher professional development is one of the most popular topics among articles published in the major science education research journals since 2001 (Chang, Chang, & Tseng, 2010).

Our call for collaborative approaches resonated with ideas that were emerging around this time. Etienne Wenger had just published his book on communities of practice (Wenger, 1998) and concepts such as professional learning communities (Dufour & Eaker, 1998) and Japanese lesson study (e.g., Fernandez & Yoshida, 2004) began to be noticed in the world of education. Although our article didn't refer to these approaches, it shared with all of these a focus on teacher collaboration to bring about educational change in a bottom-up rather than top-down manner. It is rather common these days to argue for teacher collaboration as a strategy to promote teacher professional learning, and the benefits and challenges of teacher collaboration have been well documented (Vangrieken, Dochy, Raes, & Kyndt, 2015).

In my own work since this article was published, there has often been a focus on the role of teachers in the context of reform of education. Teacher collaboration was a component of some, but not all of these projects. However, in all of them the need to capture and document teachers' practical knowledge, prior to and during the implementation of the reform, was a central idea. This idea shaped a research project on the curricular beliefs of chemistry teachers at the start of a reform of the national chemistry curriculum in the Netherlands (see Chapter 7). It was also a guiding principle of the PhD study of Ineke Henze, who investigated the development of the practical knowledge in a sample of science teachers over three years in the context of the implementation of *Algemene Natuurwetenschappen* (see Chapter 5). In other PhD studies, Tamara Platteel investigated how teachers of mother tongue language (i.e., Dutch) interpreted a curriculum innovation and how they implemented the innovation through a collaborative action research approach (Platteel, Hulshof, Van Driel, & Verloop, 2013). Michiel Dam explored biology teachers' previous success experiences as the basis of intentions to implement novel pedagogical approaches (see Chapter 10).

To me, what is most crucial about this article is that we took a particular stance. We had cited the warning that "teachers' belief systems can be ignored only at the innovators' peril" from Clark and Peterson's seminal handbook chapter on teachers' thought processes (Clark & Peterson, 1986). However, rather than considering such belief systems as conservative barriers to innovation, we advocated the need to acknowledge teachers as professionals who bring their expertise, including their personal beliefs and values, to educational innovations. Of course, we were not suggesting that teachers' existing practical knowledge should be considered as the norm per se, but we were arguing for the recognition of the wisdom that teachers accumulate across their careers.

Research since 2001 has shown that approaches that consider teachers as having deficiencies that need to be 'fixed' to enable fidelity of implementation are still very common even though they consistently fail to motivate and engage teachers intellectually (Kennedy, 2016). This leads to disappointing outcomes of educational reforms and considerable amounts of money and time being wasted. Reading the article today, I would conclude that recognition of teachers' practical knowledge implies that teachers' voices need to be incorporated in the design of reforms in education. The implementation of a reform requires teachers to be supported in ways that promote understanding of the goals and ambitions of the reform and, at the same time, allow for agency and autonomy to align the reform with their practical knowledge and personal contexts.

Professional Development and Reform in Science Education: The Role of Teachers' Practical Knowledge[1]

Jan H. van Driel, Douwe Beijaard and Nico Verloop

Abstract

In this article, professional development in the context of the current reforms in science education is discussed from the perspective of developing teachers' practical knowledge. It is argued that reform efforts in the past have often been unsuccessful because they failed to take teachers' existing knowledge, beliefs, and attitudes into account. Teachers' practical knowledge is conceptualized as action-oriented and person-bound. As it is constructed by teachers in the context of their work, practical knowledge integrates experiential knowledge, formal knowledge, and personal beliefs. To capture this complex type of knowledge, multimethod designs are necessary. On the basis of a literature review, it is concluded that long-term professional development programs are needed to achieve lasting changes in teachers' practical knowledge. In particular, the following strategies are potentially powerful: (a) learning in networks, (b) peer coaching, (c) collaborative action research, and (d) the use of cases. In any case, it is recommended that teachers' practical knowledge be investigated at the start of a reform project, and that changes in this knowledge be monitored throughout the project. In that way, the reform project may benefit from teachers' expertise. Moreover, this makes it possible to adjust the reform so as to enhance the chances of a successful implementation.

Introduction

The idea that teachers are the most influential factor in educational change is not controversial (cf. Duffee & Aikenhead, 1992). However, the crucial role of teachers in efforts to reform or innovate the curriculum may be assessed from quite different perspectives. In a traditional top-down approach, the lack of success of many innovative projects is attributed to the failure of teachers to implement the innovation in a way corresponding to the intentions of the developers. In this approach, the curriculum developers are assumed to know how the curriculum has to be changed and how teachers have to adapt their teaching practice, that is, change their classroom behavior.

This top-down approach has been criticized, for example, by Tobin and Dawson (1992). Instead of blaming teachers for the relative lack of success of many curriculum reform efforts, they suggest that curriculum developers have often failed to take into account the teachers, students, and the culture in which the new curriculum is to be embedded (cf. Wallace & Louden, 1992). In particular, teachers' beliefs are deemed important. In their influential review of research on teacher thinking, Clark and Peterson (1986) warned that "teachers' belief systems can be ignored only at the innovators' peril". To understand the role of teachers with respect to educational reform, it has been suggested that their beliefs and views (Tobin & McRobbie, 1996), or their practical knowledge (Duffee & Aikenhead, 1992) be analyzed. Practical knowledge consists of teachers' knowledge and beliefs about their own teaching practice, and is mainly the result of their teaching experience. This practical knowledge perspective is the central issue of this article, in which we address the question "What can we learn from research on teachers' practical knowledge in order to increase the success of reform in science education?" After all, as it is directly related to the teachers' behavior in classrooms (Verloop, 1992), their personal practical knowledge will exert a major influence on the way teachers respond to educational change.

Reform in Science Education

In many nations around the globe, science education is currently going through a process of change. Other articles in this series will describe the current reform from a historical perspective, and will highlight various aspects of the content of this reform (see also Bybee & DeBoer, 1994). It appears that the reform efforts in different countries share some important characteristics, which are apparently related to dissatisfaction with how science is traditionally taught. Although studies like TIMSS have revealed substantial differences in science education across countries (e.g., Stigler, Gallimore & Hiebert, 2000), in general, an emphasis seems to exist on lectures to convey science content, and technical training for acquiring practical skills. Science is usually presented as a rigid body of facts, theories, and rules to be memorized and practiced, rather than a way of knowing about natural phenomena. To an increasing extent this approach has become the subject of criticism among policy makers, teachers, educators, and researchers. First, this traditional approach has been related to the decreasing popularity of science among students, apparent from the declining numbers of students choosing science subjects as a specialization. Second, research on students' conceptions of scientific topics has convincingly demonstrated that students exposed to this approach often end up with a poor understanding of scientific concepts. Moreover, it is felt that science education in its traditional form has become outmoded, in that it does not adequately prepare future citizens to understand science and technology issues in a rapidly evolving society (Millar & Osborne, 1998). Finally, it has been argued that the culture of "school science" may restrict the professional development of science teachers (Munby, Cunningham, & Lock, 2000).

In an attempt to change this situation, a series of influential publications in the United States (Rutherford & Ahlgren, 1989; AAAS, 1993; NRC, 1996) have advocated a nation-wide reform of science education, with the following aims:
- To achieve scientific literacy as the central goal of science education ('Science for all Americans'). In this respect, it is considered particularly important to focus on students' understanding of the nature of science, for instance, by studying the history and the philosophy of science (AAAS, 1993).
- To achieve science standards for all students, implying both excellence and equity (NRC, 1996).
- To design science education to reflect the premise that science is an active process, so that both "hands-on" as well as "minds-on" activities should constitute the core of the educational process.
- To focus on inquiry as a central element of the curriculum, to promote students to actively develop their understanding of scientific concepts, along with reasoning and thinking skills.

Similar goals can be found in articles and reports documenting reform efforts in other countries, for instance, the implementation of 'Science, Technology and Society' in Canada (Aikenhead & Ryan, 1992), or a new science curriculum in Australia (Curriculum Corporation, 1994). Also, a recent report about the future of science education in the United Kingdom, called 'Beyond 2000', contains recommendations with a similar direction (Millar & Osborne, 1998). In accordance with the 'Beyond 2000' report, a new GCE syllabus has been introduced, called 'Science for Public understanding' (NEAB, 1998). This new syllabus aims to increase students' understanding of everyday science, (2) confidence in reading and discussing media reports of issues concerning science and technology, and (3) appreciation of the impact of science on how we think and act.

In the Netherlands the national curriculum traditionally only contained physics, chemistry, and biology as separate subjects. With the exception of local, small-scale projects, there is no experience with an integrated approach to science teaching. As of 1998, however, such an approach has been implemented in the national curriculum through the introduction of 'Public Understanding of Science' as a new, separate subject, alongside the traditional disciplines of physics, chemistry, and biology (De Vos & Reiding, 1999). As with 'Science for

Public understanding' (NEAB, 1998), this new subject has three main objectives: (1) to introduce *every* student to major scientific concepts (i.e., life, matter, biosphere, solar system and the universe), (2) to demonstrate the complex interactions between science, technology, and society, and (3) to make students aware of the ways in which scientific knowledge is produced and developed, that is, to promote students' understanding of the nature of science. At the same time, the curriculum of the traditional subjects has been changed to promote active learning activities by the students, especially through inquiry, and, in general, to promote students' critical thinking abilities. To facilitate these changes, in particular to reduce the amount of content which needs to be covered, some topics have been removed from the curricula (e.g., the concept of entropy was removed from the chemistry curriculum).

From a teaching perspective, the reform efforts described above share some implications for teaching science:

– Instead of transmitting content knowledge in a rigid manner, the emphasis in teaching will be on designing situations and a variety of activities which enable students to learn actively. In this respect, the teacher needs to investigate what the students already know, identify possible misconceptions, and then design an appropriate educational setting. In any case, teachers need to be able to respond to situations in their classroom they might not have anticipated (Kennedy, 1998).
– Consequently, the number of topics in the curriculum will probably have to decrease. For teachers this implies the acceptance of the idea that "less is better", and resisting "the temptation to include too much" (Millar & Osborne, 1998, p. 17).
– In general, a shift toward *reflection on science* rather than focusing solely on the content of scientific ideas is implied. Teachers will thus be asked to pay more attention to aspects of science they usually ignore, or do not feel very comfortable with, like the history and philosophy of science, or the relation between science and societal issues.
– Teachers will be confronted with the challenge of teaching science in a way which appeals to *all* students, both from a cognitive and an affective perspective, and not just students with high abilities or high motivation for science.
– A shift toward the teaching of inquiry skills, which is dehnitely more complex than the traditional training of practical skills.

Before discussing these changes from the perspective of professional development activities, we will first address the literature on educational change and teachers' cognitions in a more general way.

Implementation of the Reform

The question how to involve teachers in curriculum reform efforts so that the chances of a successful innovation are enhanced has, of course, been asked in earlier innovations. For science education, in particular, "ever since the birth of the science curricular reform movement in the late 1950s, a large portion of science teacher education has been connected in some way to attempts to introduce curricular change" (Anderson & Mitchener, 1994, p. 36). Traditionally, this process consisted roughly of the following steps:

1. The core elements of the innovation were defined by curriculum developers or policy makers.
2. A description was made of the teaching behavior expected of teachers who would loyally implement the innovation, or of the skills teachers should acquire.
3. A series of training sessions or supervision activities were designed, aimed at developing the desired teaching behavior (cf. Joyce & Showers, 1980). In particular, "single shot interventions", like inservice workshops, were used to achieve this aim.
4. Usually, the implementation was not adopted by the teachers in the manner intended, or initially observed changes in the teachers' behavior did not persist.
5. The preceding four steps were repeated, but in a modified manner, or after the innovation itself had been redefined.

Of course, not every reform effort in the past followed this scheme. There have been many attempts to improve on this outline (cf. Sparks & Loucks-Horsley, 1990), but on the whole it can be concluded that the role of teachers in the context of curriculum change usually has been perceived as 'executing' the innovative ideas of others (policy makers, curriculum designers, researchers, and the like). Recently, Ball and Cohen (1999) have argued that the role of the government should be limited to establishing a framework for reforms (e.g., by setting standards and providing useful tools, like curricular materials). The reform of actual practice, however, should be in the hands of the professional sector.

In the recent literature, there is a growing consensus that educational reform efforts are doomed to fail if the emphasis is on developing specific teaching skills, unless the teachers' cognitions, including their beliefs, intentions, and attitudes, are taken into account (Haney, Czerniak, & Lumpe, 1996). Reforms call for radical changes in teachers' knowledge and beliefs about subject matter, teaching, children, and learning. Therefore, the implementation of reforms can be seen as essentially a matter of teacher learning (Ball & Cohen, 1999). However, many authors have pointed out that teachers' ideas about subject matter, teaching, and learning do not change easily nor rapidly. There are various reasons why teachers' cognitions are usually stable and why innovative ideas are not easily applied in their teaching practice. First, teachers do not tend to risk changing their own practice which is rooted in practical knowledge built up over the course of their careers. Over the years, this knowledge has proven workable in a satisfying way. From a constructivist point of view, there is thus no need for teachers to change their conceptions (Posner, Strike, Hewson, & Gertzog, 1982). Rather, teachers tend to change their practice in a tinkering manner, picking up new materials and techniques here and there, and incorporating these in their existing practice (Thompson & Zeuli, 1999). Second, although experience contributes to an increase in the extent of a teacher's practical knowledge, at the same time, the variety within this knowledge decreases. This phenomenon is known as knowledge concentration: people gradually "feel more at home" in an area that becomes smaller (Bereiter & Scardamalia, 1993). Consequently, it becomes more and more difficult for someone to move into an area of experience he or she is not familiar with. For these two reasons, innovators often tend to consider teachers' practical knowledge conservative (cf. Tom & Valli, 1990). However, as it is the expression of what teachers really know and do, it is a relevant source for innovators when implementing educational changes.

In order to understand the role of teachers' practical knowledge in the context of educational reform, a more detailed discussion of the nature of practical knowledge seems appropriate. The next section presents a review of the research on this subject, addressing the various elements of practical knowledge and their mutual relationships, how it develops, and the research approaches that may be used to investigate practical knowledge and changes herein.

Research on Teachers' Practical Knowledge

In the past decade, the interest in teachers' practical knowledge (Carter, 1990) or craft knowledge (Grimmett & MacKinnon, 1992) has increased. This increase was influenced by a growing dissatisfaction with research which focused exclusively on teacher behavior. In particular, the results of process-product research have been criticized. By process-product research we refer to a tradition in research on teaching that was inspired by, among others, the work of Gage (1978). Its main characteristic is the search for "effective" variables in teaching behavior, that is, teacher behaviors that correspond positively to pupil achievement scores. After the correlational relationship is established, the next step typically consists of determining the exact influence of that particular variable in an experimental-control group study (Rosenshine & Stevens, 1986). Doyle (1990) has argued that the focus in process-product research on indicators of effectiveness has led to a depersonalized, context-free, and mechanistic view of teaching, in which the complexity of the teaching enterprise is not acknowledged. The underlying knowledge claim was that research could prescribe what teachers had to know and how they should act in the classroom. However, it has also been argued that, to understand the complex process of teaching, it is necessary to understand the knowledge teachers build and use "in action" (cf. Schön, 1983). In what has been labeled a "cognitive change" (Clark & Peterson, 1986), the focus in research has shifted toward the cognitions or thoughts that underlie a teacher's actions. Within this perspective, the concept of practical knowledge refers to the integrated set of knowledge, conceptions, beliefs, and values teachers develop in the context of the teaching situation. Based on the view that research cannot control practice, and prescribe what practitioners have to know and do, research on teachers' practical knowledge can be seen as a result of the criticism on process -product research, and the knowledge claim that belongs to that vision. By acknowledging the complex and context-specific nature of teaching, this research will hopefully empower teachers and enhance the status of teaching as a profession (Doyle, 1990).

The Nature of Teachers' Practical Knowledge

It is generally agreed that a teacher's practical knowledge guides his or her actions in practice (Lantz & Kass, 1987; Brickhouse, 1990; Verloop, 1992). Consequently, practical knowledge can be seen as the core of a teacher's professionality. The most important features of practical knowledge are described below:

1. It is *action-oriented* knowledge, acquired without direct help from others (Johnston, 1992). It is the accumulated wisdom of teachers on the basis of their experiences, which they can immediately use in their own teaching practice (Carter, 1990; Beijaard & Verloop, 1996).
2. It is *person- and context-bound*. It allows teachers to achieve the goals they personally value (Johnston, 1992). In addition, practical knowledge is affected by teachers' concerns about their own teaching context. Thus, practical knowledge is situation-specific, as it is adapted to a context which includes the students, the coursebooks and other learning materials, the curriculum, the school culture, and so on. This context may also vary considerably across countries (Stigler, Gallimore, & Hiebert, 2000).

Also, the teachers' disciplinary background appears to play an important role in this respect. Especially in secondary and higher education, a teacher's professional identity formation is strongly determined by the subject he or she teaches (Sikes et al., 1991).

3. It is, to a great extent, implicit or *tacit* knowledge. Teachers are not used to articulating their practical knowledge: they are more in a "doing" environment, than in a "knowing" environment (Clandinin, 1986; Eraut, 1994). Consequently, developing a shared knowledge base seems to be more problematic for teachers than for professionals in other fields.
4. It is *integrated* knowledge: scientific or formal knowledge, everyday knowledge, including norms and values, as well as experiential knowledge are part of practical knowledge (Handal & Lauvas, 1987). The process of knowledge integration is guided by experiences which play a key role in the development or change of teachers' practical knowledge. Through this process, practical knowledge encompasses elements of formal knowledge, adapted to the teaching context. Such elements may be derived from the teacher's prior formal education, as well as from inservice schooling activities (Beijaard & Verloop, 1996). However, researchers still only minimally understand how teachers integrate knowledge from different sources into the conceptual frameworks that guide their actions in practice (Eraut, 1994).
5. In building practical knowledge, teachers' *beliefs* play a very important role. As part of practical knowledge, both beliefs and knowledge are closely interwoven, but the nature of beliefs make them the filter through which new knowledge is interpreted and, subsequently, integrated in conceptual frameworks (Pajares, 1992). Beliefs, therefore, play a central role in organizing knowledge and defining behavior (Richardson, 1996). Beliefs may refer to pedagogical values as well as to teaching a specific subject or issue. Such beliefs are influenced by, among other things, a teacher's biography, for instance, by their own teachers, by raising their own children or by their disciplinary background.

One implication from the above description concerns the importance of the subject teachers teach in their practical knowledge. In this respect, it is relevant to discuss the concept of pedagogical content knowledge (PCK), which has been introduced as an element of the knowledge base for teaching (Shulman, 1986). PCK has been described as "that special amalgam of content and pedagogy that is uniquely the province of teachers, their own special form of professional understanding" (Shulman, 1987, p. 8). It refers to a transformation of the subject matter knowledge, used by teachers in the communication process with learners. PCK consists of two key elements: knowledge of instructional strategies incorporating representations of subject matter, and understanding of specific learning difficulties and student conceptions with respect to that subject matter (Van Driel, Verloop, & De Vos, 1998). As PCK refers to *particular topics* it is to be discerned from the knowledge of pedagogy, of educational purposes, and of learner characteristics in a general sense. Moreover, because PCK concerns the *teaching* of particular topics, it may turn out to differ considerably from subject matter knowledge per se. Finally, PCK is developed through an integrative process rooted in classroom practice implying that prospective or beginning teachers usually have little or no PCK at their disposal. In light of our conceptualization of practical knowledge presented earlier in this article, it follows that PCK may be perceived as a central element within teachers' practical knowledge (cf. Cochran, DeRuiter, & King, 1993).

In recent years, research in the domains discussed above has significantly promoted our understanding of the content of teachers' knowledge and beliefs, and of the relations between the elements that form teachers' cognitions. However, at this time it is not possible to characterize research on teachers' practical knowledge unequivocally. A wide range of research has already been done on teachers' practical knowledge, on teachers from different disciplinary backgrounds and countries, focusing on different aspects of a teacher's work, such as student learning, teaching of specific subject matter, collaboration with colleagues, school culture, and educational change. To understand the scope of the research on practical knowledge, we will now discuss the rationale and methodological approaches used by different investigators.

Research Rationale and Methodological Approaches

Most research on teachers' practical knowledge takes place within the hermeneutic or interpretative scientific research tradition. The studies within this tradition are usually small-scale and in-depth. Many researchers embed their studies in a narrative research approach. The underlying assumption is that narratives are not only crucial for providing insight into what teachers think and do, they also help teachers to make sense of what they think and do. Narrative research can be seen as a means of understanding teachers' culture from within (Cortazzi, 1993), by making use of personal materials such as life story, conversation, and personal writing (Connelly & Clandinin, 1990; Elbaz-Luwisch, 1997; for an example of a study in science teaching, see Osborne, 1998). The ways researchers structure their studies differ considerably. Some focus on the teacher's story applying a very loose way of collecting data, sometimes without any advance theoretical structuring of the study, whereas other researchers determine in advance which aspects of practical knowledge they want to investigate and, subsequently, use more structured methods of data collection. This is not the place to discuss and assess the various types of research on teachers' practical knowledge in detail. However, we consider it problematic if researchers merely let teachers 'talk' without interpreting their stories in terms of similarities and differences between them. We agree with Tom and Valli (1990) that such research merely leads to a collection of idiosyncratic teacher narratives, without any reference to scientific theory.

From our point of view, research on practical knowledge should aim to identify common patterns in the practical knowledge of individual teachers, and in the development of this knowledge. As a result, research in this domain can lead to the establishment of a body of knowledge which constitutes an addition to existing scientific knowledge bases for teaching (Verloop, 1992). This body of knowledge may function as a "framework for helping prospective and experienced teachers develop their repertoire of responses, understandings, and magical tricks" (Grimmett & MacKinnon, 1992, p. 441). Thus, codifying practical knowledge can help to bridge the gap between the theory and practice of teaching. For example, the results of such research may be used as case material in teacher education, and as an important source for prospective teachers to reflect upon.

To achieve this aim, various instruments and procedures have been developed to investigate teachers' knowledge and beliefs in a valid and reliable manner. In her review of methods for investigating teachers' cognitions, Kagan (1990) is rather critical of research designs in which only one method or instrument is applied. She argues that such designs are problematic, because the complexity of a teacher's practical knowledge cannot be captured by a single instrument. Instead, Kagan suggests applying multimethod designs, which focus on specific, well-defined aspects of teachers' knowledge and beliefs (e.g., PCK of particular topics). For instance, adequate designs may include Likert-type questionnaires, in combination with interviews and experimental tasks (cf. Peterson, Fennema, Carpenter, & Loef, 1989), or structured interviews, combined with teachers' logs, transcripts of actual lessons, and stimulated recall (cf. Smith & Neale, 1989). Kagan recommends the use of techniques that "yield qualitative, molar descriptions" and concludes that "the use of multimethod approaches appears to be superior, not simply because they allow triangulation of data but because they are more likely to capture the complex, multifaceted aspects of teaching and learning" (Kagan, 1990, p. 459).

A recent example of a study in which these suggestions have been applied, is found in Meijer (1999). To capture experienced teachers' practical knowledge about teaching reading comprehension in secondary education, Meijer used three instruments: (a) a semi-structured interview to elicit ideas about all possible aspects of teaching reading comprehension, (b) concept mapping, in which teachers organized and explained concepts that they viewed as important in this domain, and (c) stimulated recall interviews, in which teachers explicated what they were thinking in response to the videotape of a lesson they had just given. In a triangulation procedure, the data obtained with these instruments were combined to develop a comprehensive view of teachers' practical knowledge in the specific area of reading comprehension. It was concluded that this approach had been fruitful, as the combination of data from different sources had led to the identification of three types of practical knowledge, which could be described in detail (Meijer, 1999, p. 107).

All of the methods described so far can be used to capture teachers' practical knowledge at one point in time, or in a particular period. Obviously, in the context of curriculum reform, it is often relevant to monitor changes in teachers' practical knowledge. On the basis of her review, Kagan (1990) concludes that techniques to measure short-term changes in teachers' beliefs often suffer from a lack of ecological validity. She suggests that this may be due to short-term conceptual change being "superficial and ultimately transient" (Kagan, 1990, p. 459). A technique that has been applied frequently to investigate changes in teachers' practical knowledge, is the repeated use of concept mapping. Although Kagan is critical about how this method has been applied in many studies, she recommends the use of free-style concept maps at specific points in time, in combination with additional data sources (e.g., lesson plans, stimulated recall, or written self-evaluations). When these data sources are triangulated, an increase in the complexity of the concept maps may be indicative of an increased understanding of the topic under consideration.

A relatively new technique for investigating practical knowledge about relevant experiences and events throughout a teacher's career, is the so-called story-line method (Gergen, 1988). Beijaard et al. (1999) applied this technique in three different studies, focusing on teachers' subjective evaluation of experiences and events which pertain to a particular aspect of teaching (e.g., their interaction with students) for a period of time (e.g., the number of years they work as a teacher). By drawing a story line, teachers describe their evaluation of the aspect under consideration, on a scale from positive to negative as a function of time. Next, they are asked to clarify, in writing or orally, the high(est) and low(est) points in their story lines. Beijaard et al. concluded that the story-line method can be used efficiently and satisfactorily if certain conditions are met (e.g., addressing a limited number of aspects of teaching, drawing story lines from the present to the past). In particular, the authors value the fact that this method enables teachers to evaluate and interpret crucial experiences themselves, as an alternative to methods in which this evaluation is done by the researcher.

Science Teachers' Practical Knowledge

In this section, the attention is shifted toward science teachers' practical knowledge. For this purpose, we have selected studies in which science teachers' knowledge and beliefs are explicitly related to their classroom practice. It should be noted, however, that the expression "practical knowledge" is not used by all the scholars whose work is discussed below. From studies of *experienced* science teachers' cognitions it follows that these teachers have developed a conceptual framework in which knowledge and beliefs about science, subject matter, teaching and learning, and students are integrated in a coherent manner. Moreover, their teaching behavior usually seems consistent with this framework (Brickhouse, 1990). Individual teachers, however, may have developed quite different frameworks or "functional paradigms", even when they teach the same curriculum (Lantz & Kass, 1987). Tobin and McRobbie (1996) have identified four "cultural myths" which guide the classroom practice of experienced science teachers. Among other things, these myths concern the belief that teaching in a transmissive mode is more effective than the use of innovative teaching approaches, in which the emphasis is on facilitating and guiding student understanding, and the feeling that the mandated curriculum dominates classroom practice. From an innovative point of view, these myths are to be considered as impediments to change. For *beginning and prospective* science teachers a different picture emerges. The practical knowledge of these teachers often consists of elements which are not integrated. As a result, these teachers often seem to experience conflicts between their personal beliefs about science and science teaching on the one hand, and their own actual classroom practice on the other hand (Roberts & Chastko, 1990; Brickhouse & Bodner, 1992; Powell, 1994; Simmons et al., 1999).

Below, studies on specific aspects of science teachers' practical knowledge are discussed. This concerns studies on knowledge and beliefs about the teaching and learning of science, and about the nature of science. Next, studies on science teachers' beliefs about reform in science education are addressed. Finally, research on science teachers' PCK is discussed.

Practical Knowledge of the Teaching and Learning of Science, and the Nature of Science

Many studies on specific aspects of science teachers' practical knowledge have focused on views about the teaching and learning of science. These studies were usually conducted in the context of the implementation of constructivist teaching approaches. Some of these studies focused on the effects of inservice or preservice programs on teachers' views of teaching and learning science (e.g., Constable & Long, 1991; Hand & Treagust, 1994; Porlán Ariza & García Goméz, 1992), sometimes in connection with views on teaching science to students from various cultures (Southerland & Gess-Newsome, 1999). From the perspective of practical knowledge, studies focusing on the actual implementation of constructivist approaches in classroom practice are particularly interesting. These studies have revealed that although teachers may express cognitions about the teaching and learning of science which are consistent with constructivist ideas, their actual classroom behavior may be more or less 'traditional' (Briscoe, 1991; Johnston, 1991; Mellado, 1998). However, some studies reported changes in both teachers' cognitions and their classroom practice in the direction of constructivist ideas. These changes seemed to take place on the conditions that sufficient time, resources, and on-going professional support are available (Appleton & Asoko, 1996; Glasson & Lalik, 1993; Tobin, 1993; Radford, 1998). Hewson, Tabachnick, Zeichner, and Lemberger (1999) concluded, on the basis of a series of studies of prospective biology teachers, that specific courses within a teacher education program may substantially promote teachers' adoption of constructivist views. To help teachers to put these constructivist ideas into practice, a close cooperation between schools and universities is necessary. Adams and Krockover (1999) also reported positive outcomes in a 3-year case study of a beginning secondary biology teacher, in which a specific observation rubric was used to stimulate a constructivist teaching style.

Another strand of research on science teachers' practical knowledge is devoted to cognitions about the nature of science (Lederman, 1992). As understanding of the nature of science is a central goal of many current reform efforts, teachers' cognitions in this domain are, of course, crucial. In general, however, these studies amount to the conclusion that, irrespective of their academic background, science teachers possess limited knowledge of the history and philosophy of science (Gallagher, 1991; King, 1991) and, as a consequence, hold inadequate or naive conceptions of the nature of science (Abd-El-Khalick & BouJaoude, 1997). For example, many teachers appear to hold positivist views, believing that the substantive content of science is fixed and unchangeable rather than tentative. Moreover, it has been repeatedly found that teachers' conceptions of the nature of science "do not necessarily inhuence classroom practice" (Lederman, 1999, p. 927). In a review of teacher education progams aimed at improving science teachers' conceptions of the nature of science, Abd-El-Khalick and Lederman (1999) concluded that explicitness and rehectiveness with respect to the nature of science are the most important features of programs that appeared successful in facilitating teachers to develop conceptions of the nature of science that are consistent with those advocated by current reforms, and to translate these conceptions into an appropriate classroom approach.

Beliefs about Reform in Science Education

Given the importance of teachers' beliefs with respect to their teaching behaviors, several scholars have investigated teachers' beliefs about science education reform. The identification of teachers' beliefs is considered to be critical to the reform process. Lumpe, Haney, and Czerniak (2000) concluded that, in particular, teachers' capability beliefs in combination with their beliefs about their science teaching context are "the more precise agents of change" (Lumpe et al., 2000, p. 288). Cronin-Jones (1991) identified four categories of beliefs, which strongly influenced curriculum implementation. These categories concerned the teacher's own role, the way students learn, the abilities of particular groups of students, and the relative importance of content topics. When implementing a new curriculum, teachers appeared to adapt this curriculum according to their own context and beliefs.

Yerrick, Parke, and Nugent (1997) investigated the beliefs and knowledge of a group of experienced science teachers (n = 8) during a 2-week summer course, intended to prepare teachers to implement an inquiry-oriented science curriculum. The authors reported that teachers "began to use different ways of speaking about students and content (...) without changing fundamental views of science and teaching" (Yerrick et al., 1997, p. 14). Rather than accusing these teachers of conservatism, the authors discussed the "real dilemmas" which teachers encountered when they attempted to change their classroom practice. The authors concluded by expressing the desire to continue to collaborate with teachers, and "to continue to listen to the impact of reform in the classroom setting and then use what we hear to make shifts in staff development design" (Yerrick et al., 1997, p. 156).

Several studies have been carried out in the context of projects of local systemic science education reform. In a study aimed at assessing the impact of such a program, Levitt (2000) found that experienced teachers espoused certain non-traditional beliefs about teaching and learning of science. These beliefs concerned the use of hands-on activities, discourse and collaboration, and inquiry approaches. Similar results were obtained by Haney et al. (1996). In Levitt's study, it was also found that teachers' practices began to align with these beliefs. However, the change in teachers' beliefs was deemed "not yet strong enough". Levitt concluded that continuing professional development activities are necessary to sustain and elaborate the changes in teachers' beliefs and practices. Haney et al. (1996) suggested that such activities should be organized at a local level in a concrete and project-like manner.

Whigham, Andre, and Yang (2000) investigated the beliefs of science and mathematics teachers with respect to teaching activities that were either consistent or inconsistent with the national standards for science or mathematics education (cf. NRC, 1996). They found that teachers expressed a higher degree of belief in, and greater classroom use of, standards-consistent activities than standards-inconsistent activities. At the same time, however, many teachers, especially secondary science teachers, also expressed a strong commitment toward standards-inconsistent activities. For instance, most teachers believed that they should focus on student understanding, whereas they also believed that the curriculum should focus on student acquisition of information. These apparently inconsistent belief systems were explained by the authors in terms of science teachers struggling with the tension of pursuing science topics in depth, as required by the standards, versus pressure to "get through" the breadth of the provided curriculum materials. They suggested that teachers might beneht from inservice training, aimed at conceptual change instruction on the standards.

Science Teachers' PCK

A distinct group of studies concerns science teachers' PCK. Some of these have emphasized the importance of teachers' understanding of subject matter, which appears to function as a prerequisite before the development of PCK can take place. Smith and Neale (1989), for example, studied the effects of an inservice workshop for elementary teachers, and concluded that this program had been successful in terms of promoting teachers' knowledge of specific contents, but not with respect to the development of PCK. The authors concluded that unless teachers have acquired a "deeply principled conceptual knowledge of the content", the development of PCK is unlikely to occur (Smith & Neale, 1989, p. 17). From studies of experienced science teachers who taught topics outside their area of certification, it appeared that their general pedagogical knowledge provided them with a framework for teaching. The teachers in these studies quickly learned the new content as well as adequate content-specific instructional strategies. Sanders, Borko, and Lockard (1993) concluded that teachers integrated content knowledge and PCK in their pedagogical knowledge frameworks. In other words, it appears that both general pedagogical knowledge and subject matter knowledge can form a basis on which teachers build the development of their PCK.

The most important factor in the development of PCK is, obviously, teaching experience. For instance, Clermont, Borko, and Krajcik (1994) found that experienced chemistry teachers possessed a greater repertoire of representations and strategies of a particular topic than novices when they used chemical demonstrations as an instructional strategy. Moreover, experienced teachers were able to use certain demonstrations for various purposes, and were more successful in relating their demonstrations to specific learning difficulties of students. However, experienced science teachers' PCK may differ considerably, even when their subject matter knowledge is similar and when they teach the same curriculum. These differences are reflected by different representations and instructional strategies used in the classroom. A lack of teaching experience explains why prospective or novice science teachers usually express little to no PCK (e.g., Lederman, Gess-Newsome, & Latz, 1994). Teacher training programs are not always very successful in promoting the development of science teachers' PCK (e.g., Adams & Krockover, 1997).

Discussion and Implications
In summarizing the results of research on science teachers' practical knowledge, we may conclude that experienced science teachers, as opposed to beginning teachers, have developed an integrated set of knowledge and beliefs, which is usually consistent with how they act in practice. Factors such as the mandated (national) curriculum, and the school culture seem to determine, to a large extent, the content of their practical knowledge. Consequently, in the context of curricular change, several problems may occur. First, teachers may not possess adequate knowledge of the new content (e.g., the nature or philosophy of science) or pedagogy (e.g., conceptual change teaching) to be implemented. Second, teachers' beliefs with respect to the new content or pedagogy may differ from the intentions of the innovation. For that matter, it seems that "traditional" staff development programs, such as short-term intensive workshops can be successful in upgrading teachers' content knowledge, and in their acceptance of the ideas behind an innovation.

However, when teachers are asked to put an innovation into practice, problems are reported in all studies. For instance, inconsistencies often occur between teachers' expressed beliefs and their behavior in the classroom. It seems that long-term staff development programs are needed to actually change experienced teachers' practical knowledge. Given the nature of practical knowledge as integrated knowledge which guides teachers' practical actions, this is not surprising. From this perspective, an innovation implies not simply adding new information to existing knowledge frameworks; in fact, teachers need to restructure their knowledge and beliefs, and, on the basis of teaching experiences, integrate the new information in their practical knowledge. In the following section, types of staff development programs are discussed which have the potential to stimulate this complex process.

Reform and Professional Development Focusing on Teachers' Practical Knowledge

We perceive staff development or professionalization as a permanent process, aimed at extending and updating the professional knowledge and beliefs of teachers in the context of their work. With respect to reform efforts, we agree with Wallace and Louden (1992) that the focus "should be on facilitating the growth of the knowledge teachers have and use" (p. 518). In other words, the implementation or "scaling up" of a reform is "a process of learning rather than a process of design and engineering" (Thompson & Zeuli, 1999, p. 371). From research, it has become clear that there is not one 'ideal' way to organize staff development in the context of a reform project. Rather, multiple strategies are necessary to promote changes in teachers' knowledge and beliefs. These strategies may include: access to innovative classroom materials, opportunities to practice new ways of teaching, reflection on practical experiences, possibilities to discuss elements of the reform with others (peers, coaches, supervisors), a supportive environment, and so on (Haney et al., 1996). Below we will discuss some strategies aimed at changing teachers' existing practical knowledge (for a more detailed description of these strategies, see Beijaard, Verloop, Wubbels, & Feiman-Nemser, 2000). The elements shared by these strategies include: (a) an explicit focus on teachers' knowledge and beliefs, throughout all stages of the reform, (b) collegial cooperation or exchange between teachers, and (c) sufficient time for changes to occur, from at least one semester to several academic years.

Learning and Professional Development in Networks
In the last decade, collegial learning in school networks has emerged as a way to promote professional development (Huberman, 1995). It is generally agreed that the natural resistance to change and innovation, particularly by experienced teachers, can be reduced by learning in networks. Such networks are more or less formalized structures in which participants from different schools aim to achieve previously formulated objectives for a particular period of time. In networks, participants systematically learn from and with each other as colleagues. In other words, networking is characterized by "horizontal learning" as opposed to "vertical learning", that is, learning conducted by an external expert. Empirical research on this kind of teacher learning is beginning to appear (e.g., Galesloot, Koetsier, & Wubbels, 1997; Ryan, 1999). This research has shown that learning in networks may be particularly effective when teachers share similar school tasks, but have different experiences performing these tasks in their own schools. Specific results of learning in networks could refer

to a growth in teachers' conhdence in the value of their own practical knowledge for other teachers, and an increase in willingness to experiment with ideas from colleagues in their own classrooms. In this respect, it seems that external conditions, such as available time, need to be related to internal or personal conditions (e.g., one's expectations of a network and prior experiences) so as to create an environment of willingness to learn and to experiment.

It is important for future research to focus not only on how and what teachers learn in networks, but also on the requirements and conditions that have to be met to establish wellfunctioning horizontal learning in a network as a relatively new structure in continuing education. For instance, conversations about practice in network settings are not necessarily productive. Thus we need to know what it is that can make such conversations useful.

Peer Coaching
Horizontal learning takes place not only in networks, but in other settings as well; for example, through peer coaching. Peer coaching can be seen as a process of cooperation between two or more colleagues in which they exchange ideas, attempt to implement these ideas, reflect on their own teaching practice, and so on. Peer coaching requires interaction on an equal basis. Moreover, a strict separation from performance evaluation must be guaranteed. Being a coach for a colleague calls for a systematic approach agreed upon by all participants. This concerns, for example, the way feedback is given on a lesson observed by the coach. A teacher acting as a coach contributes not only to the professional development of a colleague, but to his or her own professional growth as well (Bergen, 1996; Philips & Glickman, 1991). In general, collegial coaching can be considered a rather simple strategy. In reality, it may have a great impact on how teachers function in schools: most teachers are "professionals in isolation", and are not used to talking about their work (Clandinin, 1986). Peer coaching, therefore, also implies that certain working conditions are met and implemented by school leaders, so that it becomes part of the school culture.

Collaborative Action Research
Collaborative action research projects can be designed as a specific form of staff development in the context of the implementation of an innovation. Although there are many variations of action research, the aim is always to yield practical, applicable results, for either personal, professional or political purposes (Noffke, 1997). Action research can have various theoretical orientations (e.g., technical, practical or emancipatory), and can imply different types of reflection (e.g., autobiographical or collaborative; Rearick & Feldman, 1999).

Common features of collaborative action research include control or ownership of the specific questions or problems teachers want to explore and the actions they carry out (e.g., developing materials, gathering information, and collecting data), in combination with group activities, such as sharing experiences and discussing or evaluating results (Cohen & Manion, 1994). The group, which may be supported or facilitated by educators or university-based researchers, constitutes a context in which the activities of individual teachers are embedded. In the case of the implementation of an innovation, the group may have a common goal, but each individual teacher is stimulated to explore this goal according to his or her own context, teaching situations, individual beliefs, and so on.

Feldman (1996) applied this approach in a group of eight physics teachers during a 3-year project. Activities included anecdote telling as a tool for teachers to share their knowledge, trying out new ideas about teaching and learning in the classroom, and systematic inquiry. Feldman concluded that since these activities were closely connected to the normal practice of the participants, they have the potential to be embedded in the practice of other science teachers, leading to the enhancement of this practice. Bencze and Hodson (1999) arrived at similar conclusions after an action research project in which two teachers and a researcher/educator cooperated in the design and implementation of more authentic science for grade 7 classrooms. In addition to other results, the project led to changes in the teachers' views about science and science teaching.

Lynch (1997) studied the effects of a collaborative project on a group of 25 beginning science teachers who were preparing for the science education reform advocated by AAAS (1993) and NRC (1996). The project consisted of a series of 3-hour-long seminars. During these seminars the intentions of the reform were discussed in relation to the participants' ideas and beliefs. Next, teachers developed their own criteria, as a tool to make sense of the reform. Finally, teams of three teachers were formed, who designed 10-day teaching units. Although these units were not actually taught, the project apparently helped the teachers to make sense of, and appreciate, the goals of the reform. In particular, the teachers' criteria appeared to be a useful tool, which they used afterward to review the goals of the reform, and specific teaching materials. Lynch concluded that developing these criteria contributed to the development of the teachers' PCK.

Parke and Coble (1997) have taken the collaborative action research approach a step further by involving teachers in curriculum development activities, which became a vehicle for professional development. Parke and Coble designed an approach in which teachers communicated continuously with colleagues as well as university staff. The development of curriculum materials was preceded by a dialogue about the reform goals. Next, in the organization of the curriculum development activities, attention was given, in particular, to the alignment of the curriculum materials teachers developed with the personal beliefs they articulated, and the school environment in which the curriculum was to be implemented. On the basis of a study involving science teachers from seven schools, Parke and Coble concluded that their approach "supported teachers to become architects for change through building upon their current conceptions instead of attempting to remediate them" (Parke & Coble, 1997, p. 785).

The Use of Cases
The use of cases as a tool to promote the development of professional knowledge of teachers has been advocated by Shulman (1986). Cases are short narratives, usually written in first-person, describing authentic or realistic classroom situations. Most cases concern problematic situations, for instance, illustrating typical problems that can occur during the teaching of specific issues. Darling-Hammond and Snyder (2000) described several professional development contexts in which cases were used. They also wrote about problems which may occur when using cases, for instance, (1) a case writer's or case user's limited knowledge or frame of reference for an adequate analysis of the nature of the issue addressed in the case, and (2) a case writer's or case user's lack of ability to generalize from the single instance represented in the case to a well-grounded set of principles for interpretation of practice. Darling-Hammond and Snyder described examples of cases, in which these problems were avoided.

In a review of the *Mathematics Case Methods Project,* Barnett (1998) concluded that teacher-authored cases can be a powerful tool to discuss content-related, pedagogical and philosophical issues in groups of teachers and university-based facilitators. Among other things, this approach appeared to stimulate (1) teachers' own understanding of mathematics, (2) the use of a student perspective as a source of feedback, and (3) a critical examination of alternative views. The latter results are relevant in particular for the development of PCK. Essential to the case-based approach was the goal to have teachers expose different ways of looking at things, rather than to impose specific views upon them.

In the held of science education, some scholars have reported that the use of vignettes which focus on content-specific teaching approaches, or on students' reasoning and misconceptions concerning a specific topic, may contribute to the development of PCK (Loughran, Gunstone, Berry, Milroy, & Mulhall, 2000; Veal, 1998). For instance, when teachers analyzed students' reasoning in such vignettes in relation to their own teaching experiences and discussed their analyses with their peers, they were stimulated to develop representations and instructional strategies with respect to the specific topics under consideration (Geddis, 1993; Van Driel et al., 1998).

Concluding Remarks

From the research discussed in this article, it follows that the practical knowledge of experienced teachers consists of an integrated set of beliefs and knowledge, which is often implicit. The research literature does not suggest, however, that this practical knowledge cannot be changed. Various methods may be applied to change teachers' practical knowledge in the course of a reform project. Preferably, a combination of methods should be used in this respect. In any case, professional development activities and reform should be linked hrmly throughout all stages of any reform project.

An essential characteristic of the strategies described in the last section is that a teacher's practice and his or her personal knowledge of this practice constitute the starting point for change. Consequently, one needs to investigate the practical knowledge of the teachers involved, including their beliefs, attitudes and concerns, at the start of a reform project (cf. Haney et al., 1996). Rather than recommending a few specific techniques, we suggest the use of multimethod designs (cf. Kagan, 1990). Obviously, the teachers' existing practical knowledge should not be considered as the norm per se. In attempts to change this knowledge, however, one should realize that the role of a teacher's practical knowledge in the context of educational reform is complex and multifaceted:

– When teachers' actual cognitions are deemed incompatible with specific ideas behind educational reform, one may attempt to create cognitive dissonance among teachers (Ball & Cohen, 1999; Thompson & Zeuli, 1999). For this purpose, strategies may be used which are similar to those in the conceptual change literature (e.g., Posner et al., 1982). Next, teachers may alter their conceptions when alternatives are in reach, which are vivid, concrete, and detailed enough to become plausible and attractive (Feiman-Nemser & Remillard, 1996).

– Some of the teachers' cognitions can be used as a source of inspiration in the design of the reform, in particular when teachers with rich expertise (cf. "wisdom of practice"; Shulman, 1987) are identified. For instance, this may occur in the context of developing curriculum materials.

– Occasionally, when a large gap is identified between innovative ideas and the practical knowledge of a vast number of teachers, one may arrive at the conclusion that the reform needs to be redefined, for instance, at a lower level of ambitions. In other words, an investigation of teachers' practical knowledge may reveal what can be achieved within the reform project.

In the course of a reform project, it is necessary to monitor the practical knowledge of the teachers to investigate the progress of the reform. Moreover, this makes it possible to adjust the project so as to enhance the chances of successful implementation.

The apparent success of some of the approaches discussed in the last section (e.g., Lynch, 1997; Park & Coble, 1997) supports our view that teachers should be involved substantially in all phases of a reform effort. Partnerships between teachers, educators, researchers, and administrators are necessary to facilitate such approaches. Moreover, time is needed, because the approaches we advocate here are not likely to bring about change in teaching practice rapidly, but rather they should lead to authentic change (cf. Thompson & Zeuli, 1999). Future research on the effectiveness of approaches like these may contribute to the design of successful reform projects in science education, in close conjunction with strategies for professional development.

Note

[1] Originally published as Van Driel, J. H., Beijaard, D., & Verloop, N. (2001). Professional development and reform in science education: The role of teachers' practical knowledge. *Journal of Research in Science Teaching*, 38(2), 137–158. Reprinted, with minor edits, with permission from the publisher.

References

AAAS (American Association for the Advancement of Science). (1993). *Project 2061: Benchmarks for science literacy.* Oxford University Press.

Abd-El-Khalick, F., & BouJaoude, S. (1997). An exploratory study of the knowledge base for science teaching. *Journal of Research in Science Teaching*, 34, 673–699.

Abd-El-Khalick, F., & Lederman, N. G. (1999). *Success of the attempts to improve science teachers' conceptions of nature of science: A review of the literature* [Paper presentation].The fifth History and Philosophy of Science & Science Teaching conference, Padova, Italy.

Adams, P. E., & Krockover, G. H. (1997). Beginning science teacher cognition and its origins in the preservice secondary science teacher program. *Journal of Research in Science Teaching*, 34, 633–653.

Adams, P. E., & Krockover, G. H. (1999). Stimulating constructivist teaching styles through use of an observation rubric. *Journal of Research in Science Teaching, 36,* 955–971.

Aikenhead, G. S., & Ryan, A. G. (1992). The development of a new instrument – Views on Science-Technology-Society (VOSTS). *Science Education, 76,* 477–491.

Anderson, R. D., & Mitchener, C. P. (1994). Research on science teacher education. In D.L. Gabel (Ed.), *Handbook of research on science teaching and learning* (pp. 3–44). Macmillan.

Appleton, K., & Asoko, H. (1996). A case study of a teacher's progress toward using a constructivist view of learning to inform teaching in elementary science. *Science Education, 80,* 165–180.

Ball, D. L., & Cohen, D. K. (1999). Developing practice, developing practitioners. In L. Darling-Hammond & G. Sykes (Eds.), *Teaching as the learning profession. Handbook of policy and practice* (pp. 3–32). Jossey-Bass.

Barnett, C. (1998). Mathematics teaching cases as a catalyst for informed strategic inquiry. *Teaching and Teacher Education, 14,* 81–93.

Beijaard, D., Van Driel, J. H., & Verloop, N. (1999). Evaluation of story-line methodology in research on teachers' practical knowledge. *Studies in Educational Evaluation, 25,* 47–62.

Beijaard, D., & Verloop, N. (1996). Assessing teachers' practical knowledge. *Studies in Educational Evaluation, 22,* 275–286.

Beijaard, D., Verloop, N., Wubbels, Th., & Feiman-Nemser, S. (2000). The professional development of teachers. In R. J. Simons, J. van der Linden, & T. Duffy (Eds.), *New learning* (pp. 261–279). Kluwer.

Bencze, T., & Hodson, D. (1999). Changing practice by changing practice: Toward more authentic science and science curriculum development. *Journal of Research in Science Teaching, 36,* 521–540.

Bereiter, C., & Scardamalia, M. (1993). *Surpassing ourselves: An inquiry into the nature and implications of expertise.* Open Court.

Bergen, T. C. M. (1996). *Docenten scholen docenten: Over de professionele ontwikkeling van docenten door middel van peer coaching* [*Teachers training teachers: About the professional development of teachers by peer coaching*]. Catholic University Nijmegen.

Brickhouse, N. W. (1990). Teachers' beliefs about the nature of science and their relationships to classroom practice. *Journal of Teacher Education, 41,* 53–62.

Brickhouse, N. W., & Bodner, G. M. (1992). The beginning science teacher: Classroom narratives of convictions and constraints. *Journal of Research in Science Teaching, 29,* 471–485.

Briscoe, C. (1991). The dynamic interactions among beliefs, role metaphors, and teaching practices: A case study of teacher change. *Science Education, 75,* 185–199.

Bybee, R. W., & DeBoer, G. E. (1994). Research on goals for the science curriculum. In D. L. Gabel (Ed.), *Handbook of research on science teaching and learning* (pp. 357–387). Macmillan.

Carter, K. (1990). Teachers' knowledge and learning to teach. In W. R. Houston (Ed.), *Handbook of research on teacher education* (pp. 291–310). Macmillan.

Chang, Y.-H., Chang, C.-Y., & Tseng, Y.-H. (2010). Trends of science education research: An automatic content analysis. *Journal of Science Education and Technology, 19*(4), 315–331.

Clandinin, D. J. (1986). *Classroom practice: Teacher images in action.* Falmer Press.

Clark, C. M., & Peterson, P. L. (1986). Teachers' thought processes. In M. C. Wittrock (Ed.), *Handbook of research on teaching* (3rd ed., pp. 255–296). Macmillan.

Clermont, C. P., Borko, H., & Krajcik, J. S. (1994). Comparative study of the pedagogical content knowledge of experienced and novice chemical demonstrators. *Journal of Research in Science Teaching, 31,* 419–441.

Cochran, K. F., DeRuiter, J. A., & King, R. A. (1993). Pedagogical content knowing: An integrative model for teacher preparation. *Journal of Teacher Education, 44,* 263–272.

Cohen, L., & Manion, L. (1994). *Research methods in education* (4th ed.). Routledge.

Connelly, F. M., & Clandinin, D. J. (1990). Stories of experience and narrative inquiry. *Educational Researcher, 19*(5), 2–14.

Constable, H., & Long, A. (1991). Changing science teaching: Lessons from a long-term evaluation of a short in-service course. *International Journal of Science Education, 13,* 405–419.

Cortazzi, M. (1993). *Narrative analysis.* Falmer Press.

Cronin-Jones, L. L. (1991). Science teacher beliefs and their influence on curriculum implementation: Two case studies. *Journal of Research in Science Teaching, 28,* 235–250.

Curriculum Corporation. (1994). *Science – A curriculum profile for Australian schools.* Curriculum Corporation.

Darling-Hammond, L., & Snyder, J. (2000). Authentic assessment of teaching in context. *Teaching and Teacher Education, 16,* 523–545.

De Vos, W., & Reiding, J. (1999). Public understanding of science as a separate subject in secondary schools in the Netherlands. *International Journal of Science Education, 21,* 711–719.

Doyle, W. (1990). Themes in teacher education research. In W. R. Houston (Ed.), *Handbook of research on teacher education* (pp. 3–24). Macmillan.

Duffee, L., & Aikenhead, G. (1992). Curriculum change, student evaluation, and teacher practical knowledge. *Science Education, 76,* 493–506.

Dufour, R., & Eaker, R. (1998). *Professional learning communities at work: Best practices for enhancing student achievement.* Association for Supervision and Curriculum Development.

Eraut, M. (1994). *Developing professional knowledge and competence*. Falmer Press.

Elbaz-Luwisch, F. (1997). Narrative research: Political issues and implications. *Teaching and Teacher Education, 13,* 75–83.

Feiman-Nemser, S., & Remillard, J. (1996). Perspectives on learning to teach. In F. B. Murray (Ed.), *The teacher educator's handbook* (pp. 63–91). Jossey Bass.

Feldman, A. (1996). Enhancing the practice of physics teachers: Mechanisms for the generation and sharing of knowledge and understanding in collaborative action research. *Journal of Research in Science Teaching, 33,* 513–540.

Fernandez, C., & Yoshida, M. (2004). *Lesson study: A case of a Japanese approach to improving instruction through school-based teacher development*. Lawrence Erlbaum.

Gage, N. L. (1978). *The scientific basis of the art of teaching*. Teachers College Press.

Galesloot, L. J., Koetsier, C. P., & Wubbels, Th. (1997). Handelingsaspecten bij wederzijds leren van ervaren docenten [Aspects of acting in reciprocal learning of experienced teachers]. *Pedagogische Studien, 74,* 249–260.

Gallagher, J. J. (1991). Prospective and practicing secondary school science teachers' knowledge and beliefs about the philosophy of science. *Science Education, 75,* 121–133.

Geddis, A. N. (1993). Transforming subject-matter knowledge: The role of pedagogical content knowledge in learning to reflect on teaching. *International Journal of Science Education, 15,* 673–683.

Gergen, M. M. (1988). Narrative structures in social explanation. In C. Antaki (Ed.), *Analysing social explanation* (pp. 94–112). Sage.

Glasson, G. E., & Lalik, R. V. (1993). Reinterpreting the learning cycle from a social constructivist perspective: A qualitative study of teachers' beliefs and practices. *Journal of Research in Science Teaching, 30,* 187–207.

Grimmett, P. P., & Mackinnon, A. M. (1992). Craft knowledge and the education of teachers. In G. Grant (Ed.), *Review of research in education* (Vol. 18, pp. 385–456). AERA.

Hand, B., & Treagust, D. F. (1994). Teachers' thought about changing to constructivist teaching/learning approaches within junior secondary science classrooms. *Journal of Education for Teaching, 20,* 97–112.

Handal, G., & Lauvas, P. (1987). *Promoting reflective teaching: Supervision in action*. SHRE and Open University Press.

Haney, J. J., Czerniak, C. M., & Lumpe, A. T. (1996). Teacher beliefs and intentions regarding the implementation of science eduction reform strands. *Journal of Research in Science Teaching, 33,* 971–993.

Hewson, P. W., Tabachnick, B. R., Zeichner, K. M., & Lemberger, J. (1999). Educating prospective teachers of biology: Findings, limitations and recommendations. *Science Education, 83,* 373–384.

Huberman, M. (1995). Networks that alter teaching: Conceptualizations, exchanges and experiments. *Teachers and Teaching: Theory and Practice, 1*, 193–211.

Johnston, K. (1991). High school science teachers' conceptualisations of teaching and learning: Theory and practice. *European Journal of Teacher Education, 14*, 65–78.

Johnston, S. (1992). Images: A way of understanding the practical knowledge of student teachers. *Teaching and Teacher Education, 8*, 123–136.

Joyce, B., & Showers, B. (1980). Improving inservice training: The message of research. *Educational Leadership, 37*, 379–385.

Kagan, D. M. (1990). Ways of evaluating teacher cognition: Inferences concerning the Goldilocks principle. *Review of Educational Research, 60*, 419–469.

Kennedy, M. M. (1998). Education reform and subject matter knowledge. *Journal of Research in Science Teaching, 35*, 249–263.

Kennedy, M. M. (2016). How does professional development improve teaching? *Review of Educational Research, 86*, 945–980.

King, B. B. (1991). Beginning teachers' knowledge of and attitudes toward history and philosophy of science. *Science Education, 75*, 135–141.

Lantz, O., & Kass, H. (1987). Chemistry teachers' functional paradigms. *Science Education, 71*, 117–134.

Lederman, N. G. (1992). Students' and teachers' conceptions of the nature of science: A review of the research. *Journal of Research in Science Teaching, 29*, 331–359.

Lederman, N. G. (1999). Teachers' understanding of the nature of science and classroom practice: Factors that facilitate or impede the relationship. *Journal of Research in Science Teaching, 36*, 916–929.

Lederman, N. G., Gess-Newsome, J., & Latz, M. S. (1994). The nature and development of preservice science teachers' conceptions of subject matter and pedagogy. *Journal of Research in Science Teaching, 31*, 129–146.

Levitt, K. (2000). *From hands-on to inquiry – Changing teachers' beliefs and classroom practice through systemic reform.* Paper presented at the annual meeting of the National Association of Research in Science Teaching, New Orleans, LA.

Loughran, J., Gunstone, R., Berry, A., Milroy, P., & Mulhall, P. (2000). *Science cases in action: Developing an understanding of science teachers' pedagogical content knowledge* [Paper presentation].The annual meeting of the National Association of Research in Science Teaching, New Orleans, LA.

Lumpe, A. T., Haney, J. J., & Czerniak, C. M. (2000). Assessing teachers' beliefs about their science teaching context. *Journal of Research in Science Teaching, 37*, 275–292.

Lynch, S. (1997). Novice teachers' encounter with National Science Education Reform: Entanglements or intelligent interconnections? *Journal of Research in Science Teaching, 34*, 3–18.

Meijer, P. C. (1999). *Teachers' practical knowledge: Teaching reading comprehension in secondary education* [PhD dissertation]. ICLON, Leiden University, the Netherlands.

Mellado, V. (1998). The classroom practice of preservice teachers and their conceptions of teaching and learning science. *Science Education, 82*, 197–214.

Millar, R., & Osborne, J. (Eds.). (1998). *Beyond 2000: Science education for the future*. King's College.

Munby, H., Cunningham, M., & Lock, C. (2000). School science culture: A case study of barriers to developing professional knowledge. *Science Education, 84*, 193–211.

NEAB (Northern Examinations and Assessment Board). (1998). *Science for public understanding* [Syllabus]. NEAB.

Noffke, S. E. (1997). Professional, personal, and political dimensions of action research. *Review of Educational Research, 22*, 305–343.

NRC (National Research Council). (1996). *National science education standards*. National Research Council.

Osborne, M. D. (1998). Teacher as knower and learner: Reflections on situated knowledge in science teaching. *Journal of Research in Science Teaching, 35*, 427–439.

Pajares, M. F. (1992). Teachers' beliefs and educational research: Cleaning up a messy construct. *Review of Educational Research, 62*, 307–332.

Parke, H. M., & Coble, C. R. (1997). Teachers designing curriculum as professional development: A model for transformational science teaching. *Journal of Research in Science Teaching, 34*, 773–790.

Peterson, P. L., Fennema, E., Carpenter, T. P., & Loef, M. (1989). Teachers' pedagogical content beliefs in mathematics. *Cognition and Instruction, 6*, 1–40.

Philips, M., & Glickman, C. (1991). Peer coaching: Developmental approach to enhancing teacher thinking. *Journal of Staff Development, 12*, 20–25.

Platteel, T., Hulshof, H., Van Driel, J. H., & Verloop, N. (2013). Teachers' interpretations of the concept-context approach for L1 education. *L1 – Educational Studies in Language and Literature, 13*, 1–25

Porlán Ariza, A., & García Goméz, M. S. (1992). The change of teachers' conceptions: A strategy for in-service science teachers' education. *Teaching and Teacher Education, 8*, 537–548.

Posner, G. J., Strike, K. A., Hewson, P. W., & Gertzog, W. A. (1982). Accomodation of a scientific conception: Toward a theory of conceptual change. *Science Education, 66*, 211–227.

Powell, R. (1994). From field science to classroom science: A case study of constrained emergence in a second-career science teacher. *Journal of Research in Science Teaching, 31*, 273–291.

Radford, D. L. (1998). Transferring theory into practice: A model for professional development for science education reform. *Journal of Research in Science Teaching, 35*, 73–88.

Rearick, M. L., & Feldman, A. (1999). Orientations, purposes and reflection: A framework for understanding action research. *Teaching and Teacher Education, 15,* 333–349.

Richardson, V. (1996). The role of attitudes and beliefs in learning to teach. In J. Sikula (Ed.), *Handbook of research on teacher education* (pp. 102–119). Macmillan.

Roberts, D. A., & Chastko, A. M. (1990). Absorption, refraction, reflection: An exploration of beginning science teacher thinking. *Science Education, 74,* 197–224.

Rosenshine, B., & Stevens, R. (1986). Teaching functions. In M. C. Wittrock (Ed.), *Handbook of research on teaching* (3rd ed., pp. 376–391). Macmillan.

Rutherford, F. J., & Ahlgren, A. (1989). *Science for all Americans.* Oxford University Press.

Ryan, S. (1999). *Constructing knowledge together: Teacher teams as learning communities* [Paper presentation]. The annual meeting of the American Educational Research Association, Montreal, Canada.

Sanders, L. R., Borko, H., & Lockard, J. D. (1993). Secondary science teachers' knowledge base when teaching science courses in and out of their area of certification. *Journal of Research in Science Teaching, 30,* 723–736.

Schön, D. (1983). *The reflective practitioner. How professionals think in action.* Basic Books.

Shulman, L. S. (1986). Paradigms and research programs in the study of teaching: A contemporary perspective. In M. C. Wittrock (Ed.), *Handbook of research on teaching* (pp. 3–36). Macmillan.

Shulman, L. S. (1987). Knowledge and teaching: Foundations of the new reform. *Harvard Educational Review, 57,* 1–22.

Sikes, P. J., Measor, L., & Woods, P. (1991). Berufslaufbahn und Identität im Lehrerberuf [Professional career and identity in the teaching profession]. In E. Terhart (Ed.), *Unterrichten als Beruf* (pp. 231–248). Bohlau.

Simmons, P. E., Emory, A., Carter, T., Coker, R., Finnegan, B., Crockett, D., Richardson, L., Yager, R., Craven, J., Tillotson, J., Brunkhorst, H., Twiest, M., Hossain, K., Gallagher, J., Duggan-Haas, D., Parker, J., Cajas, F., Alshannag, Q., McGlamery, S., Krockover, J., Adams, P., Spector, B., LaPorta, T., James, B., Rearden, K., & Labuda, K. (1999). Beginning teachers: Beliefs and classroom actions. *Journal of Research in Science Teaching, 36,* 930–954.

Smith, D. C., & Neale, D. C. (1989). The construction of subject matter knowledge in primary science teaching. *Teaching and Teacher Education, 5,* 1–20.

Southerland, S. A., & Gess-Newsome, J. (1999). Preservice teachers' views of inclusive science teaching as shaped by images of teaching, learning, and knowledge. *Science Education, 83,* 131–150.

Sparks, D., & Loucks-Horsley, S. (1990). Models of staff development. In W. R. Houston (Ed.), *Handbook of research on teacher education* (pp. 234–250). Macmillan.

Stigler, J. W., Gallimore, R., & Hiebert, J. (2000). Using video surveys to compare classrooms and teaching across cultures: Examples and lessons from the TIMSS video studies. *Educational Psychologist, 35*, 87–100.

Thompson, C. L., & Zeuli, J. S. (1999). The frame and the tapestry: Standards-based reform and professional development. In L. Darling-Hammond & G. Sykes (Eds.), *Teaching as the learning profession. Handbook of policy and practice* (pp. 341–375). Jossey-Bass.

Tobin, K. (1993). Referents for making sense of science teaching. *International Journal of Science Education, 15*, 241–254.

Tobin, K., & Dawson, G. (1992). Constraints to curriculum reform: Teachers and the myths of schooling. *Education Technology Research and Development, 40*, 81–92.

Tobin, K., & McRobbie, C. J. (1996). Cultural myths as constraints to the enacted science curriculum. *Science Education, 80*, 223–241.

Tom, A. R., & Valli, L. (1990). Professional knowledge for teachers. In W. R. Houston (Ed.), *Handbook of research on teacher education* (pp. 372–392). Macmillan.

Van Driel, J. H., Beijaard, D., & Verloop, N. (2001). Professional development and reform in science education: The role of teachers' practical knowledge. *Journal of Research in Science Teaching, 38*(2), 137–158.

Van Driel, J. H., Verloop, N., & De Vos, W. (1998). Developing science teachers' pedagogical content knowledge. *Journal of Research in Science Teaching, 35*, 673–695.

Vangrieken, K., Dochy, F., Raes, E., & Kyndt, E. (2015). Teacher collaboration: A systematic review. *Educational Research Review, 15*, 17–40.

Veal, W. R. (1998). *The evolution of pedagogical content knowledge in prospective secondary chemistry teachers* [Paper presentation]. The annual meeting of the National Association for Research in Science Teaching, San Diego, CA.

Verloop, N. (1992). Praktijkkennis van docenten: Een blinde vlek van de onderwijskunde [Craft knowledge of teachers: A blind spot in educational research]. *Pedagogische Studien, 69*, 410–423.

Wallace, J., & Louden, W. (1992). Science teaching and teachers' knowledge: Prospects for reform of elementary classrooms. *Science Education, 76*, 507–521.

Wenger, E. (1998). *Communities of practice: Learning, meaning and identity.* Cambridge University Press.

Whigham, M., Andre, T., & Yang, E. (2000). *Elementary and secondary teachers' beliefs about and instructional emphasis on the National Mathematics Education and Science Education standards* [Paper presentation]. The annual meeting of the National Association of Research in Science Teaching, New Orleans, LA.

Yerrick, R., Parke, H., & Nugent, J. (1997). Struggling to promote deeply rooted change: The "filtering effect" of teachers' beliefs on understanding transformational views of teaching science. *Science Education, 81*, 137–159.

CHAPTER 3

Teacher Knowledge and the Knowledge Base of Teaching

1   How This Article Came About

This article was published as a chapter in a special issue of the *International Journal of Education* (Volume 35, issue 5, 2001) on teacher professionalism. The special issue was situated in the ongoing debate of the status of teaching as a profession. Nico Verloop had been invited as the guest editor of this special issue, which explored teacher professionalism from different angles and included contributions from David Berliner, who described a prototypical model of teacher expertise, Andy Hargreaves who presented a study on the emotional geographies of teachers' relationships with their colleagues, and Wiske, Sick and Wirsig, who examined how new information technologies can help teachers to meet 'the challenges of this moment'.

One of the criteria for teaching to qualify as a profession is the existence of a common or shared knowledge base of teaching, conceived as all profession-related insights which are potentially relevant to a teacher's activities. Nico's contribution to the special issue would focus on the role of teachers' practical knowledge in relation to this knowledge base. He invited me and Paulien Meijer to be his co-authors. Paulien had recently finished her PhD on the practical knowledge of language teachers about teaching reading comprehension. Nico was her main supervisor and Paulien had used some of the conceptual and methodological ideas from his PhD thesis (1989) on pre-service teachers' interactive cognitions. My recent studies on science teachers' PCK and teachers' conceptions in the context of educational reform were considered to fit the broader construct of teacher practical knowledge and would complement the article.

2   What the Article Is About

The article concentrates on the knowledge base of teaching and explains the attention for this construct in relation to the shift in research on effective teaching behaviours to the knowledge and beliefs underpinning teaching behaviours. In the article, we argue that deepening teachers' knowledge has become a focus of (pre-service and in-service) teacher education. At the core of the article lies our view that the knowledge base of teaching should be broadened from research-based propositional knowledge to be prescribed to teachers, to include teacher practical knowledge, or teacher knowledge. We referred to American colleagues such as Kathy Carter in defining teacher knowledge as "the total knowledge that a teacher has at his or her disposal at a particular moment which, by definition, underlies his or her actions" (Verloop, Van Driel, & Meijer, 2001, p. 445), and Gary Fenstermacher by stating that this is 'knowledge *of* teachers' as opposed to 'knowledge *for* teachers' (Fenstermacher, 1994). Both Kathy and Gary had visited our institute in recent years. We recognised that teacher knowledge is strongly related to individual experiences and personal contexts, however, we assumed there would be elements of teacher knowledge which are shared by teachers, for instance, those who teach the same discipline or students of the same age or year level.

We explored the empirical question which elements are shared and addressed methodological issues related to how these shared elements could be identified and captured. We explained that in teacher knowledge, the concept 'knowledge' is used in an overarching, inclusive way, which combines a variety of cognitions, from conscious and well-balanced opinions to unconscious and unreflected intuitions. Consequently, teacher knowledge is a multi-dimensional concept and therefore, we argued, research on teacher knowledge requires the triangulation of data collected with a diverse set of instruments. In particular, we considered the challenges related to capturing the tacit knowledge underlying teachers' actions in practice. At this point we presented some empirical findings of the studies of Paulien and myself. We described the triangulation procedure that Paulien had developed and how that had served to identify a typology consisting of three types of practical knowledge about teaching reading comprehension (i.e., subject matter oriented, student oriented, and student learning oriented). Similarly, looking for common patterns in the PCK of individual teachers in my study (Chapter 1), we were able to identify two different teaching strategies that appeared to be particularly successful in promoting student understanding of chemical equilibrium. We concluded that rather than generating checklists with indicators of effective instruction, research on PCK contributes to establishing a knowledge base which demonstrates how specific topics can be taught "effectively and flexibly in situations that are subjected to different contextual, situational, and personal influences" (Van Driel et al., 1998, p. 691; see Chapter 1).

Finally, we addressed the implications of research on teacher knowledge for teacher education and educational innovations. For the former, we described the outcomes of a recently finished PhD study in our institute by Anneke

Zanting, who focused on the question how pre-service teachers could access and benefit from the practical knowledge of their school-based mentors. For the latter, we referred to a study I had conducted among a group of teachers in an institute for higher engineering education that was about to implement an innovation of its curriculum and pedagogical approaches (Van Driel, Verloop, Van Werven, & Dekkers, 1997). That study focused on teachers' conceptions of teaching and learning as an element of their practical knowledge and led to the identification of three types of conceptions (i.e., student-directed, teacher-centred and student-centred) which were discussed in relation to the goals of the innovation. The outcomes of the study triggered a decision to organise teachers in collaborative teams, contributing to the design and development of the new curriculum. This approach led to increased teachers' commitment to the innovation, which eventually won the national Higher Education Award (1995) from the Dutch Ministry of Education. We concluded the article by proposing directions for future research, and argued, among others, that "much more research into subject-specific aspects of teacher knowledge is needed" (Verloop et al., 2001, p. 457).

3   Impact and Follow Up

Constructing the article in the way we had done provided us with an excellent opportunity to showcase the emerging research program of our institute to a broad international audience. Being published in a special issue with contributions from eminent scholars such as Berliner and Hargreaves ensured our article to attract attention. This helps to explain that the paper has been cited over 950 times to date (compared to Berliner's and Hargreaves' articles being cited more than 1,400 and over 450 times, respectively). Interestingly, the number of annual citations of this article continued to rise, peaking at 98 in 2019. The editor of the *Peking University Education Review* proposed to translate the article in Chinese. The translated version was published in the journal in 2008 (volume 6, pp. 21–38) and has been cited 23 times to date.

To me, the article was important at the time because writing it with colleagues helped me to better understand and appreciate the nature of the research we were doing in our institute and of my own research. The discussions we had as authors were helpful to justify the rationale or purpose of conducting studies among small numbers of teachers (say, less than 15). Around the time of publication, research on teacher thinking and teacher knowledge had become quite common, however, it was not without criticism. There was a concern that research on teacher knowledge would be limited to idiosyncratic descriptions (Tom & Valli, 1990). Our aim was to try to surpass the individual level and search for the shared components of teacher knowledge or generalizable features which are common across particular groups of teachers.

Teacher knowledge was also criticized for its supposedly inherent conservativism and its tendency to mainly reflect the well-established and rigid routines of the profession (Kirk, 1986). Others pointed out that if teacher knowledge was considered without relating it to formal knowledge, it could undermine the status of teaching as a profession (Squires, 1999). For this reason, we argued that teacher knowledge draws on a variety of sources including not only practical experiences but also formal schooling such as initial teacher education or continued professional development (Calderhead, 1996). Thus, teacher knowledge should not be considered as opposite to theoretical or propositional knowledge. Instead, we argued that teachers integrate knowledge they had acquired through formal schooling into their practical knowledge and we suggested that confronting teachers with formal theoretical knowledge could enrich their practical knowledge.

However, a number of questions remained, such as, were we interested in classifying teachers or identifying types of practical knowledge (about a particular topic or issue)? What could be learned from case studies of individual teachers? How could we argue that teacher knowledge should be added to the knowledge base of teaching when teacher knowledge incorporated elements of that knowledge base? And what does that imply for Fenstermacher's distinction between 'knowledge *of* teachers' and 'knowledge *for* teachers' (Fenstermacher, 1994)? These questions would continue to inform some of the research in our institute, including my own and that of my colleagues and students. For instance, in Ineke Henze's PhD study, she traced the development of PCK about models of the solar system and the universe among a sample of nine teachers of *Algemene Natuurwetenschappen*. Ineke identified two qualitatively different types of PCK (see Chapter 5) and two different ways of teacher learning (Henze et al., 2009). However, not all teachers could be assigned unequivocally or exclusively to one of the types of PCK, or learning. Also, categorizing teachers on the basis of their PCK about one specific topic does not do justice to their broader practical knowledge.

As another example, Rosária Justi and I published a case study on the basis of her post doc project, in which we described the development of one preservice teacher's practical knowledge of models and modelling in terms of various types of knowledge – content knowledge, curricular knowledge and PCK (Shulman, 1986) – which were developed simultaneously. The study demonstrated, in considerable detail, how knowledge development was promoted as a result of participation in a specific teacher education program (Justi & Van

Driel, 2005a). Science teachers' practical knowledge of models and modelling was also central in another research project that I conducted in the context of the implementation of *Algemene Natuurwetenschappen*. This will be discussed in the next chapter.

Teacher Knowledge and the Knowledge Base of Teaching[1]

Nico Verloop, Jan van Driel and Paulien Meijer

Abstract

In this chapter, the knowledge base of teaching is conceived as all profession-related insights, which are potentially relevant to a teacher's activities. From this perspective, it is argued that teacher knowledge, or teacher practical knowledge, should be included within this knowledge base, along with formal propositional knowledge. Although teacher knowledge is strongly related to individual experiences and contexts, there are elements of teacher knowledge that are shared by all teachers or large groups of teachers, for instance, all teachers who teach pupils of a certain age level. Investigating teacher knowledge to identify these common elements so as to do justice to its complex and specific nature can be problematic from a methodological point of view. To illustrate the potential benefits and limitations of research on teacher knowledge, the results from several studies are presented. A major conclusion from these studies is that an understanding of teacher knowledge may be useful to improve teacher education and to make educational innovations more successful. Finally, three areas of interest for future research are identified.

The Knowledge Base of Teaching

A great deal of educational research has aimed at developing a knowledge base of teaching and, where possible, translating it into recommendations for teacher education (Reynolds, 1989). This knowledge base was supposedly shared by teachers and formed the basis for their behavior (Hoyle & John, 1995). Until the early 1980s, the line of reasoning in this field was rather straightforward. The goal of the research was to detect those teaching behaviors that resulted in higher pupil achievement gain scores and, subsequently, to train teachers in these desirable behaviors, either in initial teacher education programs or by means of further professional development. Inventories of variables that had "proved to be effective" (Dunkin & Biddle, 1974; Rosenshine & Stevens, 1986), such as micro-teaching, formed the basis for teacher training interventions.

This line of reasoning has come under increasing criticism during the past two decades, not only because the research led to very few generalizable results, but also, and more importantly, because, in the quest for "effective" variables comprising teaching behavior, we lost sight of the complexity and interdependency of teacher behavior as a whole. Research, and the interventions that were based on its findings, led to a fragmented and mechanistic view of teaching, in which the complexity of the teaching enterprise was not acknowledged (Doyle, 1990). Large parts of teachers' functioning were left out of consideration (see, for example, Verloop & Wubbels, 2000).

Due to the increasing criticism coming from the professionals themselves, the influence of this type of research diminished. Teachers felt that analyzing isolated behavioral components was inadequate and they resisted the prescriptive nature of this "knowledge *for* teachers" (Fenstermacher, 1994). Perhaps the most obvious place for these problems to manifest themselves was initial teacher education, where prospective teachers experienced a discrepancy between "theory" as it was treated in teacher education and the knowledge of experienced teachers at the practice schools, which they considered to be much more relevant (Kagan, 1992; Meijer, Verloop & Beijaard, 1999).

The developments described above contributed to a shift in research on teaching, following the cognitive shift in research on pupil learning. Research on teaching changed from studying teacher behavior into studying teacher cognitions and beliefs underlying that behavior, based on ideas about the interaction between them.

Centrality of Teachers

Meanwhile doubts arose also from the scientific community about a conception of professionalism that asked professionals (such as teachers) to just "apply" the theories and insights provided by others. Schön (1983, 1987) analyzed the work of various groups of professionals and concluded that they applied a certain amount of theoretical knowledge in their work, but that their behavior was not at all "rule-governed" and that they had no straightforward way to determine which behavior was adequate in specific circumstances. Schön contrasted this principle of "technical rationality" to the principle of "reflection-in-action", which pertained to the thinking of the professional during professional activity and implied a continuing dialogue with the permanently changing situation. This situation does not present itself as a well-defined problem situation. On the contrary, defining the problem is itself one of the most difficult tasks of the professional.

From this point of view, the most challenging question with respect to teacher professionality is no longer how we can best provide teachers with insights developed elsewhere, but how the process of "dialogue with the situation" takes place in a teaching context, which insights are developed in this context, and how these insights relate to insights from other sources. This recognition of the centrality of the teacher and the teacher's knowledge and beliefs regarding each educational process, including educational innovations, is relatively recent (Calderhead, 1996). Birman, Desimone, Porter, and Garet (2000), for example, searched for key features of effective professional development and, based on their research, reported that professional development should focus on deepening teacher knowledge in order to foster teacher learning and changes in practice. Similarly, Hawley and Valli (1999) considered the expansion and elaboration of teachers' professional knowledge base as essential for their professional development.

As the research on teachers' knowledge and beliefs became more prominent, it became important to identify the place of this teacher knowledge in the total knowledge base of teaching. This, of course, also meant that the conception of the "knowledge base of teaching" had to surpass restricted definitions such as "behavioral prescriptions based on effectiveness studies". For the purposes of this chapter, the knowledge base of teaching will be defined as all profession-related insights that are potentially relevant to the teacher's activities. These insights can, for example, pertain to formal theories (such as the classical theories from research on teaching), but can also pertain to information about the knowledge and beliefs of expert teachers which has emerged from more recent research. In this sense, the results of recent research on teacher knowledge are seen as an addition to the knowledge base of teaching as it was conceived until recently (see, for example, Grimmett & MacKinnon, 1992; Verloop, 1992). The main function of this newly conceived knowledge base is not prescription, but improving the "practical arguments" (Fenstermacher, 1986) in the thinking process of the teacher. Besides, this knowledge base is a public one: it is made available to all professionals, for instance, through publications and professional development activities.

Individual and Common Elements in the Knowledge Base of Teaching

This knowledge base of teaching, however, needs to be distinguished from the insights that guide an individual teacher's behavior, that is, his or her personal knowledge base. This personal knowledge of each teacher is highly determined and "colored" by his or her individual experiences, personal history (including learning processes), personality variables, subject matter knowledge, and so on. This personal knowledge based is the teacher's filter for interpreting new information (Pajares, 1992). Contrary to the earlier mentioned "knowledge *for* teachers", this is "knowledge *of* teachers" (Fenstermacher, 1994). It guides a teacher's actions in concrete and specific situations (Brown & McIntyre, 1993).

Although teacher knowledge is strongly related to individual experiences and circumstances, there will be elements of teacher knowledge which are shared by all teachers or large groups of teachers, for instance, all teachers who teach pupils of a certain age level. Which elements are shared is an empirical question. Studies in this field should honour the specific character of teacher knowledge as much as possible, although this raises large methodological problems. The basic assumption underlying this type of study is that the findings concerning common elements in teacher knowledge can, if codified adequately, become part of the overall knowledge base of teaching. This implies that the "input" for this overall knowledge base can originate both from teaching practice and from formal theories.

A Comprehensive Conception of the Knowledge Base of Teaching

This more comprehensive conception of the knowledge base of teaching has led to questions about the relationship between teacher knowledge, on the one hand, and the theoretical and propositional knowledge that had been provided previously by educational theory and research, on the other hand. These questions not only pertain to epistemological problems (cf. Fenstermacher, 1994), but also to practical implications for classroom behavior and teacher education. For instance, it is not at all clear how formal theoretical knowledge and teacher knowledge can be integrated and used as "input" in teacher education. Many authors contend that, both in professional practice and in teacher education, there should be some kind of exchange between theoretical principles on the one hand, and teacher expertise, on the other hand, whereby these two types of input interact and refine each other (Stones, 1994).

In this context, Thiessen (2000) discussed three orientations with respect to the focus of teacher education programs:
- "impactful behaviors", leading to the training of prospective teachers in behaviors that appeared to be effective in process-product research,
- "reflective practices", and
- "professional knowledge".

According to Thiessen, the final orientation is the most promising for teacher education.

> At the heart of this orientation is the image of teaching as knowledge work. Such work ... involves the interrelated use of practical knowledge (routines, procedures, processes) and propositional knowledge (discipline-based theories and concepts, pedagogical principles, situation-specific propositions). (p. 528)

For teacher education, this would imply that, at the teacher education institution, the focus should be on "practically relevant propositional knowledge", whereas at the practice school, the focus should be on "propositionally interpreted practical knowledge" (Thiessen, 2000, p. 530). Although the importance of integrating formal theoretical knowledge and teacher knowledge is evident, there are some problems with the way this integration is described by Thiessen and in much of the related literature. First, the extremely complex process of exchange and integration of formal theoretical knowledge and teacher knowledge is usually described very superficially and in a rather vague way. From our own research we learned that there is a long way to go before practising teachers can start with the explication of their personal knowledge, let alone with the confrontation of this knowledge with formal theoretical knowledge (Zanting, Verloop, & Vermunt, 2001a). Second, in most literature about the exchange of, and integration between, formal knowledge and teacher knowledge, the latter component is discussed in terms of teachers' routines and their day-to-day activities, as if it were self-evident what constitutes the essence of this teacher knowledge. We think that it is desirable, before making a plea for the integration of the formal and the practical, to get a more thorough view of this teacher knowledge, leading to a kind of equivalence between the two types of knowledge in this respect. This could help to prevent the "exchange" from amounting to just a redefining of practice in formal-theoretical terms, as has been done in previous attempts to "apply" theory in practice. This "thorough view" not only pertains to the content of teacher knowledge (Shulman, 1986), but also and particularly to the development of teacher knowledge and the way it is influenced by all kinds of contextual factors, such as innovations; that is, the teacher learning processes (Putnam & Borko, 1997). One would expect that, in investigating teacher learning, it is possible to use the huge amount of research on learning in the general sense, in which learning processes are seen as knowledge construction processes, rather than the acquisition of abstract knowledge which is subsequently "applied" (Resnick, 1987). In the context of teacher learning, Korthagen (2001) has suggested that there are various levels in the conceptions of (prospective) teachers. The learning process begins by acting on the basis of a general and intuitive idea (*Gestalt*) about a phenomenon. With the help of specific interventions in teacher education, the prospective teacher can gradually learn to articulate and elaborate on these initial ideas, thereby reaching the level of schemata or even theories. This, in turn, can lead to the formation of a more adequate *Gestalt* and, subsequently, improvements in day-to-day routine behavior.

In summary, adopting a more comprehensive conception of the knowledge base of teaching (by including teacher knowledge) implies a need to look differently at the relationship between theory and practice. Combining, integrating, and exchanging the two components become more important. Before this relationship can be studied adequately, there must be a balanced view of both theory and practice (i.e., teacher knowledge). As insight into teacher knowledge is still lacking, the first step needs to be an investigation of this component of the knowledge base of teaching.

Teacher Knowledge

Teacher knowledge is the total knowledge that a teacher has at his or her disposal at a particular moment which, by definition, underlies his or her actions (Carter, 1990). This does not imply that all the knowledge a teacher has actually plays a role in his or her actions. Teachers can, consciously or unconsciously, refrain from using certain insights during their teaching. The basic idea is that a reciprocity exists between the whole of teachers' cognition (in the broad sense) and their activities and that, consequently, it makes sense to investigate teachers' knowledge.

Teacher knowledge may have a variety of origins including both practical experiences, such as day-to-day practice, and formal schooling in the past, that is, initial teacher education or continued professional training (Calderhead, 1996). In this sense, teacher knowledge is *not* opposite to theoretical or scientific knowledge. Instead, the knowledge which teachers may derive from their teacher education may, to some extent, be absorbed and integrated into their practical knowledge. Eraut (1994) stressed that much research is needed to further understand the process by which teachers integrate knowledge from different sources into conceptual frameworks that guide their actions in practice. And, of course, teachers may differ enormously in the extent to which they absorb theoretical knowledge in their practical knowledge.

Defining Teacher Knowledge

In the literature about teacher knowledge, various labels have been used, each indicating a relevant aspect of teacher knowledge. The labels illustrate mainly which aspect is considered the most important by the respective authors. Together, these labels give an overview of the way in which teacher knowledge has been studied to date. The most commonly used labels are "personal knowledge" (Connelly & Clandinin, 1985; Elbaz, 1991), indicating that this knowledge in unique; "the wisdom of practice" (Schwab, 1971), and in more recent publications, "professional craft knowledge" (e.g., Brown & McIntyre, 1993; Shimahara, 1998), referring to a specific component of knowledge that is mainly the product of the teacher's practical experience; "action oriented knowledge", indicating that this knowledge is for immediate use in teaching practice (Carter, 1990); "content and context related knowledge" (Cochran, DeRuiter, & King,

1993; Van Driel, Verloop & De Vos, 1998); knowledge that is to a great extent "tacit" (Eraut, 1994; Calderhead & Robson, 1991); and knowledge that is based on reflection on experiences (Grimmett & MacKinnon, 1992; Gunstone, 1999). In this chapter, "teacher knowledge" or "teacher practical knowledge" is used to indicate the whole of the knowledge and insights that underly teachers' actions in practice.

It is important to realize that in the label "teacher knowledge", the concept "knowledge" is used as an overarching, inclusive concept, summarizing a large variety of cognitions, from conscious and well-balanced opinions to unconscious and unreflected intuitions. This is related to the fact that, in the mind of the teacher, components of knowledge, beliefs, conceptions, and intuitions are inextricably intertwined. As Alexander, Schallert, and Hare (1991) noted, the term "knowledge" is mostly used to encompass "all that a person knows or believes to be true, whether or not it is verified as true in some sort of objective or external way" (p. 317). This is particularly relevant with respect to research on teacher knowledge. In investigating teacher knowledge, the main focus of attention is on the complex totality of cognitions, the ways this develops, and the way this interacts with teacher behavior in the classroom. Following Pajares (1992), knowledge and beliefs are seen as inseparable, although beliefs are seen roughly as referring to personal values, attitudes, and ideologies, and knowledge to a teacher's more factual propositions (Meijer, Verloop, & Beijaard, 2001).

Using the label "teacher knowledge" or "teacher practical knowledge" as the overarching concept for teacher cognitions also means encompassing tacit forms of knowledge. This latter type of knowledge is receiving more and more attention in recent literature. Some authors welcome this increased attention as a possible answer to doubts about teachers' professionality. Furlong (2000) described the rise of three alternative conceptions of the role of knowledge with respect to teaching: (a) reflective practice, which, following Schön, is mainly focused on the knowledge that is embedded in the practice of professionals, (b) the "new rationalism", which, following Hirst, tries to develop forms of practical (rather than theoretical) reason and practical principles as the generalized outcomes of successful practice, which are subsequently confronted with theoretical critique and experiment, and (c) critical theory, aimed at revealing the assumptions behind statements about knowledge and truth and focusing on an open discourse among all professionals concerned. Furlong contended that, in fact, these three approaches all concentrate on a fairly conventional definition of professional knowledge. Therefore, he suggests using "intuition" as a totally different concept: "intuition focuses on 'ways of knowing' – obviously including knowledge, but much more besides: feelings, hunches, ways of recognizing complex patterns" (p. 28). We believe, however, that Furlong exaggerates the contrast between "intuition" and the existing research on teacher knowledge. In many studies, not only those of Schön, attention was paid to forms of cognition categorized by Furlong as "intuition", but labeled by others as "knowledge". It is important to base judgements about studies on teacher knowledge not on the labels used, but on precise examination of what the study is about. This does not alter the fact that it has appeared to be very difficult to grasp the tacit and intuitive components of teacher cognitions in research on teacher knowledge, which makes theory development and research initiatives in this field all the more important.

Shared Aspects in Teacher Knowledge

From the beginning of research into teacher knowledge, there have been differences in opinion about the question of whether these studies should be confined to describing the teacher knowledge of individuals or very small groups, such as narratives or biographies, or attention should be focused on the more general characteristics of teacher knowledge. There is no doubt that narratives and biographies can convey essential aspects of teacher knowledge, especially in teacher education settings (Merseth, 1996). However, many researchers contend that rather than describing individual manifestations of teacher knowledge, research should try to surpass the individual level. This implies that one should search for the shared components of teacher knowledge, and attempt to find "certain overarching generalizable features which are common across teachers" (Brown & McIntyre, 1993, p. 19).

In this context, three remarks need to be made. First, there is no a priori assumption that it is possible to detect such general features. This is an empirical question that needs to be answered by means of thorough research. Second, related to the previous point, the aim of this research is *not* to formulate (a new set of) prescriptions for teachers. Tom and Valli (1990) distinguished various approaches with respect to the relationship between knowledge and practice, two of which are relevant for our discourse. They are: (a) knowledge as a source of rules that specify a direct tie between knowledge and practice, and (b) knowledge as a source of schemata that can alter the perception of practitioners. The latter is related to what Grimmett and MacKinnon (1992) termed the development of a "teaching sensibility, rather than a knowledge of propositions" (p. 393), to enhance teachers' awareness of and, subsequently, their options for action. Third, in view of the way research on teaching has proceeded in the past, it is unlikely that these shared features of teacher knowledge, valid for all teachers, will be found on a large scale. Given the fact that teacher knowledge is, by definition, embedded in the personal context of the teachers, where all kinds of domain-related and pupil-related circumstances play a role, it makes sense to focus the search for shared teacher knowledge on groups of teachers that are in similar situations with respect to variables such as subject matter, level of education, and age group of students.

Keeping these three remarks in mind, we conducted a series of studies in which we tried to depict the teacher knowledge of a group of teachers who taught reading comprehension in the upper level of secondary education. The purpose of these studies was to explore the similarities (i.e., shared knowledge) and differences in language teachers' practical knowledge about the teaching of reading comprehension to 16- to 18-year-old students. First, an in-depth, qualitative study was conducted in which the practical knowledge of language teachers with respect to the teaching of reading comprehension to 16- to 18-year-old students was examined using several instruments (Meijer et al., 1999). Data were analyzed in two steps, namely the identification of substantial categories, followed by the examination of patterns in the teachers' practical knowledge. This study provided an abundance of data about teachers' practical knowledge, which could be organized according to a system of categories and subcategories of teachers' practical knowledge. The system of categories concerned teachers' practical knowledge of (a) subject matter, (b) students, (c) student learning and comprehension, (d) purposes, (e) curriculum, and (f) instructional techniques. This study also provided indications of relationships among the categories of teachers' practical knowledge. However, the group of teachers investigated was too small to allow for reliable generalizations to be made.

Consequently, a quantitative follow-up study to investigate similarities and differences in the practical knowledge of a larger group of teachers was conducted (Meijer et al., 2001). Using the system of categories from the qualitative study, a questionnaire was developed consisting of closed-format questions. Items were formulated on the basis of (a) teachers' answers to questions in the semi-structured interviews, and (b) the remarks they made during a concept mapping assignment. This was done to ensure that the questionnaire was based on teachers' own practical knowledge as much as possible.

Sixty-nine teachers, teaching at 17 different schools, returned the questionnaire. Thirty-two of the teachers were female and 37 were male. The teachers' average age was 45.4 (SD = 8.64), and ranged from 25 to 60. Twenty-six of these teachers taught Dutch (mother tongue); 21, English; 9, Latin or Greek; 8, German; and 5, French.

The analysis of the data began by identifying those items with a low variance, which were regarded as teachers' shared knowledge. Twenty-two items

TABLE 3.1 Clusters of teachers with different practical knowledge about teaching reading comprehension

Description of clusters	Number of teachers
1. Large-element view on teaching reading comprehension	11
2. Segmental view on teaching reading comprehension	25
3. Teaching reading comprehension by relating texts and students	11
4. Low appreciation for reading comprehension	20

(13.1%) were so identified. The teachers closely agreed in their responses to these items, indicating that they had rather similar opinions about these items. Principal component analyses were used with the "unshared knowledge" items to give more detailed information about the patterns in the teachers' practical knowledge. The result was a four principal component solution. These components provided insights into the relationships between the different aspects of teachers' practical knowledge.

Items related to these components were used as the basis for the construction of four scales. These scales were assumed to capture the essence of the differences in teachers' practical knowledge about teaching reading comprehension. From a cluster analysis, based on the teachers' scores on the four scales, four clusters of teachers were identified. Descriptions of the clusters are given in Table 3.1. Clusters 2 and 4 consisted of many more teachers than the other two clusters, indicating that these types of teachers were somewhat more common. We concluded that although there was shared knowledge among the teachers, there were large differences in their practical knowledge about teaching reading comprehension.

Pedagogical Content Knowledge as a Specific form of Teacher Knowledge

In research on teacher knowledge focusing on specific content domains, many investigators have built on the work of Shulman (1986) on pedagogical content knowledge. Pedagogical content knowledge (PCK) is different from content knowledge, on the one hand, because of the focus on the communication between teacher and student, and from general pedagogical knowledge, on the other, because of the direct relationship with subject matter. Shulman (1987, p. 8) described PCK as "that special amalgam of content and pedagogy that is uniquely the province of teachers, their own special form of professional understanding". PCK can be considered as a specific form of teacher knowledge, as described earlier. After analyzing the ways in which various authors have elaborated on the concept of pedagogical content knowledge, Van Driel, Verloop, and De Vos (1998) found that two elements of PCK are considered essential by all authors. They are (a) knowledge of teachers about specific conceptions and learning difficulties with respect to this particular content domain and (b) knowledge of teachers about representations and teaching strategies with respect to this particular content domain. Based on this conceptualization, several research projects have been carried out. In what follows, we give a description of one of these projects.

The project was conducted as part of a long-term research project in the Netherlands on chemical education, in which the concept of chemical reaction was central (De Vos & Verdonk, 1985). In the study reported here, the focus was on the introduction of the concept of chemical equilibrium during the second year of chemistry education (grade 10 students, aged 15–16 years). The project consisted of (a) an experimental course on chemical equilibrium, followed by (b) an in-service workshop for chemistry teachers using the experimental course in their own classes. Specifically, the aims were to improve chemistry teachers' abilities to recognize specific preconceptions and conceptual difficulties related to chemical equilibrium, and to promote their use of interventions and strategies promoting conceptual change during classroom practice.

The workshop sessions were attended by 12 participants. All had an academic background in chemistry and more than five years of experience in teaching chemistry in upper secondary education. Because the topic of chemical equilibrium is a key subject in the national curriculum, all participants were familiar with this topic, both as learners and as teachers. All participants had chosen to attend the workshop on a voluntary basis. Mostly, their choice was inspired either by interest in the topic or by the wish to innovate their educational practice.

All workshop sessions were recorded on audiotape. Additional data consisted of participants' written responses to assignments carried out during the sessions and to an evaluative questionnaire. Finally, during the implementation stage, audio recordings were made of the classroom lessons of two of the participants. The analysis of the data involved the selection of audio fragments relevant to the teachers' subject matter knowledge or PCK, followed by the transcription and analysis of these by two researchers, and then the comparison and discussion of individual interpretations until agreement occurred (researcher triangulation; Janesick, 1994). The validation of these interpretations was promoted by applying the constant comparative method (Denzin,

1994). This involved the comparison of the analyses of the transcripts with the written responses of the participating teachers.

During the first workshop session, the participants appeared to consider the introduction of chemical equilibrium problematic for many students. Moreover, most participants themselves struggled with the abstract nature of chemical equilibrium, and its relation to observations made during chemical experiments. To facilitate students' understanding, almost every participant appeared to use metaphors and analogies. Some of them used the analogies mentioned in chemistry schoolbooks. Others had worked out their own analogies. During the first workshop session, the participants discussed the strengths and weaknesses of each other's favourite analogies. Common in these analogies was the representation of molecules as people or students or the attribution of human characteristics to molecules (e.g., "molecules don't fancy changing"). It was remarkable in their discussion that chemical validity seemed to prevail. Arguments from the students' perspective were barely noticed.

Following the first workshop session, the participants implemented the experimental course in their chemistry classes. The implementation process had a great impact on the teachers. This was evidenced by the teachers' reports during consecutive workshop sessions and their responses to the questionnaire evaluating the project. First, many of them indicated that, by listening carefully to students' reasoning, their understanding of specific student conceptions and types of reasoning had improved. Many concrete examples were mentioned to demonstrate this increase in knowledge. In addition, some participants reported having extended their knowledge of successful strategies and representations with respect to chemical equilibrium. Specifically, some teachers had developed approaches that differed considerably from the representations of chemical equilibrium commonly found in chemistry schoolbooks. For instance, some teachers succeeded in promoting conceptual change by discussing the anomalous results of certain chemical experiments with students. By challenging the students' existing conceptions about chemical reactions, they provided them with a basis for the chemical equilibrium conception to become an acceptable explanation of these anomalies. However, the participants reported both successes and failures with respect to the introduction of chemical equilibrium.

Obviously, not every individual participant in our workshop reconstructed his or her PCK in a similar way. However, by looking for common patterns in the PCK of individual teachers, we were able to identify two different teaching strategies that appeared to be particularly successful in promoting student understanding of chemical equilibrium. In this way, the course and workshop contributed to the increase of knowledge about the way teachers transform subject matter knowledge and how they relate their transformations to student understanding in a particular domain, that is, the introduction of chemical equilibrium.

Studying Teacher Knowledge: Problems and Possibilities

A persistent problem in research on teacher knowledge concerns the language that should be used to describe teacher knowledge. It is unlikely that, in order to capture the "language of practice" (Yinger, 1987), the concepts of the formal theories of teaching can be used. Professionals, such as architects (Yinger, 1987), often develop a specific "way of thinking", which can be described with the help of a number of specific categories. These categories enable professionals to get a hold on their specific professional problems. Loughran (1999) argued that teachers and researchers need to develop a language to share their understanding, a language which is explicitly linked to teaching practice, in order to make sense of teaching, and to promote growth in teachers' professional knowledge. To develop such a language, it seems advisable to use predetermined categories as little as possible in research on teacher knowledge. Instead, researchers should try to develop such categories in interaction with teachers. We have begun to apply such an interpretative approach and, subsequently, to find out whether the results (i.e., the categories that emerge) can be used to describe teacher knowledge in larger groups of teachers.

We also have tried to solve another problem with this kind of research. In teacher knowledge research the key variables are multidimensional, requiring the eclectic use of multiple instruments (Calderhead, 1996). In this context, the systematic combination of various types of data is a crucial aspect. By means of multi-method triangulation, it is possible to cover not only the well-considered aspects of teacher knowledge, which are relatively stable and can be put into words rather easily, but also the ephemeral aspects. The aim is to enhance the internal validity of the research.

Since teacher knowledge is viewed as a multi-dimensional concept, requiring multiple instruments for its exploration, multi-method triangulation was applied in a qualitative study on teachers' practical knowledge (Meijer, Verloop, & Beijaard, 2002). Experienced teachers of foreign languages and the mother tongue (Dutch) were involved in this study. Their practical knowledge with respect to the teaching of reading comprehension to 16- to 18-year-old students was examined in detail using three instruments which were based on existing methods for tapping and representing the content of teachers' practical knowledge: semi-structured interviews, concept mapping assignments, and stimulated recall interviews. The semi-structured interview and the concept-mapping assignment were both meant to capture the teachers' knowledge and beliefs, whereas the stimulated recall interview was intended to examine the teachers' interactive cognitions. Together, they were thought to provide a comprehensive picture of a teacher's practical knowledge concerning the teaching of reading comprehension to 16- to 18-year-old students.

The triangulation procedure was initiated by articulating how the elements of teachers' practical knowledge are conceptually related to one another. Following a theory of human memory (Baddeley, 1990), teachers' knowledge and beliefs, on the one hand, and teachers' interactive cognitions, on the other, although different in nature, were believed to be closely related in their content. Based on this notion, a three-step procedure for triangulation was developed. The process began by looking closely at the data on the teachers' knowledge and beliefs provided by the structured open interviews and the concept mapping task. Categories from other research on the teachers' practical knowledge were used to classify the content of the teachers' practical knowledge. After analyzing all the data on the teachers' knowledge and beliefs, a set of six categories and descriptions of teachers' knowledge and beliefs were prepared.

Next, the six categories were used as a starting-point for analyzing the teachers' interactive cognitions. The result of this analysis was a refined and extended set of categories, as well as descriptions of the teachers' interactive cognitions. Finally, the results of the two previous steps were combined to gain insight into the whole of the teachers' practical knowledge, that is, the combination of their knowledge and beliefs and their interactive cognitions. A final set of categories with which we could describe the content of the teachers' practical knowledge was established. Based on patterns identified in the teachers' knowledge and beliefs as well as in their interactive cognitions, a typology consisting of three types of practical knowledge (i.e., subject matter oriented, student oriented, and student learning oriented) was developed.

From the results of this study, we concluded that the procedure of triangulation used to combine the data provided by the semi-structured interview, the concept mapping task, and the stimulated recall interview was adequate. We were able to establish a final set of categories of practical knowledge, which was based on the initial sets that were identified in the teachers' knowledge and beliefs as well as their interactive cognitions. More importantly, we were able to capture the variation in the practical knowledge of the participating teachers, on the basis of which we were able to develop a typology of the teachers' practical knowledge. Thus, the triangulation procedure provided greater insight into how the categories of the teachers' practical knowledge were related to one another, culminating in a fairly comprehensive understanding of the teachers' practical knowledge with respect to the teaching of reading comprehension to 16- to 18-year-old students.

Teacher Knowledge and Educational Innovation

So far, the discussion has focused on the relevance of teacher knowledge primarily as an element of the knowledge base of teaching. The conditions under which teacher knowledge can become a more fundamental "input" for that knowledge base of teaching, that is, in what ways the contribution of teachers as professionals to their common knowledge base can become more substantial, has also been addressed. Obviously, this can have important consequences for teacher education. There is another area where research on teacher knowledge can potentially be relevant, that is, the field of educational innovations.

In many past educational innovations, the teacher was seen as the executor and implementer of innovations that were devised by others. Teachers were supposed to implement these innovations in accordance with the intentions of the developers as much as possible, and, if there was additional time and money available, it was spent on training the teachers to acquire the skills needed in order to demonstrate the required behavior. The vast majority of the educational innovations did not materialize at all or failed after some time because the teachers, after a period of change, abandoned the new behavior and returned to the old routines with which they were comfortable. There is a growing consensus that educational innovations are doomed to fail if the emphasis remains on developing specific skills, without taking into account the teachers' cognitions, including their beliefs, intentions, and attitudes (Trigwell, Prosser, & Taylor, 1994). Many innovations are considered impractical by the teachers concerned because, for instance, they are unrelated to familiar routines (leading to strong feelings of uncertainty and insecurity), do not fit in with their own perceptions of the domain, or conflict with the existing school culture (Brown & McIntyre, 1993; Carlgren & Lindblad, 1991). This does not mean that the knowledge and beliefs of teachers should be the standard, but it certainly means that they must be the starting point for any successful intervention or innovation. To identify their authentic beliefs with respect to the basic ideas behind the innovation, a thorough investigation into the knowledge of the teachers themselves is required.

In every specific innovation, one must decide what role the information gathered about teacher knowledge will play. In some cases, the conclusion may be that the essence of the innovation appears to be so remote from the teacher knowledge at hand that the planned innovation needs to be substantially adjusted, or even cancelled. In other cases, the conclusion might be that the intended innovation can be brought in harmony with the teachers' ideas and the next question then might be how to further develop teachers' cognitions (and subsequently their actions). To achieve the latter, not only insight into teacher knowledge is necessary, but also in the way teacher knowledge can be changed, in other words, into the learning processes of teachers (Putnam & Borko, 1997). Recently, some experiences with learning environments for teachers became available, such as peer coaching, the use of case studies and learning in groups (Van Driel, Beijaard, & Verloop, 2001). In all interventions, it is important to realize that teacher cognitions have taken years to take shape and are, consequently, not easily changed. Another complicating factor is that "these beliefs are assumed to be implicit or tacit because teachers may not be aware of how they influence their behavior" (Patrick & Pintrich, 2001, p. 118). Moreover, many authors have indicated that knowledge and beliefs function as filters for interpreting new experiences, or making a selection from new information (Pajares, 1992; Putnam & Borko, 1997), for instance, about innovative instructional approaches. Thus, before every major change or innovation, it makes sense to at least examine the filters or lenses of the teachers concerned. Below we report how, in the context of a specific innovation in higher engineering education, teachers' conceptions and beliefs about teaching and learning were investigated, and in what way this information affected the subsequent innovation (Van Driel, Verloop, Van Werven, & Dekkers, 1997).

This project took place in a Dutch institute of higher education that provides courses in technical disciplines, like mechanical and electrical engineering. The management of the institute had several reasons for deciding to participate in a large-scale innovation project. Most important was the fact that, especially during the first year, many students were unsuccessful, resulting in poor success rates and a large number of "drop outs". The curriculum needed to be redesigned in order to make it more student-centered, implying an emphasis on process-oriented instruction and self-regulated study activities (Vermunt & Verloop, 1999). It was obvious that the proposed reform would strongly affect the existing teaching practice (teaching methods, testing procedures) of the teachers of first-year courses. Therefore, it was decided to conduct a study among the teachers involved in the reform. Two questions were central in this study. First, what conceptions about teaching and learning are held by the teachers of first-year courses? Second, how do these conceptions relate to the goals of the curriculum innovation project?

Sixty teachers participated in this study, all teaching first-year courses. The average age of the teachers was approximately 45 years. With few exceptions, they possessed ample teaching experience (15–25 years). Teachers were interviewed in small groups. This choice was made because we were particularly interested in the conceptions occurring in the population of teachers as a whole, rather than in each teacher's conceptions and beliefs. Besides, one purpose of the study was to describe the culture existing within this group of teachers. Interviewing groups is known to be an adequate method of achieving this aim (Merton, Fiske, & Kendall, 1990).

Fifteen interviews with duos and ten interviews with trios were conducted. The mean length of an interview session was 75 min. A semi-structured interview format was chosen in order to acknowledge the expertise of the respondents on the subject and to allow them to tell and discuss "their own stories" and to introduce issues the interviewers had not thought of (Smith, 1995). The data were analyzed from an interpretative phenomenological perspective, and consisted of an iterative process which included both data triangulation (comparing interview reports with written answers on the questionnaire) as well as investigator triangulation (comparing analyses of individual researchers; Janesick, 1994).

The teaching conception that occurred most frequently was labelled *student-directed*. In this teaching conception, teachers carefully plan and control students' learning activities in order to cover a fixed amount of subject matter. According to this conception, students are supported as much as possible by teachers, who offer explanations, present demonstrations, give feedback, and so on. This conception appeared to be adopted by about two-thirds of the respondents. Two other teaching conceptions were identified: a *teacher-centered* conception, adopted by about one quarter of the respondents, and a *student-centered* conception, which emerged from the answers of about one-tenth of the teachers. The teacher-centered conception reflects the image of the teacher as an expert in the subject matter, who imparts information to students. Rather than supporting students as much as they can, teachers who have a teacher-centered conception expect their students simply to study hard. This conception appeared to be adopted mostly by some of the oldest and most experienced respondents. The student-centered conception was found among a relatively small group of about 6–8 teachers. Unlike most of their colleagues, these teachers seemed to be more inclined to promote self-regulated student activities. Also, they adapted their teaching practice to fit with the goals of the institute as a whole, and with the qualifications required from the field of professional engineering, as well as with their students' prior education.

With a few exceptions from the teacher-centered category, all teachers indicated that, on the whole, they supported the proposed curriculum innovation, and expressed a desire to implement a "student-centered" approach. However, for the teachers adopting the student-directed conception, this implied the need for frequent interactions with small groups of students, in order to offer as much "service" to students as possible. In fact, most teachers appeared to be very sceptical about students' abilities to perform self-regulated activities without teachers' constant support and control.

The results of this study had a large impact on the course of the innovation project. The will the teachers generally expressed to support this project was considered, in principle, to be a reinforcement of the major goal of the project (i.e., redesigning the first year of the curriculum in order to enable more students to study successfully). Moreover, it was felt that the desire of the majority of the teachers to teach small groups and to maintain a relatively large number of teaching periods per week had to be acknowledged. As these desires reflected basic aspects of their conceptions of teaching, it was considered unwise to provoke dilemmas regarding these matters (Duffee & Aikenhead, 1992). On the other hand, it was considered necessary to promote teachers' conceptions with regard to a student-centered teaching approach. In addition to conventional staff development activities, it was decided to organize the design and the development of the new curriculum in teams of teachers. This collaborative approach took the teachers' current conceptions as a starting point, while the development of these conceptions was supposed to be inspired by collegial interaction. Five teams of 5–8 teachers more or less successfully designed elements of the new first-year curriculum.

Concluding Remarks

From the theoretical developments and empirical investigations with respect to teacher knowledge, the efforts to broaden the knowledge base of teaching to include teacher knowledge are promising. A number of illuminating studies, depicting teachers' knowledge with respect to a range of phenomena, are available. As it has become clear that the greater part of teacher knowledge is strongly related to specific domains or contexts, much time-consuming research will be needed in order to depict the relevant aspects of teacher knowledge for a wide range of specific topics and contexts. Those who had hoped that, on the basis of a couple of large-scale general investigations into teacher cognition, we would find the holy grail, that is, the essence of teacher knowledge in the general sense, will be disappointed. It is to be expected that, in order to describe teacher knowledge, much perseverance will be required, not unlike the work devoted in the past to other components of the knowledge base of teaching, such as the formal teaching theories.

The main question concerning the role of teacher knowledge in teacher education is in what ways this teacher knowledge can be made available, or accessible, to prospective teachers. We have known for a long time that for a prospective teacher to observe a mentor is not sufficient to reach this goal (Calderhead, 1988). In past years, successful attempts were made to provide prospective and beginning teachers with teacher knowledge in the form of case descriptions and narratives (Noddings, 1996; Levin, 1995). However, it is still unclear how teacher knowledge can be made clear by mentors during practice teaching. One of the problems is that, for experienced mentor teachers (like for most experienced professionals, for that matter), it is often unclear to them exactly how they proceed in a particular task and what knowledge is involved. This is because separate elements from their knowledge and insights gradually become parts of a larger whole and become inseparable from that larger whole, a process which can be described as "knowledge encapsulation" (Van de Wiel, 1997). Confronting beginners with these end-products of experienced teachers often is more confusing than illuminating (Borko, 1989).

It is clear that explicating teacher knowledge is not done by mentor teachers spontaneously, and happens only in exceptional cases (Brown, 1995). As Brown and McIntyre (1993) stated, for teachers, it holds that "to them most of what has happened in their lessons, and especially almost everything which they themselves have done in the classroom, is so ordinary and so obvious as not to merit any comment. ... They are seldom asked to articulate and elaborate on what they do in their ordinary, everyday teaching. For such reasons, this part of the professional knowledge of experienced teachers is communicated to beginning teachers only to a very limited extent, and the wheels of teaching have to be reinvented by each new generation" (p. 13).

In our research program, various procedures have been applied to help prospective teachers elucidate the teacher knowledge of their mentors and to investigate the effects of these procedures (Meijer, Zanting, & Verloop, 2002; Zanting, 2001; Zanting, Verloop, & Vermunt, 2001b). On the basis of these investigations, it was possible to give prospective teachers access to the teacher knowledge of their mentor teachers, but it was also clear that specific interventions were needed to achieve this. Especially eliciting the tacit elements in mentor teachers' practical knowledge appeared to be time consuming. Moreover, there were indications that the prospective teachers could use the teacher knowledge of their mentor teachers as a source for their own knowledge development. Finally, following this path would seem to be necessary if one is to accomplish the often advocated exchange between formal theory, on the one hand, and teachers' practical knowledge, on the other. This also calls on the mentor's ability to relate his or her explicated teacher knowledge to these formal theories. It is evident that this ability requires additional and thorough training of the mentor teachers.

Confronting teachers' practical knowledge with formal theory might also be an answer to those who criticize teacher knowledge for its inherent conservative character and its tendency to mainly reflect the well-established and rigid routines of the profession (Kirk, 1986). Approaches that value both teachers' practical knowledge and formal theories as relevant components of the knowledge base of teaching, and which confront each element with the other, might enhance the quality of both. This might help to bring about the situation described by Thiessen (2000): the development of "practically relevant propositional knowledge" at the university and the development of "propositionally interpreted practical knowledge" in schools (p. 530).

Given the present state of the art, future research on teacher knowledge should be concentrated in three areas. First, procedures and techniques needed to grasp the more tacit and intuitive aspects of teacher knowledge need to be developed; procedures and techniques focused on both the exploration and extension of the knowledge base of teaching. At this moment, the importance of these tacit and unconscious elements is insufficiently translated into research efforts. Second, much more research into subject-specific aspects of teacher knowledge is needed, especially concerning new and innovative issues. Not only should this information be used to optimize innovations but, conversely, it should also be determined what effects specific innovations have on teacher knowledge in particular domains. Third, studies of learning conceived as a change in the teacher knowledge of an individual teacher need to be conducted. At this moment, there is only scant information about environments that can successfully trigger teacher learning, and about the kinds of circumstances that cause particular kinds of change. In the past, teacher learning was mainly studied as a change in teacher behavior. It has already been acknowledged that deepening teacher knowledge is the key feature for enhancing teacher learning (Birman et al., 2000). The recent developments with respect to teacher knowledge research make it possible to study teacher learning from a knowledge development perspective.

Note

1 Originally published as Verloop, N., Van Driel, J. H., & Meijer, P. (2001). Teacher knowledge and the knowledge base of teaching. *International Journal of Educational Research, 35*(5), 441–461. Reprinted, with minor edits, with permission from the publisher.

References

Alexander, P. A., Schallert, D. L., & Hare, V. C. (1991). Coming to terms: How researchers in learning and literacy talk about knowledge. *Review of Educational Research, 61*(3), 315–343.

Baddeley, A. (1990). *Human memory. Theory and practice.* Lawrence Erlbaum.

Birman, B. F., Desimone, L., Porter, A. C., & Garet, M. S. (2000). Designing professional development that works. *Educational Leadership, 57*(8), 28–33.

Borko, H. (1989). Research on learning to teach: Implications for graduate teacher preparation. In A. E. Woolfolk (Ed.), *Research perspectives on the graduate preparation of teachers* (pp. 69–87). Prentice Hall.

Brown, S. (1995). The professional craft knowledge of teachers: Student teachers gaining access to it. In R. Hoz & M. Silberstein (Eds.), *Partnerships of schools and institutions of higher education in teacher development* (pp. 25–38). Ben-Gurion University of the Negev Press.

Brown, S., & McIntyre, D. (1993). *Making sense of teaching.* Open University Press.

Calderhead, J. (1988). The contribution of field experiences to student primary teachers' professional learning. *Research in Education, 40,* 34–49.

Calderhead, J. (1996). Teachers: Beliefs and knowledge. In D. C. Berliner & R. C. Calfee (Eds.), *Handbook of educational psychology* (pp. 709–725). MacMillan.

Calderhead, J., & Robson, M. (1991). Images of teaching: Student teachers' early conceptions of classroom practice. *Teaching and Teacher Education, 7*(1), 1–8.

Carlgren, I., & Lindblad, S. (1991). On teachers' practical reasoning and professional knowledge: Considering conceptions of context in teachers' thinking. *Teaching and Teacher Education, 7,* 57–516.

Carter, K. (1990). Teachers' knowledge and learning to teach. In W. R. Houston (Ed.), *Handbook of research on teacher education* (pp. 291–310). MacMillan.

Cochran, F. K., DeRuiter, J. A., & King, R. A. (1993). Pedagogical content knowing: An integrative model for teacher preparation. *Journal of Teacher Education, 44,* 261–272.

Connelly, F. M., & Clandinin, D. J. (1985). Personal practical knowledge and the modes of knowing: Relevance for teaching and learning. In E. Eisner (Ed.), *Learning and teaching the ways of knowing* (pp. 174–198). University of Chicago Press.

De Vos, W., & Verdonk, A. H. (1985). A new road to reactions, part 1. *Journal of Chemical Education, 62,* 238–240.

Denzin, N. K. (1994). The art and politics of interpretation. In N. K. Denzin & Y. S. Lincoln (Eds.), *Handbook of qualitative research design* (pp. 500–515). Sage.

Doyle, W. (1990). Themes in teacher education research. In W. R. Houston (Ed.), *Handbook of research on teacher education* (pp. 3–23). MacMillan.

Duffee, L., & Aikenhead, G. (1992). Curriculum change, student evaluation, and teacher practical knowledge. *Science Education, 76,* 493–506.

Dunkin, M. J., & Biddle, B. J. (1974). *The study of teaching.* Holt, Rinehart and Winston.

Elbaz, F. (1991). Research on teachers' knowledge: The evolution of a discourse. *Journal of Curriculum Studies, 23*(1), 1–19.

Eraut, M. (1994). *Developing professional practice and competence.* Falmer Press.

Fenstermacher, G. D. (1986). Philosophy of research on teaching: Three aspects. In M. C. Wittrock (Ed.), *Handbook of research on teaching* (3rd ed., pp. 37–49). MacMillan.

Fenstermacher, G. D. (1994). The knower and the known: The nature of knowledge in research on teaching. In L. Darling-Hammond (Ed.), *Review of research in education* (Vol. 20, pp. 3–56). AERA.

Furlong, J. (2000). Intuition and the crisis in teacher professionalism. In T. Atkinson & G. Claxton (Eds.), *The intuitive practitioner. On the value of not always knowing what one is doing* (pp. 15–31). Open University Press.

Grimmett, P. P., & MacKinnon, A. M. (1992). Craft knowledge and the education of teachers. In G. Grant (Ed.), *Review of research in education* (Vol. 18, pp. 385–456). AERA.

Gunstone, R. (1999). Content knowledge, reflection, and their intertwining: A response to the paper set. *Science Education, 83*(3), 393–396.

Hawley, W. D., & Valli, L. (1999). The essentials of effective professional development. A new consensus. In L. Darling-Hammond & G. Sykes (Eds.), *Teaching as the learning profession. Handbook of policy and practice* (pp. 127–179). Jossey-Bass.

Henze, I., Van Driel, J. H., & Verloop, N. (2009). Experienced science teachers' learning in the context of Educational Innovation. *Journal of Teacher Education, 60*(2), 184–199.

Hoyle, E., & John, P. D. (1995). *Professional knowledge and professional practice.* Cassell.

Janesick, V. J. (1994). The dance of qualitative research design. In N. K. Denzin & Y. S. Lincoln (Eds.), *Handbook of qualitative research design* (pp. 209–219). Sage.

Justi, R., & Van Driel, J. H. (2005a). A case study on the development of a beginning chemistry teacher's knowledge on models and modelling. *Research in Science Education, 35*(2–3), 197–219.

Kagan, D. M. (1992). Implications of research on teacher belief. *Educational Psychologist, 27*(1), 65–90.

Kirk, D. (1986). Beyond the limits of theoretical discourse in teacher education: Towards a critical pedagogy. *Teaching and Teacher Education, 2,* 155–167.

Korthagen, F. A. J. (2001). *Linking practice and theory. The pedagogy of realistic teacher education.* Lawrence Erlbaum.

Levin, B. B. (1995). Using the case method in teacher education: The role of discussion and experience in teachers' thinking about cases. *Teaching and Teacher Education, 11*(1), 63–79.

Loughran, J. J. (1999). *Understanding and articulating teacher knowledge* [Paper presentation]. The biennial conference of the International Study Association on Teachers and Teaching (ISATT), Dublin, Ireland.

Merseth, K. K. (1996). Cases and case methods in teacher education. In J. Sikula, T. J. Buttery, & E. Guyton (Eds.), *Handbook of research on teacher education* (2nd ed., pp. 722–744). MacMillan.

Merton, R. K., Fiske, M., & Kendall, P. L. (1990). *The focused interview: A manual of problems and procedures.* The Free Press, Collier Macmillan.

Meijer, P. C., Verloop, N., & Beijaard, D. (1999). Exploring language teachers' practical knowledge about teaching reading comprehension. *Teaching and Teacher Education, 15,* 59–84.

Meijer, P. C., Verloop, N., & Beijaard, D. (2001). Similarities and differences in teachers' practical knowledge about teaching reading comprehension. *The Journal of Educational Research, 94*(3), 171–184.

Meijer, P. C., Verloop, N., & Beijaard, D. (2002). Multi-method Triangulation in a qualitative study on teachers' practical knowledge: An attempt to increase internal validity. *Quality & Quantity, 36*(2), 145–167.

Meijer, P. C., Zanting, A., & Verloop, N. (2002). How can student teachers elicit experienced teachers' practical knowledge. Tools, suggestions and significance. *Journal of Teacher Education, 53*(5), 406–419.

Noddings, N. (1996). Stories and affect in teacher education. *Cambridge Journal of Education, 26*(3), 435–447.

Pajares, M. F. (1992). Teachers' beliefs and educational research. Cleaning up a messy construct. *Review of Educational Research, 62,* 307–332.

Patrick, H., & Pintrich, P. R. (2001). Conceptual change in teachers' intuitive conceptions of learning, motivation and instruction: The role of motivational and epistemological beliefs. In B. Torff & R. J. Sternberg (Eds.), *Understanding and teaching the intuitive mind. Student and teacher learning* (pp. 117143). Lawrence Erlbaum.

Putnam, R. T., & Borko, H. (1997). Teacher learning: implications of new views of cognition. In B. Biddle, T. L. Good, & I. F. Goodson (Eds.), *International handbook of teachers and teaching* (Vol. II, pp. 1223–1296). Kluwer Adademic Publishers.

Resnick, L. (1987). *Education and learning to think.* National Academy Press.

Reynolds, M. C. (Ed.). (1989). *The knowledge base for the beginning teacher.* Pergamon Press.

Rosenshine, B., & Stevens, R. (1986). Teaching functions. In M. C. Wittrock (Ed.), *Handbook of research on teaching* (3rd ed., pp. 376–391). MacMillan.

Shulman, L. S. (1986). Those who understand: Knowledge growth in teaching. *Educational Researcher, 15*(2), 4–14.

Shulman, L. S. (1987). Knowledge and teaching: Foundations of the new reform. *Harvard Educational Review, 57,* 1–22.

Schön, D. A. (1983). *The reflective practitioner. How professionals think in action.* Basic Books.

Schön, D. A. (1987). *Educating the reflective practitioner.* Jossey-Bass.

Schwab, J. J. (1971). The practical: Arts of the eclectic. *School Review, 79*(4), 493–542.

Shimahara, N. K. (1998). The Japanese model of professional development: Teaching as craft. *Teaching and Teacher Education, 14*(5), 451–462.

Smith, J. A. (1995). Semi-structured interviewing and qualitative analysis. In J. A. Smith, R. Harre, & L. Van Langenhove (Eds.), *Rethinking methods in psychology* (pp. 9–26). Sage.

Squires, G. (1999). *Teaching as a professional discipline*. Falmer Press.

Stones, E. (1994). Assessment of a complex skill: Improving teacher education. *Assessment in Education, 1,* 235–251.

Thiessen, D. (2000). A skillful start to a teaching career: A matter of developing impactful behaviors, reflective practices, or professional knowledge? *International Journal of Educational Research, 33*(5), 515–537.

Tom, A. R., & Valli, L. (1990). Professional knowledge for teachers. In W. R. Houston (Ed.), *Handbook of research on teacher education* (pp. 372–392). MacMillan.

Trigwell, K., Prosser, M., & Taylor, P. (1994). Qualitative differences in approaches to teaching first year university science. *Higher Education, 27,* 75–84.

Van de Wiel, M. (1997). *Knowledge encapsulation. Studies on the development of medical expertise* [Doctoral dissertation]. Maastricht University, The Netherlands.

Van Driel, J., Beijaard, D., & Verloop, N. (2001). Professional development and reform in science education: The role of teachers' practical knowledge. *Journal of Research in Science Teaching, 38*(2), 137–158.

Van Driel, J. H., Verloop, N., & De Vos, W. (1998). Developing science teachers' pedagogical content knowledge. *Journal of Research in Science Teaching, 35*(6), 673–695.

Van Driel, J. H., Verloop, N., Van Werven, H. I., & Dekkers, H. (1997). Teachers' craft knowledge and curriculum innovation in higher engineering education. *Higher Education, 34,* 105–122.

Verloop, N. (1992). Praktijkkennis van docenten: Een blinde vlek van de onderswijskunde [Craft knowledge of teachers: A blind spot in educational research]. *Pedagogische Studien, 69,* 410–423.

Verloop, N., & Wubbels, T. (2000). Some major developments in teacher education in the Netherlands and their relationship with international trends. In G. Willems, J. Stakenborg, & W. Veugelers (Eds.), *Trends in Dutch teacher education* (pp. 19–32). Garant.

Vermunt, J. D., & Verloop, N. (1999). Congruence and friction between learning and teaching. *Learning and Instruction, 9,* 257–280.

Yinger, R. J. (1987). Learning the language of practice. *Curriculum Inquiry, 17,* 295–318.

Zanting, A. (2001). *Mining the mentor's mind. The elicitation of mentor teachers' practical knowledge by prospective teachers* [Doctoral dissertation]. Leiden University, The Netherlands.

Zanting, A., Verloop, N., & Vermunt, J. (2001a). Student teachers' beliefs about mentoring and learning to teach during teaching practice. *British Journal of Educational Psychology, 71,* 57–80.

Zanting, A., Verloop, N., & Vermunt, J. (2001b). Student teachers eliciting mentors' practical knowledge and comparing it to their own beliefs. *Teaching and Teacher Education, 17*(6), 725–740.

CHAPTER 4

Teachers' Knowledge of Models and Modelling in Science

1 Why I Conducted the Study

My interest in the use of models and modelling in science goes back a long way. As part of my studies for a Master of Chemistry, I engaged in a research project on the teaching and learning of models in chemistry for grade 9. The project was initiated by Wobbe De Vos who had developed a syllabus for grade 9 Chemistry. As a chemistry teacher, Wobbe had observed that the common presentation in textbooks of molecules and atoms as the smallest particles that make up substances typically led students to think that, for example, a molecule of water is a miniscule drop of water. To avoid these misconceptions, Wobbe decided to present molecules and atoms as models, that is, human constructions that could help to understand, explain and predict the behaviour of substances. Wobbe referred to these models as corpuscular models rather than particle models. I was attracted to his ideas and familiarised myself with the syllabus. Next, I observed a few lessons in which the syllabus was used and I became fascinated by the discussions that grade 9 students had with each other and their teachers, where they used the notion of molecules to explain phenomena they had observed, such as evaporation or chemical reactions. My participation in the project led to my first academic publication, which was entitled after a quote from a student: "Als het een geur heeft, dan moeten er toch moleculen zijn, die jij dus waarneemt met de neus" ("If it has a smell, then there must be molecules that you observe with the nose"; Van Driel & De Vos, 1983). Incidentally, this paper was published as the opening article of the first issue of a new journal for science education research in Dutch language, *Tijdschrift voor Didactiek der ß-wetenschappen* (Journal for Didactics of Science and Mathematics), which was published between 1983 and 2014.

When I decided to do a PhD study (see Chapter 1), I was keen to further explore the teaching and learning of chemistry through models and modelling. The opportunity to work again with Wobbe De Vos, as the main supervisor of my study, strongly motivated me to take this perspective. In particular, the focus was on the use of models to understand the dynamic nature of chemical equilibrium, that is, the idea that in a state of chemical equilibrium two opposing reactions take place at the same rate. This idea is counterintuitive;

however, it helps to explain why and how a state of equilibrium is established in a chemical system and restored after a disruption. I published a few articles that demonstrate how these model-based approaches can assist and challenge student learning of basic ideas in chemistry (e.g., Van Driel, De Vos, & Verloop, 1999; Van Driel, 2002).

As I became more interested in teachers' implementation of these approaches (Chapter 1) and had begun my research on teacher practical knowledge in the context of the Leiden research program *The Knowledge Base of Teaching*, I was keen to make teachers' practical knowledge of models and modelling in science a central topic of my research.

2   Context

Around this time, the second half of the 1990s, a number of national innovations were taking place in secondary education in the Netherlands, mandated by the Dutch government. As explained in Chapter 2, one of these innovations concerned the introduction of a new subject called *Algemene Natuurwetenschappen* (ANW; General Science) in the national curriculum for grades 10–12. The subject had the following main objectives:

1. Introducing every student to major scientific concepts (i.e., life, matter, the biosphere, the solar system and the universe);
2. Demonstrating the complex interactions between science, technology and society;
3. Making students aware of the ways in which scientific knowledge is produced and developed.

Models and modelling in science were prominent in all these objectives. For instance, models of matter and of the solar system were taught in relation to the first objective and the role of models and modelling was highlighted to explain scientific knowledge development.

ANW was introduced in the curriculum for grades 10–12 *alongside* physics, chemistry and biology and it was going to be taught by teachers who were qualified for one or more of these science subjects. I was very interested to investigate how such teachers would implement the new subject, in particular, how they would embed the role of models and modelling in their teaching of it. A national program for teacher professional development was being set up aimed to provide teachers with a qualification that was required to teach ANW. A pilot version of the program took place in the first half of 1997 and I contacted the program leaders to discuss how models and modelling in science could be included. It was agreed that I would provide a workshop on this topic. Prior to that, participants were asked to complete a homework assignment. This consisted of seven open items, inspired by and covering the same themes as an instrument by Grosslight et al. (1991), namely: (1) types of representations of models, (2) goals and functions of models in science, (3) characteristics of scientific models and (4) modelling in science, that is, the design and revision of models. In addition, I invited participants for an interview about their current teaching practice with respect to the teaching of models and modelling in science and their ideas and expectations concerning the role of models and modelling in the new subject. Fifteen teachers completed the written assignment and seven volunteered to be interviewed (three of whom had also done the assignment). All of them had taught physics, chemistry or biology for at least five years.

The findings of this study were published in *Tijdschrift voor Didactiek der ß-wetenschappen* (Van Driel, 1997) and demonstrated a large variety in the practical knowledge of the participating teachers. For instance, teachers expressed very different views about characteristics and functions of models and how they included models and modelling in their teaching practice. A common element, however, was that they seemed to focus on the content rather than the nature of models. The study concluded with implications for the national professional development program and further research. I was keen to explore the practical knowledge about models and modelling among a larger cohort of science teachers, first at the start of their participation in the professional development program and next during the implementation of ANW. To conduct a baseline measurement, I decided to develop a survey instrument with Likert type items. The survey consisted of two parts, designed to capture teachers' practical knowledge about 1) models and modelling in science and 2) teaching and learning of models and modelling. Part 1 was set up according to the themes of Grosslight et al. (1991) which had also been used to design the homework assignment and consisted of 32 items. Part 2 (30 items) was based on themes that had emerged from the analysis of the abovementioned interviews.

As all secondary schools had to offer ANW from 1999 onwards, each school in the country had to nominate teachers to obtain the qualification through completing the professional development program. The program itself was organised across a school year and consisted of a range of workshops and seminars (60 hours) and tasks that teachers had to complete as part of their assessment (estimated at 60 hours). My institute was selected as one of the providers of this program. Cohorts of around 100 teachers per year enrolled. In the first iteration of the program (1998/99), I provided a workshop on models and modelling in science. To prepare for this, I asked the participants to complete Part 1 of the survey prior to the session. At the conclusion of the workshop, I asked them to complete Part 2. This approach allowed me to collect the responses of 71 teachers to Part 1 and 74 to Part 2. I decided to report the findings in two separate papers, to be co-authored with Nico Verloop. The first was going to focus on teachers' practical knowledge about models and modelling in science and would be based on the data from the homework assignment from the pilot version of the professional development program, combined with the 71 responses to Part 1 of the survey from the first cohort of the program. The second paper would concentrate on science teachers' knowledge of teaching and learning of models and modelling and was based on the interviews and part 2 of the survey. The idea behind this was that, rather than writing separate papers on qualitative data and quantitative data, it would be more interesting to combine different data sources to explore different aspects of teachers' practical knowledge.

3   Reflection and Follow Up

Around this time, I had met Professor John Gilbert (University of Reading, UK) at a NARST conference. John was very interested in the use of models and visualisation in science education and led an international research group, MISTRE (Models in Science and Technology; Research in Education). He was familiar with the work of Wobbe De Vos in this field and was keen to hear about the new subject ANW and my research project in this context. As John was the editor of the *International Journal of Science Education*, it seemed logical to submit the manuscript on teachers' practical knowledge about models and modelling in science to this journal. After a round of revisions, it was accepted and published in late 1999. To date, it has accumulated more than 480 citations in Google Scholar. It is interesting to see that in the first 10 years after it was published it attracted only modest attention, but since 2009 it has been cited consistently around 30 times per year (33 in 2019). Most of the authors who have cited the article, representing a wide range of countries and languages, included the word 'model' or 'modelling' in the title of their paper, indicating that this topic continues to be relevant around the world.

Reflecting on the article and on the study on which it was based, a few things can be noted. In terms of strengths, I think the article did a good job in framing the topic of models and modelling in science by relating it to the history and philosophy of science while taking an explicit science education perspective. I must credit Wobbe De Vos for sharing his wisdom about this topic with me. His work in this area is cited heavily in the first half of the article. The combination of two instruments (small scale – open assignment and larger scale – survey) is another strength. Both instruments covered the same ground and the teachers participating in the two studies were very similar in terms of background and experience. This enabled an interesting comparison of data: where the teachers who did the homework assignment could frame their responses in their own words, those who participated in the survey study were limited to pick one score on a four-point scale ranging from (1) 'never', through (2) 'sometimes' and (3) 'usually', to (4) 'always'. Interestingly, both types of data showed that the participating science teachers shared the general idea that a model is a simplified representation of reality. The responses to the homework assignment showed that teachers used different criteria to determine whether or not a specific example (e.g., a toy car) qualified as a scientific model. Also, these teachers emphasized different functions and characteristics of models. The analyses of the survey indicated that the practical knowledge of models and modelling in science of the teachers, on the whole, was not very pronounced. That is, most items were scored between (2) and (3) and there were no significant differences between teachers with different years of experience or disciplinary backgrounds. A cluster analysis revealed two subgroups of teachers, the smaller of the two expressing more outspoken but also inconsistent views. We accounted for this by arguing that these teachers may have integrated different perspectives about models and modelling in science in their practical knowledge, for instance, drawing on their disciplinary education and later professional experience. This could have resulted in inconsistencies of which they may not have been aware. Looking back on the study, I must admit that a Likert scale survey, although it allows the use of statistical techniques, isn't the most appropriate instrument to study teachers' practical knowledge. In the paper on teacher knowledge that was published in 2001 (see Chapter 3), we would argue that studies on teachers' practical knowledge require triangulation of data collected with a diverse set of instruments.

Despite these and other limitations, for me, this article is important as it marks my first major publication with an explicit focus on models and modelling in science. It was followed by a number of articles based on this and subsequent projects. First, Nico Verloop and I wrote an article focusing on teaching and learning of models and modelling in science education based on data from interviews and responses to Part 2 of the survey. In this article, which was also published in the *International Journal of Science Education* (Van Driel & Verloop, 2002), we reported that teachers differed in the extent to which they used teaching activities focusing on models and modelling in science and that their knowledge of students' views of models and modelling abilities was either limited or not very well integrated with their knowledge of teaching activities. To address the latter problem, we recommended teachers to study students' knowledge and abilities about models, preferably through collecting data in their own classrooms. This idea would be incorporated in future projects with Onno De Jong and Rosária Justi. Also, I wrote a couple of short articles based on the study in publications for science teachers and teacher educators.

Next, I joined Wobbe De Vos and Ton Van Der Valk on a project that aimed to result in a validated set of common characteristics of scientific models. This project originated from Wobbe's earlier work and was inspired by his idea that definitions of scientific models in textbooks failed to capture the essence of the way current scientists use and develop models. Rather than looking for one consensus definition of a scientific model, Wobbe proposed a set of common characteristics that might apply to models with different purposes and formats that were used across scientific disciplines. This list of seven characteristics came out of his own PhD thesis (1985) and was included in the article that is central to this chapter. To validate the list, Wobbe had selected 77 articles from different scientific disciplines, published in Scientific Citation Index (SCI) journals, that had the word 'model' or 'mode(l)ling' in the title. Based on the preliminary list of seven characteristics, a set of ten statements about the role of models and modelling in science research was designed. The first author of each of the 77 articles was invited to indicate whether these statements were correct, or not, from the point of view of their own research and to provide an explanation for their response. Unfortunately, Wobbe became sick around this time and sadly passed away in 2002. After a while, Ton and I decided to complete the project and on the basis of 24 responses (31%), we concluded that the consulted scientists mostly agreed with the initial list of common characteristics of models and modelling in science. However, some of these needed to be amended or revised. We recommended that in science education more attention should be paid to current uses of models in scientific research, and that the nature of models needed to be addressed more explicitly. An article was finally published in 2007 (Van Der Valk, Van Driel, & De Vos, 2007).

My research on teachers' practical knowledge about models and modelling in science continued in two different ways. First, I was keen to follow up on the baseline studies with the ANW teachers, by tracing the development of the practical knowledge of teachers who were implementing ANW in their own classes. Nico Verloop and I obtained a research grant which funded the salary of a PhD candidate (4 years fulltime; note that in the Netherlands most PhD candidates are not students but employees of universities at a specified salary rate). So instead of doing the research myself, I became the supervisor of a PhD researcher who would investigate the development of ANW teachers' practical knowledge about models and modelling. This project will be discussed in the next chapter.

Second, I had become very interested in investigating the development of the practical knowledge of secondary pre-service science teachers' during their teacher education program. I had set up a partnership with Onno De Jong at Utrecht University. Onno was one of the teacher educators when I did my teacher education program at Utrecht. We shared a background in chemistry and were both interested in the development of PCK in pre-service teachers of chemistry. We agreed that the relationship between (macroscopic) phenomena and (sub-microscopic) models constituted a central topic in the chemistry curriculum, so we designed a joint research project on pre-service chemistry teachers' PCK development on that topic. In Chapter 6, this project will be discussed in detail.

Teachers' Knowledge of Models and Modelling in Science[1]

Jan H. van Driel and Nico Verloop

Abstract

This study investigated the knowledge that experienced science teachers have of models and modelling science in the context of a school curriculum innovation project in which the role and the nature of models and modelling in science are emphasized. The subjects in this study were teachers of biology, chemistry and physics preparing for the curriculum innovation. Two instruments were used: a questionnaire with seven open items on models and modelling, which was completed by 15 teachers, and a questionnaire consisting of 32 items on a Likert-type scale ($n = 71$). Results indicated that the teachers shared the same general definition of models. However, the teachers' content knowledge of models and modelling proved to be limited and diverse. A group of teachers who displayed more pronounced knowledge appeared to have integrated elements of both a positivist and a social constructivist epistemological orientation in their practical knowledge. Implications for the design of teacher education interventions are discussed.

Introduction

Models play a central role in science education. Usually, the focus is on the content of the models being taught and learned. Yet the nature of the models is not always explicitly discussed. Moreover, in spite of the current emphasis on constructivist teaching strategies, it seems to be unusual to invite the students to actively construct and revise models. Instead, teachers usually present the models to be learned as static facts. However, a new Dutch curriculum innovation project was recently initiated which is aimed at, among other things, focusing more attention on the role and the nature of models and modelling in science. In this context, the knowledge and beliefs science teachers hold about models and modelling are of crucial importance, since they will influence the teachers' perception of the curriculum innovation project, and, ultimately, the way they will implement the innovation.

The study in this paper was carried out in the context of this innovation project. The theoretical framework of the study draws upon the concept of teachers' practical knowledge or craft knowledge. Practical knowledge consists of the accumulated and integrated set of knowledge and beliefs teachers develop with respect to their teaching practice (Grimmett & MacKinnon, 1992). Teachers' practical knowledge is derived from teaching experience and formal education, and is ready to be used in their own practice (Beijaard & Verloop, 1996). As it is assumed to be the dominant factor in guiding the teacher's behaviour (Verloop, 1992), the personal practical knowledge of teachers exerts a major influence on the way they respond to a new curriculum (Duffee & Aikenhead, 1992).

The rationale of this study is connected to one of the aims of the curriculum innovation project, that is, to shift the focus of attention in science teaching from the content to the nature of scientific models. In this respect, teachers' practical knowledge of models and modelling in science is important. Thus, the focus in this study was on investigating the knowledge of experienced science teachers in this domain.

Models in Science and in Science Education

Models and Modelling in Science

Models in science differ in terms of physical appearance and cover a large range of applications. Several categorizations of scientific models have been described (e.g., Black, 1962; J. K. Gilbert, 1994), dividing models in terms of appearance (e.g., physical models and mathematical models) or functions. From the latter perspective, models may be characterized as descriptive, explanatory, or predictive. A descriptive model is characterized by a large degree of 'positive analogy' between model and target (Hesse, 1966). An example is the heliocentric model, describing the orbits of the planets in our solar system. Through the implementation of a theory, an explanatory model may be designed. In the example, the concept of gravity, derived from Newtonian theory, may be used to design a model which explains the movements of the planets. Moreover, the inclusion of theoretical notions in a model enables the formulation of predictions. For instance, Adams and Le Verier could predict the existence of the eighth planet, Uranus, on the basis of a model which included the concept of gravity. Shortly after this prediction was made, Uranus was indeed identified by observation.

Categorizing models serves to emphasize the differences between scientific models. Yet these models share several common characteristics. Instead of presenting a general definition of a scientific model, some authors have tried to identify the common characteristics which apply to all scientific models (De Vos, 1985; Van Hoeve-Brouwer, 1996).

1. A model is always related to a target, which is represented by the model. The term 'target' refers to either a system, an object, a phenomenon or a process.

2. A model is a research tool which is used to obtain information about a target which cannot be observed or measured directly (e.g., an atom, a dinosaur, a black hole). Thus, a scale model, that is, an exact copy of an object (e.g., a house, a bridge) on another scale, is not considered to be a *scientific* model.
3. A model cannot interact directly with the target it represents. Thus, a photograph or a spectrum does not qualify as a model.
4. A model bears certain analogies to the target, thus enabling the researcher to derive hypotheses from the model which may be tested while studying the target. Testing these hypotheses produces new information about the target.
5. A model always differs in certain respects from the target. In general, a model is kept as simple as possible. Dependent on the specific research interests, some aspects of the target are deliberately excluded from the model.
6. In designing a model, a compromise must be found between the analogies and the differences with the target, allowing the researcher to make specific choices. This process is guided by the research questions.
7. A model is developed through an iterative process, in which empirical data with respect to the target may lead to a revision of the model, while in a following step the model is tested by further study of the target.

In any case, models play an important role in the *communication* between scientists. Individuals may have a mental model, that is, a personal, private representation of a target. Through speech or writing, a mental model may be expressed by an individual. This expressed model is available for discussion with others. Through comparison and testing of their personal, expressed models, scientists may reach agreement on consensus models. Such models belong to the main products of science (Gilbert *et al.*, 1998). The process of construction of consensus models is fundamental to the understanding of scientific progress (Van Oers, 1988). As the choice for a specific model depends on the context and the purpose of the research, several consensus models may coexist with respect to the same target. For example, biochemists and theoretical chemists may use quite different models for the corpuscular structure of water.

Models in Science Education

Many studies have been conducted on the teaching and learning of the *content* of specific models, for instance, studies on corpuscular models (e.g., De Vos & Verdonk, 1987; Harrison & Treagust, 1996). Thus far, only a few studies have focused on the process of modelling (e.g., S. W. Gilbert, 1991) and on students' conceptions about models and their use in science (Grosslight *et al.,* 1991). The students in the latter study often held conceptions that corresponded with a 'naive realist' epistomology. That is, the students usually considered models to be exact copies of reality, albeit on a different scale. However, the older students in this study appeared to understand that models are designed for specific purposes, and that a model may change in the course of time, for instance when new empirical data have been analysed. The functions of models in explaining and predicting observable phenomena were only rarely acknowledged by these students. It appears that, until now, there have been no investigations of teachers' knowledge of models and modelling in science.

Purpose and Context of This Study

The purpose of this study was twofold. From a theoretical perspective, this study aimed at contributing to a better understanding of specific aspects of the practical knowledge of experienced science teachers, that is, their knowledge concerning models and modelling in science. A practical purpose of this study was to contribute to the design of specific activities and interventions, aimed at developing science teachers' knowledge in this domain.

To understand the context of this study, it is important to know that in the Netherlands, the national curriculum traditionally contains physics, chemistry and biology as separate subjects. With the exception of local, small-scale projects, there is no experience with an integrated approach to teaching science. As of 1998, however, such an approach is being implemented in the national curriculum through the introduction of Public Understanding of Science as a new, separate subject, alongside the traditional disciplines of physics, chemistry and biology (De Vos and Reiding, 1999). The new subject has three main objectives: (1) to introduce *every* student to major scientific concepts (i.e., life, matter, biosphere, solar system and the universe); (2) to demonstrate the complex interactions between science, technology and society; and (3) to make students aware of the ways in which scientific knowledge is produced and developed. The emphasis on models and modelling is most apparent within the latter objective.

To illustrate the role of models and modelling in the new subject, some elements of the curriculum are concisely portrayed. In the *Life* domain, for instance, students are asked to design a model for the human immunity system. Reflecting on this assignment, the students are encouraged to discuss questions on the nature and the use of models in general. In the *Solar system and universe* domain, the students compare and discuss several models for the solar system from the history of science, such as Ptolemaeus' geocentric model and Copernicus' heliocentric model. In the *Biosphere* domain, finally, students study the role of predictive models with respect to the greenhouse effect. This study also serves to illustrate the role of simultaneous models (Van Hoeve-Brouwer, 1996), that is, the use of different models for the same target alongside one another.

The implementation of the new subject is supported by an in-service programme for teachers with teaching experience in either physics, chemistry or biology. This programme was started in 1997 and is conducted on a nationwide scale. It was decided that the in-service programme should consist of workshops and conferences (60 hours altogether) plus self-regulated study activities, also amounting to approximately 60 hours.

In the present study, the knowledge of experienced science teachers was investigated at the start of this programme in order to ascertain these teachers' practical knowledge as a result of prior education and teaching experience, before specific interventions took place in the in-service programme. Thus, the results of the study could actually inform the design of such activities. Specifically, data were collected in order to map the participants' practical knowledge with respect to models and modelling in science, in terms of the common characteristics of models (see above), the roles, and the functions of models in science.

Design of the Study

Two instruments were designed to investigate teachers' knowledge of models and modelling in science. The first instrument was a questionnaire with seven open items, while the other instrument consisted of a Likert-type scale questionnaire.

Open-Item Questionnaire
The design of the questionnaire was inspired by an instrument developed by Grosslight *et al.* (1991). The questionnaire used in the present study addressed the same themes, namely: (1) types of representations of models; (2) goals and functions of models in science; (3) characteristics of scientific models; and (4) modelling in science, that is, the design and revision of models. The questionnaire consisted of seven open items. The first item addressed the first theme, i.e., the respresentations of models. The respondents were presented with seven specific examples, including a toy car, a picture of a house, Ohm' s law, and a water molecule. They were asked to indicate whether they considered

each example a model, and why. The six other items addressed the remaining three themes, each theme being covered by two questions. For example, one item was 'How would you describe what a model is to someone who is not familiar with models?' (theme (3)).

The questionnaire was administered to a group of teachers ($n = 15$) at the start of the in-service programme, to be completed by them individually at home. With two exceptions, all of them had more than five years teaching experience in physics, chemistry or biology. No information about models in science was given to them in advance.

The teachers' written answers were analysed applying an interpretative phenomenological approach (Smith *et al.,* 1995). First, the answers of every individual teacher were interpreted in terms of the themes mentioned above. Next, it was investigated within every theme whether the teachers' answers could be categorized. For every theme, global descriptions of categories were used as a starting point (e.g., 'describing' and 'explaining' for theme (2), and the common characteristics mentioned above for theme (3)). Comparing the teachers' formulations with these global descriptions resulted in a more detailed description of the categories. After the categorization of the teachers' answers, an attempt was made to identify the existence of specific patterns in these answers. It was explored whether the teachers' answers within a certain category were related to their answers in other specific categories.

Likert-Type Scale Questionnaire

The four themes that inspired the design of the open-item questionnaire were also used as the starting point for the development of the Likert-type scale questionnaire. Initially, 8 to 12 statements about models and modelling in science were formulated for each theme (e.g., 'a model is a simplified reproduction of reality'). Two fellow researchers were asked to comment upon these statements. This resulted in the rejection of five statements, and changes in the formulation of almost every other statement. The final set of statements consisted of 32 items, distributed among the respective themes as follows: (1) types of representation: 5; (2) goals and functions: 8; (3) characteristics: 9, and (4) design and development: 10. Respondents were asked to indicate to what extent each statement was valid for models and modelling in science, using a four-point scale ranging from: (1) 'never', through; (2) 'sometimes'; and (3) 'usually', to (4): 'always'. Finally, the respondents were asked to indicate their gender, their number of years of teaching experience, and the subject in which they taught the most hours (either chemistry, biology, or physics).

This questionnaire was administered to a group of science teachers ($n = 71$), again at the start of the in-service programme and to be completed by them individually at home. This group did not include teachers who had previously completed the open-item questionnaire. This choice was made to avoid possible effects of testing. Given the similarities between the two instruments, teachers' answers to the Likert-type scale questionnaire otherwise might have been influenced by their previously answering the open-item questionnaire. The majority of the respondents were male (80%). The average number of years of teaching experience was 17.5 (standard deviation: 7.5 years). More than a quarter (27%) of the respondents were physics teachers, 35% had a background in biology and 37% taught chemistry (1% unknown).

The analysis of the data included several statistical procedures. After the usual descriptive statistics (frequencies, mean scores, and standard deviations) had been obtained, principal components analyses with varimax rotation were performed. This resulted in the extraction of three factors. These factors were subsequently treated as scales, and subjected to the analyses of reliability. Moreover, Pearson correlations, both within and between scales, were computed. Next, analyses of variance (ANOVA) were performed to investigate whether teachers' scores on the three scales and on the individual items differed significantly with respect to subject and teaching experience. For the latter purpose, the teachers were divided into four groups of roughly equal sizes, that is, (1): less than 10 years, (2): 11–15 years, (3): 16–20 years, and (4): more than 20 years. Levene statistics were incorporated to test for homogeneity of variances, as well as Tukey HSD (honest significant difference) tests for multiple comparisons. Finally, a hierarchical cluster analysis was carried out on the group respondents as a whole to explore whether they could be divided into homogeneous subgroups with distinctive knowledge of models and modelling in science. Squared Euclidian distances were calculated as a measure of distance, and average linkage between groups was applied as a clustering method. This analysis was followed by a series of T-tests, incorporating Levene's test for equality of variances, to explore differences in scores on scales and individual items between groups of respondents. Ultimately, analyses of crosstabs were performed to check whether the teachers were distributed evenly over clusters with respect to subject and teaching experience. All statistical analyses were performed using SPSS, version 7.5.

Results

Open-Item Questionnaire on Models and Modelling
All the teachers produced a general description of a model. These descriptions appeared to be very similar and could be summarized as follows: 'A model

is a simplified or schematic representation of reality'. Specific results, however, indicated a large degree of variety of the teachers' knowledge of models and modelling in science. This variety became apparent when the teachers' answers were analysed per theme:

1. The teachers held different beliefs with respect to the *representational modes* of scientific models. When asked to respond to seven specific examples, one teacher classified all these, including a picture of a house and a toy car, as a model, referring to each example's potential to represent specific aspects of reality. On the other hand, other teachers rejected almost all the examples, including a molecule of water. In the view of these teachers, explanatory potential appeared to be an important criterion for an example to qualify as a model.

2. The teachers emphasized different *functions* of models. Specifically, the explanatory function and the descriptive function of models were stressed. However, some important functions (e.g., using models to make predictions) were rarely mentioned. Three teachers discussed the exemplary function of models, which does not seem appropriate within the context of science. Teachers emphasizing the explanatory function would normally accept only a few of the given examples as models (see point 1), whereas teachers stressing the descriptive function seemed to accept most of the examples mentioned above as scientific models.

3. The teachers mentioned different *characteristics* of models. All the teachers mentioned the relation between model and target (first characteristic; see above). Three of the teachers only mentioned this aspect. Others, however, mentioned five to six of the seven characteristics listed earlier. The latter group was expected to have rejected most of the examples of models presented earlier, arguing that these examples would not comply with all the characteristics. No relation could be found, however, between the number of characteristics the teachers mentioned, and the number of examples (see point 1) they classified as models.

4. Differences between the teachers' epistemological orientation became apparent from their answers to questions about *modelling in science* (i.e., designing and revising models). Most of the teachers displayed a constructivist orientation, indicating, for instance, that different models can co-exist for the same target, dependent on the researchers' interest or theoretical point of view. A minority of the teachers, however, reasoned in termed of logical postivism. These teachers stated that a model should always be as close to reality as possible and that a model may become 'outdated' when new data are obtained. However, it was not possible to identify relations between the teachers' epistemological orientations and the other themes discussed above.

Likert-Type Scale Questionnaire

Mean values for individual items varied from 1.65 to 3.39, whereas standard deviations ranged between 0.32 and 1.01. The highest number of missing values was four for one item. All 32 items were thus entered in principal components analyses with varimax rotation. These analyses resulted in the extraction of three factors. Eleven items had high loadings (> 0.40) on Factor 1, eight items loaded similarly high on Factor 2 and another eight items on Factor 3. Five items remained that had low loadings (< 0.25) on all three factors. These items were not used during further analyses.

Cronbach alpha values of the three scales constructed in correspondence with the factor solution were 0.75 (Factor 1:11 items), 0.67 (Factor 2: 8 items), and 0.64 (Factor 3: 8 items). Given the numbers of items per scale, plus the fact that the questionnaire was administered for the first time, these Cronbach alpha values may be considered acceptable (Pedhazur & Pedhazur Schmelkin, 1991, pp. 109–110). On the basis of the analysis of item-total statistics, it was concluded that no items had to be removed from one of the three scales: not a single case of elimination of items resulted in the rise of the Cronbach alpha. Moreover, all the Pearson correlations of individual items with their respective scales were significant at the 0.001 level (2 tailed). The values of these correlations ranged between 0.42 and 0.69. Next, the respondents' scores on a scale were divided by the number of items per scale. For every scale, mean scores and standard deviations were then calculated.

The interpretation of the scales identified in the process described above revealed three distinctive aspects of models and modelling in science. The first scale grouped statements referring to the relations between models and targets in a positivist way. These statements scored relatively high (M = 2.99, SD = 0.40), indicating that, in general, the respondents would support the idea that a model is a simplified reproduction of reality, whose most important function is to enable causal explanations of phenomena. Moreover, a high score on this scale is indicative of the belief that the development of models is a straightforward, rational process.

The items with high loadings on the second scale referred to the physical appearance of models. These items had in common that they concerned the manner in which models are represented, through the use of drawings, pictures, analogies, or scale models. The mean score for this scale was 2.21 (SD = 0.35), suggesting that the respondents allotted a large variety of representational modes to scientific models. For example, 63% of the respondents believed that 'sometimes' even a photograph can be a model.

The third scale grouped items that referred to the use and the construction of models in a social context. Characteristic of these items was the recognition of the idea that models are the products of human thought, creativity and

TABLE 4.1 Scales within the Likert-type scale questionnaire on models and modelling, and sample items

Scales	Sample scale-items
Relating models and targets	'A model is a simplified reproduction of reality' 'A model corresponds with the target as much as possible' 'One attempts to keep a model as simple as possible' 'In the course of its development, the correspondence between a model and its target is increased'
Physical appearance of models	'A model has the shape of a drawing' 'Analogies are used in the development of models' 'The most important difference between a model and the target concerns the scale'
Social context of models	'The development of a model is guided by the questions of the researcher' 'A model depicts the ideas of scientists' 'Creativity is a major factor in the development of models'

communication. The statement with the highest loading on this factor (0.66), read 'A model depicts the ideas of scientists'. The mean score of this scale was 2.76 (SD = 0.38). In particular, statements referring to the role of creativity (M = 3.24), and questions posed by the researcher (M = 3.30) with respect to developing models received strong support. Table 4.1 presents the scales and sample items.

Pearson correlations between the three scales were calculated, which identified a significant correlation (0.33, significant at the 0.01 level: 2-tailed) only between the first and the third scale. This indicates a tendency among the respondents to combine the notion that a model is a simplified reproduction of reality with the idea that models are used and constructed in a social context.

The analyses of variance revealed that the teachers' scores on the three scales did not differ significantly with respect to years of teaching experience. With respect to the subject the teachers taught, however, a significant difference emerged. Specifically, the teachers of chemistry scored higher than the physics teachers on the first scale, relating models and targets in a positivist fashion (M = 3.15 and 2.80, respectively, $p < 0.05$; for biology teachers M was 2.96). The teachers' subject accounted for 12% of the observed variance in the respondents' scores on this scale. For a better understanding of this difference, multiple comparisons were performed at the item level, focusing on the 11 items of which this scale consisted.

The analysis showed that the chemistry teachers scored significantly higher ($p < 0.05$) than the physics teachers on two items:
1. The assessment of models focuses on truth, rather than usefulness;
2. Scientists use the most advanced models available.

Mean scores for chemistry teachers on these items were (1): 2.48 and (2): 2.85, whereas the physics teachers' mean scores were (1): 1.84 and (2): 2.37. These results indicate that the chemistry teachers were more strongly committed to logical positivism than the physics teachers, whereas the biology teachers held an intermediate position.

Out of the sample of 71 respondents, 59 appeared to have completed all 27 items comprising the three scales. These 59 respondents were entered in a hierarchical cluster analysis. On inspection of the squared Euclidean distance coefficients, a five-cluster solution was chosen. The increase in the value of this distance measure was relatively large from a five-cluster to a four-cluster solution (Norušis/ SPSS Inc. 1992). The respondents were distributed among these five clusters as follows: 37 were classified as cluster 1; 19 were grouped together in cluster 2; whereas the remaining three were assigned one each to clusters 3, 4 and 5. These latter clusters were not used in further analyses. The interpretation of clusters 1 and 2 is discussed below.

Clusters 1 and 2 were entered in a series of T-tests to explore whether they scored differently with respect to the three scales, and with respect to individual items. It appeared that cluster 2 ($n = 19$) scored significantly higher ($p < 0.001$) than cluster 1 ($n = 37$) on scales (1), relating models and targets, and (3), social context of models, and significantly lower ($p < 0.05$) on scale (2), physical appearance of models. These results are summarized in Table 4.2. For this table, the respondents' scores on a scale were divided by the number of items per scale. Then, mean scores (M) and standard deviations (SD) were calculated. T-tests at the item level revealed that cluster 2 scored significantly higher than cluster 1 on almost every individual item belonging to scales (1) and (3), the differences of the item means ranging between 0.25 and 0.84.

The statements with the largest differences of the means were:
1. The assessment of models focuses on truth, rather than usefulness (0.84); and
2. Creativity is a major factor in the development of models (0.71).

These results indicate that the teachers in cluster 2 seemed to hold a positivist view of models, on the one hand, while recognizing the idea that models are

TABLE 4.2 Scores of clusters 1 and 2 on the three scales: means (M), standard deviations (SD) and differences between the means (Diff. means)

Scales	Cluster	M	SD	Diff. means
Relating models and targets	1 (n = 37)	2.82	0.29	−0.53***
(11 items)	2 (n = 19)	3.35	0.26	
Physical appearance of models	1 (n = 37)	2.25	0.27	0.18*
(8 items)	2 (n = 19)	2.07	0.34	
Social context of models	1 (n = 37)	2.63	0.28	−0.51***
(8 items)	2 (n = 19)	3.14	0.24	

*The difference of the means is significant at the 0.05 level (T-test; 2-tailed). ***The difference of the means is significant at the 0.001 level (T-test; 2-tailed).

constructed in a social context, on the other hand. In the next section, this paradoxical finding is discussed in more depth. Moreover, compared with the teachers in cluster 1, their ideas about the ways models are represented are less specific.

Finally, analyses of crosstabs were performed to check whether the teachers were distributed evenly over the two clusters with respect to their subject, and teaching experience. These analyses showed that physics teachers were slightly over-represented in cluster 1 (13 observed, whereas 10 were expected), and that teachers of chemistry were over-represented in cluster 2 (9 observed; 6 expected). However, the results of chi-square tests revealed that these differences between observed and expected frequencies were not significant (> 0.1).

Conclusions

Understanding Science Teachers' Knowledge of Models

The results of the present study indicate that experienced science teachers, though they share the general notion that a model is a simplified representation of reality, may have quite different cognitions about models and modelling in science. For instance, the results of the open-item questionnaire revealed a large variation in the criteria the teachers used to determine whether or not specific examples qualified as scientific models. Moreover, from the same questionnaire it appeared that the teachers emphasized different functions and characteristics of models. Some functions and characteristics of models were rarely mentioned by these teachers (e.g., using models to make predictions, or perceiving a model as a tool for obtaining information about a target which is inaccessible for direct observation).

From the Likert-type scale questionnaire, three scales emerged for the characterization of the teachers' knowledge of models and modelling in science. With one exception, the scores on these scales did not differ significantly with respect to the teachers' subject or experience. The only exception concerned the scores of the chemistry teachers as compared with the physics teachers on the scale associated with the relation between models and targets. The results suggested that the chemistry teachers more strongly supported the positivist notions that the quality of a model is determined by the extent of positive correspondence with its target, and that the development of models is a straightforward, rational process. It is unclear whether this difference between teachers of chemistry and physics was associated with their prior education or with teaching experience in their respective subjects.

On the whole, the results of this study indicate that the knowledge of the majority of the teachers of models and modelling in science was not very pronounced. For instance, the mean scores of the teachers in cluster 1 (see above), who constituted two-thirds of the respondents to the Likert-type scale questionnaire, ranged between '2' and '3' on all scales. On the other hand, about one third of the teachers (associated with cluster 2) displayed significantly more distinct cognitions with respect to models and modelling, scoring either higher (> 3.0) or lower (< 2.1) on the three scales. The alternation between high and low scores suggests that this subgroup held particular ideas with respect to all scales. As stated previously, this difference in knowledge between the two subgroups appeared *not* to be related to the teachers' subject or experience.

Interestingly, the teachers in cluster 2 scored high on two scales, that is, scale (1), relating models and targets, and scale (3), social context of models. These scales appeared to be significantly correlated. A high score on scale (1) is considered to be indicative of a strong commitment to logical positivism, whereas a high score on scale (3) is in support of the notion that models are used and developed in a social context. The latter notion may be associated with a (social) constructivist epistemology. Thus, one may conclude that the knowledge of the teachers in cluster 2 is internally inconsistent. From a practical knowledge perspective, however, this result may be explained as follows. As practical knowledge is often 'tacit' or implicit, these teachers may have integrated different perspectives about models and modelling in science in their conceptual frameworks, or 'functional paradigms' (Lantz & Kass, 1987), thus resulting in inconsistencies of which they are not aware. Possibly, their high scores on scale (1) are related to their prior, disciplinary education, whereas the social constructivist notion has been added due to the influence of the recent educational literature. Anyway, we are not suggesting that a high score on either scale is indicative of an epistemological misconception. One could even argue that the teachers in cluster 2, more or less implicitly, combine 'the best' of two orientations.

Implications for the Design of Interventions

This study makes it clear that teachers' knowledge of models and modelling in science is often limited, and may include inconsistencies. To extend science teachers' knowledge in this domain, they could, of course, be provided with specific information and relevant literature. Specific activities may be designed, however, to deal more effectively with respect to developing the teachers' practical knowledge. For instance, teachers may be asked to discuss specific examples with each other, focusing on the reasons why they consider an example to be a model or not. Such discussions may facilitate the identification of common characteristics of scientific models. Moreover, teachers may be asked to analyse models in textbooks from various domains within science with respect to these models' functions and characteristics. In particular, the predictive function of models should be emphasized, as this function appeared to be underexposed in the teachers' cognitions. In the context of the innovation project focused on in the present study, the predictive function is particularly important when models of the biosphere are the focus of attention. In addition, teachers could focus on a specific target and analyse different models and their development throughout the history of science with respect to this target. Through this analysis, the role of creativity and other aspects of the social context of models may be illuminated.

Specific activities may be designed to anticipate teachers' epistemological orientations. For example, the co-existence of various models of the same target may be analysed to demonstrate that a model does not necessarily bear as much positive correspondence to a target as it possibly could. Many physical and chemical phenomena, for instance, can be adequately explained with a 'simple' stick-and-ball model to represent moecules, in preference to a more advanced model, incorporating quantum mechanics. Such examples may promote the teachers' understanding of the role of the questions or the purposes of the researchers in relation to the choice or the design of a model. Specifically, the limitations of a model, and the deliberate inclusion in a model of differences between this model and its target, should receive attention. In addition, discussing their analyses of these, and other, examples with each other may contribute to teachers becoming aware of possible inconsistencies in their knowledge of models and modelling in science.

Acknowledgement

The authors wish to thank Ben Smit and Douwe Beijaard of ICLON Graduate School of Education, Leiden University, for their assistance in designing the instruments and analysing the data.

Note

1 Originally published as Van Driel, J. H., & Verloop, N. (1999). Teachers' knowledge of models and modelling in science. *International Journal of Science Education, 21*(11), 1141–1153. Reprinted, with minor edits, with permission from the publisher.

References

Beijaard, D., & Verloop, N. (1996). Assessing teachers' practical knowledge. *Studies in Educational Evaluation, 22*, 275–286.

Black, M. (1962). *Models and metaphors. Studies in language and philosophy.* Cornell University Press.

De Vos, W. (1985). *Corpusculum delicti* [PhD dissertation]. University of Utrecht.

De Vos, W., & Reiding, J. (1999). Public Understanding of Science as a separate subject in secondary schools in the Netherlands. *International Journal of Science Education, 21*, 711–719.

De Vos, W., & Verdonk, A. H. (1987). A new road to reactions, Part 4: The substance and its molecules. *Journal of Chemical Education, 64*, 692–694.

Duffee, L., & Aikenhead, G. (1992). Curriculum change, student evaluation, and teacher practical knowledge. *Science Education, 76*, 493–506.

Gilbert, J. K. (Ed.). (1994). *Models and modelling in science education.* Association for Science Education.

Gilbert, J. K., Boulter, C., & Rutherford, M. (1998). Models in explanations, Part 1: Horses for courses? *International Journal of Science Education, 20*, 83–97.

Gilbert, S. W. (1991). Model building and a definition of science. *Journal of Research in Science Teaching, 28*, 73–79.

Grimmett, P. P., & Mackinnon, A. M. (1992). Craft knowledge and the education of teachers. In G. Grant (Ed.), *Review of research in education, 18* (pp. 385–456). American Educational Researcher Association.

Grosslight, L., Unger, C., Jay, E., & Smith, C. L. (1991). Understanding models and their use in science: Conceptions of middle and high school students and experts. *Journal of Research in Science Teaching, 28*, 799–822.

Harrison, A. G., & Treagust, D. F. (1996). Secondary students' mental models of atoms and molecules: Implications for teaching chemistry. *Science Education, 80*, 509–534.
Hesse, M. B. (1966). *Models and analogies in science.* Sheen & Ward.
Lantz, O., & Kass, H. (1987). Chemistry teachers' functional paradigms. *Science Education, 71*, 117–134.
Norušis, M. J./SPSS Inc. (1992). *SPSS/PC + Professional statistics, version 5.0.* SPSS Inc.
Pedhazur, E. J., & Pedhazur Schmelkin, L. (1991). *Measurement, design and analysis: An integrated approach.* Lawrence Erlbaum Associates.
Smith, J. A., Harris, R., & Van Langenhove, L. (Eds.). (1995). *Rethinking methods in psychology.* Sage.
Van Der Valk, T., Van Driel, J. H., & De Vos, W. (2007). Common characteristics of models in present-day scientific practice. *Research in Science Education, 37*, 469–488.
Van Driel, J. H. (1997). Het onderwijzen van modellen binnen ANW [Teaching of models within General Science]. *Tijdschrift voor Didactiek der β-wetenschappen, 14*(2), 177–196.
Van Driel, J. H. (2002). Students' corpuscular conceptions in the context of chemical equilibrium and chemical kinetics. *Chemistry Education Research and Practice in Europe, 3*(2), 201–213.
Van Driel, J. H., & De Vos, W. (1983). "Als het een geur heeft, dan moeten er toch moleculen zijn, die jij dus waarneemt met de neus" ["If it has a smell, then there must be molecules that you observe with your nose"]. *Tijdschrift voor Didactiek der Natuurwetenschappen, 1*(1), 3–13.
Van Driel, J. H., De Vos, W., & Verloop, N. (1999). Introducing dynamic equilibrium as an explanatory model. *Journal of Chemical Education, 76*(4), 559–561.
Van Driel, J. H., & Verloop, N. (2002). Experienced teachers' knowledge of teaching and learning of models and modelling in science education. *International Journal of Science Education, 24*(12), 1255–1272.
Van Hoeve-Brouwer, G. M. (1996). *Teaching structures in chemistry* [PhD dissertation]. CDβ-Press.
Van Oers, B. (1988). Modellen en de ontwikkeling van het natuurwetenschappelijk denken van leerlingen [Models and the development of scientific thinking among students]. *Tijdschrift voor Didactiek der β-wetenschappen, 6*, 115–143.
Verloop, N. (1992). Praktijkkennis van docenten: een blinde vlek van de onderwijskunde [Practical knowledge of teachers: A blind spot in educational research]. *Pedagogische Studien, 69*, 410–423.

CHAPTER 5

Development of Experienced Science Teachers' Pedagogical Content Knowledge of Models of the Solar System and the Universe

1   How the Study Came About

The introduction of *Algemene Natuurwetenschappen* (ANW) in 1998/99 was interesting for a number of reasons:
– Given a decline of Dutch students interested to pursue science in grades 10–12, in particular physics and chemistry, ANW was set up to provide all students with a basic understanding of some of the big ideas in science, demonstrate the importance of these ideas for students' lives and explain how they had been developed. ANW had a strong science-technology-society (STS) flavour and probably the label Public Understanding of Science covers the subject better than the literal translation General Science (De Vos & Reiding, 1999).
– The introduction of ANW was part of an ambitious innovation of (upper) secondary education in the Netherlands, mandated by the government, which aimed to promote self-regulated learning by students. The idea underlying this innovation was that if students aged 15–18 years take responsibility for their own learning, in terms of active construction of knowledge, this would increase their motivation and foster metacognitive skills, leading to better learning outcomes.
– Science teachers were presented with an opportunity to implement a new subject with specific learning objectives and a curriculum that contained unfamiliar content for most of them, while also required to contribute to the broader innovation, that is, promoting self-regulated student learning.

To prepare and support teachers, professional development programs were set up. Most of these were aimed at the goals of the overall innovation, for instance, on pedagogical approaches that would contribute to students taking responsibility for their learning, regardless of the subject or discipline they were studying. Also, the overall innovation inspired various research projects, for instance, focusing on the effects of specific interventions on the development of students' metacognitive skills.

As explained in the previous chapter, a national approach was taken to the qualification of teachers for ANW. The research I had done in that context, provided a snapshot of some of the knowledge and beliefs that experienced science teachers brought to ANW, specifically with respect to models and modelling, which is a prominent theme in the ANW syllabus. I was very interested to investigate how teachers, once they had obtained their ANW qualification, would implement ANW. First, how would their existing practical knowledge guide the initial implementation, and subsequently, how would their teaching experiences impact on their practical knowledge? Rather than exploring these questions broadly, I decided to keep a focus on the theme models and modelling and – with Nico Verloop – wrote an application for a PhD project entitled "The role of teachers' practical knowledge in the context of educational innovation" for a very competitive scheme funded by the Dutch Research Council. The application was successful and allowed us to hire a fulltime PhD candidate for a period of four years. Given the nature of the project, we were looking for someone who combined knowledge of educational theories and research methods with experience as a science teacher. Such people are rare, but once I had met Ineke Henze, it was clear that we had found the ideal candidate. Ineke was a chemistry teacher with more than 20 years experience and she had recently completed a Master's in Educational Science. It was agreed that Nico Verloop and I would supervise Ineke's project.

2   How the Study Was Conducted ...

The project started in 2001 and aimed to capture the practical knowledge of experienced science teachers who had begun to implement ANW very recently and monitor the development of these teachers' practical knowledge during the next two years. Given our interest in the theme models and modelling, it was decided to focus on one of the four content domains within ANW, that is Solar System and Universe. A particular textbook was selected which contained several strategies to teach the role and the nature of scientific models. For instance, it addressed historical models of the solar system and contained an assignment for students to develop a model to explain the earth's seasons and discuss their models in the classroom. Ineke wrote to 10 schools that used this textbook to invite teachers to her project and secured the participation of nine teachers from five schools. At the start of the study, these teachers had 8 to 26 years of experience teaching chemistry, physics or biology. All of them had started to teach ANW two or three years ago.

A number of instruments were developed to investigate different aspects of teachers' practical knowledge. Data collection included the following: (1) an initial semi-structured interview focusing on general pedagogical knowledge and PCK about models and modelling (specifically related to the topic Solar System and Universe); (2) a questionnaire focusing on subject matter knowledge about models and modelling in science (see previous chapter); (3) a Repertory Grid to capture teachers' personal knowledge about teaching models and modelling; and (4) story lines to elicit teachers' perceptions of their learning from teaching the topic Solar System and Universe and ANW more broadly. To trace changes in their practical knowledge, Ineke visited every teacher multiple times over a period of 2.5 years. She interviewed them three times on their PCK about models and modelling (1), when they had just finished teaching the topic Solar System and Universe. The questionnaire (2) and Repertory Grid (3) were administered on each of these occasions. The story lines (4) were conducted with 8 of the 9 teachers, about six months after the last PCK interview. Data collection was always done at a location chosen by the teacher, usually their classroom or an office space in their school.

3   ... And What Was Found

As per the norm in our institute, it was agreed that Ineke would do a PhD thesis by publications. Therefore, once data collection was concluded, Nico and I worked with her on the outlines of four articles to report the findings of the study. The first article (Henze, Van Driel, & Verloop, 2007a) focused on the teachers' practical knowledge at the start of the study, using data from the first interview (1) and questionnaire (2). Combining an analysis of the ideas the teachers expressed about teaching and learning in general, with those related to four elements of PCK (i.e., knowledge about (a) instructional strategies concerning a specific topic, (b) students' understanding of this topic, (c) ways to assess students' understanding of this topic, and (d) goals and objectives for teaching this topic in the curriculum) and their responses to the questionnaire about models and modelling in science, two types of practical knowledge were identified across the sample. Both types portrayed teachers' practical knowledge about teaching models and modelling to consist of a configuration of general pedagogical knowledge, subject matter knowledge and PCK. Interestingly, it was found that within each of these domains of teacher knowledge, a combination of different perspectives was apparent. For example, in Type A general pedagogical knowledge was a hybrid of behaviourist and cognitive perspectives on learning and teaching and in Type B subject matter knowledge combined a positivist epistemological view with the idea that models are constructed in a social and cultural context. In both Type A and Type B, PCK was found to be consistent with general pedagogical knowledge. We concluded the article by comparing both types of knowledge to the goals of ANW and wondered what would happen over time, for instance, would individual teachers' practical knowledge develop from Type A into B, or would other types of knowledge emerge?

In the second article (Henze, Van Driel, & Verloop, 2007b), teacher knowledge was considered through the construct of personal knowledge, drawing on George Kelly's personal construct psychology. Kelly developed the Repertory Grid method as a highly structured clinical interview procedure, which enables individuals to articulate and interrogate their system of personal constructs. The Repertory Grid is essentially a matrix consisting of a set of 'elements' and a set of bipolar 'constructs'. For the purpose of this study, the elements consisted of 12 teaching activities focusing on models and modelling, which were selected and amended from the ANW textbook. Teachers were asked to rate each of these activities against a set of 15 constructs, such as *'Teacher-centred'* versus *'Student-centred'*, or *'Suitable for 16-year-olds'* versus *'Suitable for older students'*. By looking for similarities and differences in the teachers' clustering of elements and constructs, three qualitatively different types of teachers' personal knowledge about teaching models and modelling were identified. Type 1, for instance, displayed a teacher-led perspective that combined the learning of model content with a critical reflection on the role and nature of models in science, whereas Type 3 reflected a teaching approach that favoured students' model production and revision to promote the learning of specific model content. Comparing the outcomes of the study with one of my baseline studies (i.e., Van Driel & Verloop, 2002), we found that, across the board, teaching activities such as modelling by students and reflection on the nature of models were much more common in the teaching practice of the participants in this study. This could be an indication of a successful implementation of ANW, however, the use of different instruments and samples obviously limit making comparisons between the two studies. We also noticed that working with the Repertory Grid enhanced teachers' reflections on their teaching practice and suggested using this instrument as a resource in professional development programs.

For the third article, which is included in this chapter, it was decided to focus on the development of the teachers' pedagogical content knowledge. Each teacher had been interviewed by Ineke three times, in 2002, 2003 and 2004, respectively, when they had just finished teaching of the chapter on Solar System and Universe in their ANW textbook. Interview questions covered the four elements of PCK mentioned above (first article) and addressed teachers' experiences in detail, for instance, 'In what activities, and in what sequence, did your students participate in the context of this chapter?' (Knowledge of instructional strategies) or 'On what, and how, did you assess your students in the context of this chapter?' (Knowledge about assessing students' understanding). Starting with the analysis of the interview data from the year 2002, two types of teachers' PCK of models of the Solar System and the Universe were identified. Type A of PCK appeared to be focused mainly on model content, while Type B of PCK was focused on model content, model production, and thinking about the nature of models. These two types formed the starting point for analysing the development of teachers' PCK in subsequent years. Comparing the data from the years 2002, 2003, and 2004 revealed that all teachers had extended their initial knowledge. In Type A, some of the elements of PCK (especially knowledge about instructional strategies) had become more sophisticated, but integration of PCK elements was limited. In contrast, the elements of PCK in Type B had developed in interaction with each other, for instance, the development of knowledge about students' understanding of models was reciprocally related to the teachers' knowledge about instructional strategies as well as to their knowledge of assessment of understanding models.

The final article focused on the learning process of the teachers. This article drew on the data that were obtained through the story line method. The choice of this method was inspired by experiences of our colleague Douwe Beijaard (Beijaard, Van Driel, & Verloop, 1999). In this method, teachers evaluate and classify their experiences and present this by drawing a story line and commenting on its shape (e.g., peaks or lows). The storyline method is selective in that it focuses on what is found relevant to teachers themselves. We found that, after a few years of teaching the ANW syllabus and the specific subject of solar system and universe, all teachers perceived themselves as competent in subject matter as well as in teaching methods. Comparing the data across the sample of teachers, two qualitatively different variations in learning processes were identified. Type II teachers learned collaboratively and preferred teaching methods in which collaboration and discussion between students are prominent. In contrast, Type I teachers learned mainly individually and favoured teaching methods that aim to make difficult and abstract issues concrete for students. Given the focus on *how* teachers learned rather than *what* they learned, we decided to submit the article to the *Journal of Teacher Education*. It was accepted and published in 2009 (Henze, Van Driel, & Verloop, 2009).

4   Reflection and Follow Up

To me, this project stands out in several ways. It was the most comprehensive effort that I have been involved in to capture the practical knowledge of teachers by combining a variety of theoretical and methodological perspectives, and to follow the development of practical knowledge over a considerable period of time (2.5 years). Also, it was the first PhD study that I (co-)supervised that resulted in four articles in high quality international journals (*International Journal of Science Education, Research in Science Education* and *Journal of Teacher Education*). Obviously, Ineke Henze deserves the credits for these achievements, and it was a pleasure to work closely with her and Nico Verloop on this project. After her graduation, Ineke and I would continue to collaborate resulting in a number of joint publications and conference presentations and eventually we would co-supervise a PhD candidate.

As for the four articles summarised above, three of them have accumulated around 100 citations in Google Scholar, while the article on PCK development that is included in this chapter stands out with more than 280 citations. This article appeared in a Special Issue of the *International Journal of Science Education*, entitled 'Developments and challenges in researching science teachers' Pedagogical Content Knowledge: An international perspective' (2008, volume 30, issue 10). Together with Australian colleagues Amanda Berry and John Loughran, I was co-editor of this special issue which came out of symposia on PCK research at the ESERA conference in 2005 (Barcelona) and the NARST annual meeting in 2006 (San Fransisco). These symposia brought together scholars from a range of countries, including the USA, Mexico, South Africa, Australia, Sweden and the Netherlands, and attracted large audiences. Amanda, John and I proposed the idea of a special issue based on these symposia to John Gilbert, editor-in-chief of the *International Journal of Science Education*, who gave us the green light. Working together with Amanda and John, reviewing and editing the papers that were submitted to be considered, proved to be a very enjoyable and rewarding professional experience and inspired future collaborations.

The fact that this article was included in a special issue on PCK will have helped to attract attention to it. Also, and maybe more importantly, where most studies on PCK are limited to a description or measurement of PCK at a certain moment in time, this is one of few articles to date that portrayed the development of PCK over time. Of course, the study had a number of limitations: the sample consisted of only nine teachers and all the data were drawn from interviews. I think these limitations were compensated by the richness and depth of the interview data. Through visiting the teachers multiple times and showing a genuine interest in their ideas and their practice, Ineke had established strong relationships with the teachers. With her long experience as a chemistry teacher, she understood teachers' work thoroughly and spoke the same language. As a result, the conversations became more personal over time and teachers were better able and probably felt more confident to explicate their professional practical knowledge.

Considering the different typologies of knowledge and professional learning that were reported in these papers, we were keen to explore how these applied to the teachers in the study. We were invited to contribute a chapter to a book (edited by Khine and Saleh) in the series *Models and Modeling in Science Education* and used that opportunity to combine the outcomes of the Rep Grid study with the study on PCK development and found that all four teachers who were most representative of Type B in the latter study displayed personal knowledge Type 3 in the former. Compared to these four, the other five teachers, representative of personal knowledge Types 1 or 2 and PCK Type A, were found to have less extended practical knowledge about models and modelling and were less successful in realising the aims of ANW. One possible explanation for the difference between the two groups was that the latter group had taught ANW only to grade 10 students, whereas the others also taught ANW to grades 11 and 12 and had implemented more student-led modelling activities with these older students. In addition, the differences appeared to be related to teachers' initial pedagogical perspectives, epistemological views, and subject matter knowledge (Henze & Van Driel, 2011).

As implications for professional development broadly, we suggested to take differences between teachers, in terms of existing practical knowledge and preferred learning activities as a starting point rather than adopting a one-size-fits-all approach. To extend teachers' practical knowledge, we recommended to engage them in collaborative learning activities to make them experience that professional learning is not only individual but also social in nature. A collaborative approach would assist teachers in explicating and sharing their practical knowledge with colleagues which, we argued, could be the main driver of effective professional learning of science teachers. In later years, another PhD candidate, Monika Louws, would follow up on these ideas by considering teachers as agents of their own professional development and investigating what it is that teachers want to learn, and why and how they want to learn this (see e.g., Louws et al., 2017).

Development of Experienced Science Teachers' Pedagogical Content Knowledge of Models of the Solar System and the Universe[1]

Ineke Henze, Jan H. van Driel and Nico Verloop

Abstract

This paper investigates the developing pedagogical content knowledge (PCK) of nine experienced science teachers in their first few years of teaching a new science syllabus in the Dutch secondary education system. We aimed to identify the content and structure of the PCK for a specific topic in the new syllabus, 'Models of the Solar System and the Universe', describing the PCK development in terms of relations between four different aspects: knowledge about instructional strategies; knowledge about students' understanding; knowledge about assessment of students; and knowledge about goals and objectives of the topic in the curriculum. Semi-structured interviews were conducted in three subsequent academic years. From the analysis of the data, two qualitatively different types of PCK emerged. Type A can be described as oriented towards model content, while Type B can be typified as oriented towards model content, model production, and thinking about the nature of models. The results also indicate that these two types of PCK developed in qualitatively different ways.

Introduction

Pedagogical content knowledge (PCK) has held an important position since it was introduced to describe the 'missing paradigm' in research on teaching several decades ago (Shulman, 1986, 1987). Various scholars (e.g., Cochran, deRuyter, & King, 1993; Grossmann, 1990; Marks, 1990) elaborated on Shulman's work and described PCK in different ways; that is, incorporating different attributes or characteristics (van Driel, Verloop, & De Vos, 1998, p. 676). In the present study, we defined PCK as teacher knowledge about (a) instructional strategies concerning a specific topic; (b) students' understanding of this topic; (c) ways to assess students' understanding of this topic; and (d) goals and objectives for teaching the specific topic in the curriculum. In this, we largely agree with the categorisations of Grossman (1990) and Magnusson, Krajcik, and Borko (1999, p. 99). Compared with Shulman's original construct (Shulman, 1986), these authors adopted a somewhat broader definition of PCK. Acknowledging that the various components of teachers' PCK may interact in very complex ways, Magnusson et al. claimed, "Effective teachers need to develop knowledge with respect to all of the aspects of pedagogical content knowledge, and with respect to all of the topics they teach" (1999, p. 115).

While PCK has been a subject of research since the 1980s, and much has been written about its importance as a foundational knowledge base for teaching, little is known about the process of PCK development, especially in experienced teachers and in the context of educational innovation. Up to now, few empirical investigations have been conducted into how different aspects of this knowledge are connected and may influence each other's growth.

The innovation in this study concerned the introduction of Public Understanding of Science (PUSC) as a new science subject in secondary education in the Netherlands. Among its other objectives, the new syllabus is intended to make students aware of the ways in which scientific knowledge is produced and developed. Students should gain a clear understanding of a scientist's activities; for example, designing and using models, developing theories, and carrying out experiments (De Vos & Reiding, 1999). In this respect, the introduction of PUSC is close to the vision on science education reform in many other countries, such as Canada (Aikenhead & Ryan, 1992), the USA (American Association for the Advancement of Science, 1994), and the UK (Northern Examinations and Assessment Board, 1998), which requires students to become knowledgeable in varied aspects of scientific inquiry and the nature of science. Moreover, the introduction of the new science syllabus overlaps with a move towards a social constructivist view on knowing and learning in Dutch secondary education (cf. Greeno, Collins, & Resnick, 1996), as a result of which science teachers have their students learn the subject matter through classroom activities that support the active construction of knowledge and understanding in social interaction with other students, instead of providing all the answers themselves (cf. Van der Valk & Gravemeyer, 2000).

Aim of the Study

The aim of this study was to investigate the developing PCK of a small number of experienced science teachers in their first few years of teaching the new syllabus on PUSC. We followed these teachers for a period of 3 years in their natural settings to see if, and how, their initial PCK developed. We aimed to identify the content and structure of their PCK of a specific topic in the PUSC syllabus – namely, 'Models of the Solar System and the Universe' – describing its development in terms of relations between its different components (Magnusson et al., 1999). We did not intend to describe in detail the PCK development of each individual participant, but to identify possible common patterns across the knowledge development of different teachers (Verloop, van Driel, & Meijer, 2001).

The following research question was central to the study:
— How can science teachers' PCK of the specific topic of 'Models of the Solar System and the Universe' in the PUSC syllabus be typified at a time when they still have little experience of teaching PUSC, and how does this PCK develop when teachers become more experienced in teaching this particular topic?

Context of the Study

In 1999, a new syllabus on PUSC (in Dutch: ANW) was introduced, for all students aged 15–17 years in upper secondary education in the Netherlands. The programme (curriculum) of this new syllabus is divided into six domains, Domain A to Domain F (SLO, 1996).

General skills (Domain A), such as language skills, computer skills, and research skills, should be developed in combination with the learning of specific subject matter that is introduced in relevant context issues of Life, Biosphere, Matter, and Solar System and Universe (i.e., Domains C-F).

The development of students' capacity to reflect critically on scientific knowledge and procedures (Domain B) requires them to become able, among other things, to explain how scientists obtain a specific kind of knowledge that (by its very nature) is always limited and context bound, and how observation, theory formation, and technology are influenced by each other as well as by cultural, economic, and political factors. students' reflection on scientific knowledge and procedures should be linked to specific science topics; for example, 'Health care' (Domain C: Life), 'The earth climate' (Domain D: Biosphere), 'Radiation risks' (Domain E: Matter), and 'Understanding the universe' (Domain F: Solar System and Universe).

Models and Modelling in PUSC

Aiming to improve the comprehensive nature of students' understanding of the main processes and products of science, Hodson (1992) proposed three purposes for science education: to learn science – that is, to understand the ideas produced by science (concepts, models, and theories); to learn about science – that is, to understand important issues in the philosophy, history, and methodology of science; and to learn how to do science – that is, to be able to take part in those activities that lead to the acquisition of scientific knowledge.

TABLE 5.1   PUSC as a framework to improve students' understanding of science

	PUSC domains		
	A	C–F	B
Hodson (1992)	Learn how to do science	Learn science	Learn about science
Justi and Gilbert (2002)	Learn to produce and revise models	Learn the major models	Learn the nature of models

In general, all natural sciences can be thought of as an attempt to model nature in order to understand and explain phenomena. Models and modelling are, as a consequence, applied and used extensively by natural scientists. Therefore, the key to Hodson's purposes (i.e., improving students' comprehensive understanding of science) is a central role for models and modelling in science education (cf. Justi & Gilbert, 2002).

In this light, the subject PUSC may offer an appropriate framework (see Table 5.1). To help students gain a rich understanding of the main products and processes of science, the learning of scientific models (Domains C-F) and the act of modelling – that is, the production and revision of models (Domain A) – should go hand in hand with critical reflection on the role and nature of models in science (Domain B).

The above implies, for example, that in the PUSC domain entitled 'Solar System and Universe' (Domain F), students could be asked to compare and discuss several models for the solar system from the history of science (Domain B). In addition, students could be challenged to design models (Domain A) for the earth's seasons, or the phases of the moon. Reflecting on such an assignment, students could be encouraged to discuss the functions and characteristics of models in general (Domain B).

From a constructivist view on knowing and learning, models can be used as cognitive tools to promote students to think deeply, instead of the teacher supplying all the answers. In addition, students' modelling activities may offer valuable opportunities for teachers to monitor students' progress in changing their initial mental models to an understanding of particular models (i.e., 'consensus models'; Gilbert & Boulter, 2000), which are generally accepted in physics, chemistry, or (biotechnology (Duit & Glynn, 1996) and astronomy (cf. Lemmer, Lemmer, & Smit, 2003). Moreover, by encouraging students to reflect on their personal learning process, they may be able to draw meaningful parallels between the development of their personal understandings and the growth of scientific knowledge (Hodson, 1992).

Traditionally, science teachers have devoted little explicit attention to the nature of scientific models; that is, their hypothetical character and the ways in which they gradually develop (Vollebregt, Klaassen, Genseberger, & Lijnse, 1999). Science textbooks for secondary education contain many examples of scientific models, usually presenting these models as static facts or as final versions of our knowledge of matter (Erduran, 2001). Although various teaching strategies have been described in the literature, designed specifically to promote students' understanding of 'consensus models', current textbooks rarely include assignments inviting students actively to construct, test, or revise their own models as part of the learning process (cf. Barab, Hay, Barnett, & Keating, 2000).

De Jong, van Driel, and Verloop (2005) explored pre-service science teachers' PCK of models and modelling. The research findings indicated, among other things, that a majority of the teachers intended to pay attention to models as constructs, invented by scientists, but in their teaching practice appeared to have discussed models as objects or facts that are given. A similar discrepancy has also been found among experienced teachers (Koulaidis & Ogborn, 1989), De Jong et al. (2005) suggested that pre-service and experienced teachers generally lack sufficient knowledge of strategies for teaching models as constructs.

Owing to the emphasis the new syllabus places on new content and new teaching strategies concerning the role and nature of scientific models, teachers' PCK of models and modelling in science may be subject to change. We followed nine experienced teachers over a period of 3 years to investigate their developing PCK in the context of teaching a chapter on PUSC Domain F. The teachers were questioned about the four afore-mentioned knowledge elements of PCK. The topic focused on was 'Models of the Solar System and the Universe', which is one of the more unusual and difficult topics in the entire syllabus.

Method and Research Design

This section starts with a description of the participants in the study and how they were selected. We then turn to the description of the research instrument used in this study to investigate the teachers' PCK, and an explanation of the research procedure.

Participants in the Study

The study was conducted among nine PUSC teachers working at five different schools. They were users of the teaching method 'ANtWoord' (in English: 'Answer'). We selected this method to be used by the participants in our study because its workbook contained many strategies emphasising the role and nature of scientific models. This book has, for instance, a chapter on 'Solar System and Universe' (Domain F), in which students have to develop models to describe and explain the earth's seasons, and discuss them in the classroom afterwards. Students also learn different models of the solar system, such as Ptolemy's geocentric model and Copernicus' heliocentric model, and debate their strengths and weaknesses (cf. Albanese, Danhoni Neves, & Vicentini, 1997).

The nine teachers responded to a written invitation we sent to 10 different schools using the ANtWoord method. After meetings we organised at their schools (to explain the purposes and conditions of the study), they all agreed to join in. The teachers varied with regard to their backgrounds, years of teaching experience, and original teaching disciplines. Among the participants were three teachers of physics, three teachers of chemistry, and three teachers whose original discipline was biology. Their teaching experiences ranged from 8 to 26 years at the start of the study. To become qualified to teach the new science subject, the teachers had taken part in a 1-year course, which was conducted nationwide. The participants happened to be all male, which can be seen as a limitation of the study. They were all among the first PUSc teachers at their schools.

Data Collection

The data collection consisted of a semi-structured interview to investigate the teachers' PCK of 'Models of the Solar System and the Universe'. The interview was conducted among the teachers by the first author of this article, in three subsequent academic years.

Semi-structured interview. With all teachers, a semi-structured interview was held in February 2002, 2003, and 2004. The interview questions were developed on the basis of the results of a study of the relevant literature on PCK, on the one hand, and models and modelling in science and astronomy education, on the other hand. The initial interview schedule was tested on four PUSc teachers (not among the nine participants in the study). As a result of this pilot study, some interview questions were rephrased or replaced in the schedule, and some new questions were added to the scheme.

The final interview included questions, which aimed at eliciting the teachers' PCK of models and modelling in PUSc. In the context of teaching Chapter 3 of the ANtWoord workbook, entitled 'Solar System and Universe', the teachers were questioned about the four knowledge elements of PCK mentioned in the Introduction (see Table 5.2).

All interviews took place privately in a place chosen by the teacher (e.g., the teacher's classroom, or a small office), each year shortly after he had finished the lessons about the chapter on the solar system and universe. An

TABLE 5.2 General phrasings of the interview questions

PCK elements	Questions about teaching 'Models of the solar system and the universe'
(a) Knowledge about instructional strategies	1. In what activities, and in what sequence, did your students participate in the context of this chapter? Please explain your answer 2. What was (were) your role(s) as a teacher, in the context of this chapter? Explain your answer
(b) Knowledge about students' understanding	3. Did your students need any specific previous knowledge in the context of this chapter? Explain your answer 4. What was successful for your students? Explain your answer 5. What difficulties did you see? Explain your answer
(c) Knowledge about ways to assess students' understanding	6. On what, and how, did you assess your students in the context of this chapter? Explain your answer 7. Did your students reach the learning goals with regard to this chapter? How do you know? Explain your answer
(d) Knowledge about goals and objectives of the topic in the curriculum	8. What was (were) your main objective(s) in teaching the topic of 'Models of the Solar System and the Universe'? Explain your answer

audiocassette recorder was used to tape the conversation. The interviews took 30 min to 1 hr. Afterwards, all interviews were transcribed verbatim.

Analysis

The analysis of the data started with the interviews conducted in 2002. Codes were developed for the four elements of PCK and tested on the interview data of two teachers, to see whether all the variations in the statements could be covered. As a result of this test, some codes had to be reformulated. The final codebook (Henze, Van Driel, & Verloop, 2007a) was the result of different steps of testing and adapting the codes, until the first and second author reached consensus on all codes to be used.

Knowledge about Instructional Strategies and about students' Understanding

The authors concluded that similar codes could be employed for knowledge about instructional strategies concerning 'Models of the Solar System and the Universe' and knowledge about students' understanding of this topic (PCK elements a and b). These knowledge elements were typified by three codes: (i) a code representing the content of models (teachers have knowledge about the teaching of specific concepts in relation to certain models, and have knowledge about students' understanding of these concepts); (ii) a code standing for the thinking about the nature of models (teachers know how to make students reflect on the nature of models, and have knowledge about their students' understanding of the nature of models); and (iii) a code related to the production of models; that is, teachers know how to stimulate students' model production (i.e., students thinking up, and construction of physical models) and testing, and have specific knowledge about students' modelling skills (e.g., students' creativity and coming up with new possibilities, which is an important step in the modelling process). These three codes can be linked, roughly, to the PUSC Domains C-F (i), Domain B (ii), and Domain A (iii), respectively.

Knowledge about Ways to Assess students' Understanding

After reading and discussing the teachers' responses to the interview questions about ways of assessment in the context of teaching 'Models of the Solar System and the Universe', it was found that the teachers' knowledge about ways to assess students' understanding (PCK element c) of this topic could be typified using the following codes referring to various ways of assessment: written test on model content; oral and poster presentation, or account, as products of self-directed work; paper or essay on the students' reflection upon the nature of models; students' modelling activities; classroom debate on the heliocentric and geocentric models; portfolio on the preparation of the debate on models; and observation of group work.

Knowledge about Goals and Objectives of the Topic in the Curriculum

Regarding the knowledge about goals and objectives for teaching the topic in the curriculum (PCK element d), it was decided, following repeated reading and discussion of the teachers' responses, to typify their answers using two different kinds of codes. First, generally speaking, the teachers expressed their epistemological perspectives. In analysing these perspectives, Nott and Wellington's (1993) classification of epistemological views was applied, on the basis of which three codes were developed: (i) positivist, in which models are seen as simplified copies of reality (e.g., Teacher 1: 'Students have to understand that models are reductions of reality and not the truth'); (ii) relativist, in which models are seen as one way to view reality (e.g., Teacher 3: 'It should not be taken for granted that a phenomenon can be modelled in one way: you can look to things from different perspectives'); and, (iii) instrumentalist, in which the question is whether models 'work', instead of 'being true' (e.g., Teacher 5: 'I want my students to understand that a model does not have to be real and true to be useful'). Second, teachers' statements about the purposes of using models in the classroom were coded in terms of the various functions of models in science (Giere, 1991): (i) to visualise and describe phenomena; (ii) to explain phenomena; (iii) to obtain information about phenomena that cannot be observed directly; (iv) to derive hypotheses that may be tested; and (v) to make predictions about reality.

After coding the teachers' interview responses, we put together, per PCK element, the coded statements. With this, the variety of statements within each PCK element became clear (see Table 5.3, columns). We examined carefully the various sets of statements and identified for each teacher the combinations of codes that arose across the different elements (see Table 5.3, rows). Next, we compared these combinations across the nine teachers, and two patterns (i.e., specific combinations of codes, which recurred – more or less – strictly) emerged. From these two patterns, which indicate/represent different contents of the PCK elements, we constructed two types of PCK with regard to 'Models of the Solar System and the Universe': Type A and Type B (see Results section, Table 5.4). To see how these types of PCK developed over the years 2003 and 2004, the interview fragments involved were read, thoroughly, and we used the same codebook that was developed to code the interview data from the year 2002. Finally, we examined the combinations of codes applied, per teacher, over the years. By focusing on the relationships between the different PCK elements, the results (discussed in the next section) indicate that Type A and Type B of PCK developed in qualitatively different ways.

In the Results section, we first describe the two types of PCK in the year 2002. Next, we describe the PCK development of two teachers, each of whose knowledge was more or less representative of one of the PCK types. Finally, we present our general conclusions with regard to the PCK development of the teachers in the study.

Results

As a result of the analysis of the interview data from the year 2002, we identified two types of teachers' PCK of 'Models of the Solar System and the Universe'

EXPERIENCED SCIENCE TEACHERS' PEDAGOGICAL CONTENT KNOWLEDGE 141

TABLE 5.3 Codes applied to the teachers' interview responses (2002)

Teacher, original discipline (years of teaching experience a)	Knowledge about instruction	Knowledge about students' understanding	Knowledge about assessment	Knowledge about goals and objectives
Teacher 1, biology (15 years)	Model content	Model content	Examinations on model content; Oral presentations; Reports on group work; Essay	Positivist/Instrument view; Models used to explain phenomena
Teacher 2, chemistry (8 years)	Model content	Model content	Examinations on model content; Oral presentations; Poster presentations	Positivist/Instrument view; Models used to explain phenomena
Teacher 3, biology (25 years)	Model content; Model production; Thinking about the nature of models	Model content; Model production; Thinking about the nature of models	Examinations on model content; Observation of modelling and debating activities; Portfolio	Relativist/Instrument view; Models used to explain phenomena, obtain information, test hypotheses
Teacher 4, physics (11 years)	Model content	Model content	Examinations on model content; Oral presentations; Poster presentations	Positivist/Instrument view; Models used to explain phenomena
Teacher 5, chemistry (9 years)	Model content; Model production; Thinking about the nature of models	Model content; Model production; Thinking about the nature of models	Examinations on model content; Observation of group work, modelling and debating activities;	Relativist/Instrument view; Models used to explain phenomena, obtain information, test hypotheses

(*cont.*)

TABLE 5.3   Codes applied to the teachers' interview responses (2002) (cont.)

Teacher, original discipline (years of teaching experience[a])	Knowledge about instruction	Knowledge about students' understanding	Knowledge about assessment	Knowledge about goals and objectives
Teacher 6, biology (11 years)	Model content; Model production; Thinking about the nature of models	Model content; Model production; Thinking about the nature of models	Examinations on model content; Observation of group work, modelling and debating activities	Relativist/Instrument view; Models used to explain phenomena, obtain information, test hypotheses
Teacher 7, chemistry (22 years)	Model content	Model content	Examinations on model content; Reports on group	Positivist/Instrument view; Models used to explain phenomena
Teacher 8, physics (23 years)	Model content; Thinking about the nature of models	Model content	Examinations on model content; oral presentations; Reports on group work	Positivist/Relativist/Instrument view; Models used to explain phenomena
Teacher 9, physics (26 years)	Model content; Model production	Model content; Model production	Examinations on model content; Observation of group work, modelling and debating activities; Reports on group work	Positivist/Relativist/Instrument view; Models used to explain phenomena, test hypotheses

a   In the original discipline.

TABLE 5.4 PCK Types A and B (2002)

PCK element	Type A of PCK	Type B of PCK
Knowledge about instructional strategies	Knowledge about specific multi-media (film, video) and concrete materials to support students' understanding of *model content*, and knowledge of ways to connect models with reality.	Knowledge of motivating and challenging assignments to promote students' learning of *model content*. Knowledge about effective ways/methods to promote students' *thinking about the nature of models* (e.g., debating, *modelling activities*, computer simulation); Knowledge about ways to stimulate students' creativity.
Knowledge about students' understanding	Knowledge about students' difficulties with the *content of specific models*, and inability to connect models with reality.	Knowledge of students' motivation to discover things (*model content*) themselves; Knowledge of students' motivation and abilities to participate in modelling and related thinking activities (*modelling skills*); Knowledge of student's affinity with specific models (*understanding of the nature of models*).
Knowledge about ways to assess students' understanding	Knowledge about examinations of *model content* and application using written examinations, oral presentations, posters, and reports.	Knowledge of how to evaluate model content, model production, and *thinking about the nature of models* using examinations, oral presentations, reports, portfolios, and group observations.
Knowledge about goals and objectives in the curriculum	Epistemological views that can be understood as positivist and instrumentalist; Knowledge about the use of models to visualise and explain phenomena.	Epistemological views: Instrumentalist and Relativist; Knowledge about the use of models to visualise and explain phenomena, to formulate and test hypotheses, and to obtain information about phenomena.

(see Table 5.4). These two types were considered different starting points for the development of teachers' PCK in subsequent years. Type A of PCK appeared to be focused mainly on model content, while Type B of PCK was focused on model content, model production, and thinking about the nature of models (cf. Henze et al., 2007a). We compared the answers and reactions of the nine teachers with the characteristics of Type A and Type B, and as a result we considered the PCK of five teachers (i.e., Teacher 1, Teacher 2, Teacher 4, Teacher 7, and Teacher 8), to be more or less indicative of Type A, while the PCK of the other four teachers (i.e., Teacher 3, Teacher 5, Teacher 6, and Teacher 9) was classified as representative of Type B.

Type A: Focused on Model Content

In Type A PCK, knowledge about instructional strategies includes knowledge that is aimed at the transmission of the content of certain models (of the solar system), and knowledge about effective methods and materials to support students' understanding of the content of these models and to help students connect the models with reality. Knowledge about students' understanding (e.g., knowledge about students' abilities to think three-dimensionally, or to connect models with reality) is not very specific. Knowledge about ways to assess students' understanding includes knowledge of examinations, (oral) presentations, and reports, to assess both students' content knowledge of models and their use of models as 'tools'. Knowledge about goals and objectives in the curriculum with regard to models and modelling reflects a combination of positivist and instrumentalist views. In general, models are seen as reductions of reality, aimed at visualising and explaining different phenomena (cf. van Driel & Verloop, 1999).

Type B: Focused on Model Content, Model Production, and Model Thinking

In Type B PCK, knowledge about instructional strategies includes knowledge about motivating and challenging tasks that are aimed at supporting students' understanding of model content and model production or comparison (e.g., debating), and about effective ways to promote students' thinking about the nature of models and creativity in model production. Knowledge about students' understanding includes knowledge about students' motivation, specific difficulties and inabilities concerning the content of scientific models and modelling activities, and knowledge about students' understanding of the nature of specific models and their affinity with these models. Knowledge about ways to assess students' understanding includes knowledge of examinations, students' presentations, reports, modelling and debating activities, and portfolios to assess students' knowledge about the content of models, the production of models, and thinking about the nature of models. In the knowledge about goals and objectives for teaching models and modelling in the curriculum, not only the visualisation and explanation of phenomena are emphasised, but also how to formulate and test hypotheses, and how to obtain information about phenomena. Models are conceived of as instruments but also as ways to view reality (i.e., a relativist epistemological view; cf. van Driel & Verloop, 1999).

Development of PCK

Comparison of the data from the years 2002, 2003, and 2004 revealed the following with respect to the development of the teachers' PCK. Firstly, the results of the study indicated that, in developing their PCK, all teachers extended their initial knowledge, over time. In addition, the ways in which the two types of PCK developed over the years appeared to be qualitatively different in terms of relations between the four components. To illustrate our findings, we describe the PCK development of two teachers in the following sections. The description of their development is based on their reactions to the interview questions about the learning and teaching of models and modelling with regard to the solar system and the universe, in the context of the ANtWoord workbook Chapter 3 on 'Solar System and Universe'. Even though the results of the teachers representing one of both Types A and B are quite similar (in general), the PCK development of each of these two teachers was considered the most pronounced example of the two types of PCK. We have called one teacher 'William' (representing PCK Type A, in 2002; Teacher 8, see Table 5.3) and the other teacher 'Andrew' (representing PCK Type B, in 2002; Teacher 5, see Table 5.3).

PCK Development of William (Type A)
Knowledge about instructional strategies. In 2002 and 2003, William's instruction in models of the solar system started with the observation of phenomena (positions of moon, sun, stars) by his students (Grade 10, upper secondary education). From this, he explained Copernicus' heliocentric model of the solar system using a PowerPoint presentation and a variety of concrete examples and visual tools, applied in front of the class. Next, the students set to work, carrying out different tasks; for example, building the model (constructing it using foam balls, or creating it from cardboard), and manipulating wooden sticks and balls and a lamp. These activities were aimed at connecting students' observations of phenomena with the heliocentric model. Students did

not design their own models (based on their observations). According to William, a classroom debate on the geocentric and heliocentric models of the solar system was of no use: his students lacked the knowledge, the understanding, and the level of abstract reasoning required. In 2002 and 2003, William also paid attention to other models of the solar system (ideas of Pythagoras, Aristotle, and Ptolemy), and to the key roles played by Tycho Brahe, Johannes Kepler, and Galileo Galilei in getting the heliocentric model accepted in preference to the geocentric model by astronomers.

In 2004, his lessons on the solar system were confined to the teaching of the heliocentric model. The teaching of other (historic) models appeared to be too timeconsuming for him, and too difficult for his students: 'I hardly understand the geocentric models myself, so, what about the students' understanding?' Due to a lack of time, he had stopped reflecting on the ideas of an expanding universe that began in a 'big bang'. He still emphasised students' observations of natural phenomena (stars, planets, eclipses of sun and moon). Observations (and, in addition, computer simulations) of the phases of Venus appeared to be very helpful in finding arguments in favour of the heliocentric model.

Over the years, William put much time into developing various materials, tools, and instruction methods to explain the content of the heliocentric model to his students.

Knowledge about students' understanding. In 2002, William showed little specific knowledge of his students' understanding of the different models of the solar system. He said, 'All they need to learn from the models is some basic knowledge of geometry' and 'Some students' general inability for three-dimensional thinking hinders their gaining in-depth understanding'. Over the years, he mainly based his knowledge about students' understanding of, and difficulties with, specific concepts on the results of written examinations.

> Some pupils really didn't get what I meant when I asked questions like 'Why are the observations about the phases of Venus along with its relative size the main arguments in favour of the heliocentric model?' This made me feel dissatisfied with my teaching and with the teaching materials I've been using. (William)

To address this problem, William introduced the computer simulation programme 'Red-shift' to have students 'observe (by manipulation of time) the phases of Venus, showing that Venus is sometimes on the opposite side of the sun, just as the heliocentric model predicts and in contrast to the geocentric model'. In addition, William understood that some students had difficulties with the scientific contingency of models; that is, their hypothetical character, and the ways in which they gradually develop. He said that these students complained "Why should we learn something that will change, anyway?"

Knowledge about ways to assess students' understanding. In 2002, William evaluated every task (observations of phenomena, practical work) of his students in order to get them working and keep them working. To save time, he gradually diminished the number of students' oral and poster presentations in the lessons, and reports on practical work to be evaluated. His assessment of students' work was confined to a written report of a group study on a specific topic, and a written examination, which consisted of questions on knowledge of facts (model content) and on application of this knowledge (e.g., the interpretation of newspaper reports). The topics and questions in his examinations did not change very much throughout the years. From his interpretations of the results of the exams, William realised that, 'to better understand the heliocentric model, the students need more concrete experiences'. For this reason, he started to use a number of planetaries, a solar scope, and a computer simulation programme (cf. Bakas & Mikropoulos, 2003) in his lessons.

Knowledge about goals and objectives in the curriculum. From 2002 to 2004, William insisted that his students understood that knowledge of the structure and the size of the universe was not based on solid data drawn from experiments: 'It is only if you start from certain assumptions that the models will work' (i.e., relativist and instrumentalist epistemological views). In 2002, William held the view that students had to know that models of the solar system were not the same as reality: 'It is always a simplified reduction', which is aimed at describing and explaining certain phenomena (i.e., positivist epistemological view).

In the course of time, William became aware of his understanding that, in the case of the heliocentric model of the solar system, the model is simply a smaller copy of reality:

> I think that we know rather precisely how planets rotate around the sun, for example. Actually, I don't believe that reality is any different from the model. Speaking of atoms, neutrons, and electrons, however, I do understand that reality is much more complex than the model. I really think that it's due to my lack of knowledge of the universe's complexity.

In 2004, William was satisfied with the results of his lessons:

> Students look at the starry sky, more often; they show more interest in that part of reality. So, one of my teaching objectives has been achieved (i.e., students' wonderment and respect for the creation of 'heaven and earth').

PCK Development of Andrew (Type B)
Knowledge about instructional strategies. In 2002, Andrew and his colleagues had developed their own workbook (which they used alongside the ANtWoord book) 'to stimulate the students to go deeply into the material, being aware that they are really learning things'. The ANtWoord workbook did not meet their requirements on this point. Over the years, Andrew developed knowledge to adapt his lessons on the solar system and universe to suit students of different ages and levels of education and with different interests:

> I really like to talk to young people about their motives. So what I like to do is just to sit down with my class or have a classroom discussion about how the topic relates to their own lives. I introduce the assignments from there.

Andrew insisted from the beginning that his students designed and understood their own models:

> Making different models from the same data. I really pushed them to think about it themselves: for example, making and testing their models to explain the phases of the moon, using two balls (moon and earth) and a lamp (sun).

Andrew spent much time introducing the heliocentric and geocentric models of the solar system, putting a 'House of Commons-like' classroom debate on the models' strengths and weaknesses central: "It's a good experience for them that the 'best' model doesn't always win. In the history of science this has happened, too: the 'best' science hasn't always been recognised".

Over the years, he improved the organisational part of the debate: "Small things count, like how I arrange the tables. Or how I use the blackboard or where I am myself, standing or sitting". In summary, Andrew developed his knowledge about instructional strategies with regard to model content, model production, and thinking about the nature of models mainly based on his interpretation of students' responses to his lessons, indicating their motivation, abilities, and understanding.

Knowledge about students' understanding. According to Andrew, in 2002, his students were not generally used to thinking on a high level of abstraction. It was difficult for them to understand that a phenomenon can be modelled in more than one way, and that different models can be 'true': "For instance, one model is more complex than another, allowing for prediction of different things". Students did not need specific previous knowledge for the learning of models of the solar system and the universe. Andrew added: "Some pupils have a natural inclination to look around and notice things. Some pupils are interested in reading what others have written. And you do have some who are just not interested at all ...".

Over the years, Andrew mainly developed his knowledge about students' understanding by observing their work in the classroom as part of his instruction. In their making and testing of different models to explain the seasons on earth, for example, Andrew noticed that the students showed more sympathy for an earth (or a sun) that moves up and down than for a tilting earth's axis.

> They (the students) explained the earth's seasons as being caused by differences in the distance from the sun through the year, instead of different parts of the globe facing towards the sun, at different times of the year, which is caused by a tilt of the earth's axis. (cf. Kikas, 1998, 2004)

Knowledge about ways to assess students' understanding. At first (in 2002 and 2003), Andrew and his colleagues held only one major test (not on separate chapters, but on the whole book) in June. Andrew explained (in 2002):

> As a part of this test, they (the students) just have to know how a specific model works and be able to reproduce it, that's all. But that is still hard for a lot of pupils who can't explain the eclipses of the sun and moon. I don't think it's really a problem, they pass anyway because they know other things.

He preferred to evaluate his students' understanding of certain models by observation of group work and interpretation of their modelling and debating activities. In 2004, Andrew also started to give students marks for work in class and for their workbook tasks, because he had come to the conclusion that adding external motivation by giving marks, is an effective way to stimulate students to make progress.

Knowledge about goals and objectives in the curriculum. In 2002, Andrew had a relativist and instrumental epistemological view on models, which did not change over the years: "I want them (the students) to understand that a model doesn't have to be real and true to be useful. It's an interesting thought that an 'incorrect' model can still predict things (phenomena) correctly". This was important to him, because, "In the end, pupils have to understand how science works and the impact it has on society and especially on their daily lives".

Conclusions

From the results of the study, we conclude that, initially, teachers' PCK could be described in two qualitatively different varieties (see Table 5.4). In 2002, Type A could be typified as mainly oriented towards the teaching of science as 'a body of established knowledge', while Type B could be typified as more oriented towards 'the experience of science as a method of generating and validating such knowledge' (Hodson, 1992, p. 545).

The focus in our study was on how teachers' PCK developed over the course of three academic years. With regard to Type A, we conclude that in particular the knowledge about instructional strategies further developed. The results of the study indicate that this development was mainly influenced by the teachers' interpretation of students' results on written examinations (focusing on facts and application of knowledge) and reports on group work. In 2004, the teachers' PCK Type A was still mainly focused on model content. Knowledge about goals and objectives of the learning and teaching of 'Models of the Solar System and Universe' did not change significantly; that is, this knowledge still reflected a combination of positivist and instrumentalist epistemological views.

Figure 5.1 illustrates the development of the PCK elements in Type A, over time. The results of the study indicate that the development of teachers' knowledge about instructional strategies in the content of 'Models of the Solar System and the Universe' (i.e., ideas about materials to support students' understanding of model content and ways to connect models with reality) was consistent with their knowledge about goals and objectives of teaching the topic in the curriculum (i.e., based on their view on models as reductions of reality), and was also related to their knowledge about students' understanding of the subject (e.g., knowledge about students' difficulties with specific topics,

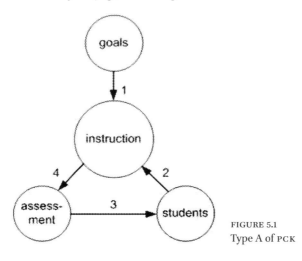

FIGURE 5.1
Type A of PCK

and inabilities to connect models with reality). (See Figure 5.1, arrows 1 and 2.) The teachers' developing knowledge about students' understanding of specific topics with regard to 'Models of the Solar System and Universe' (e.g., the rotations of the planets, or the concept of 'parallax') was, generally, associated with their interpretations of students' responses in written tests and group reports. (See Figure 5.1, arrow 3.) The knowledge of ways to assess their students' understanding – that is, using examinations on knowledge and applications of model content – was consistent with their ideas about instruction (i.e., also in the content of models). (See Figure 5.1, arrow 4.) However, although the teachers' knowledge of instruction methods developed substantially over time, in general their knowledge about ways of assessment did not change greatly.

From our results, we conclude that in the development of PCK in Type A, some of the elements of PCK (especially knowledge about instructional strategies) have become more sophisticated or expanded, but the interaction between these elements is rather static.

With regard to the development of PCK elements in Type B over the years, we conclude that changes in the knowledge about instructional strategies, the knowledge about students' understanding, and the knowledge about assessment were mutually related. The knowledge about goals and objectives of the learning and teaching of 'Models of the Solar System and the Universe' did not change significantly; that is, not only the visualisation and explanation of phenomena were still emphasised in this PCK element, but also how to formulate and test hypotheses, and how to obtain information about phenomena. Models were still conceived of as instruments, but also as ways to view reality (i.e., a relativist epistemological view).

Figure 5.2 illustrates the development of the PCK elements in Type B, over time. The results of the study indicate that the development of the teachers' knowledge about instructional strategies (e.g., ideas about the organisation of students' activities on model content, production, and thinking about the nature of models) was consistent with their knowledge about goals and objectives of teaching 'Models of the Solar System and Universe' in the curriculum (i.e., based on a relativist and instrumentalist view on models and modelling) and also related to their knowledge about students' understanding of the topic (e.g., knowledge about students' motivation and abilities to participate in modelling and debating activities, and knowledge about students' affinity with specific models). (See Figure 5.2, arrows a and b.) The development of knowledge about students' understanding was related to the teachers' knowledge about instructional strategies (i.e., an interpretation of the students' responses to classroom activities), as well as to the teachers' knowledge about assessment (e.g., using group observations, portfolios, presentations, and written exams).

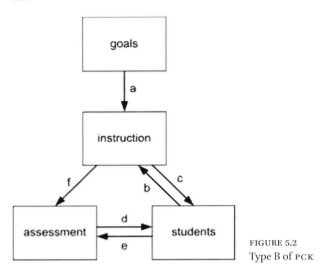

FIGURE 5.2
Type B of PCK

(See Figure 5.2, arrows c and d.) The knowledge about assessment (i.e., knowledge about how to evaluate model content, model production, and thinking about models) generally developed under the influence of the teachers' growing knowledge with regard to students' understanding (i.e., knowledge about students' motivation and abilities to participate in different kinds of activities), as well as the teachers' developing knowledge about instructional strategies (i.e., knowledge about how to promote students' learning of model content, model production and thinking about the nature of models). (See Figure 5.2, arrows e and f.)

From the results, we conclude that in Type B the elements of PCK seem to be developing in such a way that the content of the different elements is consistently and dynamically related to each other and to the teaching of 'Models of the Solar System and Universe'.

In the next section, we discuss the results of the study, and some implications for the teachers' professional development.

Discussion and Implications

In the theoretical models of Grossman (1990) and Magnusson et al. (1999, p. 99), the development of PCK is seen as (mostly) an autonomous process, influenced, among other things, by the teachers' general pedagogical knowledge and relevant subject matter knowledge. From this, we hypothesised that both types of PCK development were related to the teachers' general pedagogical knowledge and beliefs. In particular, given the differences between their knowledge about instructional strategies and student understanding, we expect teacher-directed pedagogical perspectives for Type A, and more or less student-directed pedagogical perspectives for Type B. Furthermore, for Type A both the knowledge about goals and objectives of teaching 'Models of the Solar System and the Universe' in the curriculum, and the knowledge about instructional strategies were generally restricted to an explanation of the heliocentric model of the solar system. Based on this, it may be suggested that Type A of PCK development was related to a teacher's limited subject matter knowledge and his mainly positivist view on models and modelling. In the same way, the more extended knowledge about goals and objectives of teaching 'Models of the Solar System and the Universe' in the curriculum and the knowledge about instructional strategies, shown by teachers representing Type B of PCK development, suggests a more comprehensive subject matter knowledge and a relativist and instrumentalist view on models and modelling in science (cf. van Driel, De Jong, & Verloop, 2002; Wallace & Loughran, 2003).

As the teachers' PCK development seems to be related to their initial pedagogical perspectives, epistemological views, and subject matter knowledge about models of the solar system and universe, interventions aimed at the development of teachers' professional understanding (especially those teachers representing PCK Type A) could involve opportunities and facilities for teachers to reflect on teaching experiences in order to articulate and share their pedagogical and epistemological ideas, and their knowledge of the history and philosophy of science (cf. Fullan & Hargreaves, 1992).

Different tools have been developed for documenting science teachers' understanding of their own professional practice and their students' learning of particular science (and astronomy) content. For example, the use of Resource Folios (Berry et al., 2006; Loughran et al., 2006) has been advocated as a way to make teachers' tacit knowledge explicit. In this approach, teachers represent the key concepts attached to a certain science topic, in connection to the teaching/learning practice of this topic or phenomenon (e.g., earth seasons, moon phases), thus explicating their own (developing) PCK. We think that explicating personal professional knowledge, and sharing it with colleagues or student-teachers, could be the main key to effective professional development of (experienced) science teachers (cf. Wallace & Louden, 1992).

Acknowledgement

The present study was funded by the Dutch Association for Scientific Research: NWO (grant number 411-21-201).

Note

1 Originally published as Henze, I., Van Driel, J. H., & Verloop, N. (2008). Development of experienced science teachers' pedagogical content knowledge of models of the solar system and the Universe. *International Journal of Science Education, 30*(10), 1321–1342. Reprinted, with minor edits, with permission from the publisher.

References

Aikenhead, G. S., & Ryan, A. G. (1992). The development of a new instrument. Views on Science-Technology-Society (VOSTS). *Science Education, 76,* 477–491.

Albanese, A., Danhoni Neves, M. C., & Vicentini, M. (1997). Models in science and in education: A critical review of research on students' ideas about the earth and its place in the universe. *Science and Education, 6,* 573–590.

American Association for the Advancement of Science. (1994). *Benchmarks for science literacy.* Oxford University Press.

Bakas, C., & Mikropoulos, T. (2003). Design of virtual environments for the comprehension of planetary phenomena based on students' ideas. *International Journal of Science Education, 25*(8), 949–967.

Barab, S., Hay, K., Barnett, M., & Keating, T. (2000). Virtual Solar System project: Building understanding through model building. *Journal of Research in Science Teaching, 37*(7), 719–756.

Beijaard, D., Van Driel, J. H., & Verloop, N. (1999). Evaluation of story-line methodology in research on teachers' practical knowledge. *Studies in Educational Evaluation, 25,* 47–62.

Berry, A., Loughran, J., & Mulhall, P. (2006, April). *Developing science teachers' pedagogical content knowledge using resource folios* [Paper presentation]. The annual meeting of the National Association for Research in Science Teaching (NARST), San Francisco, CA.

Cochran, F. K., DeRuiter, J. A., & King, R. A. (1993). Pedagogical content knowing: An integrative model for teacher preparation. *Journal of Teacher Education, 44,* 261–272.

De Jong, O., van Driel, J. H., & Verloop, N. (2005). Preservice teachers' pedagogical content knowledge of using particle models in teaching chemistry. *Journal of Research in Science Teaching, 42*(8), 947–964.

De Vos, W., & Reiding, J. (1999). Public understanding of science as a separate subject in secondary schools in the Netherlands. *International Journal of Science Education, 21,* 711–719.

Duit, R., & Glynn, S. (1996). Mental modelling. In T. Welford, J. Osborne, & P. Scott (Eds.), *Research in science education in Europe: Current issues and themes* (pp. 166–176). Falmer.

Erduran, S. (2001). Philosophy of chemistry: An emerging field with implications for chemistry education. *Science & Education, 10,* 581–593.

Fullan, M., & Hargreaves, A. (1992). *Teacher development and educational change.* Falmer Press.

Giere, R. (1991). *Understanding scientific reasoning* (3rd ed.). Holt, Rinehart & Winston.

Gilbert, J. K., & Boulter, C. J. (2000). *Developing models in science education.* Kluwer.

Greeno, J. G., Collins, A. M., & Resnic, L. B. (1996). Cognition and learning. In D. C. Berliner & R. C. Calfee (Eds.), *Handbook of educational psychology* (pp. 15–46). Simon & Shuster Macmillan.

Grossman, P. L. (1990). *The making of a teacher: Teacher knowledge and teacher education.* Teachers College Press.

Henze, I., & Van Driel, J. H. (2011). Science teachers' knowledge about learning and teaching models and modeling in public understanding of science. In M. S. Khine & I. M. Saleh (Eds.), *Models and modeling: Cognitive tools for scientific enquiry* (pp. 239–261). Springer.

Henze, I., Van Driel, J. H., & Verloop, N. (2007a). Science teachers' knowledge about teaching models and modelling in the context of a new syllabus on public understanding of science. *Research in Science Education, 37*(2), 99–122.

Henze, I., Van Driel, J. H., & Verloop, N. (2007b). The change of science teachers' personal knowledge about teaching models and modelling in the context of science education reform. *International Journal of Science Education, 29*(15), 1819–1846.

Henze, I., Van Driel, J. H., & Verloop, N. (2009). Experienced science teachers' learning in the context of Educational Innovation. *Journal of Teacher Education, 60*(2), 184–199.

Hodson, D. (1992). In search of a meaningful relationship: An exploration of some issues relating to integration in science and science education. *International Journal of Science Education, 14,* 541–562.

Justi, R. S., & Gilbert, J. K. (2002). Science teachers' knowledge about and attitudes towards the use of models and modelling in learning science. *International Journal of Science Education, 24,* 1273–1292.

Kikas, E. (1998). Pupils' explanations of seasonal changes: Age differences and the influence of teaching. *British Journal of Educational Psychology, 68,* 505–516.

Kikas, E. (2004). Teachers' conceptions and misconceptions concerning three natural phenomena. *Journal of Research in Science Teaching, 41*(5), 432–448.

Koulaidis, V., & Ogborn, J. (1989). Philosophy of science: An empirical study of teachers' views. *International Journal of Science Education, 11,* 173–184.

Lemmer, M., Lemmer, T. N., & Smit, J. J. A. (2003). South African students' views of the universe. *International Journal of Science Education, 25*(5), 563–582.

Loughran, J. J., Berry, A., & Mulhall, P. (2006). *Understanding and developing science teachers pedagogical content knowledge.* Sense Publishers.

Louws, M. L., Meirink, J. A., Van Veen, K., & Van Driel, J. H. (2017). Teachers' self-directed learning and teaching experience: What, how, and why teachers want to learn. *Teaching and Teacher Education, 66*, 171–183.

Magnusson, S., Krajcik, J., & Borko, H. (1999). Nature, sources and development of pedagogical content knowledge. In J. Gess-Newsome & N. G. Lederman (Eds.), *Examining pedagogical content knowledge* (pp. 95–132). Kluwer.

Marks, R. (1990). Pedagogical content knowledge: From a mathematical case to a modified conception. *Journal of Teacher Education, 41*(3), 3–11.

Northern Examinations and Assessment Board. (1998). *Science for public understanding* [*Syllabus*]. NEAB.

Nott, M., & Wellington, J. (1993). Your nature of science profile: An activity for science teachers. *School Science Review, 75*, 109–112.

Shulman, L. S. (1986). Those who understand: Knowledge growth in teaching. *Educational Researcher, 15*, 4–14.

Shulman, L. S. (1987). Knowledge and teaching: Foundations of the new reform. *Harvard Educational Review, 35*, 637–695.

SLO. (1996). *Voorlichtingsbrochure HAVO/VWO Algemene natuurwetenschappen* [Information brochure on Public Understanding of Science]. SLO.

Van der Valk, T., & Gravemeijer, K. (2000, May). *Het Studiehuis vanuit B-didactisch perspectief* [*The Study House seen from a science education perspective*] [Paper presentation]. The Onderwijs Research Dagen (ORD), Leiden, The Netherlands.

Van Driel, J. H., De Jong, O., & Verloop, N. (2002). The development of preservice chemistry teachers' PCK. *Science Education, 86*(4), 572–590.

Van Driel, J. H., & Verloop, N. (1999). Teachers' knowledge of models and modelling in science. *International Journal of Science Education, 21*, 1141–1153.

Van Driel, J. H., & Verloop, N. (2002). Experienced teachers' knowledge of teaching and learning of models and modelling in science education. *International Journal of Science Education, 24*(12), 1255–1272.

Van Driel, J. H., Verloop, N., & De Vos, W. (1998). Developing science teachers' pedagogical content knowledge. *Journal of Research in Science Teaching, 35*(6), 673–695.

Verloop, N., Van Driel, J. H., & Meijer, P. (2001). Teacher knowledge and the knowledge base of teaching. *International Journal of Educational Research, 35*, 441–461.

Vollebregt, M., Klaassen, K., Genseberger, R., & Lijnse, P. (1999). Inzichtelijk een deeltjesmodel leren [A problem posing approach to teaching an initial particle model]. *Tijdschrift voor Didactiek der β-Wetenschappen, 16*(1), 12–26.

Wallace, J., & Louden, W. (1992). Science teaching and teachers' knowledge. Prospects for reform of elementary classrooms. *Science Education, 76*, 507–521.

Wallace, J., & Loughran, J. (Eds.). (2003). *Leadership and professional development in science education: New possibilities in enhancing teacher learning*. Routledge/Falmer.

CHAPTER 6

The Development of Preservice Chemistry Teachers' Pedagogical Content Knowledge

1 How the Study Came About

As explained in previous chapters, I had developed an interest in investigating the development of the practical knowledge of secondary pre-service science teachers during their teacher education program. Specifically, I was keen to study the development of PCK in the context of the method courses that are a prominent component of the teacher education program at Leiden University. To understand the context, it is important to note that the Netherlands has a higher education system that offers programs at two levels: higher professional education and university education. Teacher education for early childhood, primary and lower secondary education (grades 7–9) is offered in the higher professional stream by institutes that are now called universities of applied sciences. Teacher education for upper secondary education (grades 10–12) is traditionally the domain of (research) universities. Universities such as Leiden offer a one-year postgraduate teacher education program for students who have obtained a Master's degree in Science or Arts, specialising in a school subject such as chemistry, history, or English language and culture.

Given my background in chemistry and my previous research, I planned to set up a study with pre-service teachers (PSTs) of chemistry, focusing on learning to teach about models and modelling. Since our cohorts were small (typically between 5–10 chemistry PSTs per year), I contacted Onno De Jong at Utrecht University. Onno had been a teacher educator when I did my teacher qualification course in the early 1980s and we had both been working on our PhD thesis in the second half of the 1980s at the department of chemistry education at Utrecht. Given this shared background and experience, we had many similar ideas about research topics, methods and theories so we decided to join forces and designed a study on the development of PCK on what we called *macro-micro*, that is, the relation between observable phenomena, like chemical changes, and macroscopic properties (e.g., solubility) and their interpretation and explanation in terms of corpuscular models. The Utrecht cohort was about the same size as in Leiden, so working together doubled the number of participants. More important than that, collaborating implied combining our expertise and sharing the work.

Our first study took place in the academic year 1997/98. Twelve PSTs participated, seven of whom were enrolled in Leiden, the other five in Utrecht. Our programs were structured quite similarly. Both had a 50/50 distribution of the time dedicated to university coursework, including seminars and workshops, and school placements. The method course ('Chemiedidactiek') was organised as a series of workshops, scheduled over the two semesters of the program. Onno taught the Utrecht course; my colleague Theo Mulder was the chemistry educator in Leiden. The three of us had a few meetings and designed a protocol to ensure that we would take a very similar approach to the topic *macro-micro*. Underlying our approach was our belief that PCK is something beginning teachers cannot learn from a university course or textbook only. Rather, they need to plan and conduct the teaching of specific topics in classrooms and reflect on the impact of their teaching on students. As detailed in the article in this chapter, we agreed to introduce *macro-micro* during a university workshop. The aim of this workshop was to make the PSTs aware that relating the macro and micro levels and using adequate representations may be a natural thing for them as qualified chemists but is often problematic for secondary students. To prepare for the workshop, PSTs were asked to study a paper from the research literature which described some of these difficulties (i.e., Harrison & Treagust, 1996). During the workshop, this paper was discussed in relation to the PSTs' classroom experiences during the first two months of the semester. After the workshop, we asked them to select a topic from the chemistry curriculum with a strong *macro-micro* presence and consult with their school-based mentor to plan and teach one to three lessons about this topic.

The study aimed to capture the influence of the elements of our approach (i.e., the workshop, classroom experiences and feedback from mentors) on the development of the PCK about models and modelling of the PSTs. We agreed to embed data collection as much as possible in the method course, so that from the perspective of the PSTs, their participation in the study seemed part of the course. We video recorded both the Leiden and the Utrecht delivery of a university workshop on *macro-micro* and we interviewed each PST individually about their experiences and reflections concerning *macro-micro* during the semester, both at university and in their schools. In addition, we asked them to respond to a questionnaire about 'phenomena and particles in chemistry education', at the start and at the end of the semester. Finally, we interviewed their school-based mentors. Obviously, this multimethod design was time-consuming and labour intensive, however, we deemed it necessary "given the complex nature of PCK as a construct, plus our desire to capture the *development* of PCK" (Van Driel, De Jong, & Verloop, 2002, p. 578).

2 Reflection and Follow Up

In the article, the findings were reported through a combination of tables and quotes from interviews with PSTs and their mentors. In two tables we aimed to demonstrate the changes in the PCK of the PSTs by comparing and coding their responses to the pre- and post-questionnaire (Table 6.1) and by analysing their interview responses (Table 6.2). The influences of the different elements of our design (i.e., workshop, classroom experiences, mentor) on PCK development were inferred mainly from the interviews with the PSTs and their mentors. We concluded the PSTs had become aware, to different extents, of their tendency to make connections between the macro and micro levels in a quick and implicit manner, and most of them had noticed that this could cause confusion among students. Thus, they formulated intentions to be much more mindful about their use of language, "in particular by dealing explicitly with the distinction between the macro and the micro level, and the relation between these levels" (Van Driel et al., 2002, p. 585). In terms of PCK development, we concluded that classroom experiences more than the other factors had contributed to the PSTs' increased knowledge of specific conceptions and learning difficulties of students, one of the main components of PCK. We also observed that some PSTs had expanded their content knowledge about *macro-micro*.

Onno and I presented the findings at the 1999 NARST annual meeting and proceeded to write a manuscript which was submitted to *Science Education* in early 2000 and, after a round of revisions, was accepted a year later. In the meantime, encouraged by the outcomes of the study, we had begun to plan a follow-up project. More than in the first study, we aimed to offer PSTs opportunities to learn *from* teaching, rather than learn about teaching. Therefore, we decided to amend our teaching approach as follows:

- Instead of confronting PSTs with a paper from the research literature, we decided to start by asking them to explicate their existing PCK by remembering their own learning experiences about *macro-micro* when they were students.
- Prior to planning and teaching a lesson series of three to six lessons on *macro-micro*, we organised a workshop session during which PSTs could expand their PCK by analysing and discussing common chemistry schoolbooks, focusing on examples of how *macro-micro* was taught or represented (e.g., in diagrams or drawings).
- PSTs were required to collect and analyse data from their students related to the lesson series they taught, specifically by audio recording the lessons

and by collecting student work, including written responses to a test with a *macro-micro* focus.
- Rather than interviewing PSTs on the basis of their experiences, we asked them to write a reflective report and share this during a final meeting of the method course.

We hoped that these changes would increase the impact of our approach on the PCK development of the PSTs. One of the recommendations of our previous study to achieve this was to organise specific field-based activities, in particular, asking PSTs to analyse students' answers to written tasks in the domain of *macro–micro* to enhance their understanding of students' conceptions and learning difficulties.

The amended approach was offered to the combined cohorts of chemistry PSTs of the universities of Leiden (n = 4) and Utrecht (n = 8) in the academic year 1999/2000. Two workshops were organised to prepare PSTs for designing and teaching their lesson series. For each workshop a detailed scenario was written to ensure that they would be delivered in very similar ways in the two locations. PSTs received three written assignments; the first two were discussed during the workshops, the third one related to the lesson series PSTs had taught and asked them to write a concise report about "the most remarkable episodes and events during the lessons, including the analysis of the students' mistakes in a test at the end of the lessons" (De Jong, Van Driel, & Verloop, 2005, p. 953). During a final workshop, these reports were presented and discussed plenary. Data collection, more than in the first study, was closely connected to the design of the course. Instead of using questionnaires and interviews, we collected the written responses of the PSTs to the three assignments and made audio recordings of all university workshops.

The different data sources employed in this round resulted in a different approach to presenting the findings. We distinguished between PSTs' *initial* PCK in terms of their understanding of student learning difficulties related to *macro-micro* and instructional strategies they considered useful to overcome such learning difficulties, and their PCK *after* teaching the lesson series. Initial PCK results were based on PSTs' written responses to the two assignments and recordings of the discussions during the workshops about these assignments. Instead of using tables, these findings were reported in a narrative format, using quotes from PSTs as illustrations. We concluded that all PSTs remembered specific learning difficulties, and that, although their recollections were rather fragmented and often a bit vague, they seemed to be aware of problems associated with understanding the relation between macroscopic phenomena and microscopic entities (i.e., atoms or molecules). In the discussion of their

PCK post-teaching, we distinguished between PSTs who focused on learning difficulties they had observed among their students, and those who mainly focused on instructional strategies. The first group (n = 7) described learning difficulties, expressed by students either in written or oral form, in different levels of detail or specificity. The second group (n = 5) described their teaching approach and, to different extents, the responses of their students to their approach. In both groups, two PSTs formulated explicit intentions for future teaching. We concluded that our 'learning from teaching' approach, consisting of the sequence of activities outlined above, had met our expectations. Specifically, "writing a reflective lesson report, and discussing these reports with each other, turned out to be useful in helping the P[S]Ts to explicate, and further develop, their ideas about students' learning difficulties and instructional strategies – in other words, their PCK" (De Jong, Van Driel, & Verloop, 2005, p. 962). Although this conclusion applied to all PSTs, the development of PCK varied quite a bit between individual PSTs. This was consistent with the 1998 PCK article (Chapter 1), in which we acknowledged that the impact of participating in our project on PCK was different for individual teachers. To account for these personal differences, we referred to the then recently published Interconnected Model of Teacher Professional Growth (IMTPG; Clarke & Hollingsworth, 2002). This model highlights that teacher learning occurs along non-linear pathways that are shaped by teachers' personal and professional experiences. The IMTPG and its application in my research will be discussed in more detail in Chapter 9.

The outcomes of this study were presented at the 2001 NARST annual meeting before we started to write a new journal article. This time, we decided to target a Dutch language journal on education research called *Pedagogische Studiën*. We reckoned that many Dutch and Flemish colleagues who were not specialising in chemistry or science education, might be interested to learn from our study about the impact of teacher education on PCK development more broadly. I took the lead in the writing of this paper, which was published in 2004 (Van Driel, De Jong, & Verloop, 2004). At the same time, Onno led the writing of a manuscript that we would submit to the *Journal of Research in Science Teaching*. This was accepted late 2004 and appeared in print in 2005 (De Jong, Van Driel, & Verloop, 2005). Please notice the time between data collection (1999/2000) and the publication of this paper! I think it is fair to say that presenting the results at a conference, and then writing an article in Dutch, helped us to frame the article in a way that made it attractive for a journal like *Journal of Research in Science Teaching*. Since Onno retired from the university around this time, this second study concluded our joint research project. However, we would continue to work and publish together, our last collaborative effort was a book chapter on chemistry teachers' learning (Van Driel & De Jong, 2015). Of the papers we wrote together and with Nico Verloop, the one in *Science Education* (this chapter) and the one in the *Journal of Research in Science Teaching* were by far the most impactful in terms of citations: nearly 600 and 375, respectively. For both articles, the number of citations has grown steadily over time, peaking around 2013–14 and continuing to be cited often since then. It's not easy to understand why some articles pick up so many citations and others don't. Clearly, articles published in high ranked journals such as *Science Education* and *Journal of Research in Science Teaching* are read more widely than those in local journals and that increases their likelihood of being cited. Also, both articles followed up on the PCK article in the *Journal of Research in Science Teaching* (Van Driel et al.,1998; see Chapter 1), so it is reasonable to assume that many people who read, downloaded or cited that article, would be interested in these papers.

3   Next Steps

At the NARST annual meeting in 2001, Onno and I discussed our project with several international colleagues, including John Gilbert and Rosária Justi. Rosária had completed her PhD on models and modelling in science teaching at the University of Reading (UK) with John as her supervisor and was now working at the Federal University of Minas Gerais in Belo Horizonte, Brazil. Obviously, the four of us shared a common research interest. Rosária was keen to do a post-doc project and she and I discussed opportunities for her to do this at Leiden University. She wrote a project proposal and secured funding from CAPES, a Brazilian agent, and I was able to obtain additional funding from the Dutch Research Council. This enabled her to live and work in Leiden for a full year, which coincided with the academic year 2002/03. We designed a research project on the development of pre-service science teachers' knowledge of models and modelling. The design followed that of the studies I had conducted with Onno, with a few changes:
– Rather than embedding the project in the method course, we situated it in the research component of our teacher education program. Each pre-service teacher in our program was required to conduct a study on a topic of their interest, with a load of 300 hours. We offered all pre-service teachers of science the opportunity to do their study in a collaborative manner, supervised by Rosária and myself. Five of them volunteered to participate (four were specialising on chemistry, one on physics).

- We organised four workshops (3 hours each) over a period of six weeks for this group, devoted to models and modelling in science and addressing philosophical, historical and pedagogical aspects. In addition, we scheduled a meeting to support the PSTs with the planning and methodological aspects of their studies. After these sessions, PSTs designed a lesson series on models and modelling and a plan for a study connected to these lessons.
- Data collection included recordings of the workshops, research plans and reports written by the PSTs (complemented by video recordings of their lessons and materials produced by their students), questionnaires and interviews.

I consider this design a progression of the two rounds of studies with Onno De Jong. Central in each study was that PSTs designed and taught a number of lessons on models and modelling in their placement schools. In the first study with Onno, we interviewed the PSTs about their experiences. In the second study, we asked them to record the lessons and collect artefacts from their students. In the project with Rosária, we took this one step further: Each PST investigated their own research question, conducted a brief literature study and systematically collected data in their classrooms. The studies with Onno and Rosária were not set up to compare the impact of the different designs on the PSTs' development of PCK, however, Rosária and I concluded on the basis of our data that the combination of workshops, lesson planning, teaching experiences, and research-based reflections – mediated by us as researchers and in a group context – had supported a comprehensive development of the PSTs' content knowledge, curricular knowledge and PCK about models and modelling. The obvious limitation, as in almost any study in the context of a teacher education program, was that PSTs could not apply what they had learned in a next iteration of designing, teaching and researching their lesson series about models and modelling.

Rosária and I presented the outcomes of the project at the biannual conference of ISATT (International Study Association on Teachers and Teaching) which was organised in Leiden in 2003 and then wrote three journal articles, with different foci: a) the development of PSTs' knowledge about models and modelling in science, aimed at a science education audience and accepted for publication by the *International Journal of Science Education* (Justi & Van Driel, 2005b); b) the use of the Interconnected Model of Teacher Professional Growth (IMTPG; Clarke & Hollingsworth, 2002) to analyse knowledge development in PSTs, aimed at a teacher education audience and published in *Teaching and Teacher Education* (Justi & Van Driel, 2006; see also Chapter 9); and c) a case study describing in detail the stepwise development of content knowledge, curricular knowledge and PCK about models and modelling of one of the PSTs (Justi & Van Driel, 2005a). These three articles have been quite successful in terms of citations, especially the article published in the *International Journal of Science Education* (Justi & Van Driel, 2005b) with nearly 200 citations in Google Scholar to date. It is interesting, however, to note that whereas I think that the studies with Onno and Rosária became more sophisticated over time, the numbers of citations of the respective articles decreased. Maybe the novelty factor was wearing off?

Finally, and importantly, Rosária and I encouraged the five PSTs to collectively write an article to showcase the outcomes of their projects, which was published in *NVOX*, the national science teacher journal in the Netherlands. It is not very common for pre-service teachers to publish in this journal, but it seemed an appropriate outlet for their efforts. More generally, I think there is a lot of value in teachers conducting research in their own practice and sharing the outcomes with their colleagues. In future years, this would become a central idea in the PhD study of Tamara Platteel, who studied the implementation of a curriculum innovation in mother tongue education in a group of teachers who were involved in a collaborative action research approach (Platteel, Hulshof, Van Driel, & Verloop, 2013).

The Development of Preservice Chemistry Teachers' Pedagogical Content Knowledge[1]

Jan H. van Driel, Onno De Jong and Nico Verloop

Abstract

This study investigated the development of pedagogical content knowledge (PCK) within a group of 12 preservice chemistry teachers (all M.Sc.) during the first semester of their one-year post-graduate teacher education program. The study focused on PCK with respect to a central issue in science teaching, that is, the relation between observable phenomena, like chemical reactions, and macroscopic properties (e.g., boiling point, solubility) on the one hand, and their interpretation in terms of corpuscular characteristics on the other hand (*macro-micro*). For secondary school students, shifting mentally between the macro and micro levels is usually problematic, whereas their teachers are often unaware of students' learning difficulties in this domain. The collection of data involved two written questionnaires, interviews with each preservice teacher and their respective mentors, and an audio recording of a specific workshop session in the teacher education program. Results indicated a growing awareness among the preservice teachers concerning the need, in teaching situations, to explicitly relate the macro and micro levels to each other. Moreover, the importance of the careful and consistent use of language was noticed by many preservice teachers. The growth of PCK was influenced mostly by the preservice teachers' teaching experiences. Also, the workshop contributed substantially. Finally, for some preservice teachers, their mentors had influenced the growth of PCK. Implications for science teacher education are discussed.

Introduction

In recent years, researchers have shown a growing interest in the knowledge base of preservice science teachers. Many studies have addressed fairly general aspects of teaching and learning science. For instance, researchers have investigated preservice teachers' conceptions of teaching and learning science (Brickhouse & Bodner, 1992; Mellado, 1998; Simmons et al., 1999) or their views on teaching science to students from various cultures (Southerland & Gess-Newsome, 1999), or the ways preservice teachers construct practical knowledge about teaching (Zuckerman, 1999). Other researchers, however, have investigated the subject matter knowledge of preservice science teachers in the context of learning to teach (Gess-Newsome, 1999; Haidar, 1997). To acknowledge the importance of the transformation of subject matter knowledge *per se* into subject matter knowledge *for teaching,* Shulman (1987) introduced the concept of pedagogical content knowledge (PCK). He described PCK as "... that special amalgam of content and pedagogy that is uniquely the province of teachers, their own special form of professional understanding". Accordingly, PCK encompasses teachers' knowledge of representations and instructional strategies in relation to knowledge of student learning, both with respect to a specified content area. In the field of science education, so far only a few studies have focused on teachers' PCK and its development (Magnusson, Krajcik, & Borko, 1999).

In this study, the development of PCK was explored within a group of preservice teachers of chemistry. Moreover, we have tried to identify the influence of certain components of the preservice teacher education program (viz., specific workshops, student teaching experiences, and feedback from mentors) on this development. The purpose of the study was twofold. From a theoretical point of view, we aimed to gain a better understanding of factors which either promote or hinder the development of PCK (Grossman, 1990; Veal, 1998). Moreover, our study aimed to contribute to the research-based design of science teacher education courses.

Pedagogical Content Knowledge

According to Shulman (1986), research on pedagogical content knowledge (PCK) may contribute to resolving the "blind spot" which results from a relative lack of research focusing on the content of the lessons taught. In the last decade, numerous studies on PCK have been published (e.g., Gess-Newsome & Lederman, 1999; Van Driel, Verloop, & De Vos, 1998). Various scholars, elaborating on Shulman's work, have proposed different conceptualizations of PCK, in terms of the features they include or integrate (e.g., Cochran, DeRuiter, & King, 1993; Grossman, 1990; Magnusson, Krajcik, & Borko, 1999; Marks, 1990; Veal, 1998). Yet it seems that the two following elements are central in any conceptualization of PCK, that is, knowledge of representations of subject matter and instructional strategies incorporating these representations on the one hand, and understanding of specific student conceptions and learning difficulties on the other hand, both with respect to a specified content area. Obviously, these elements are intertwined and should be used in a flexible manner: the more representations and strategies teachers have at their disposal within a certain domain, and the better they understand their students' learning processes in the same domain, the more effectively they can teach in this domain. In addition, there appears to be agreement on the nature of PCK. Firstly, since PCK refers to *particular topics,* it is to be discerned from knowledge of pedagogy, of educational purposes, and of learner characteristics in a general sense. Secondly, because PCK concerns the *teaching* of particular topics, it may turn out to differ considerably from subject matter knowledge per se. Finally, all scholars suggest that PCK is developed through an integrative process rooted in classroom practice, and that PCK guides the teachers' actions when dealing with subject matter in the classroom. The latter supports the view of Van Driel, Verloop, and De Vos (1998) that PCK is a central component of teachers' practical knowledge or craft knowledge (cf. Grimmett & MacKinnon, 1992).

Pedagogical content knowledge has been described as "the transformation of several types of knowledge for teaching" (Magnusson, Krajcik, & Borko, 1999, p. 95). These types of knowledge include subject matter knowledge, pedagogical knowledge (classroom management, educational aims), and knowledge about context (school, students). Grossman (1990) has identified four sources that are potentially important with respect to the development of PCK: (a) disciplinary education, which may lead to personal preferences for specific educational purposes or topics, (b) observation of classes, both as a student and as a preservice teacher, often leading to tacit and, sometimes, conservative PCK, (c) classroom teaching experiences, and (d) specific courses or workshops during teacher education, of which the impact is normally unknown.

Within the domain of science teaching, several studies have been performed on the development of teachers' knowledge, in the context of bothpreservice and inservice teacher education. With respect to the development of PCK, the following results from these studies seem relevant:

– *Knowledge of subject matter.* According to Smith and Neale (1989), the development of PCK depends on teachers having a "deeply principled conceptual knowledge of the content". As for preservice teachers, the subject matter knowledge they have acquired during disciplinary education usually contains misconceptions and deficiencies (Smith, 1999). For instance, Gess-Newsome and Lederman (1993) noted that the subject matter structures of preservice biology teachers, who had nearly completed the requirements for a BS in Science Education, was often vague and fragmented at the start of their teacher education program. During this program, the preservice teachers developed more coherent and integrated subject matter structures. However, the development of PCK was hindered by the complexity of teaching practice.

– *Teaching experience with respect to specific topics.* According to Lederman, Gess-Newsome, and Latz (1994), the development of PCK among preservice science teachers is promoted by the constant use of subject matter knowledge in teaching situations. Initially, preservice teachers separate subject matter knowledge from general pedagogical knowledge. As a result of teaching experiences however, these types of knowledge are being integrated.

- *Knowledge of students' conceptions and learning difficulties.* By getting acquainted with the specific conceptions and ways students reason, preservice teachers may start to restructure their subject matter knowledge into a form that enables productive communication with their students (Lederman, Gess-Newsome, & Latz, 1994). In addition to field-based experiences, preservice teachers may benefit from studying students' preconceptions with respect to a specific topic during teacher education courses, and comparing and discussing these preconceptions in relation to their own conceptions (Geddis, 1993). Such activities may stimulate preservice teachers to generate transformations of subject matter knowledge and topic specific teaching strategies. Van Driel, Verloop, and De Vos (1998) have described the influence of inservice chemistry teachers' analyses of students' conceptions and types of reasoning concerning a specific topic (i.e., chemical equilibrium) on the development of their PCK on this topic.
- *Participating in specific workshops.* Clermont, Krajcik, and Borko (1993) have studied the effects of a short, intensive workshop on specific teaching strategies (i.e., chemical demonstrations). They found that the PCK of preservice science teachers participating in this workshop developed towards that of expert teachers. On the other hand, Adams and Krockover (1997) found that workshops can have a negative effect because they can stimulate preservice teachers to copy conventional instructional strategies, stressing procedures rather than student understanding.

Comparing these factors with the sources for PCK development described by Grossman (1990), we may suggest that (a) disciplinary education, naturally, constitutes the basis for knowledge of subject matter, (b) observation of classes may promote the knowledge of students' conceptions, (c) classroom teaching experiences may stimulate the integration of subject matter knowledge and general pedagogical knowledge, thus contributing to the development of PCK, and (d) specific courses or workshops during teacher education have the potential to affect PCK, for instance, by extending preservice teachers' knowledge of students' preconceptions or their knowledge of specific representations of subject matter. The present study aims to improve our understanding of the nature of the development of PCK among preservice science teachers, in particular, the factors influencing this development.

Context and Scope of the Present Study

The present study was situated in the context of the first semester of a one-year postgraduate teacher education program, qualifying for the teaching of chemistry at preuniversity level (cf. grades 10–12 of secondary education). Before entering this program, participants need to have obtained a Master's degree in chemistry. Generally speaking, the development of knowledge and beliefs during the program is seen as an individual process of knowledge construction. This process is guided by teaching experiences as a preservice teacher in a secondary school, supervised by a mentor, on the one hand, and by institutional meetings and workshops and individual study of the literature on the other hand.

During the first semester of the teacher education program, the preservice teachers work in couples or trios at the same school. In the first weeks of the course, the preservice teachers' school activities mainly consist of observing and discussing their mentor's lessons. Next, they begin to teach their own classes (about four to eight lessons per week). These classes are regularly observed by their mentors. Meetings of the preservice teachers with their mentors include preparatory talks, during which the preservice teacher's lesson plans are discussed, and meetings focusing on the evaluation of specific lessons taught by the preservice teacher. During this semester, the preservice teachers also take part in institutional meetings and workshops, for two afternoons per week on average. The main aim of these meetings and workshops is to stimulate the reflection on teaching experiences in relation to the relevant literature (e.g., on science education, pedagogy, educational psychology), as a result of which preservice teachers make their teaching concerns and intentions more explicit.

With respect to the development of PCK, the ideas from the previous section have been incorporated in the program as follows. Before they begin teaching a specific topic, the preservice teachers' subject matter knowledge of this topic is addressed by encouraging them to reflect on their own learning process as a student (*Knowledge of subject matter*). Next, during *specific workshop sessions,* they are asked to relate these reflections to their experiences during classroom lessons as an observer, and their study of the literature, in order to identify specific teaching and learning difficulties (*Knowledge of students' conceptions and learning difficulties*). Subsequently, the preservice teachers formulate teaching concerns, which then form the basis for their preparation of lesson plans focusing on the topic under consideration. After teaching these lessons (*Teaching experience with respect to specific topics*), the preservice teachers are encouraged to share their reflections and formulate new teaching concerns (De Jong et al., 1999).

The present study focuses on a central issue in science teaching, that is, relating macroscopic phenomena to microscopic particles (Lijnse et al., 1990). We shall refer to this theme as *macro-micro*. The *macro-micro* perspective concerns the relation between observable phenomena, like chemical reactions, and macroscopic properties (e.g., boiling point, solubility) on the one hand, and their interpretation in terms of corpuscular characteristics on the other hand (De Vos & Verdonk, 1996). Obviously, representations (such as models and analogies) serve as an intermediate between these two levels. Because learning to relate these levels to each other is one of the most important objectives of chemistry education, preservice teachers need to develop PCK in this domain. However, Gabel (1999) found that chemistry teachers are often unaware of these levels and their mutual relations. Accordingly, we assumed that the preservice teachers in this study, being educated as chemists, had developed a habit of "jumping" between the macro and micro level in a flexible, fast, and often implicit way (Johnstone, 1993). For secondary school students, however, relating the macro and micro levels and using adequate representations is often problematic. The conceptual demands of shifting between these levels can be overwhelming (see e.g., Andersson, 1990). Specifically, students tend to mix up these levels, for instance, by attributing macroscopic properties to atoms or molecules (De Vos & Verdonk, 1987; Lee et al., 1993). As students' learning difficulties in this domain have been investigated in several studies, it was decided to discuss some findings from the research literature during one of the institutional workshops, after 2 months in the first semester. For this purpose, every preservice teacher was asked to study the paper by Harrison and Treagust (1996) as a preparation for the workshop. During the workshop, this paper was discussed in relation to the preservice teachers' classroom experiences in the first 2 months of the semester. After the workshop, the preservice teachers chose a topic from the chemistry curriculum in which the relation between macroscopic phenomena and corpuscular explanations was dominantly present (e.g., explaining the precipitation of inorganic salts in terms of ionic bonding). They planned and taught one to three lessons on this topic and discussed them with their mentor.

This paper describes the development of PCK in the domain of macro-micro *among the preservice chemistry teachers in this study. In particular, the following research question is addressed:* What development of the preservice teachers' PCK can be identified and what is the influence of specific factors (i.e., teaching experience, institutional workshops, and the mentor) on this development?

Design and Procedure

The subjects in the study were a group of 12 preservice teachers of chemistry. Shortly before entering a one-year post-graduate teacher education program, all participants had obtained a Master's degree in chemistry. Seven preservice teachers were female, 5 were male. Their ages varied from 22 to 28 years. All of them had little or no teaching experience. Five preservice teachers followed the institutional program at Utrecht University, while the others participated in the program at Leiden University. The programs were taught by two different teacher trainers, the second author of this paper being the Utrecht instructor. The instructor at Leiden University met regularly with the first author to discuss the design and the progress of the program. It was decided early on to follow a similar approach with respect to *macro-micro*.

A qualitative in-depth study was designed. In order to monitor the development of PCK, we chose a multimethod approach (Baxter & Lederman, 1999). Data were collected at specific moments during the first semester of the teacher education program:

- In October '97, all preservice teachers responded to a written questionnaire, aimed as a baseline measurement of their subject matter knowledge and pedagogical content knowledge with respect to the *macro-micro* issue (see Appendices I and IA). Although at this time, the preservice teachers had only very limited teaching experience, we wanted to investigate to what extent they had already developed PCK and preconceptions about teaching *macro-micro* issues, for instance, on the basis of earlier experiences as a learner of chemistry (e.g., in secondary school), or due to their first teaching experiences.
- In November '97, the workshop sessions devoted to *macro-micro* were recorded on videotape and subsequently transcribed. Two sessions took place: one for the group of 7 preservice teachers at Leiden University and the other for the group of 5 preservice teachers at Utrecht University. The sessions were led by the respective teacher trainers, the second author of this paper leading the Utrecht session. The first author was present during the Leiden session, observing the discussion and taking notes. Identical procedures and written instructions for the teacher trainers were used to guarantee that both sessions took place in a similar manner.
- From December '97 to January '98, every preservice teacher was interviewed individually about his or her practical experiences and reflections concerning *macro-micro* during the whole of the first semester (see Appendix II). All interviews were conducted in a semistructured way that allowed the respondents to tell "their own stories" and to introduce issues the interviewers had not thought of (Smith, 1995). The first author interviewed the preservice teachers at Leiden University, whereas the second author interviewed Utrecht preservice teachers.
- In the same period, we interviewed the mentors of these preservice teachers to investigate their view on the preservice teachers' knowledge and

development concerning *macro-micro* (see Appendix III). The first author interviewed the mentors of the Leiden group, and the second author interviewed the Utrecht mentors.
– Finally, in the same period, the preservice teachers responded to a second questionnaire. This was similar to the first questionnaire, but focused on pedagogical content knowledge only (see Appendices I and IB).

We analyzed the data from an interpretative phenomenological perspective. Smith (1995) characterized this view on qualitative analysis as follows: "While one is attempting to capture and do justice to the meanings of the respondent, to learn about his or her mental and social world, those meanings are not transparently available, they must be obtained through a sustained engagement with the text and a process of interpretation" (p. 18). Accordingly, the analysis of all data (both written and verbal) focused on the identification of regularities or patterns in the statements made by the respondents, without the use of an *a priori* established system of categories or codes. Instead, we developed categories on the basis of the data, through an iterative process during which the data were constantly compared with each other, as well as with theoretical notions, in particular, concerning the nature of PCK (cf. Denzin, 1994).

The data from the two questionnaires were analyzed first. We compared the answers to the first and the second questionnaire to identify changes in the preservice teachers' PCK, particularly in their knowledge of specific learning difficulties of students. Comparing and discussing our individual analyses, three categories emerged during the analysis process to describe these changes. We then assigned the changes found with individual respondents to these categories, resulting in a numerical overview of the results.

In the analysis of the other data, the interviews with the individual preservice teachers formed the starting point. All these interviews were audio taped and transcribed verbatim. We then analyzed the interviews, focusing on the factors contributing to the development of elements of PCK. Next, the interview data were connected with the data from the remaining sources (data triangulation; Janesick, 1994). Thus, we analyzed the interviews with the mentors, mostly to validate the preservice teachers' descriptions of their own development. Finally, the transcripts of the workshop sessions were analyzed, mainly to check the references preservice teachers made to these sessions during the interviews. Subsequently, we compared the results concerning individual preservice teachers to identify common patterns in their development, and factors influencing these developments. In this step, investigator triangulation (Janesick, 1994) was applied by comparing and discussing the interpretations of the first and the second author of this paper.

The multimethod approach described above is inherently time-consuming and laborintensive. In our view, an approach like this is necessary given the complex nature of PCK as a construct, plus our desire to capture the *development* of PCK. According to Baxter and Lederman (1999), PCK is hard to assess because it is constituted by "what a teacher knows, what a teacher does, and the reasons for the teacher's actions" (Baxter & Lederman, 1999, p. 158). In the present study we have focused on preservice teachers' growing awareness of what they know, and how their awareness grew. To account for possible inconsistencies between what they reported and what they did during their lessons, the interviews with the mentors were included.

Results

In this section, the results of the comparison of the two questionnaires are described first. These results give an indication of the changes in the preservice teachers' knowledge of specific conceptions and learning difficulties of students, and, sometimes, of changes in their subject matter knowledge. Next, the results of the analysis of the other data (interviews with preservice teachers and mentors, workshop sessions) are presented. This presentation consists of two parts. In the first part, results are discussed which provide more insight in the changes in the preservice teachers' PCK, that is, not only their knowledge of specific conceptions and learning difficulties of students, but also their knowledge with respect to the use of specific teaching activities and strategies. Observed changes in the preservice teachers' subject matter knowledge are also briefly described. In the second part, results are addressed which contribute to an understanding of the factors that have contributed to the changes in the preservice teachers' PCK. These factors concern (1) classroom teaching experience, (2) university-based workshop, and (3) meetings with mentors.

Questionnaires: Changes in Knowledge of Specific Conceptions and Learning Difficulties of Students, and Changes in Subject Matter Knowledge

Comparing the answers of the preservice teachers on the first and second questionnaire, more learning difficulties were described in the latter. In addition, learning difficulties and students' conceptions were often described in more detail and more specifically in the second questionnaire. To illustrate the increase of the number of learning difficulties described, we compare the numbers of blank responses in the two questionnaires. In the first questionnaire, Question 2 was left unanswered by the 12 preservice teachers 30 times (out of 108, that is 12 times 9; 28%), which corresponds to an average of 2.5 unanswered items out of 9 (see Appendix 1A). This number of blank responses may be considered high, but it must be remembered that this question addressed aspects of PCK at a time when the preservice teachers had only very limited teaching experience. In the second questionnaire, only 15 times (14%) preservice teachers did not respond to an item, corresponding to 1.3 unanswered items on average (Appendix 1B).

The results of the comparison of the two questionnaires have been summarized in Table 6.1. To construct this table, the answers of the preservice teachers to Question 2 with respect to the 9 items in the first questionnaire (Appendix 1A) have been compared with their responses to the respective items in the second questionnaire (Appendix 1B). Analyzing the content of the preservice teachers' answers revealed that in 16 cases (15%) the answers to the two questionnaires were phrased in identical or similar terms, so we concluded that in fact, a change was not detectable ("Ident" in Table 6.1). In most cases, however, differences were observed between the answers to the two questionnaires. These changes could be grouped into three categories. Although it was sometimes difficult to categorize a difference between two answers unequivocally

TABLE 6.1   Differences in the answers of the preservice teachers to the two questionnaires

Preservice Teacher	Item 1	Item 2	Item 3	Item 4	Item 5	Item 6	Item 7	Item 8	Item 9
PT-1	LD-s	Ident	Ident	Ext	LD-g	Ext	–	LD-g	Ext
PT-2	LD-s	–	Ext	LD-s	–	LD-g	–	–	–
PT-3	LD-s	LD-s	LD-s	Ext	LD-g	LD-g	LD-g	LD-s	LD-g
PT-4	LD-g	LD-g	LD-s	LD-s	LD-g	LD-g	–	LD-g	–
PT-5	LD-s	LD-s	LD-g	Ident	LD-s	LD-g	LD-s	LD-s	–
PT-6	Ident	LD-s	Ident	LD-s	Ident	LD-s	Ident	Ident	LD-s
PT-7	LD-s	–	Ext	–	Ext	LD-s	LD-g	Ext	–
PT-8	LD-s	LD-g	Ext	Ident	LD-s	Ident	LD-g	LD-s	Ext
PT-9	LD-s	Ident	LD-s	Ident	LD-g	LD-s	Ident	LD-s	Ext
PT-10	Ident	–	Ident	Ext	Ext	LD-g	LD-g	Ext	Ident
PT-11	LD-g	Ext	LD-g	Ext	LD-s	Ext	–	LD-s	Ext
PT-12	LD-s	Ext	LD-s	LD-s	LD-s	Ext	LD-g	LD-g	–

Ext: More extensive description; LD-g: Addition of a description of learning difficulties in general terms; LD-s: Addition of a description of specific learning difficulties; Ident: Answers were (more or less) identical; –: Item was unanswered in both questionnaires.

into one of these three categories, it was possible for us to achieve consensus about all differences.

1. *More extensive description.* ("Ext"; figures 20 times in Table 6.1; 19%). This category consisted of changes in terms of a more extensive description, which was not explicitly related to problems or conceptions students might have. For instance, one preservice teacher (PT-7 in Table 6.1) answered item 5 (dissolving of salt in water) with a short reference to a solution containing ions in the first questionnaire, whereas his answer to this item in the second questionnaire was: "Extending particulate model with ions and non-molecular substances".

    Sometimes, changes in this category reflected a growth in the preservice teachers' subject matter knowledge. In particular, this was noted several times with respect to item 9 (Mixing of monochloromethane and sodium hydroxide in ethanol). For instance, one preservice teacher (PT-1 in Table 6.1) had only written a question mark as a response to item 9 in the first questionnaire, while her answer to the second questionnaire referred to the possibility of the reaction being of the S_N1- or S_N2-type and how to distinguish between these possibilities, without any reference to students.

2. *Addition of a description of learning difficulties in general terms.* ("LD-g"; figures 24 times in Table 6.1; 22%). This category concerned changes which consisted of the addition of an explicit reference to students' problems or conceptions, but in a rather general or unspecific way. Changes of this type occurred relatively often for most of the items throughout the questionnaire. For example, a preservice teacher (PT-5) added: "It willbe difficultforthemtounderstandwhat happens at the molecular level", to his response to item 3 (dissolving sugar). Other examples included: "Comparing it to the melting of ice", by PT-4 as a response in the second questionnaire to item 2 (melting of stearic acid), or adding: "Students may confuse this process with a decomposition reaction", (PT-1) in response to item 5 (dissolving salt in water).

3. *Addition of a description of specific learning difficulties.* ("LD-s"; figures 33 times in Table 6.1; 31%). Changes in this category consisted of the addition of specific learning problems and conceptions of students. Typically, such learning problems would be stated in terms of a question students might ask with respect to the topic under consideration (e.g., "Why does the water evaporate, although its boiling point is 100°C?", in the case of heating water to 60°C; PT-2; item 1).

    Examples in this category could be further divided into additions indicating an increased understanding of learning difficulties (a) in a *macro*-context, for instance the statement quoted above, or: "In my class, students find it difficult to see that oxygen has been consumed. They think it's a decomposition reaction" (PT-2; referring to the burning of magnesium; item 4), (b) in a micro-context, for instance: "Students have difficulties understanding that individual molecules of water have different velocities at the same temperature" (PT-9; item 1; heating water to 60°C), and (c) with respect to *relating the macro and micro level to each other*. Typical of the latter category were answers (in the second questionnaire) like: "Students ask why you don't feel anything when you put your finger in a solution of salt, whereas this solution is supposed to consist of positively and a negatively charged particles" (dissolving salt in water; PT-8; item 5), or: "Students hold conceptions like 'the molecules become warmer'" (heating water to 60°C; PT-7; item 1).

Interviews with Preservice Teachers and Mentors; Workshop Sessions (1): Changes in the Preservice Teachers' PCK and Subject Matter Knowledge

From the interviews with the preservice teachers and their mentors, it became clear that for most preservice teachers changes in their pedagogical content knowledge had occurred. These changes could be described adequately with the use of two categories, according to Shulman's two key elements of PCK, that is (1) knowledge of specific conceptions and learning difficulties of students and (2) knowledge of instructional strategies incorporating representations of subject matter. In Table 6.2, the changes for each individual preservice teacher have been summarized. Below, the different types of changes are discussed in more detail and illustrated with concrete examples from the interviews.

1. Knowledge of specific conceptions and learning difficulties of students.
   - Ten of the preservice teachers reported that they had become aware that students often have problems to relate or distinguish the macro and micro levels. For example, PT-3 had experienced that "students have difficulties to switch, and we haven't, when something is at the micro level or at the macro level". Most of them had noticed that when they would switch from one level to the other quickly and implicitly, this would usually create confusion among students. In this context, some mentioned that students often had problems understanding chemical formulas. As an example, PT-4 had experienced that students did not understand the difference between "Na^+ (aq) + Cl^- (aq)" and "NaCl (aq)" to represent an aqueous solution of sodium chloride. In particular, PT-4 had noticed that students would argue that the notation

TABLE 6.2   Growth of the preservice teachers' PCK inferred from interview data

	Knowledge of students' conceptions/difficulties		Knowledge of instructional strategies	
Preservice teacher	Conf. M-M	Unad. micro	Use visual.	Use language
PT-1	+	+	o	+
PT-2	+	o	+	o
PT-3	+	+	+	+
PT-4	+	+	+	+
PT-5	+	+	+	o
PT-6	+	o	+	o
PT-7	+	+	+	o
PT-8	+	o	o	o
PT-9	+	o	o	+
PT-10	o	o	o	o
PT-11	o	o	o	o
PT-12	+	o	o	+

Conf. M-M: Increased awareness of confusion about micro and macro levels; Unad. micro: Understanding of problems caused by unadequate use of micro level; Use visual.: Successful use of visualizations and multiple modes of representation; Use language: Increased awareness of the need to use language carefully and consistently; +: Growth detected; o: No growth detected.

including charged ions was at odds with their experience that "nothing happens" when you put a finger in a solution of sodium chloride.
- In addition, 3 of these 10 teachers (PT-1, PT-5, and PT-7) had observed that their preference to reason in corpuscular terms often hindered their students' understanding, especially when discussing chemical experiments. However, as academic chemists, these teachers had experienced difficulties in refraining from the use of such terms. For instance, PT-1 explained that "normally, I immediately reason in terms of models, instead of first discussing what has happened, like, out of two clear solutions a solid substance has been formed, and then using that as a starting point to discuss an explanation".

Alternatively, 3 preservice teachers (PT-3, PT-4, and PT-5) had noticed that students were inclined to interpret reaction equations in a microscopic context only. As one preservice teacher, PT-3, commented:

"They do not see that a reaction equation refers not only to molecules, but also to larger quantities ...".

2. Knowledge of instructional strategies incorporating representations of subject matter. Specifically
   – Six of the teachers (PT-2, PT-3, PT-4, PT-5, PT-6, and PT-7) reported the successful use of specific teaching strategies, such as the use of visualizations, or the use of multiple modes of representation. The use of visualizations refers to, for instance, using the blackboard to make connections between a drawing of a test tube (macro level) and a drawing of particles (micro level). During the interview, PT-4 gave a detailed description of such an example. Multiple representations were used in particular to promote students' understanding of the micro level, by providing them simultaneously with various modes to represent molecules and atoms, such as chemical symbols, drawings in which atoms are represented by circles, together with material models, students could manipulate themselves. PT-6 had used this strategy on several occasions, observing that different representations (of a water molecule) facilitated the understanding of different subgroups of students within a class, because some students would benefit from one particular mode of representation, whereas others were able to understand the relations between the various modes of representation. PT-7 had successfully encouraged his students to design their own models to explain a specific phenomenon.
   – Five of the teachers (PT-1, PT-3, PT-4, PT-9, and PT-12) concluded that, when communicating with students about *macro-micro* issues, it is necessary to use specific terms in a clear and consistent manner. This was noted especially in cases which require a careful distinction between, as one preservice teacher (PT-9) remarked, "the things we see" on the one hand, and "our explanations in terms of atoms and molecules" on the other hand. PT-3 explained: "I have tried to avoid expressions such as 'so here we can *see* the ions'". Instead, PT-3 would rather explicitly refer to models, saying things such as "we can explain this by assuming ...". As another example, PT-1 stated that he would not use words referring to models in the context of discussing "the reality", because this would confuse the students enormously.

From the analysis of the interview data, it became clear that all but two of the participating preservice teachers had expanded their PCK concerning *macro-micro* (PT-10 and PT-11 in Table 6.2). One of them, PT-10, stated that for her the most important result of the *macro-micro* assignments had been that she had become aware, in a general sense, that students might have their own conceptions. For her, this was an eye-opener as she had always been taught chemistry in a traditional, "delivery" mode. According to her mentor, PT-10 had also experienced serious difficulties because of a lack of sound subject matter knowledge. As a result, she had often been embarrassed by unexpected questions of her students. Later during the semester, PT-10 could better handle such situations. Thus, it seemed that for this preservice teacher, the emphasis had been on improving her subject matter knowledge and gaining PCK of a very general nature. For PT-11, the emphasis on *macro-micro* had been "too early", as her concerns had been with issues related to classroom management. According to her mentor, she had "grown as a person", and she had become more selfassertive. In addition, PT-11 remarked that she had become aware that "as a teacher, you sometimes contribute to the creation of misconceptions among students", for instance, by not using models carefully enough.

In addition to developing their PCK, some preservice teachers had also extended their subject matter knowledge. In particular, some demonstrated an increased awareness of the nature of atoms and molecules as models. For instance, PT-3 explained that he had become more aware of the difference between observable phenomena on the one hand, and models of tiny particles, which have been "invented by chemists to explain" such phenomena. Moreover, 4 preservice teachers (PT-1, PT-3, PT-4, and PT-6) had been inspired to think critically and deeply about the ontological status of atoms and molecules. In particular, the Utrecht group had discussed the question "Do atoms really exist?" during their workshop session. Consequently, the participating preservice teachers reported an increased awareness of the role of models and representations in relating the macro and micro levels. In Leiden, PT-6 had similar discussions with his mentor at school.

Interviews with Preservice Teachers and Mentors; Workshop Sessions (2): Factors Contributing to Changes in Preservice Teachers' PCK

So far, we have focused on the *content* of the changes in the preservice teachers' PCK. Below, the focus of attention is shifted to the *factors* contributing to the growth of PCK. The most important source of data for this discussion was Question 6 of the interviews with the preservice teachers (Appendix II). The analysis of these data was validated by the results of Question 4 of the interviews with the mentors (Appendix III) and by checking the data from the workshop sessions (see the previous section Design and Procedure). The factors contributing to the growth of PCK are discussed in order of decreasing impact:

1. *Classroom teaching experience.* Classroom experiences refer both to the observation of lessons given by the mentor or by a peer preservice

teacher, as well as to lessons the preservice teachers taught themselves. Such experiences with respect to *macro-micro* were considered by the preservice teachers to have had the strongest impact on their PCK in this domain. These experiences had an impact on both elements of PCK, in particular on the preservice teachers' knowledge of students' learning difficulties. This knowledge was promoted by:

- *The questions students posed during lessons* directly at the preservice teachers. For instance, one preservice teacher (PT-12) had taught a group of students who would ask for an explanation at any time when they thought her explanation became unclear. These responses had alerted PT-12 to various specific misunderstandings.
- *Correction of students' answers to written tests.* As an example, 2 preservice teachers (L-6 and L-12) explicitly described the specific learning difficulties they had recognized while correcting students' written answers to test questions about chemical formulas and reaction equations (e.g., confusion between indices in formulas and stoichiometric coefficients).
- *The responses of students to specific assignments.* For instance, 1 preservice teacher (L-6) had asked his students to draw pictures of a water molecule. He had been very surprised by some of the results, for instance, of a student who had drawn tiny particles surrounded by a liquid. Subsequently, he had discussed these results with the students.
- *The observation of students' behavior during lessons taught by the mentor or a peer.* Three preservice teachers (PT-6, PT-7, and PT-9) discussed this factor explicitly. One of them, PT-9, explained that observing the students' responses to another teacher's approach had facilitated her understanding of students' learning difficulties much more than teaching her own lessons, because then "She did not have enough time and space in her mind" to observe the students' responses.

In addition to this, some preservice teachers also described the ways in which classroom experiences had affected their knowledge of representations of subject matter and related teaching strategies. For instance, the conclusion of PT-1, described above, to start by focusing on phenomena, like observations during a chemical experiment, before discussing explanations in terms of models, was mainly inspired by students' initial responses to his way of teaching, which had indicated confusion or misunderstanding. Also, the knowledge PT-6 and PT-7 gained about the use of several representational modes (see above) was based on trying out particular strategies during the lessons they taught themselves and observing their students' responses to their approach.

2. *University-based workshop.* All preservice teachers mentioned the impact of the university-based workshop. Prior to the workshop, all had studied the paper by Harrison and Treagust (1996; see section 1.2, Context and Scope of the Present Study). In a general sense, the discussion during the workshop had contributed to the preservice teachers' understanding that students develop their own conceptions, and that a teacher's approach may sometimes unintentionally promote specific misconceptions among students.

In addition, most of the preservice teachers mentioned that reading and discussing the paper had promoted their understanding of specific learning difficulties and misconceptions of students. In particular, some preservice teachers described parallels between the description of students' misconceptions in the paper, and their own observations in the classroom. One of them, PT-12, could use the paper to explain some of the problems she had experienced. When she first observed students having difficulties relating the macro and micro levels to each other, she hypothesized that her way of explaining had been deficient. After reading and discussing the paper, she could interpret her students' problems in terms of limited abilities to deal with abstractions. This insight had served as an inspiration for her teaching approach in the following period.

With respect to their knowledge of teaching strategies, the impact of the workshop had been modest. This impact was described in rather general terms, for instance, "the workshop made me realize I need to be careful with models" (PT-11). Three preservice teachers (PT-8, PT-10, and PT-11) explicitly stated that, at this stage of their development, they were not yet able to apply the content of the paper to their teaching practice. It must be noted, however, that the paper of Harrison and Treagust (1996) focuses on the description of students' conceptions and abilities and contains only a small section on recommendations for classroom instruction.

For some preservice teachers, the workshop had apparently affected their subject matter knowledge. In particular, the preservice teachers of the Utrecht group reported that their discussion about the ontological status of atoms and molecules (see above) had urged them to explore the edges of their subject matter knowledge. For one of them, PT-5, the workshop had been the most significant influence on his knowledge of the *macro-micro* relationship. He described the workshop as "annoying, but in a positive sense".

3. *Meetings with mentor.* Five preservice teachers explicitly described a positive impact of discussions with their mentors concerning *macro-micro*. A couple of them (PT-6 and PT-7), who were supervised by the same mentor, had had lengthy and extensive discussions with this mentor about the relationship between the macro and micro levels. These discussions had stimulated their awareness of students' problems in this domain, and of the necessity to be explicit about these levels and their relationship. Moreover, the mentor had suggested specific teaching strategies (e.g., using multiple representational modes), which the preservice teachers had applied in their lessons. Two other preservice teachers (PT-1 and PT-4) stated that they had benefited from the knowledge their mentor had of specific learning difficulties concerning *macro-micro*.

One mentor had noticed that, discussing the observed use of language with a preservice teacher, PT-12, resulted in a more thoughtful and explicit use of language by this preservice teacher. The mentor suggested that this improvement was partly due to the effect of the workshop, which had occurred in the same period. Another mentor noticed many inaccuracies and mistakes in the explanations presented by a preservice teacher (PT-10). He spent much time discussing these flaws with the preservice teacher, initially aiming mainly at improving her subject matter knowledge. In the end, the mentor observed a progression both in the field of subject matter knowledge as well as PCK. He, too, suggested that this progression was also influenced by the university workshop.

Conclusions and Discussion

Most of the preservice teachers in this study displayed a distinct development of PCK about *macro-micro*. The PCK developed by the preservice teachers may be summarized as follows. To different extents they had become more aware of their own habit to "jump" between the macro and the micro level in a fast and implicit manner. Moreover, most of them had observed that their usual way of reasoning often caused problems for students, who, for instance, became confused by the mixing of terms from a macro context and a micro context. Thus, preservice teachers concluded that they should be very strict in their use of language, in particular by dealing explicitly with the distinction between the macro and the micro level, and the relation between these levels. In addition, some had apparently also developed subject matter knowledge in this area.

In terms of the factors contributing to this development, it became apparent that, according to the preservice teachers and their mentors, classroom experiences had had the strongest impact. In the first place, different activities and events during classroom teaching had affected the preservice teachers' knowledge of specific learning difficulties of students. In the second place, their knowledge of representations and teaching strategies had benefited from experiences during classroom practice. This strong impact of teaching experiences is consistent with the findings of other scholars (e.g., Grossman, 1990; Lederman, Gess-Newsome & Latz, 1994; Smith, 1999).

The preservice teachers also attributed a substantial effect to the university-based workshop session on the development of their PCK. It is suggested that this impact may be explained by (a) the timing of the session, about half-way through the semester, and (b) the format, which focused on the preservice teachers' interpretations of the research literature in relation to their own beliefs and teaching experiences at the time. Thus, most preservice teachers could relate the content of the paperby Harrison and Treagust (1996) to the learning difficulties and types of reasoning of their own students. In addition, the workshop session had had a minor impact on the preservice teachers' knowledge of specific teaching strategies. At the same time, however, reading and discussing the paper had triggered the development of subject matter knowledge for at least some of the participating preservice teachers.

Finally, about half of the participants indicated that their mentor had been a major influence in developing their PCK in the domain of *macro-micro*. Mentor influence varied greatly, because of (a) differences in the frequencies and intensities of the meetings between mentors and preservice teachers, and (b) variations in the extent to which the mentors were interested or involved in the *macro-micro* perspective. Possibly, the mentors' own PCK in this domain may vary considerably.

From the analysis of the data from the questionnaires and the interviews, differences between the preservice teachers became apparent with regard to the *extent* of their development of PCK about *macro-micro*. As the preservice teachers' PCK about *macro-micro* at the start of the program was, without exceptions, very limited, these differences must have been created during the course of the program. At the end of this program, some preservice teachers described specific learning difficulties and conceptions of students in considerable detail, or gave a precise description of a teaching strategy they had developed on the basis of their experiences. Others, however, reported rather general notions, for instance, in terms of having observed students' limited abilities to deal with models, or having become more aware of their own inaccurate use of language in the domain of *macro-micro*. Two preservice teachers, rather than developing PCK about *macro-micro,* had been occupied mainly with developing their self-images as teachers (Kagan, 1992), in relation to developing general pedagogical knowledge (PT-11; i.e., in the area of classroom management), or in relation to improving subject matter knowledge (PT-10). To account for these differences between the preservice teachers' development, several aspects are important. In the first place, as each preservice teacher had taught various topics to different classes, his/her individual experiences had led to differences in their specific knowledge. For instance, while PT-6 and PT-7 had taught the basic ideas of molecules and atoms in grade 9, PT-3, PT-4, and PT-5 had focused on the interpretation of precipitation experiments in terms of the ions involved (grade 10), and PT-9 had taught molecular structures of organic substances in relation to macroscopic properties of these substances in grade 10. Secondly, differences between the subject matter knowledge of the preservice teachers were noted. Although all participants had recently obtained a Master's degree in chemistry, they apparently differed in their knowledge of the domain of *macro-micro*. This may be explained by the fact that the relationship between macroscopic phenomena and microscopic explanations is usually not emphasized in the chemistry curricula of our universities. For instance, courses on the philosophy or nature of chemistry are not compulsory in these curricula. This may explain why some preservice teachers reported to have developed subject matter knowledge about *macro-micro,* whereas others were already more knowledgeable in this field, for instance, because of their intrinsic interest in these issues. As the subject matter knowledge of a specific domain forms a basis for the development of PCK in this domain (Grossman, 1990), it is clear that differences in subject matter knowledge may have played an important role in the observed variations in the preservice teachers' PCK. Thirdly, differences in the extent of the development of PCK are due to variations in the influence of the preservice teachers' mentors. As discussed above, for half of the participants their mentor had not been very influential as far as the teaching of *macro-micro* issues was concerned, whereas the other half had discussed the *macro-micro* perspective often and extensively with their mentors.

Obviously, the exploratory nature of the present study, and the small number of preservice teachers involved, do not allow us to generalize these conclusions. In future research, we will continue to study the development of PCK in other groups of preservice teachers of chemistry.

To conclude this paper, we present a number of implications for science teacher education derived from this study. Firstly, we recommend organizing specific field-based activities. In particular, the preservice teachers could be asked to analyze their students' answers to written tests or specifically designed assignments in terms of students' learning difficulties and conceptions in the domain of *macro-micro*. In the present study, several preservice teachers had accidentally carried out this type of activity and reported they had benefited from it. Eventually, the preservice teachers could be stimulated to carry out small-scale action research activities, for instance, interviewing students to investigate their conceptions and ideas about *macro-micro* (cf. Smith, 1999).

Secondly, the use of articles from the educational research literature in university-based workshops is recommended, provided that the timing and the format of these sessions enables the preservice teachers to relate their own experiences and beliefs to such articles. In the domain of *macro-micro*, a rich base exists of useful literature, for instance, documenting specific misconceptions, the effects of certain teaching approaches, etc.

Finally, the role of the mentors should be given special attention. The observed variation in the mentors' approach and involvement indicates that they *potentially* have a strong impact on the development of preservice teachers' PCK. Thus, we recommend integrating the role of the mentors systematically in the program. On the one hand, the mentors' knowledge of the university-based elements of the teacher education program needs to be improved, while on the other hand, the mentors' ideas and experiences should be used as input in this program.

When formulated in more general terms, the above recommendations can also be applied to other domains than *macro-micro*. As mentioned earlier, in several studies it was found that teachers' pedagogical content knowledge could be improved when teachers studied or analyzed students' preconceptions and types reasoning in a specific domain (Geddis, 1993; Van Driel, Verloop, & De Vos, 1998). As for the role of mentors, Zanting et al. (1998) reported that preservice teachers may benefit from studying their mentors' practical knowledge. Thus, we recommend that the meetings between mentors and preservice teachers be structured in a way that stimulates the preservice teachers to inquire and explore their mentors' pedagogical content knowledge about specific topics.

As pedagogical content knowledge refers to the ability to transform subject matter knowledge in a manner accessible to learners, the development of PCK depends to a large extent on preservice teachers' subject matter knowledge. Like other scholars, mentioned earlier in this paper (viz., Gess-Newsome & Lederman, 1993; Smith, 1999), we have found in this study that this subject matter knowledge often contains deficiencies. One way to tackle this problem is to reconceptualize science teacher education programs in a way which integrates courses on subject matter, pedagogy, and field experiences. Recently, such programs have been developed at Oregon State University (Lederman & Gess-Newsome, 1999; Niess & Scholz, 1999). In teacher education programs such as ours, however, we have to work with the subject matter knowledge which preservice teachers possess upon entrance as a result of preceding disciplinary education. In such programs, we recommend to address this subject matter knowledge explicitly as a basis for the development of their PCK. That is, through specific assignments (e.g., analyzing text books or reflecting on field experiences), preservice teachers' may become aware of certain deficiencies in their subject matter knowledge. When these deficiencies are discussed with preservice teachers in the context of the *teaching* of the topics under consideration, this may contribute to a simultaneous development of more adequate subject matter knowledge and PCK. In future work, we will study the development of preservice teachers' PCK in relation to their subject matter knowledge in more detail.

Note

1   Originally published as Van Driel, J. H., De Jong, O., Verloop, N. (2002). The development of preservice chemistry teachers' PCK. *Science Education, 86*(4), 572–590. Reprinted, with minor edits, with permission from the publisher.

References

Adams, P. E., & Krockover, G. H. (1997). Beginning science teacher cognition and its origins in the preservice secondary science teacher program. *Journal of Research in Science Teaching, 34,* 633–653.

Andersson, B. (1990). Pupils' conceptions of matter and its transformations (Age 12–16). In P. L. Lijnse, P. Licht, W. De Vos, & A. J. Waarlo (Eds.), *Relating macroscopic phenomena to microscopic particles* (pp. 12–35). CDβ-Press.

Baxter, J. A., & Lederman, N. G. (1999). Assessment and measurement of pedagogical content knowledge. In J. Gess-Newsome & N. G. Lederman (Eds.), *Examining pedagogical content knowledge* (pp. 147–161). Kluwer Academic Publishers.

Brickhouse, N. W., & Bodner, G. M. (1992). The beginning science teacher: Classroom narratives of convictions and constraints. *Journal of Research in Science Teaching, 29,* 471–485.

Clarke, D., & Hollingsworth, H. (2002). Elaborating a model of teacher professional growth. *Teaching and Teacher Education, 18,* 947–967.

Clermont, C. P, Krajcik, J. S., & Borko, H. (1993). The influence of an intensive in-service workshop on pedagogical content knowledge growth among novice chemical demonstrators. *Journal of Research in Science Teaching, 30,* 21–43.

Cochran, K. F., DeRuiter, J. A., & King, R. A. (1993). Pedagogical content knowledge: An integrative model for teacher preparation. *Journal of Teacher Education, 44,* 263–272.

De Jong, O., Ahtee, M., Goodwin, A., Hatzinikita, V., & Koulaidis, V. (1999). An international study of prospective teachers' initial teaching conceptions and concerns: The case of teaching 'combustion'. *European Journal of Teacher Education, 22*, 45–59.

De Jong, O., Van Driel, J. H., & Verloop, N. (2005). Preservice teachers' pedagogical content knowledge of using particle models in teaching chemistry. *Journal of Research in Science Teaching, 42*(8), 947–964.

De Vos, W., & Verdonk, A. H. (1987). A new road to reactions, part 4: The substance and its molecules. *Journal of Chemical Education, 64*, 692–694.

De Vos, W., & Verdonk, A. H. (1996). The particulate nature of matter in science education and in science. *Journal of Research in Science Teaching, 33*, 657–664.

Denzin, N. K. (1994). The art and politics of interpretation. In N. K. Denzin & Y. S. Lincoln (Eds.), *Handbook of qualitative research design* (pp. 500–515). Sage.

Gabel, D. (1999). Improving teaching and learning through chemistry education research: A look to the future. *Journal of Chemical Education, 76*, 548–554.

Geddis, A. N. (1993). Transforming subject-matter knowledge: The role of pedagogical content knowledge in learning to reflect on teaching. *International Journal of Science Education, 15*, 673–683.

Gess-Newsome, J. (1999). Secondary teachers' knowledge and beliefs about subject matter and their impact on instruction. In J. Gess-Newsome & N. G. Lederman (Eds.), *Examining pedagogical content knowledge* (pp. 51–94). Kluwer Academic Publishers.

Gess-Newsome, J., & Lederman, N. G. (1993). Preservice Biology teachers' knowledge structures as a function of professional teacher education: A year-long assessment. *Science Education, 77*, 25–45.

Gess-Newsome, J., & Lederman, N. G. (Eds.). (1999). *Examining pedagogical content knowledge*. Kluwer Academic Publishers.

Grimmett, P. P., & MacKinnon, A. M. (1992). Craft knowledge and the education of teachers. In G. Grant (Ed.), *Review of research in education* (Vol. 18, pp. 385–456). AERA.

Grossman, P. L. (1990). *The making of a teacher: Teacher knowledge and teacher education*. Teachers College Press.

Haidar, A. H. (1997). Prospective chemistry teachers' conceptions of the conversation of matter and related concepts. *Journal of Research in Science Teaching, 34*, 181–197.

Harrison, A. J., & Treagust, D. F. (1996). Secondary students' models of atoms and molecules: Implications for teaching chemistry. *Science Education, 80*, 509–534.

Janesick, V. J. (1994). The dance of qualitative research design. In N. K. Denzin & Y. S. Lincoln (Eds.), *Handbook of qualitative research design* (pp. 209–219). Sage.

Johnstone, A. H. (1993). The development of chemistry teaching: A changing response to changing demand. *Journal of Chemical Education, 70*, 701–705.

Justi, R., & Van Driel, J. H. (2005a). A case study on the development of a beginning chemistry teacher's knowledge on models and modelling. *Research in Science Education*, 35(2–3), 197–219.

Justi, R., & Van Driel, J. H. (2005b). The development of science teachers' knowledge on models and modelling – Promoting, characterising, and understanding the process. *International Journal of Science Education*, 27(5), 549–573.

Justi, R., & Van Driel, J. H. (2006). The use of the IMTPG as a framework for understanding the development of science teachers' knowledge on models and modelling. *Teaching & Teacher Education*, 22(4), 437–450.

Kagan, D. M. (1992). Professional growth among preservice and beginning teachers. *Review of Educational Research*, 62(2), 129–169.

Lederman, N. G., & Gess-Newsome, J. (1999). Reconceptualizing secondary science teacher education. In J. Gess-Newsome & N. G. Lederman (Eds.), *Examining pedagogical content knowledge* (pp. 199–213). Kluwer Academic Publishers.

Lederman, N. G., Gess-Newsome, J., & Latz, M. S. (1994). The nature and development of preservice science teachers' conceptions of subject matter and pedagogy. *Journal of Research in Science Teaching*, 31, 129–146.

Lee, O., Echinger, D. C., Anderson, C. W., Berkheimer, G. D., & Blakeslee, T. D. (1993). Changing middle school students' conceptions of matter and molecules. *Journal of Research in Science Teaching*, 30, 249–270.

Lijnse, P. L., Licht, P., De Vos, W., & Waarlo, A. J. (Eds.). (1990). *Relating macroscopic phenomena to microscopic particles*. CDβ-Press.

Magnusson, S., Krajcik, J., & Borko, H. (1999). Nature, sources and development of pedagogical content knowledge. In J. Gess-Newsome & N. G. Lederman (Eds.), *Examining pedagogical content knowledge* (pp. 95–132). Kluwer Academic Publishers.

Marks, R. (1990). Pedagogical content knowledge: From a mathematical case to a modified conception. *Journal of Teacher Education*, 41, 3–11.

Mellado, V. (1998). The classroom practice of preservice teachers and their conceptions of teaching and learning science. *Science Education*, 82, 197–214.

Niess, M. L., & Scholz, J. M. (1999). Incorporating subject matter specific teaching strategies into secondary science teacher preparation. In J. Gess-Newsome & N. G. Lederman (Eds.), *Examining pedagogical content knowledge* (pp. 257–276). Kluwer Academic Publishers.

Platteel, T., Hulshof, H., Van Driel, J. H., & Verloop, N. (2013). Teachers' interpretations of the concept-context approach for L1 education. *L1 – Educational Studies in Language and Literature*, 13, 1–25.

Shulman, L. S. (1986). Those who understand: Knowledge growth in teaching. *Educational Researcher*, 15(2), 4–14.

Shulman, L. S. (1987). Knowledge and teaching: Foundations of the new reform. *Harvard Educational Review*, 57, 1–22.

Simmons, P. E., Emory, A., Carter, T., Coker, R., Finnegan, B., Crockett, D., Richardson, L., Yager, R., Craven, J., Tillotson, J., Brunkhorst, H., Twiest, M., Hossain, K., Gallagher, J., Duggan-Haas, D., Parker, J., Cajas, F., Alshannag, Q., McGlamery, S., Krockover, J., Adams, P., Spector, B., LaPorta, T., James, B., Rearden, K., & Labuda, K. (1999). Beginning teachers: Beliefs and classroom actions. *Journal of Research in Science Teaching*, *36*, 930–954.

Smith, D. C. (1999). Changing our teaching: The role of pedagogical content knowledge in elementary science. In J. Gess-Newsome & N. G. Lederman (Eds.), *Examining pedagogical content knowledge* (pp. 163–197). Kluwer Academic Publishers.

Smith, D. C., & Neale, D. C. (1989). The construction of subject matter knowledge in primary science teaching. *Teaching and Teacher Education*, *5*, 1–20.

Smith, J. A. (1995). Semi-structured interviewing and qualitative analysis. In J. A. Smith, R. Harre, & L. Van Langenhove (Eds.), *Rethinking methods in psychology* (pp. 9–26). Sage.

Southerland, S. A., & Gess-Newsome, J. (1999). Preservice teachers' views of inclusive science teaching as shaped by images of teaching, learning, and knowledge. *Science Education*, *83*, 131–150.

Van Driel, J. H., & De Jong, O. (2015). Empowering chemistry teachers' learning: Practices and new challenges. In J. Garcia-Martinez & E. Serrano-Torregrosa (Eds.), *Chemistry education: Best practices, opportunities and trends* (pp. 99–121). Wiley-VCH.

Van Driel, J. H., De Jong, O., & Verloop, N. (2002). The development of preservice chemistry teachers' PCK. *Science Education*, *86*(4), 572–590.

Van Driel, J. H., De Jong, O., & Verloop, N. (2004). De Pedagogical Content Knowledge (PCK) van scheikundedocenten-in-opleiding over het gebruik van deeltjesmodellen [The Pedagogical Content Knowledge (PCK) of chemistry pre-service teachers about the use of particle models]. *Pedagogische Studiën*, *81*(4), 273–289.

Van Driel, J. H., Verloop, N., & De Vos, W. (1998). Developing science teachers' pedagogical content knowledge. *Journal of Research in Science Teaching*, *35*(6), 673–695.

Veal, W. R. (1998). *The evolution of pedagogical content knowledge in prospective secondary chemistry teachers* [Paper presentation]. The Annual Meeting of the National Association of Research in Science Teaching, San Diego.

Zanting, A., Verloop, N., Vermunt, J. D., & Van Driel, J. H. (1998). Explicating practical knowledge: An extension of mentor teachers' roles. *European Journal of Teacher Education*, *21*(1), 11–28.

Zuckerman, J. T. (1999). Student science teachers constructing practical knowledge from inservice science supervisors' stories. *Journal of Science Teacher Education*, *10*(3), 235–245.

Appendix I: Questionnaire about Phenomena and Particles in Chemistry Education

Below nine processes are listed which are included in the chemistry syllabus for specific grades

Item 1	Grade 9	Heating a beaker with 100 ml water to approximately 60°C
Item 2	Grade 9	Melting stearic acid
Item 3	Grade 9	Dissolving 5 grams of sugar in 100 ml of water at room temperature
Item 4	Grade 9	Burning 8 grams of solid magnesium
Item 5	Grade 10	Dissolving 5 grams of salt in 100 ml of water at room temperature
Item 6	Grade 10	Dissolving 0.10 mole pure acetic acid in 100 ml of water
Item 7	Grade 11	Mixing 50 ml of acetone with 50 ml of water
Item 8	Grade 11	Electrolysis of a solution of copper bromide
Item 9	Grade 12	Dissolving monochloromethane gas and sodium hydroxide in ethanol

Appendix IA: First Questionnaire

Question 1: Describe each process in terms of both phenomena and particles.

Question 2: Note for each process specific learning difficulties or preconceptions you expect for students of the respective grades.

Appendix IB: Second Questionnaire

Note for each process specific learning difficulties or preconceptions for students of the respective grades. You may refer to your experiences or observations during classroom teaching.

Appendix II: Questions during the Interviews with the Preservice Teachers

1. How would you – as a chemist – describe the relation between macroscopic phenomena and microscopic particles? Use examples to clarify your answer.
2. Why is it important to pay attention to this relationship: [a] during chemistry lessons at secondary schools, and [b] in institutional workshops in the teacher education program?
3. In what manner have you taught this relationship during your lessons?
4. What learning difficulties and conceptions of students did you observe during these lessons?
5. Which specific aspects of the *macro-micro* relationship did you find difficult to teach?

6. To what extent and in what way have your ideas about this relationship been influenced by: [a] reading and discussing the literature (i.e., the Harrison and Treagust (1996) article), [b] your experiences during classroom teaching, [c] discussions with your mentor, and [d] other factors?

Appendix III: Questions during the Interviews with the Mentors of the Preservice Teachers

1. In what manner(s) did the preservice teacher teach the *macro-micro* relationship during his or her lessons?
2. To what extent was the preservice teacher capable of diagnosing learning difficulties and conceptions of students with respect to this relationship?
3. What teaching difficulties did you observe in the preservice teacher in this respect?
4. To what extent and in what way did the preservice teacher develop his or her ideas about teaching this relationship? How was a development expressed in the way the preservice teacher taught and discussed his or her lessons?

CHAPTER 7

The Conceptions of Chemistry Teachers about Teaching and Learning in the Context of a Curriculum Innovation

1 How the Study Came About

As part of the broader innovation of upper secondary education in the Netherlands in the late 1990s, that led to the introduction of *Algemene Natuurwetenschappen* (see Chapter 5), the curricula of school subjects were critically examined. The curriculum for chemistry in grades 9–12 was identified as problematic, mainly because of the increasing number of students opting out of chemistry from grade 10 onwards and the decline of students pursuing chemistry in higher education. Wobbe De Vos demonstrated that since its introduction in 1863, this curriculum had always had an emphasis on fundamental chemical knowledge and skills. On the basis of an analysis of the historical development of the curriculum, Wobbe argued that it had become overcrowded and inconsistent due to numerous additions of topics to keep up with the explosive growth of chemical knowledge during the 20th century. As a result, he concluded, the current curriculum "confronts all students with theoretical abstractions […], detached from their daily lives and irrelevant for their lives as future citizens" (De Vos et al., 2002, p. 110). Wobbe's analysis was shared by practising chemistry teachers, some of whom had formed a group that published a paper in *NVOX*, the journal of the national science teacher association on 'dilemmas in school chemistry' (Eenhoorngroep, 1999). This article was discussed at meetings of chemistry teachers and triggered many responses. Although many teachers appeared to share concerns about the chemistry curriculum, their ideas about solutions and ways forward appeared to be rather diverse.

In this context, I became interested to conduct a large-scale investigation of the beliefs of chemistry teachers about the curriculum. First, I thought it was important to understand the beliefs that underpinned the ideas that teachers were advocating in the discussions. Second, only a small percentage of all chemistry teachers in the country was represented in the discussions. What was the silent majority thinking? I designed a project on teachers' curricular beliefs as a component of teacher practical knowledge. This project was similar to the study on teachers' knowledge of models and modelling in science (Chapter 4) in that the aim was to capture an aspect of their practical knowledge that was essential in the context of an innovation that was about to be implemented. It was more ambitious in that I planned to reach out to the entire population of chemistry teachers in upper secondary education in the country. Data from the Dutch Ministry of Education (October 2001) indicated that this population consisted of around 1000 individuals. I contacted NVON, the national science teacher association, and explained the project. They endorsed the study and granted me permission to use their member directory. This included 966 people who were registered as chemistry teachers. Although this sample included a number of retired chemistry teachers, it was considered the best approximation of the population.

Obviously, the size of the population had ramifications for the design of the study. It was decided to develop a questionnaire with (mostly) closed response items. To compensate for the limitations of an instrument like this in a study on teacher beliefs, the following measures were taken:
– Rather than attempting to capture teachers' belief systems comprehensively, the focus would be on two specific components, that is, (a) teachers' beliefs about the chemistry curriculum and (b) teachers' general beliefs about the goals of education. For both components, previous research and theoretical frameworks were available.
– The development process consisted of three steps: (1) an initial version of the questionnaire was sent out for feedback to five expert chemistry teachers; (2) a revised version of the questionnaire was piloted among a group of 112 in-service chemistry teachers, with a response rate of 56%; (3) a final version of the questionnaire was based on the qualitative and quantitative analysis of the pilot response.

Theoretically, the questionnaire was based on the concept 'curriculum emphases' which was introduced by Doug Roberts in the 1980s and defined as

> a coherent set of messages to the student about science, rather than within science. Such messages constitute objectives which go beyond learning the facts, principles, laws and theories of the subject matter itself – objectives which provide an answer to the student question: "Why am I learning this?" (Roberts, 1982, p. 245)

One of the PhD students of Wobbe De Vos, Berry Van Berkel, had used this concept in his study in the 1990s to analyse chemistry curricula. Van Berkel identified three curriculum emphases that focused on different aspects of chemistry, that is, fundamental theoretical chemical concepts (*Fundamental Chemistry*), the role of technological and societal issues in chemistry

(*Chemistry, Technology and Society*) and how knowledge in chemistry is developed in socio-historical contexts (*Knowledge Development in Chemistry*). Van Berkel's study demonstrated how the first emphasis dominated the Dutch chemistry curriculum and raised questions about whether the role of the other emphases should be enhanced and how that might be done (Van Berkel, 2001). I decided to include a section in the questionnaire on curricular beliefs, based on these three curriculum emphases.

Another study that inspired the design of the questionnaire was published in 1987 by Lantz and Kass, who reported that chemistry teachers developed quite different frameworks or "functional paradigms", even if they were teaching the same curriculum. These frameworks consisted of coherent sets of beliefs about their subject, teaching and learning, and students, and were aligned with their teaching behaviour (Lantz & Kass, 1987). This triggered a decision to include a section in the questionnaire on teachers' general education beliefs. For this purpose, I was attracted to a recently completed Dutch PhD study by Eddie Denessen (Radboud University, Nijmegen). Denessen's study built on previous studies in this field, going back to John Dewey. In line with Dewey, Denessen demonstrated that subject-matter oriented educational beliefs and learner-centred beliefs were not mutually exclusive ideological stances, but that people, teachers as well as the general public, typically combine elements of both ideologies in their belief systems. Denessen had developed a Likert-type scale questionnaire with 25 items, distributed over six scales, which seemed to complement the curriculum emphasis items very well. Whereas the latter all had an explicit focus on chemistry education, for instance, starting with a phrase such as 'I think it is an important task of chemical education …', the items from Denessen's questionnaire formulated educational goals and objectives in a general way, for instance, 'It is a task of the school to develop students' social skills'. I contacted Eddie and he was happy to approve the use of his questionnaire as a section in my instrument.

At this time, 2003, the use of email and online surveys was not as common as it is today, and I was anxious about excluding teachers by adopting an electronic approach to data collection. Therefore, it was decided to mail a hard copy of the questionnaire to the 966 people from the NVON directory whose addresses I was allowed to use. An envelope to return the questionnaire, free of charge, was included, as was a non-response form to allow addressees to indicate that they were not or no longer active as chemistry teachers in upper secondary education or didn't have the time or motivation to participate. In total, 495 (51%) people responded, of whom 348 (36%) completed the questionnaire, while 147 (15%) returned the non-response form.

2   Impact and Follow Up

Based on the general characteristics of the respondents, such as number of years of teaching experience, it was concluded that they constituted about one third of the entire population of Dutch chemistry teachers at the time and were representative of this population. Statistical analyses of the data, including principal component and correlation analysis, resulted in the identification of two distinct and independent belief structures: one that combined the curriculum emphasis *Fundamental Chemistry* with a subject-matter oriented educational belief, and another in which the curriculum emphasis *Chemistry-Technology-Society* was combined with a learner-centred educational belief. The curriculum emphasis *Knowledge Development in Chemistry* was associated with both these belief structures. It appeared that about three-quarters of the respondents combined elements of the two belief structures. However, a cluster analysis revealed two relatively small subgroups whose members' beliefs could be described more or less in terms of one of these two belief structures.

These findings were in line with previous research which had led to the identification of distinct belief structures, and groups of teachers combining these structures in hybrid ways (e.g., Denessen, 1999; Lantz & Kass, 1987; Van Driel & Verloop, 2002). An important question, obviously, is what such outcomes imply for the innovation, in this case the innovation of the Dutch chemistry curriculum for grades 10–12. To do justice to teachers' different belief structures, it was recommended that the new curriculum should preferably have a flexible organization, which provides teachers with the possibility to teach topics in a way that is consistent with the curriculum emphasis they value most. In this way, teachers' commitment to, and ownership of the new curriculum could grow, increasing the chances of a successful and enduring innovation.

The national committee that led the innovation defined the basic chemistry concepts that constituted the core of the revised curriculum. The committee mandated that these concepts should be taught in relation to contexts that students can relate to. This context-based approach indicated a shift from *Fundamental Chemistry* to *Chemistry-Technology-Society*. To implement the innovation, it was decided to organise the development, trialling and evaluation of context-based curriculum materials in regional networks of chemistry teachers. This was consistent with recommendations from the literature (see Chapter 2) which found that teachers with different belief structures and experiences can inspire and learn from each other, thus contributing to the simultaneous development of teachers' beliefs and practice. The process started in 2003/2004 and was concluded in 2008/2009.

As the project was a baseline study, it was concluded around the time the regional networks started. I wanted to disseminate the outcomes of the study among teachers and others who were involved in the innovation as soon as possible. Therefore, I wrote an article about the study that was published in NVOX (Van Driel, 2003). The main message was that a context-based approach to teaching chemistry doesn't imply a straitjacket and that the required shift from *Fundamental Chemistry* to *Chemistry-Technology-Society* can be realised in different ways for different chemical topics drawing on the expertise of teachers with different belief structures.

To publish the outcomes of the study in academic journals, it was decided to target three different audiences, using different selections of the data set and applying different approaches to data analysis. First, the article included in this chapter was written to reach out to a science education audience, aiming to contribute to the international discourse on reform in science education and the role of science teachers. By doing this, the article, published in the *International Journal of Science Education* (2005), followed up on the paper published in the *Journal of Research in Science Teaching* in 2001 (Van Driel et al., 2001; see Chapter 2). Second, an article was written for a general educational audience which focused on the role of teachers' beliefs in relation to educational innovation more broadly. In this paper, a sophisticated approach to data analysis was applied to reveal a deeper understanding of the subgroups or clusters of teachers with similar belief structures. For this purpose, I was assisted by a colleague from the faculty of Social and Behavioural Sciences at Leiden University who was an expert on a technique called PRINCALS. Without going into details, this technique reveals the data's underlying structure by examining both objects and variables in relation to each other within one analysis. The article was submitted to *Learning and Instruction*, the journal of the European Association for Research on Learning and Instruction (EARLI). After several rounds of revision, the paper was accepted and published in 2007 (Van Driel et al., 2007). Finally, a paper was submitted and accepted by the *Journal of Curriculum Studies* (Van Driel et al., 2008). In this article, the concept of curriculum emphasis was central and only the data from this section of the questionnaire were included. In the analysis, teachers' beliefs about the chemistry curriculum for two streams of upper secondary education were compared, which revealed that the curriculum emphasis *Knowledge development in chemistry* was considered much more important for pre-university education than for senior general secondary education.

All three papers have picked up substantial numbers of citations. The article in *Learning and Instruction* has been cited 244 times to date, the ones in *International Journal of Science Education* and *Journal of Curriculum Studies* 168 and

102 times, respectively. These numbers are possibly reflective of the size of the readership and the impact factors of the respective journals. As the home journal of EARLI, *Learning and Instruction* is distributed to its 2,700 members and has an impact factor well above 3. It's interesting to reflect on the publication strategy. Obviously, there is considerable overlap between the three articles, in particular in the sections on context, instrument development and data collection. The two articles that were published later both reference the 2005 article in *International Journal of Science Education*, for instance: "Elsewhere (Van Driel et al., 2005) we have reported about this study, focusing on teachers' domain specific beliefs which were operationalised in terms of the aforementioned curriculum emphases" (Van Driel et al., 2007, p. 159). It should be noted that these articles were submitted at a time (2006–2007) when publishers did not yet apply similarity checks. Had such checks been conducted, I assume it would have led to some communication with the editors about the nature of the overlap and, possibly, a requirement to reduce the similarity. Looking back, I admit that this publication strategy is akin to what is sometimes called 'salami slicing', that is, collecting data in one research project and reporting this (wholly or in part) in multiple publications. However, given the siloed nature of our research communities, I wish to argue that the study was worth reporting to different audiences who would not normally read each other's research journals. This is confirmed by the fact that the different articles were accepted by top journals in their respective fields, after having gone through a rigorous process of double-blind peer review. Also, the numbers of citations of all three articles demonstrate that many readers of those journals found the study relevant to their research.

I wasn't able to follow up this baseline study with a research project, for instance, to investigate the development processes in the teacher networks. Colleagues and PhD students from the Chemistry Education group at Utrecht University conducted a number of such projects, some of which included Onno De Jong (for instance, see Stolk et al., 2011). Nevertheless, the study was followed up in later years in a variety of ways. First, my German colleagues, Silvija Markic, Ingo Eilks and Bernd Ralle, reached out to me. They were interested to translate the questionnaire from Dutch into German to conduct a study among German in-service chemistry teachers. We decided to collaborate, and it was interesting to compare the outcomes of the German study (more than 1,100 respondents) to the Dutch study. For instance, it was found that *Chemistry-Technology-Society* was valued much less by the German teachers, which was considered problematic given that the debate in Germany also focused on increasing the relevance of chemistry education through enhancing the societal orientation by implementing context-based curricula (Markic et al., 2009).

Second, in 2005 I became one of the supervisors of Tamara Platteel who did a PhD project on the knowledge and beliefs of teachers of mother tongue education (L1). The study was inspired by a recent report of the Royal Netherlands Academy of Arts and Sciences which proposed two ways to improve secondary education in the Netherlands, that is, context-based education and the teacher as curriculum developer. Tamara was interested to explore these ideas with a group of eleven L1 teachers who developed curriculum materials in ways that were similar to those in the regional networks of chemistry teachers and with a similar objective, that is, increasing the relevance of mother tongue education by teaching it through contexts that are meaningful to students. Although the teachers expressed different ideas about context-based education, they shared the view that this approach would increase student motivation and engagement and, consequently, their own motivation (Platteel et al., 2013).

A few years later, a National Reform Committee for Biology Education proposed a context-based reform to secondary biology education. Working with my colleague Fred Janssen and PhD candidates, we developed and trialled a so-called bridging methodology to support biology teachers to gradually change their current practice towards a context-based teaching approach (Janssen, Westbroek, Doyle, & Van Driel, 2013). The gist of this methodology was making the innovation practical and attractive to implement for teachers while respecting and building on their existing practical knowledge. This work will be highlighted in Chapter 10.

Finally, and more recently, I co-supervised the PhD study of a Dutch chemistry teacher, Hans Vogelzang, who investigated the implementation of Scrum methodology to facilitate a context-based approach to teaching the revised chemistry curriculum (Vogelzang et al., 2020). This study explored the knowledge and practice of twelve chemistry teachers who had been teaching the revised chemistry curriculum for a number of years. Teachers were offered professional development to implement a novel methodology, called Scrum. Scrum capitalises on students working in autonomous groups on complex, real-world tasks while teachers scaffold their learning process mostly through formative assessments. Rather than focusing on the content of the curriculum, or the curriculum emphases, this study highlighted the role of teachers' pedagogical and didactical expertise which was key during the implementation process. Instead of subject matter expertise or teaching experience, pedagogical expertise distinguished teachers in terms of the effectiveness of their implementation of Scrum.

The Conceptions of Chemistry Teachers about Teaching and Learning in the Context of a Curriculum Innovation[1]

Jan H. van Driel, Astrid M. W. Bulte and Nico Verloop

Abstract

In this paper, we report on a study of the beliefs of chemistry teachers about the teaching and learning of chemistry in upper secondary education in the Netherlands. This study was conducted in the context of the planning of a national revision of the chemistry curriculum towards a context-based approach. Chemistry teachers' beliefs were investigated using a questionnaire that focused on both content-related ideas about the chemistry curriculum and general educational beliefs. The questionnaire was administered to a sample of Dutch chemistry teachers (n = 966), with a response of 348 (36%). On the basis of factor analysis, two distinct and independent belief structures were found: (1) a belief that combines the curriculum emphasis Fundamental Chemistry with a subject-matter-oriented educational belief, and (2) a belief that combines the curriculum emphasis Chemistry, Technology and Society with a learner-centred educational belief. In a cluster analysis, it was found that most teachers (about three-quarters of the respondents) combined elements of the two belief structures. However, two relatively small subgroups were identified whose beliefs could be described in terms of one of these two belief structures. Implications for the innovation of the chemistry curriculum are discussed.

Introduction

There is growing consensus that educational reform can only be successful if the knowledge, beliefs, and attitudes of the teachers who are involved in the reform are taken into account (Haney et al., 1996). In the past, however, the lack of success of many educational reform projects has often been attributed to the failure of teachers to implement the innovation according to the intentions of the curriculum developers. In such a view, the curriculum developers assume they know how the curriculum must be changed and expect teachers to adapt their classroom behaviour accordingly. However, when new curriculum materials are imposed upon teachers, they may implicitly and intuitively, or even explicitly, resist implementing such materials. Teachers will accept a new curriculum more easily when it is in accordance with learning goals they themselves personally value (Johnston, 1992) or when it is perceived by them as a possible solution to problems they currently experience. In other words, teachers interpret and integrate new curricular materials according to their own beliefs (Pajares, 1992). Therefore, Clark and Peterson concluded that 'teachers' belief systems can be ignored only at the innovators peril' (1986, p. 291). So far, studies of teachers' beliefs have focused mainly on aspects of general educational beliefs, such as beliefs about teaching and learning, children and the school (for example, Boulton-Lewis et al., 2001; Pratt, 1992). Little is known, however, about teachers' content-related beliefs, for instance, about subject matter, and the importance of teaching specific topics or curricular goals, and the relation of such content-related beliefs to general educational beliefs. Given the current emphasis on reform in science education (for example, Millar & Osborne, 1998; National Research Council, 1996) and the importance of teachers' beliefs, research on science teachers' content-related beliefs should serve to promote a better understanding of the content and the nature of such beliefs, which may contribute to the success of curriculum innovation projects.

The present study focused on teachers' beliefs about the teaching and learning of chemistry in the context of an innovation of the chemistry curriculum in upper secondary education in the Netherlands. This innovation was mainly inspired by the fact that the number of students who choose chemistry in upper secondary education has dropped substantially in the past decade. This problem has been explained in terms of a lack of perceived relevance of the content of the curriculum by the students (De Vos, 2001). A committee, appointed by the Ministry of Education, has been installed to design a blueprint for a new chemistry curriculum for the upper-level secondary school. The new curriculum should make chemistry more attractive and interesting for students, in particular, by connecting chemical knowledge with contexts that are relevant to them. Therefore, the new curriculum could have a context-based approach to the teaching of chemistry (cf. *ChemCom* in the US, or *Chemistry: The Salters Approach* in the UK – a review of these and similar approaches is provided by Bennett and Holman, 2002). In contrast to these new ideas, the chemistry curriculum for upper secondary education in the Netherlands has traditionally focused on the learning of fundamental chemical concepts and skills (De Vos et al., 2002). Although after 1980 attempts were made to pay more attention in the curriculum to applications of chemical knowledge in society (e.g., industrial chemistry), such contexts and their consequences for students' daily lives are still only dealt with in the margins. For the present discussion, it is important to note that the vast majority of chemistry teachers developed their professional classroom knowledge and beliefs within a tradition focusing on the acquisition of chemical concepts and skills.

The purpose of the work presented in this paper was to a gain a better understanding of the content and the nature of the beliefs of experienced chemistry teachers about the teaching and learning of chemistry. This is relevant given the aforementioned absence of studies in this area. Also, this work may contribute to the process of innovation of the chemistry curriculum in the Netherlands by taking the conceptions of chemistry teachers into account.

The Theoretical Basis Underlying the Empirical Study

The main idea underlying the present empirical study was that, within the whole of teachers' educational beliefs, beliefs about the curriculum, and the learning and teaching of particular subject matter, are connected with beliefs about teaching, learning, children, and the school in a more general sense (Calderhead, 1996, Pajares, 1992). To investigate teachers' beliefs specifically with respect to the chemistry curriculum, we adopted the concept of curriculum emphases (Roberts, 1982, 1988) as a theoretical basis. In addition, a pedagogical framework based on the ideas of Dewey was used (Shen, 1997) to explore these specific beliefs in relation to chemistry teachers' general educational beliefs. Both theoretical frameworks are discussed below.

The Curriculum Emphasis Concept

By analysing North American science curricula that were in use over a period of 80 years, Roberts and coworkers identified seven different so-called curriculum emphases. Roberts defined a *curriculum emphasis* as a consistently related set of explicit or implicit meta-lessons, in which a substantial sequence of science topics are taught. The term 'meta-lesson' refers to objectives of the science curriculum, such as '… to promote understanding of [...] processes in scientific enquiry such as observing, hypothesizing, classifying, experimenting, and interpreting data' (Roberts, 1988, p. 31). Roberts stressed that the number of seven curriculum emphases is not a historically, let alone theoretically, fixed number. New emphases have been developed since (Fensham, 1998) and emphases have been combined under a new umbrella. Van Berkel (2001), elaborating on the work of Roberts in the context of analysing chemistry curricula, limited the number of curriculum emphases from seven to three. In the present study, the categorization of Van Berkel et al. was adopted, albeit with slightly different labels. These three emphases are discussed in the following.

The first curriculum emphasis was called 'Fundamental Chemistry' (FC) and is identical with what Van Berkel (2001) labelled 'Normal Chemistry Education'. The meta-lesson corresponding to this emphasis may be summarized as follows: theoretical notions, in particular about the corpuscular nature of matter, are taught first, because it is believed that such notions can later on provide a basis for understanding the natural world, and are needed for the students' future education. The second emphasis, 'Chemistry, Technology, and Society' (CTS) implies an explicit role of technological and societal issues within the chemistry curriculum. The meta-lesson implied by this emphasis is that students should learn to communicate and make decisions about social issues involving chemical aspects. Examples of such issues can be found in textbooks, albeit often in the margins. Nevertheless, it may be expected that this emphasis plays a role, at least in some chemistry teachers' beliefs. The third and final curriculum emphasis, 'Knowledge Development in Chemistry' (KDC), corresponds with what Van Berkel (2001) labelled 'History and Philosophy of Science'. This emphasis is connected with the meta-lesson that students should learn how knowledge in chemistry is developed in socio-historical contexts, so that they learn to see chemistry as a culturally determined system of knowledge, which is constantly developing.

These three curriculum emphases are illustrated in Box 1.

General Educational Beliefs

Research on general educational beliefs has a long history. Many scholars in this area have distinguished between two prototypic ideologies, one of which is sometimes called 'traditional', 'transmission-oriented', or 'subject-matter oriented' (Billig et al., 1988; Shen, 1997). On the other hand, a 'progressive' or 'learner-centred' ideology is usually considered, the origins of which, at least in the North-American literature, are commonly attributed to the work of John Dewey (Shen, 1997). An important element of the discussion in the literature concerns the relation between these two ideologies: are they to be considered as two opposite extremes of the same dimension, or do these ideologies represent two independent dimensions? The first idea implies that educational beliefs can be placed at some position on a scale ranging from, for example, 'subject-matter oriented' at one extreme to 'learner-centred' at the other end. The latter idea, however, implies that the two ideologies are not mutually exclusive, but that people can combine elements of both ideologies; that is, they can, in principle, support both ideologies. Dewey, indeed, 'held that the two dimensions could be harmonious' (Shen, 1997, p. 343). In a recent study in the Netherlands (Denessen, 1999), it was found that many people held to a large extent both subject-matter oriented beliefs and learner-centred beliefs.

> **Box 1. Example to illustrate the three curriculum emphases**
>
> Consider the following chemistry topic: calculations in chemistry, more specifically, the principle that two chemicals react in fixed mass ratios and that during such a chemical reaction the total mass is conserved. This topic can be treated in completely different situations with completely different meta-lessons.
>
> *Fundamental chemistry:* Within this emphasis, an approach could, for instance, be as follows. The textbook and/or the teacher provide the students with the theory; that is, the fixed ratios in which chemicals react. The following assignment may be formulated for students: 'Use these ratios and perform the textbook calculations'. Two types of (implicit) messages or meta-lessons may get across. Firstly, students will receive the theory as something that is correct and true. Secondly, students may feel that this is what needs to be learned in order to be successful in education and proceed to a higher level. Although such messages are seldom explicitly expressed in curriculum guidelines, many science curricula appear to be founded on these emphases.
>
> *Chemistry, Technology, and Society:* Within this emphasis, a possible approach could include a classroom discussion about the safety regulations for the use of food preservatives; for example, 'How much sulphite is required to preserve white wine, and how much is safe?'. Students also investigate the properties of chemicals and search for explanations. This time, however, they do this in the light of a socio-scientific question. Students now receive the following message about the school subject: there is a socially and/or personally relevant question, and chemical knowledge is needed to find an answer. Roberts called this emphasis 'Science, Technology, Decisions', and it received a great deal of attention as 'Science-Technology-Society' (STS) in the late 1970s and early 1980s (Solomon & Aikenhead, 1994).
>
> *Knowledge Development in Chemistry*: An approach within this emphasis may consist of students doing experiments and finding out that the same 'law' applies in different circumstances. Students carry out the experiments and calculations to discover themselves the same chemical foundations as Lavoisier found in the eighteenth century. An implicit metalesson of this approach is to show students that, just as they themselves did, chemists throughout history were able to discover certain laws that can be considered important foundations of present-day chemistry. Roberts (1982) described such an emphasis as 'The Self as Explainer', and identified this emphasis from the analysis of different textbooks over the years.

Context and Research Questions

At the start of the present study, the following information was available about the problems chemistry teachers perceived while teaching the present upper secondary chemistry curriculum and their beliefs about how to solve those problems. First, during a national conference of chemistry teachers in 1999, participants (n = 164) were asked to respond to several statements. It appeared that they supported the idea of reducing the number of (theoretical) topics in the curriculum, thus trying to make the curriculum less overloaded. At the same time, they expressed the desire to pay more attention to the relation between chemistry and society. In addition, they also wished to have more opportunities for laboratory work, aiming at the development of students' inquiry skills (Pilot & Van Driel, 2001).

Next, some chemistry teachers expressed their concerns about the upper secondary chemistry curriculum during meetings of regional networks (1999–2001). These teachers appeared to consider the present chemistry curriculum to be problematic. However, they analysed the problem in different ways, and consequently suggested different solutions. For instance, some teachers advocated reform of the chemistry curriculum in close conjunction with similar reforms of the curricula for physics and biology, thus trying to strengthen the connections between the curricula of the individual disciplines. In this context, it is important to note that, in the Netherlands, the national curriculum traditionally contains physics, chemistry, and biology as separate subjects. In 1998, however, an integrated approach to teaching science in upper secondary education was implemented in the national curriculum through the introduction of Public Understanding of Science as a new, separate subject, alongside the traditional disciplines of physics, chemistry, and biology (De Vos & Reiding, 1999). Since then, a substantial number of chemistry teachers has obtained a qualification to teach Public Understanding of Science, and, subsequently, has taught this subject.

Finally, in an ongoing discussion in a Dutch science teachers' journal (Eenhoorngroep, 1999; Kerkstra & Jansen, 2001; Van Driel, 2000), some chemistry teachers argued that a shift is needed in chemical education from focusing on cognitive outcomes to a more holistic approach, which also addresses students' affective skills and attitudes.

Most teachers who participated in the aforementioned discussions seemed to support the idea that a change in upper secondary chemical education is necessary. However, they did not advocate starting a large-scale innovation of chemical education. This reluctance may be explained by problems of teacher workload: many teachers argued that they needed more time and facilities to do their work adequately. In this context, a reform project was considered an extra burden on their already busy scheme (Pilot & Van Driel, 2001).

To obtain a more comprehensive and systematic understanding of the existing beliefs of the population of chemistry teachers in upper secondary education in the Netherlands, it was decided to conduct a survey among this population. The following research questions guided the empirical study:

1. What beliefs do chemistry teachers in upper secondary education in the Netherlands hold with respect to the teaching and learning of chemistry in terms of the curriculum emphases 'Fundamental chemistry', 'Chemistry, technology, and society', and 'Knowledge development in chemistry'?
2. How do these teachers' specific beliefs relate to their general educational beliefs about teaching, students, and the school?
3. Can subgroups of chemistry teachers be distinguished that are characterized by different belief patterns, and, if so, are the subgroups related to specific background variables (e.g. years of experience, prior education, academic background) of the teachers within certain subgroups?

It was expected that the answers to these questions could be helpful in taking teachers' existing beliefs into account when developing a new chemistry curriculum for upper secondary education, and in the planning of future staff-development programmes related to this innovation.

Design

Instrument

As we were interested in investigating the beliefs of the *whole* population of chemistry teachers in the country, a large-scale survey was necessary to answer the research questions. For this purpose, it was decided to design a questionnaire. Obviously, this type of instrument has certain shortcomings in investigating teachers' beliefs (see, for example, Kagan, 1990). In particular, a questionnaire study is limited in taking into account the complexity of people's personalities and their belief systems (Pajares, 1992). Given our research questions and aims, however, which implied a large number of teachers to be involved in the study, it seemed the most attractive option. The choice for this design was supported by the following: (1) the availability of theoretical frameworks and previous studies (Denessen, 1999; Van Berkel, 2001), which seemed useful to investigate teachers' beliefs, both with respect to the chemistry curriculum and to education in a general sense; (2) the fact that, in the present context, there was already some information available about chemistry teachers' conceptions (see earlier); and (3) the fact that, in the research literature, there are many examples of studies on teacher beliefs using questionnaires (for example, Boulton-Lewis et al., 2001; Haney et al., 1996).

The design of the questionnaire could thus be based on the theoretical and practical information already mentioned. The questionnaire consisted of three parts: (1) a series of questions focusing on teachers' experience, prior education and academic background, and qualifications; (2) a series of items consisting of statements about the teaching and learning of chemistry; and (3) a series of items consisting of general statements about teaching, learning, students, and the school. Part 1 included a question on whether the respondent had a formal qualification to teach 'PublicUnderstanding of Science'. Since this qualification could be obtained through an inservice course only, teachers with this qualification also had experiences teaching 'Public Understanding of Science'. This question was included because it was expected that such experiences could have an impact on teachers' ideas about teaching chemistry. This expectation was based on the different emphases in the syllabus for 'Public Understanding of Science' compared with the emphases in the existing chemistry curriculum (De Vos & Reiding, 1999).

The design process consisted of three phases. A first draft of the questionnaire was designed by the authors. Part 2 of the questionnaire focused on the three curriculum emphases discussed earlier (FC, CTS, and KDC). For each of these emphases, a scale of 9–11 items was initially constructed focusing on the goals of teaching chemistry in upper secondary education (cf. A-level chemistry in the UK). Our idea was that, in a teacher's understanding, a curriculum emphasis is characterized by trying to achieve certain objectives. In Roberts' terms, such objectives reflect a set of meta-lessons, which are indicative of a specific curriculum emphasis. Examples of items in each of the three scales are presented in Table 7.1. Each item had to be scored on a five-point scale, ranging from 1 'completely disagree', through 3 'do not agree, but do not disagree either', to 5 'completely agree'. In addition, a sixth option ('Not applicable') could be chosen.

The items of Part 3 were taken from an existing instrument, which was developed and tested to investigate general educational beliefs (Denessen, 1999). This instrument consisted of six scales: Career, Discipline, Product, Pedagogy, Democracy, and Process. A description of these scales, including examples of items, is presented in Table 7.2. Again, each item had to be scored on the same five-point scale. There was also a sixth option ('Have never thought about this'). In his study, Denessen (1999) found that high scores on the Career, Discipline, and Product scales were typical of an educational orientation focusing on subject matter. On the other hand, high scores on the Pedagogy, Democracy, and Process scales were associated with a learner-centred educational orientation.

TABLE 7.1 Examples of items in Part 2 of the questionnaire

Fundamental Chemistry (FC)
  It is the task of chemical education to prepare students for further education in chemistry or a related domain, such as pharmacy or medicine
  Knowledge of acids and bases is important, in my view, for students because these are fundamental concepts within chemistry
  I think it is an important task of chemical education to provide students with an understanding of the structure and the internal coherence of chemical knowledge

Chemistry, Technology, and Society (CTS)
  I think it is an important task of chemical education to ensure that students learn how chemical knowledge is applied to develop new products, such as plastics and medicines
  I think it is an important task of chemical education to ensure that students learn how to use chemical knowledge to make personal choices; in particular, concerning food and health
  I think that the objectives of chemical education should be based on an analysis of situations in society in which chemistry plays an important role

Knowledge Development in Chemistry (KDC)
  I think it is an important task of chemical education to ensure that students gain insight into the historical development of chemical knowledge
  I think it is an important task of chemical education to ensure that students learn that chemists design and use models as tools to solve theoretical and practical problems
  I think it is an important task of chemical education to ensure that students come to understand that chemical knowledge is never definitive, but can always be changed

---

This version of the questionnaire was then sent to five expert chemistry teachers. These teachers were chosen because they were actively involved, for instance, in organizing the annual meeting of chemistry teachers, in designing and presenting new educational materials, or in a committee on the national examination of chemistry. These five teachers were asked to comment on the general structure of the questionnaire and to give comments and suggestions regarding specific items. Their responses varied in length and detail, but, in general, were of a positive and supportive nature. All made many specific comments concerning the types of items, and their formulation. Each teacher's response was used to make changes in the questionnaire, specifically in Part 2.

TABLE 7.2 Scales and examples of items in Part 3 of the questionnaire

Scale	Example of an item
Career represents the belief that education serves mainly to prepare children for a future career	If children want to achieve something later in life, they have to learn a lot now at school
Discipline is focused on obedience, order, and the will to work on the part of the students	In school, students should obey the teachers
Product emphasizes the importance of achievement and good marks	Giving students marks is a good way to stimulate them to learn
Pedagogy concerns the importance of students' development as people, both as individuals and in society	It is a task of the school to develop students' social skills
Democracy acknowledges the students' opinions and desires	I think it is normal for students to criticise a teacher
Process emphasizes the importance of the learning process, for instance, in autonomous and cooperative settings	Students can learn much from each other

In particular, it was decided to delete items that were misunderstood or ambiguous. The formulation of almost every item in Part 2 was changed.

In the second phase of the design process, the revised version of the questionnaire was piloted. For this purpose, a sample of 112 chemistry teachers was composed by selecting at random about one-half of the participants in the 2002 annual meeting of chemistry teachers (Woudschoten, the Netherlands). This version of the questionnaire consisted of the same three parts and was mailed to this sample with an accompanying letter explaining the purpose and the procedure of the pilot study. Teachers were asked to answer all items in the questionnaire and to add their comments and suggestions, both at a general level and about specific items. Finally, they were asked to mention how much time it had taken to complete the questionnaire.

In the third phase, the results of the pilot study were used to revise the questionnaire once again. The useful response (63 respondents; 56%) was analysed both statistically and in a qualitative manner. The former concerned analysis of descriptive statistics (frequencies, means, standard deviation, missing values) and the reliability of the scales (homogeneity, Cronbach's alpha). One item from the FC scale in Part 2 received so much support (mean score, 4.6) that it was concluded that almost all teachers (completely) agreed with this statement. This statement was thus eliminated from the final version. For all scales, the values for Cronbach's alpha ranged from 0.71 to 0.78 and were considered satisfactory. Thus, it was decided to use the same scales in the final version of the questionnaire. However, on the basis of analysis of homogeneity, focusing on the item-total correlations and on the effect on the value of Cronbach's alpha of deleting items, five items in the scales of Part 2 appeared to not fit well in their scales (i.e. Cronbach's alpha increased on the deletion of these items by more than 0.02; item-total correlations fell below 0.25), and were subsequently removed from the questionnaire. The qualitative analysis focused on the comments and suggestions written by the respondents. One item received comments from five respondents; two other items were criticised by four respondents. All in all, 12 items in Part 2 were changed, because the original formulation was either ambiguous or unclear. As for Part 3, it was concluded that it was not necessary to make changes in the scales or the individual items as they had been designed by Denessen (1999).

Sample

The National Association of Science Education in the Netherlands (NVON) included 966 members who were registered as teachers of chemistry in Spring 2003. After contacting the board of the association, it appeared that the large majority (estimated at approximately 75–80%) of these members were actively teaching chemistry in upper secondary education. Compared with the total number of (qualified) chemistry teachers working in upper secondary education in the Netherlands (n = 1001, according to data from the Ministry of Education, 1 October 2001), it was concluded that the sample of 966 association members contained a large enough number of active chemistry teachers in upper secondary education to be considered a representative sample of all such teachers in the country. For that reason, it was decided to mail the final version of the questionnaire to this sample. However, as this sample also contained association members who taught chemistry at lower levels of secondary education, and members who formerly taught chemistry but had moved to other jobs, or retired, a non-response form was designed to ensure that the respondents had (recent) experience in teaching chemistry in upper secondary education (see later).

The questionnaire was mailed in April 2003 with an accompanying letter, in which addressees were invited to return the questionnaire. In the letter, attention was focused on the current discussion about the curriculum for chemical education, mentioning the ministerial committee that was preparing a blueprint for a new curriculum. It was argued in the letter that it is important for this innovation for teachers' voices to be heard. In this respect, the approval by NVON of this study was mentioned, as was the fact that NVON had agreed to provide its directory of chemistry teachers for the mailing of the questionnaire. Finally, the letter referred to the possibility that people could not, or would not, return the questionnaire. In that case, they were asked to return a non-response form, which contained four possible reasons for not responding – (a) I am not a chemistry teacher in upper secondary education, (b) These days, I am far removed from the practice of chemical education, (c) I don't have time to answer the questions, (d) I never participate in studies such as this – plus an open alternative ('Other reason, that is ...').

Data analysis

For the items of Part 1, only descriptive analyses were performed, to characterize the composition of the response group in terms of years of teaching experience, prior education, academic background, and qualifications.

For the items of Parts 2 and 3, mean scores, standard deviations, and missing values were investigated. Next, the mean scores and the standard deviations of the scales were computed. Following this, each scale was subjected to an analysis of homogeneity, focusing on the item-total correlations, the value of Cronbach's alpha, and the effect on this value of deleting items. The results thus obtained with respect to the scales in Part 2 were used to answer the first research question.

Next, relations between the scales within Part 2 and between the scales across Parts 2 and 3 of the questionnaire were explored. For this purpose, Pearson correlations were calculated and a principal component analysis was conducted. The results of these analyses are relevant to the second research question.

To answer the third research question, first, a series of t-tests were performed to investigate whether the teachers' scores on the scales differed significantly with respect to teaching experience, prior education, academic background, and qualifications. Levene statistics were incorporated to test for equality of variances. Next, hierarchical cluster analysis was carried out on the group of respondents as a whole to explore whether they could be divided into homogeneous subgroups with distinctive scores on the scales in Parts 2 and 3 of the questionnaire. Squared Euclidian distances were calculated as a measure of distance, and Ward's method was applied as a clustering method. This was followed by a series of analyses of variance to investigate whether cluster averages were significantly different on the scales in Parts 2 and 3, incorporating Levene statistics as well as Tukey Honest Significant Difference tests for multiple comparisons. Finally, analyses of crosstabs were performed to check whether the teachers were distributed evenly over clusters with respect to teaching experience, prior education, academic background, and qualifications. All statistical analyses were performed using SPSS software, version 11.0.

Results and Discussion

Respondents

In total, 495 persons responded (51%). The useful response of people who completed the questionnaire was 348 (36%). On the other hand, 147 (15%) respondents did *not* fill out the questionnaire, but returned the non-response form instead. As expected, the sample contained a fairly large number of people who did not belong to the target group of the present study (i.e., active chemistry teachers in upper secondary education): 65 persons indicated that they were not chemistry teachers (in upper secondary education), whereas 45 people considered themselves too far removed from the practice of chemical education (e.g., due to retirement, or having moved to other jobs). Only nine people indicated that they had either no time to participate, or never participated in such studies. Overall, the useful response (n = 348) concerned about one-third of the entire target group of chemistry teachers working in upper secondary education in the Netherlands, that is compared with the data of the Ministry of Education, according to which the total number of such teachers was 1001 (October 2001).

The answers to Part 1 of the questionnaire are summarized in Table 7.3. From this table, it can be seen that the large majority of the respondents (more than 90%) had an academic background in chemistry, or chemical engineering, mostly holding a degree at master's level (81%) or Ph.D. level (12%). Almost all respondents were (formally) qualified to teach chemistry at the upper secondary level; about one-third were also qualified to teach 'Public Understanding of Chemistry'. The finding that 72% of the respondents had more than 15 years of teaching experience seems in accordance with data from the Ministry of Education, which indicated that the mean number of years of teaching experience of chemistry teachers in the Netherlands is 18 years (standard deviation 11 years).

Initial Analyses (Parts 2 and 3)

On the basis of examination of the mean values and standard deviations of individual items, it was decided that the whole set of items was suitable for further analyses, without elimination of any individual item. To explore the adequacy of the scales in Parts 2 and 3 of the questionnaire, these scales were subjected to a series of analyses of reliability and correlation. Analysis of homogeneity

TABLE 7.3　General characteristics of the respondents

Item	Options	Number	Percentage
Experience as a chemistry teacher in upper secondary education	< 1 year	5	1
	1–5 years	33	10
	5–15 years	57	16
	> 15 years	250	72
Highest level of prior education	Ph.D.	40	12
	Master of science	283	81
	Other/unknown	25	7
Major in prior education	Chemistry	261	75
	Chemical engineering	51	15
	Other/unknown	36	10
Formal qualification to teach chemistry in upper secondary education	Yes	332	95
	Other qualification	10	3
	No qualification	6	2
Formal qualification to teach 'Public Understanding of Science'	Yes	121	35
	No	225	65

TABLE 7.4　Mean score, standard deviations, and values of Cronbach's alpha for the scales in Part 2

Scale	Number of items	Mean score	Standard deviation	Cronbach's alpha
FC	8	3.9	0.5	0.73
KDC	7	3.6	0.5	0.72
CTS	8	3.8	0.5	0.71

revealed no items, in any scale, which fitted problematically. Most values of Cronbach's alpha ranged from 0.69 to 0.73 (see Table 7.4 and, later, Table 7.6), with one exception of 0.54 for a scale with only three items ('Product'). These values were considered adequate, considering the small number of items for some scales (Pedhazur & Pedhazur Schmelkin, 1991, pp. 109–110).

Research Question 1: What Beliefs do Chemistry Teachers Hold about the Teaching and Learning of Chemistry?

To answer the first research question, the emphasis was on the results concerning the scales in Part 2 of the questionnaire. For this purpose, the respondents' scores on each scale were divided by the number of items per scale. For every scale, mean scores and standard deviations were then calculated. In Table 7.4, the number of items per scale, the mean scores and their standard deviations, plus the internal consistencies (Cronbach's alpha) of these scales, are shown.

From this table, it is evident that all three scales obtained mean scores between 3.5 and 4.0, indicating that, on the whole, all three curriculum emphases were valued in a positive sense by the respondents. Although all the differences between the mean scores were statistically significant, these differences were small in an absolute sense. The highest score (3.9) was received by the curriculum emphasis FC. As said before, this emphasis, which places great importance on the learning of fundamental concepts, such as acids and bases, and skills, such as making calculations involving concentrations or amounts of substances, has been dominant in the curriculum of chemical education in the Netherlands, as well as in many other countries over the world. There was almost equally strong support for the other two curriculum emphases; that is, CTS (mean score 3.8), and KDC (3.6). This indicates that the respondents considered it also important to pay attention to the 'meta-lessons' implied by these two emphases; that is, that students should learn to communicate and make decisions about social issues involving chemical aspects, and that they should learn to see chemistry as a culturally determined system of knowledge, which is constantly developing. These mean scores concern the group of respondents as a whole. Obviously, it is possible that subgroups with more distinctively different scores on these emphases exist. This is discussed later (see research question 3). First, to explore possible relationships between the opinions on the three curriculum emphases, the Pearson correlations between the scales in Part 2 were calculated. The results are summarized in Table 7.5.

From this table, it appears that the correlations both between the KDC and the CTS scales, and between the FC scale and the KDC scale were significant at the 0.01 level, whereas the correlation between the FC scale and the CTS scale was almost zero. These results suggest that the FC and CTS scales refer to different dimensions of teachers' beliefs about the curriculum for chemical education, whereas the KDC scale may have a relationship with both dimensions. In the following, we discuss the relationships between the scales in more detail.

TABLE 7.5   Pearson correlations between the scales in Part 2 and Part 3

	FC	KDC	CTS	Career	Discipline	Product	Pedagogy	Democracy	Process
FC	1								
KDC	0.24**	1							
CTS	0.04	0.35**	1						
Career	0.39**	0.20**	0.11**	1					
Discipline	0.43**	0.20**	0.11*	0.58**	1				
Product	0.30**	0.18**	0.07	0.51**	0.39**	1			
Pedagogy	0.07	0.18**	0.31**	0.13*	0.24**	0.08	1		
Democracy	0.06	0.16**	0.21**	-0.02	-0.02	-0.01	0.36**	1	
Process	0.02	0.25**	0.37**	-0.09	-0.01	-0.07	0.45**	0.58**	1

*Correlation was significant at the 0.05 level (two-tailed). **Correlation was significant at the 0.01 level (two-tailed).

Research Question 2: How Do Teachers' Content-Specific Beliefs Relate to Their General Educational Beliefs?

In this subsection, the results with respect to teachers' general educational beliefs, as revealed by their scores on the scales in Part 3 of the questionnaire, are discussed first. Again, the respondents' scores on each scale in Part 3 were divided by the number of items per scale. For every scale, mean scores and standard deviations were then calculated. In Table 7.6, the number of items per scale, the mean scores and their standard deviations, plus the internal consistencies (Cronbach's alpha) of these scales, are presented.

From Table 7.6, it can be seen that the mean scores on the Pedagogy, Democracy, and Process scales were substantially higher, ranging from 3.9 to 4.2, than the mean scores on the three other scales in this table, which ranged from 3.3 to 3.8. In other words, the respondents seemed to favour a learner-centred educational orientation. Next, the results of this part of the questionnaire were compared with those of Denessen (1999) – in particular to check whether scores on the Career, Discipline, and Product scales were strongly related to each other, and whether the same was true for scores on the Pedagogy, Democracy, and Process scales. For this purpose, Pearson correlations were calculated (see Table 7.5), from which it followed that, indeed, the correlations between the scales followed a pattern similar to that in Denessen's study. However, the Pedagogy scale, apart from being rather strongly correlated to Democracy and

THE CONCEPTIONS OF CHEMISTRY TEACHERS 215

TABLE 7.6 Mean score, standard deviations, and values of Cronbach's alpha for the scales in Part 3

Scale	Number of items	Mean score	Standard deviation	Cronbach's alpha
Career	4	3.6	0.7	0.84
Discipline	5	3.8	0.5	0.73
Product	3	3.3	0.6	0.54
Pedagogy	6	3.9	0.5	0.71
Democracy	3	3.9	0.6	0.69
Process	4	4.2	0.5	0.69

Process (0.36 and 0.45, respectively), also appeared to have a moderate correlation with the Career and Discipline scales (0.13 and 0.24, respectively).

Table 7.5 also indicates moderate to strong relationships between the Career, Discipline, and Product scales on the one hand, and the curriculum emphasis scales of FC and KDC on the other. In addition, Career and Discipline were also significantly correlated with CTS (both 0.11). On the other hand, the Pedagogy, Democracy, and Process scales were moderately to strongly correlated with KDC and CTS, respectively, but all had a correlation of almost zero with FC.

To explore the relationships between content-specific beliefs and general educational beliefs in more detail, a principal component analysis was performed. The first two extracted components had Eigenvalues higher than 1.0, and together explained 53% of total variance. The rotated component matrix is presented in Table 7.7.

This table indicates that the CTS, Pedagogy, Democracy, and Process scales had high loadings (0.63–0.83) on the *second* component and low loadings (0.16 at a maximum) on the *first* component, whereas the opposite was true for the FC, Career, Discipline, and Product scales. The only scale with about equally high scores (0.35 and 0.46, respectively) on both components was KDC. We therefore interpreted the two components in terms of two different belief structures: (1) a belief that combines the curriculum emphasis CTS with a learner-centred educational belief, and (2) a belief that combines the curriculum emphasis FC with a subject-matter oriented educational belief. The curriculum emphasis KDC could not be assigned exclusively to one of these belief structures. As is evident from the factor loadings, these two beliefs may, to a large extent, be considered independent of each other. This implies that teachers' scores on the scales that represent one belief were not related to their scores on the scales representative of the other belief.

TABLE 7.7 Rotated component matrix*

	Scale	Component 1	Component 2
Part 2	FC	**0.68**	0.07
	KDC	**0.35**	**0.46**
	CTS	0.11	**0.63**
Part 3	Career	**0.82**	0.01
	Discipline	**0.79**	0.10
	Product	**0.71**	−0.01
	Pedagogy	0.16	**0.69**
	Democracy	−0.09	**0.74**
	Process	−0.12	**0.83**

Note: All scores higher than 0.3 in bold. *Rotation method: Varimax with Kaiser normalization.

Research Question 3: Can Subgroups of Chemistry Teachers with Different Belief Patterns Be Identified?

First, whether the scores on the various scales were related to teachers' variables, such as years of teaching experience, prior education, academic background, and qualifications, was investigated. For this purpose, a series of t-tests were performed, incorporating Levene statistics for equality of variances. The results of these analyses are summarized as follows:

1. The scores of teachers with more than 15 years of teaching experience (n = 250) were not significantly different from those of teachers with 1–5 years of teaching experience (n = 33) – with the exception of their mean scores on the Product scale, where the latter group scored significantly *lower* (2.9) than did the more experienced group (3.4).
2. The scores of teachers with a Ph.D. (n = 40) were not significantly different from those of teachers with a master's in science (n = 283) on any of the scales.
3. The scores of teachers with a major in chemistry (n = 261) were not significantly different from those of teachers with a major in chemical engineering (n = 51) on any of the scales.
4. Teachers who only taught chemistry (n = 225) scored significantly *higher* than teachers who also had a qualification to teach 'Public Understanding of Science' (n = 121) on the curriculum emphasis CTS: 3.8 versus 3.7. On all other scales, the scores of these two subgroups were not significantly different.

Next, we investigated whether subgroups could be identified within the group of respondents that corresponded to the two belief structures described earlier. Out of the sample of 348 respondents, 325 (93%) appeared to have completed all the items comprising the nine scales. These 325 respondents were entered in a hierarchical cluster analysis. In such an analysis, no *a priori* criterion is used to divide the respondents into clusters. Instead, similarities between the respondents' answer patterns are analysed in order to group individual respondents into clusters. Ward's method, which is designed to optimize the minimum variance within clusters (Aldenderfer & Blashfield, 1984), was used as a clustering method. On inspection of the dendogram, focusing on the increase of the squared Euclidean distance in each stage of the agglomeration process, a four-cluster solution was chosen (Norušis/SPSS Inc. 1992). The respondents were distributed among these three clusters as follows: 147 were classified as cluster 1 (45% of the 325 respondents used in this analysis), 94 teachers formed cluster 2 (29%), 48 were grouped together in cluster 3 (15%), whereas the remaining 36 respondents (11%) were assigned to cluster 4.

The mean scores of these four clusters on the scales in Part 2 and Part 3 are presented in Table 7.8. This table reveals that the mean scores of the two largest clusters (clusters 1 and 2) followed the same pattern, although the scores of the largest cluster (cluster 1) were substantially lower on all scales than those of cluster 2. These two subgroups did not display a distinct preference for one of the curriculum emphases, nor could they be characterized as having either a subject-matter or a learner-centred orientation. Members of cluster 2 had relatively high scores on *all* scales, whereas the scores of members of cluster 1 were about 0.1–0.2 lower on all the scales than the mean scores of the whole sample (see final row of Table 7.8; note that some scores are slightly different

TABLE 7.8 Mean scores of the clusters on the scales in Part 2 and Part 3

Cluster	n	FC/subject-matter orientation				CTS/learner-centred orientation				
		FC	Career	Discipline	Product	CTS	Pedagogy	Democracy	Process	KDC
1	147	3.9	3.4	3.7	3.1	3.6	3.8	3.9	4.1	3.5
2	94	**4.2**	**4.1**	**4.2**	**3.7**	**4.1**	**4.2**	**4.2**	**4.5**	**4.0**
3	48	*3.4*	*2.9*	*3.2*	*3.0*	4.0	4.0	4.2	**4.6**	3.6
4	36	**4.2**	3.8	3.9	3.5	*3.1*	*3.5*	*3.4*	*3.8*	3.6
Total	325	3.9	3.6	3.8	3.3	3.8	3.9	4.0	4.3	3.6

Note: Relatively high scores are in bold; relatively low scores are in italics.

from those in Table 7.6 because not all respondents were involved in the cluster analysis).

The other two clusters that were formed during cluster analysis were not only smaller, but seemed to have a more specific score pattern. Cluster 3 had relatively *high* mean scores both on the curriculum emphasis CTS and on the scales that are representative of a learner-centred orientation (i.e., Pedagogy, Democracy, and Process), whereas the members of this cluster had relatively *low* scores on FC, and on Career, Discipline, and Product; that is, the scales representative of a subject-matter orientation. For cluster 4, the situation was the opposite. The differences between the mean scores of clusters 3 and 4 were statistically significant for all scales, with the exception of the scores on the curriculum emphasis KDC. Therefore, it was concluded that these two clusters consisted of teachers who displayed one of the typical belief structures identified earlier: cluster 3 represented the belief that combines the curriculum emphasis CTS with a learner-centred educational belief, whereas cluster 4 stood for the combination of the curriculum emphasis FC with a subject-matter-oriented educational belief. It must be remembered, however, that these two clusters together consisted of about one-quarter of the respondents. In other words, the majority of the respondents could *not* be assigned to one of these belief structures.

In a final series of analyses, whether cluster membership was related to general teacher characteristics was investigated; that is, years of teaching experience, prior education, academic background, and qualifications. For this purpose, analyses of cross-tabs were performed to check whether the teachers were distributed evenly over the four clusters with respect to these variables. This was indeed the case, as the results of chi-square tests showed no significant differences between observed and expected frequencies in the clusters, for any of the variables.

Conclusions and Implications

Conclusions

About one-third of the total population of chemistry teachers in upper secondary education in the Netherlands participated in this study. Based on their general characteristics (i.e., years of teaching experience), we have reason to believe that the group of respondents was representative of this population. This, in combination with the size of the sample, allows us to make generalizations about the population of Dutch chemistry teachers.

It was found that, on the whole, the respondents tended to support all of the three curriculum emphases to which they were asked to respond. The strongest support was given to the curriculum emphasis 'Fundamental Chemistry', in which the main aim is to introduce students to the fundamental concepts and skills within chemistry, so as to prepare them for future training. However, there was almost equally strong support for the curriculum emphasis 'Chemistry, Technology, and Society', where the main aim is for students to learn to communicate and make decisions about social issues involving chemical aspects. Finally, as the mean score on the curriculum emphasis 'Knowledge Development in Chemistry' was only slightly lower, the respondents indicated that they considered it also important that students learn to see chemistry as a culturally determined system of knowledge, which is constantly developing.

The general educational beliefs of the respondents could be interpreted in terms of a subject-matter orientation and a learner-centred orientation (cf. Denessen, 1999). The latter orientation received substantially more support than did the former, indicating that the respondents valued the importance of their students' opinions and their learning process, including the development of their social skills.

On the basis of analysis of correlation and principal component analysis, two distinct and independent belief structures were found: (1) a belief that combines the curriculum emphasis FC with a subject-matter-oriented educational belief, and (2) a belief that combines the curriculum emphasis CTS with a learner-centred educational belief. The curriculum emphasis KDC could not be assigned exclusively to one of these belief structures. In a cluster analysis, two relatively small subgroups were identified whose members' beliefs could be described more or less in terms of one of these two belief structures. However, it appeared that most teachers (about three-quarters of the respondents) combined elements of the two belief structures.

We did not find relationships between teachers' general characteristics, such as (recent) teaching experience, prior education, academic background, and qualifications, and their content-specific or general educational beliefs. One interesting exception concerned the finding that teachers with a qualification to teach 'Public Understanding of Science' scored significantly *lower* on the curriculum emphasis CTS in comparison with teachers who taught only chemistry. This result may be considered a surprise, because in the curriculum for 'Public Understanding of Science' an emphasis on relationships between science, technology, and society is evident (De Vos & Reiding, 1999). Since chemistry teachers who are qualified to teach 'Public Understanding of Science' have at least some experiences teaching this subject, an explanation of their lower scores on this emphasis may be that these teachers had negative experiences focusing on relationships between science, technology, and society. Alternatively, they may consider it less important to pay attention to this emphasis when teaching chemistry, because this emphasis is already a central element of 'Public Understanding of Science'. From the data collected in this study, it is not possible to draw a clear conclusion concerning this finding.

Implications for the Innovation of the Curriculum for Chemical Education

The support for FC may be explained as a result of the teachers' commitment to the present curriculum, which most of them had taught for a long time. Also, teachers may value this curriculum emphasis because, from this perspective, the design of the curriculum is based primarily on the internal relationships of chemical concepts and skills, thus leading to a coherent structure. At the same time, the almost equally strong support for CTS may be considered congruent with the proposed shift towards a more context-based curriculum. Finally, the finding that KDC received only slightly less support shows that the new curriculum should also pay attention to the nature of chemical knowledge as something that constantly develops in a social-cultural context.

To accommodate teachers' support for *all* these curriculum emphases, the new curriculum should preferably have a flexible organization, which leaves room for individual teachers to make choices according to their own preferences. A possible design could focus on the selection of contexts, which could form the starting point of the learning process, leading the students to understand the underlying fundamental chemical concepts and skills, their internal relationships, and, if possible, how these concepts and skills have been developed. Contexts can vary from school to school, and from year to year. Thus, teachers will have the possibility of selecting those contexts that they value, or which they think are most relevant to their students. In this respect, examples from other countries can be used as input or inspiration (e.g., 'Ideas about Science' from the UK; Millar & Osborne, 1998).

The strong support for a learner-centred orientation implies that the design of learning activities for the new curriculum should focus on activities that value the input from students, and their ideas and opinions, and that leave room for students to work on the problems of their choice.

The fact that about three-quarters of the respondents had more than 15 years of teaching experience implies that the large majority of chemistry teachers are thoroughly familiar with the present curriculum and may find it difficult to change their practice in the context of a new curriculum. Preliminary experiences in the Netherlands have revealed difficulties both in the design of context-based modules and in the use of such modules in practice

(Stolk et al., 2003; Westbroek et al., 2003). In any case, a system of professional development activities will be needed to support chemistry teachers in this respect (Van Driel et al., 2001). An organization in regional networks of chemistry teachers, designers of educational materials, teacher educators, and researchers offers possibilities of combining and aligning the process of developing and evaluating new curriculum materials together with professional development processes. Within such an approach, teachers could be facilitated to carry out action research projects to further support them 'to become architects for change through building upon their current conceptions instead of attempting to remediate them' (Parke & Coble, 1997, p. 785).

Implications for Further Research

The study reported in this paper is limited in various ways. First, the use of a questionnaire with Likert-type items to investigate teachers' beliefs has certain disadvantages. In the literature on teacher beliefs, many references have been made to the implicit or tacit nature of such beliefs, which make them difficult to investigate (for example, Pajares, 1992). Although the reliability of this instrument was considered satisfactory in statistical terms, we are aware that the teachers, to some extent, may have interpreted items in other ways than they were meant. Therefore, a follow-up study is necessary to validate and further explore the outcomes of the present study. In particular, we intend to use the results obtained with this questionnaire as the starting point for an in-depth investigation of particular aspects of chemistry teachers' beliefs. For instance, the unclear position in our findings of the curriculum emphasis KDC with respect to the two belief structures warrants further research. What ideas do teachers have about this curriculum emphasis, and how do these relate to the other curriculum emphases? Also, the finding that most teachers (clusters 1 and 2) apparently combined elements of the two belief structures should be investigated more thoroughly. For instance, how can we interpret teachers' strong support for the curriculum emphasis FC, on the one hand, and their relatively high scores for the learner-centred scales (e.g., democracy, pedagogy), on the other? Finally, it will be interesting to explore the position of teachers with a qualification to teach 'Public Understanding of Science' in more depth. To explore these and other issues, a small-scale study using other types of instruments (e.g., metaphors or concept maps) is planned.

In addition to this, we plan research activities in connection with the curriculum innovation process. Now that the ministerial committee has produced its blueprint for the design of the new curriculum (Driessen & Meinema, 2003), curriculum development activities started in the summer of 2004. We intend to examine the development of the knowledge and beliefs of certain groups of chemistry teachers when they start working with new curricular materials, over a period of several years, to investigate whether, and how, their knowledge and beliefs change, and how such changes are related to changes in teaching practice. For such a study, it may be particularly interesting to focus on teachers with distinct belief patterns (cf. clusters 3 and 4).

Acknowledgment

The authors wish to thank Ben Smit of ICLON Graduate School of Education, Leiden University, for his assistance in designing the instruments and analysing the data.

Note

1   Originally published as Van Driel, J. H., Bulte, A. M. W., & Verloop, N. (2005). The conceptions of chemistry teachers about teaching and learning in the context of a curriculum innovation. *International Journal of Science Education, 27*(3), 303–322. Reprinted, with minor edits, with permission from the publisher.

References

Aldenderfer, M. S., & Blashfield, R. K. (1984). *Cluster analysis.* Sage.

Bennett, J., & Holman, J. (2002). Context-based approaches to the teaching of chemistry: What are they and what are their effects? In J. K. Gilbert et al. (Eds.), *Chemical education: Towards research-based practice* (pp. 165–184). Kluwer Academic Publishers.

Billig, M., Condor, S., Edwards, D., Gane, M., Middleton, D., & Radley, A. (1988). *Ideological dilemmas: A social psychology of everyday thinking.* Sage.

Boulton-Lewis, G. M., Smith, D. J. H., McCrindle, A. R., Burnett, P. C., & Campbell, K. J. (2001). Secondary teachers' conceptions of teaching and learning. *Learning and Instruction, 11*, 35–51.

Calderhead, J. (1996). Teachers: Beliefs and knowledge. In D. C. Berliner & R. C. Calfee (Eds.), *Handbook of educational psychology* (pp. 709–725). MacMillan.

Clark, C. M., & Peterson, P. L. (1986). Teachers' thought processes. In M. C. Wittrock (Ed.), *Handbook of research on teaching* (3rd ed., pp. 255–296). Macmillan.

Denessen, E. (1999). *Opvattingen over onderwijs: Leerstof- en leerlinggerichtheid in Nederland* [*Beliefs about education: Subject matter and student orientations in the Netherlands*] [Ph.D. dissertation]. Garant, Leuven.

De Vos, W. (2001). *De toestand van de school scheikunde* [The situation of school chemistry]. Utrecht University, Department of Chemical Education.

De Vos, W., Bulte, A. M. W., & Pilot, A. (2002). Chemistry curricula for general education: Analysis and elements of a design. In J. K. Gilbert et al. (Eds.), *Chemical education: Towards research-based practice* (pp. 101–124). Kluwer Academic Publishers.

De Vos, W., & Reiding, J. (1999). Public understanding of science as a separate subject in secondary schools in the Netherlands. *International Journal of Science Education, 21*, 711–719.

Driessen, H. P. W., & Meinema, H. A. (2003). *Chemistry between context and concept. Designing for renewal.* SLO. http://www.slo.nl/e22/Slo21/guest/000/031/000/003?ECT=22&iConId=7292

Eenhoorngroep. (1999). Dilemma's in de schoolscheikunde [Dilemma's in school chemistry]. *NVOX, 24*, 289–291.

Fensham, P. J. (1998). The politics of legitimating and marginalizing companion meanings: Three Australian case stories. In D. A. Roberts & L. Oestman (Eds.), *Problems of meaning in science curricula* (pp. 178–192). Teachers' College, Columbia University.

Haney, J. J., Czerniak, C. M., & Lumpe, A. T. (1996). Teacher beliefs and intentions regarding the implementation of science eduction reform strands. *Journal of Research in Science Teaching, 33*, 971–993.

Janssen, F. J. J. M., Westbroek, H., Doyle, W., & Van Driel, J. H. (2013). How to make innovations practical? *Teachers College Record, 115*(7), 1–42.

Johnston, S. (1992). Images: A way of understanding the practical knowledge of student teachers. *Teaching and Teacher Education, 8*, 123–136.

Kagan, D. M. (1990). Ways of evaluating teacher cognition: Inferences concerning the Goldilocks principle. *Review of Educational Research, 60*, 419–469.

Kerkstra, A., & Jansen, K. (2001). Discussie 'nieuwe scheikunde' [Discussion 'New chemistry']. *NVOX, 26*, 73–75.

Lantz, O., & Kass, H. (1987). Chemistry teachers' functional paradigms. *Science Education, 80*, 509–534.

Markic, S., Eilks, I., Van Driel, J. H., & Ralle, B. (2009). Vorstellungen deutscher Chemielehrkräfte über die Bedeutung und Ausrichtung des Chemielernens [Views of German chemistry teachers about the relevance and orientation of learning chemistry]. *Chemie Konkret, 16*(2), 90–95.

Millar, R., & Osborne, J. (Eds.). (1998). *Beyond 2000: Science education for the future.* King's College.

National Research Council. (1996). *National science education standards.* National Research Council.

Norušis, M. J./SPSS Inc. (1992). *SPSS/PC+ Professional statistics, version 5.0.* SPSS Inc.

Pajares, M. F. (1992). Teachers' beliefs and educational research: Cleaning up a messy construct. *Review of Educational Research, 62*, 307–332.

Parke, H. M., & Coble, C. R. (1997). Teachers designing curriculum as professional development: A model for transformational science teaching. *Journal of Research in Science Teaching, 34*, 773–790.

Pedhazur, E. J., & Pedhazur Schmelkin, L. (1991). *Measurement, design and analysis: An integrated approach.* Lawrence Erlbaum Associates.

Pilot, A., & Van Driel, J. H. (2001). Ontwikkeling van een vernieuwd vak scheikunde in het voortgezet onderwijs [The development of a new secondary school subject chemistry]. *Tijdschrift voor Didactiek der β-wetenschappen, 18*, 41–58.

Platteel, T., Hulshof, H., Van Driel, J. H., & Verloop, N. (2013). Teachers' interpretations of the concept-context approach for L1 education. *L1 – Educational Studies in Language and Literature, 13*, 1–25.

Pratt, D. D. (1992). Conceptions of teaching. *Adult Education Quarterly, 42*, 203–220.

Roberts, D. A. (1982). Developing the concept of 'curriculum emphases' in science education. *Science Education, 66*, 243–260.

Roberts, D. A. (1988). What counts as science education? In P. J. Fensham (Ed.), *Development and dilemmas in science education* (pp. 27–54). Palmer Press.

Shen, J. (1997). Structure of the theoretical concept of educational goals: A test of factorial validity. *The Journal of Experimental Education, 64*, 342–352.

Solomon, J., & Aikenhead, G. (1994). *STS education – International perspective on reform.* Teachers College Press.

Stolk, M. J., Bulte, A., de Jong, O., & Pilot, A. (2003, August 20–23). *Professional development of chemistry teachers: Contextualizing school chemistry* [Paper presentation]. The 4th ESERA conference, Noordwijkerhout, The Netherlands.

Stolk, M. J., De Jong, O., Bulte, A. M. W., & Pilot, A. (2011). Exploring a framework for professional development in curriculum innovation: Empowering teachers for designing context-based chemistry education. *Research in Science Education, 41*, 369–388.

Van Berkel, B. (2001). *To escape from and to escape to.* Centre for Science and Mathematics Education.

Van Driel, J. H. (2000). *Vernieuwing van scheikunde onderwijs. Een samenvatting en een aanzet tot vervolg van de discussie* [Innovation of chemical education. A summary and an attempt to continue the discussion]. http//www.nvon.nl/scheik/vernieuwing.htm

Van Driel, J. H. (2003). Opvattingen van docenten scheikunde over het scheikunde curriculum [Chemistry teachers' beliefs about the chemistry curriculum]. *NVOX, 28*(8), 375–377.

Van Driel, J. H., Beijaard, D., & Verloop, N. (2001). Professional development and reform in science education: The role of teachers' practical knowledge. *Journal of Research in Science Teaching, 38*, 137–158.

Van Driel, J. H., Bulte, A. M. W., & Verloop, N. (2005). The conceptions of chemistry teachers about teaching and learning in the context of a curriculum innovation. *International Journal of Science Education, 27*, 3, 303–322.

Van Driel, J. H., Bulte, A. M. W., & Verloop, N. (2007). The relationships between teachers' general beliefs about teaching and learning and their domain specific curricular beliefs. *Learning and Instruction, 17*(2), 156–171.

Van Driel, J. H., Bulte, A. M. W., & Verloop, N. (2008). Using the curriculum emphasis concept to investigate teachers' curricular beliefs in the context of educational reform. *Journal of Curriculum Studies, 40*, 107–122.

Van Driel, J. H., & Verloop, N. (2002). Experienced teachers' knowledge of teaching and learning of models and modelling in science education. *International Journal of Science Education, 24*(12), 1255–1272.

Vogelzang, J., Admiraal, W. A., & Van Driel, J. H. (2020). A teacher perspective on Scrum methodology in secondary chemistry education. *Chemistry Education Research and Practice, 21*, 237–249.

Westbroek, H., Klaassen, K., Bulte, A., & Pilot, A. (2003, August 20–23). *Characteristics of meaningful chemistry education* [Paper presentation]. The 4th ESERA conference, Noordwijkerhout, The Netherlands.

CHAPTER 8

Taking a Closer Look at Science Teaching Orientations

1 How the Article Came About

Disseminating research through publications in journals and books and presentations at conferences, obviously, is essential for the recognition of the research and for establishing an international reputation as a researcher. Although journal articles are usually held in higher esteem than conference papers, the latter tend to be more important in building relationships with researchers with similar research interests. I presented my studies at nearly every annual meeting of NARST and biannual conference of ESERA in the past 20 years and, as explained in Chapter 1, this has been incredibly important in building connections with international colleagues. These connections have led to joint projects and publications and also to enduring friendships.

Among those whose research has been relevant and inspirational to me were Sandra Abell and Patricia Friedrichsen. Sandi was Professor of science education and Director of the Science Education Center at the University of Missouri-Columbia (USA). A former elementary school science teacher, she had conducted numerous teaching and research projects in elementary and middle level science classrooms in collaboration with classroom teachers. She was a very prolific author, and among many other roles, she had been co-editor of the first *Handbook of Research on Science Education* (2007), and past president of NARST. Pat is currently a Professor of science education in the same institution. Her research focuses on secondary science teacher learning across the professional continuum, using a variety of frameworks, including pedagogical content knowledge and skills, teacher beliefs, communities of practice, and core science teaching practices. It was during a NARST or ESERA conference around 2005 that Sandi invited me to visit their institute. Around the same time, I asked her to co-author an encyclopedia chapter on science teacher education with me (Van Driel & Abell, 2010).

In 2008, immediately after that year's NARST meeting, I travelled with Sandi and her husband Mark Volkmann to Columbia. During my stay I gave a few presentations and met with most of the researchers and PhD students of the Science Education Center. Also, Sandi, Pat and I had several meetings to take a closer look at some of the research the three of us had been and were doing.

We shared an interest in science teacher learning and in pedagogical content knowledge. One of the issues that emerged was a shared frustration about the loose or vague use of definitions and conceptual models in the research literature, in particular, on teacher knowledge and beliefs. Authors used the same definitions and models in rather different ways. We had to admit that, looking at our own publications, we had also been guilty of selectively or inconsistently referring to particular conceptualisations of teacher knowledge and beliefs. We decided to use our frustration as the basis for a jointly written position paper.

The focus of the paper was the PCK model published by Shirley Magnusson, Joseph Krajcik and Hilda Borko in 1999 in a book *Examining Pedagogical Content Knowledge*, edited by Julie Gess-Newsome and Norman Lederman (Magnusson et al., 1999). In the first decade after it was published, this model had gained substantial attention from researchers in PCK in science education; it has been cited more than 3,000 times to date. In her PhD dissertation (Pennsylvania State University, 2002), Pat had focused on secondary biology teachers' science teaching orientations and analysed the model and its historical origins. Reflecting on her research trajectory, Pat would later describe how the model had both inspired and frustrated her (Friedrichsen, 2015). Ineke Henze in her PhD study had used the model to analyse the PCK development among teachers of *Algemene Natuurwetenschappen* (see Chapter 5). In selecting the model, often referred to as 'the Magnusson et al. model', we didn't mean to criticize the model as such. Instead, our aim was to highlight how the different applications of the model hindered progress in research on science teachers' knowledge and beliefs, which in turn made it difficult to apply this research in pre-service and in-service teacher education.

2   What the Article Is About

The Magnusson et al. model distinguishes four components of pedagogical content knowledge, that is, knowledge of (i) instructional strategies, (ii) students' understanding of science, (iii) science curricula and (iv) assessment of scientific literacy. All these components are shaped by teachers' *orientations to science teaching*, defined as "knowledge and beliefs about the purposes and goals for teaching science at a particular grade level" (Magnusson et al., 1999, p. 97). These orientations became a specific focus of our article. We had noticed that many researchers had included orientations to science teaching in their studies, however, they would often define these differently, if they defined orientations at all. We were concerned that the research suffered from this lack of a shared definition. Our paper therefore aimed "to clarify the orientations construct and offer a view of orientations to science teaching that can be of use to researchers and science teacher educators" (Friedrichsen, Van Driel, & Abell, 2011, p. 359).

Based on Pat Friedrichsen's PhD study, we demonstrated that whereas Shulman's original model did not include an element such as orientations to teaching a subject, this was added by one of his doctoral students, Pamela Grossman in her seminal book *The Making of a Teacher* (Grossman, 1990). Grossman had argued how conceptions of purposes for teaching specific subject matter influence other PCK components. We showed how Magnusson et al. combined some of Grossman's ideas with those of others, notably Ed Smith and Charles Anderson, to introduce nine distinct orientations to teaching science. We analysed these nine orientations and highlighted the variety of sources they drew on: whereas some were based on curriculum orientations others originated from empirical studies, for example, of goals of science teachers.

Turning to the research literature that had used Magnusson et al.'s orientations to teaching science, we identified four issues: (1) the construct was defined in substantially different ways, (2) very few studies addressed the relationship between orientations and the other PCK components that are supposedly shaped by these orientations, (3) researchers often assigned science teachers to one of the nine orientations, ignoring that teachers can hold multiple orientations and (4) some researchers who had applied the Magnusson et al. model focused on the four PCK components, omitting the overarching science teaching orientations. We asserted that these issues could be related to the inherent complexity of studying science teachers' knowledge, beliefs and practice. We argued that whereas eliciting teachers' knowledge (e.g., of instructional strategies) from their practice may be fairly straightforward, "beliefs about purposes and goals for teaching science are often implicit, unobservable, and difficult to elicit" (Friedrichsen et al., 2011, p. 370).

To move the field forward, we reviewed the literature searching for consensus on the dimensions of teachers' beliefs that influence practice. Among others, we turned to Doug Roberts' idea of curriculum emphases (see Chapter 7) and used this to propose that orientations to science teaching should be reconceptualized as consisting of interrelated sets of beliefs. Based on Roberts' curriculum emphases, we suggested the following three dimensions for science teaching orientations: (i) beliefs about the goals or purposes of science teaching, (ii) beliefs about the nature of science, and (iii) beliefs about science teaching and learning. In future empirical research, patterns or profiles could be revealed, which if interpreted from a theoretical point of view, could lead to the identification of labels or categories of distinctly different science teaching orientations. Such research would require the development of new and specific instruments. We concluded the article with the view that our recommendations would contribute to conceptual and methodological clarity in research on science teachers' knowledge, beliefs and practice.

3   Impact and Follow Up

While we were working on the manuscript, Sandi was unwell and her condition worsened during the process. We finished the paper early 2010 and decided to submit it to *Science Education*. The three of us met at the NARST meeting in Philadelphia in March of that year and celebrated the finishing of the paper. That was the last time I saw Sandi. We received feedback from reviewers, revised the manuscript and resubmitted it in August. Four days later, Sandi passed away. The article was accepted in September and published online the next month.

The article started to pick up citations quickly. Three years after it was published online, it was already cited more than 50 times. It has been cited 30 to 50 times per year since then, cites totalling 370 to date. Although these numbers demonstrate that our paper is recognised as relevant by scholars who study science teachers' knowledge and beliefs, I don't think it has made a big change to the ways that teachers' orientations have been conceptualised and investigated. Reflecting on the article and the collaboration with Pat and Sandi, it has helped me to improve my understanding of the complexities inherent in the relationships between what teachers know and believe, what they want to achieve and what they actually do in their classrooms. In my research, I had tended to focus on teachers' knowledge, or particular aspects of it, without paying much attention to their beliefs. In other studies (see Chapter 7), teacher beliefs were the focus, however, these were studied in isolation of teachers' knowledge and practice. The work on the article in this chapter convinced me that to understand teachers' work, it is essential to investigate affective and cognitive aspects in relation to each other, as challenging as that may be. Teachers' beliefs, their goals, motivation and contexts together with specific aspects of their knowledge, determine their actions. This understanding would inspire future projects such as the PhD study of Monika Louws (Louws et al., 2017).

As for the Magnusson et al. model, although it recognises the importance of teachers' orientation related to their PCK, it remained unclear how orientations 'shape' PCK components. Moreover, it represented the PCK components as isolated silos or containers, thus failing to acknowledge that, for instance, a teacher's topic-specific knowledge of instructional strategies needs to be related to their understanding of how their students learn that topic for their teaching to be potentially effective. For instance, a physics teacher may know twenty strategies to explain Ohm's law, but to know which strategy is appropriate or helpful requires knowledge of their learners' actual understanding of relevant physical concepts at a particular time and in a particular context. In short, as Pat would argue in her reflection (Friedrichsen, 2015), the Magnusson et al. model lacks explanatory power.

More broadly, the work on this paper highlighted how research on teachers' knowledge and beliefs, PCK in particular, was hindered by a lack of shared ideas about concepts, theories and methods within the research community. Our 1998 PCK article (Chapter 1) had already drawn attention to the variety of published PCK models in terms of knowledge aspects that were included or excluded. In 2010, the landscape had become even more diffuse. For instance, colleagues in mathematics education had published a Mathematics Knowledge for Teaching (MKT) model (Ball, Thames, & Phelps, 2008) which aimed to highlight the complex relationships between subject matter knowledge and PCK. This model has become hugely influential in research on mathematics teaching (nearly 8,000 citations to date!), however, it is rarely referred to in science education research.

The lack of a shared definition and the existence of multiple conceptualisations of PCK inspired colleagues from the USA (Julie Gess-Newsome, Janet Carlson and April Gardner) to organise a PCK Summit in Colorado Springs, USA, in October 2012. The aims of the summit were to form "a professional learning community to explore the potential of a consensus model of PCK" and identify specific next steps that would move science education research in this field forward (Carlson et al., 2015, p. 15). I was fortunate to be invited to participate in this summit and very happy to see some of the colleagues I had worked with (Ineke Henze, Pat Friedrichsen, Kira Padilla, John Loughran, Amanda Berry) among the participants, as well as scholars whose work I had read, including researchers in mathematics education. The summit was an incredible experience: to be able to spend five whole days in a beautiful environment with 22 colleagues from all over the world to share research findings, theoretical ideas and methodological insights focused on a topic (i.e., PCK) that everyone is passionate about, is rather unique! The summit resulted in a consensus definition of PCK and a comprehensive model of teacher professional knowledge and skill (TPK&S) that were published in a book edited by Berry, Friedrichsen and Loughran (2015). One chapter in the book explains how the new model aims to address the weaknesses in PCK research identified by Lee Shulman in his opening address to the summit. The TPK&S model locates

PCK in the context of teacher classroom practice, while positioning teacher orientations and beliefs as a filter or amplifier between (public) topic-specific professional knowledge and personal PCK (Gess-Newsome, 2015). To illustrate this, from a variety of strategies to introduce a science topic, say chemical equilibrium, made available through a teacher education program, a teacher with a conceptual change orientation would apply different strategies compared to someone who believes that teaching is telling. Gess-Newsome argued:

> The removal of teacher orientations and beliefs from the construct of PCK and placing it as an amplifier or filter for classroom practice is a contribution of the model of TPK&S. Removing orientations and affect outside the realm of PCK is more consistent with the literature that has carefully considered this topic (Friedrichsen, Van Driel, & Abell, 2011) and provides greater explanatory power than when embedded within the PCK construct. (2015, p. 35)

To me, the new model was a step forward. It is comprehensive and more complex than existing models of PCK or teacher knowledge more broadly, however, this enables scholars to situate their research and explain its purpose. For instance, I recognised that some of my studies had focused on the interaction between topic-specific professional knowledge and personal PCK, whereas other scholars had investigated the impact of personal PCK on student achievement. The model helped to identify which variables would be relevant to include in the design of future studies.

The PCK summit as a whole was very inspirational and motivating, and for many participants a highlight in their career. It surely was for me! However, it had raised new questions, for instance, about the development of PCK in relation to or influenced by other variables, and how to measure PCK quantitatively in a meaningful way. Moreover, it turned out that the consensus about the new model was not as strong or clear as we had hoped for. Different versions of the model were shared at conferences and in publications, both by summit participants and others. Talking with colleagues at international conferences, there was a growing sense that a follow-up conference might be helpful. I took it upon me to lead the organisation of a second PCK summit, together with Amanda Berry, Sophie Kirschner, Andreas Borowski and Janet Carlson. The summit was organised as a five-day seminar with 24 participants and took place in December 2016 at Leiden University.

The idea of the second PCK summit was to build an understanding of each other's research by focusing on research instruments and data obtained with these instruments to learn how scholars infer PCK from their data. We made it a priority to bring in new participants, both senior and beginning, in an effort to broaden the thinking power of the group. The aims of this summit were to:

> [D]evelop a shared set of criteria to identify PCK for each kind of instrument through collectively analysing data that were obtained with the respective instrument; make accessible and comprehensible these instruments to the wider PCK research community; and reach consensus on a model of PCK that is strongly connected with empirical data of varying nature and can be used as a framework for the design of future PCK studies. (Cooper & Van Driel, 2019, pp. 307–308)

At the end of the summit, the consensus model that resulted from the first summit was revisited during a model-building session that included all participants. This session resulted in a preliminary version of a revised model, which would be further developed and refined in the months after the summit and presented at the NARST and ESERA conferences in 2017. Based on the feedback of participants to the summit and these conferences, this resulted in the publication of a Refined Consensus Model of PCK (Carlson & Daehler et al., 2019). This refined model is now quickly gaining traction in current and emerging PCK research.

I believe that the process of the two PCK summits and sharing their outcomes with the broader research community through conference presentations and publications, has made a valuable contribution to progress in this research field. Like many constructs in educational research, PCK has been defined, theorised and investigated in a variety of ways. Although it is not necessary, and practically impossible, that all researchers commit themselves to adopting the same conceptualisation, it is vital that they understand each other's positions and that there is a sense of agreement about what a construct represents, and what it does not. Crucially, participants in this process need to be open to the views of other researchers, senior or more junior to the research field, and willing to understand the contexts (national, institutional) in which their research is done. I consider myself very fortunate to be part of a community that operates on this basis. Implications of the PCK summits for my current and future research will be discussed in the final chapter of this volume.

Taking a Closer Look at Science Teaching Orientations[1]

Patrica Friedrichsen, Jan H. van Driel and Sandra K. Abell

Abstract

In this position paper, we examine the science teaching orientation component of the S. Magnusson, J. Krajcik, and H. Borko (1999) pedagogical content knowledge (PCK) model for science teaching. We trace the origin of the construct in the literature, identifying multiple definitions that have led to ambiguity. After examining published studies using the PCK model, we identified the following methodological issues: (a) using orientations in different or unclear ways, (b) unclear or absent relationship between orientations and the other model components, (c) simply assigning teachers to one of nine categories of orientations, and (d) ignoring the overarching orientation component. To bring clarity to the literature, we propose defining science teaching orientations as a set of beliefs with the following dimensions: goals and purposes of science teaching, views of science, and beliefs about science teaching and learning. Consequently, there is a need for new instruments to elicit these dimensions. We conclude by making recommendations to address the four issues identified in the literature.

Introduction

Science teacher practices are influenced by a number of factors, including the social and policy context in which they teach (Little, 2003), subject matter knowledge (Abell, 2007; Gess-Newsome, 1999), their beliefs about teaching (Jones & Carter, 2007; Pajares, 1992), and their pedagogical content knowledge (PCK; Abell, 2007; Davis, Petish, & Smithy, 2006). Thus, research in these areas forms a significant corpus of science education research. Like a number of science education researchers (Lee & Luft, 2008; Loughran, Milroy, Berry, Gunstone, & Mulhall., 2001; Loughran, Mulhall, & Berry, 2008; Nilsson, 2008), we have been interested particularly in examining PCK as an aspect of teacher learning and practice (De Jong, van Driel, & Verloop, 2005; Friedrichsen et al., 2009; Henze, van Driel, & Verloop, 2008; van Driel, De Jong, & Verloop, 2002). In fact, the construct of PCK has been a fruitful framework for science teacher education research over the past two decades. Many of these researchers have used the Magnusson, Krajcik, and Borko (1999) model of PCK for science teaching as a foundation. One component of this model is what the authors called orientations to science teaching. They viewed orientations as influencing teacher practice by shaping other components of PCK. A number of researchers have examined teachers' orientations to science teaching, sometimes using different terms to define what appears to be a similar construct (Abell, 2007). As researchers, we are concerned that the orientations research suffers from this lack of shared definition. Our aim in this paper is to clarify the orientations construct and offer a view of orientations to science teaching that can be of use to researchers and science teacher educators. For this purpose, we begin by reviewing the historical roots of the orientations construct and the origins of several proposed science teaching orientations. We then discuss a set of issues in the recent research related to the orientations construct. Finally, we offer our view of the orientations construct and suggest avenues for future research.

Orientations to Science Teaching: A Historical Overview

Roots: Lee Shulman and Pamela Grossman
Lee Shulman introduced PCK as a central element in the knowledge base of teaching. His original emphasis (Shulman, 1986, 1987) was on various knowledge elements. This led to research conceptualized by a variety of elements included in the teacher knowledge model (for an overview, see, e.g., van Driel, Verloop, & de Vos, 1998). In a recent interview, Shulman, reflected on the origins of PCK, saying that the questions that had inspired the construct were, on the one hand, "What is it that a teacher knows and is able to do that a specialist in the subject matter that that teacher is teaching, no matter how smart they are, doesn't understand and can't do?" and, on the other hand, "What is it that a mathematics teacher can do and understand that a history teacher can't?" (Shulman, quoted in Berry, Loughran, & Van Driel, 2008, p. 1275). Early PCK research revealed the influence of the ways teachers understood their subject on how they taught it. However, the research also indicated the complexity of the interaction of different knowledge elements: "Just knowing the content well was really important, just knowing general pedagogy was really important and yet when you added the two together, you didn't get the teacher" (Shulman, quoted in Berry et al., 2008, p. 1274). Shulman's original model did not include an element such as orientations to teaching a subject.

Pamela Grossman, a doctoral student of Lee Shulman, built upon and further delineated Shulman's knowledge base for teaching in her dissertation and subsequent book, *The Making of a Teacher: Teacher Knowledge and Teacher Education* (1990). Grossman proposed a model of teacher knowledge that included four components: subject matter knowledge, general pedagogical knowledge, knowledge of context, and PCK. She placed PCK in the center of the model, and represented it as influenced by and influencing the other three domains. Within the PCK portion of the model, she identified an overarching component, *conceptions of purposes for teaching subject matter*, defined in the following way: "The first component includes knowledge and beliefs about the purposes for teaching a subject at different grade levels. These overarching conceptions of teaching a subject are reflected in teachers' goals for teaching particular subject matter" (p. 40). Most of the beginning English teachers in her study held multiple goals. For example, Kate's goals were to help students develop analytical and communication skills, as well as develop self-awareness. Later in the text, Grossman added a third part to the component: "Conceptions of what it means to teach English include teachers' beliefs about the central purposes for studying English, their goals for students, *and their beliefs about the nature of English as a secondary-school subject*". According to Grossman, this component of PCK, conceptions of purposes for teaching subject matter, influences three other PCK components: knowledge of students' understanding, curricular knowledge, and knowledge of instructional strategies:

> Although beginning teachers may lack the managerial skills necessary to implement their plans successfully, their beliefs about the goals for teaching their subject become a form of conceptual map for instructional decision making, serving as the basis for judgments about textbooks, classroom objectives, assignments, and evaluation of students. (p. 86)

Grossman's view of this component parallels what Magnusson et al. (1999) would later label orientations to science teaching.

Additional Influences: Charles Anderson and Ed Smith

During the early 1980s, Ed Smith, Charles Anderson, and colleagues moved away from the prevailing process-product research with its focus on teacher behavior (Brophy & Good, 1986; Rosenshine & Stevens, 1986) to study science teaching in action. In their research project, "The Planning and Teaching Intermediate Science Study" (PTIS), Smith and Anderson (1984a) observed fifth-grade teachers as they taught science units. One group of teachers used the Laidlaw Brothers *Exploring Science* textbook (Blecha, Gega, & Green, 1979), whereas the other group used revised versions of the Science Curriculum Improvement Study (SCIS) *Communities* unit (SCIS, 1971). The researchers noted that within each curriculum group teachers differed in how they implemented the curriculum. In the *Educator's Handbook: A Research Perspective* (Richardson-Koehler, 1987), Anderson and Smith introduced the term "teachers' orientations toward science teaching and learning" to refer to different approaches to teaching they observed in the PTIS project. They defined teachers' orientations as "general patterns of thought and behavior related to science teaching and learning" (p. 99), as a combination of a teacher's cognition and action. In the *Handbook*, Anderson and Smith described four different science teacher orientations: (1) activity-driven teaching, (2) didactic teaching, (3) discovery teaching, and (4) conceptual-change teaching. In contrast to Grossman's conceptions of purposes for teaching subject matter, Anderson and Smith defined orientations toward science teaching and learning as including teaching behavior.

Magnusson, Borko, and Krajcik's View of Orientations

Magnusson et al. (1999) proposed a science-specific PCK model in the book, *Examining Pedagogical Content Knowledge* (Gess-Newsome & Lederman, 1999) (see Figure 8.1). The model drew heavily on Grossman's (1990) work while borrowing terminology from Anderson and Smith (1987).

Magnusson and colleagues retain Grossman's PCK components in their model of PCK for science teaching – curricula, students' understanding [of science], and instructional strategies. Magnusson et al. made two notable changes to Grossman's model. The first was the addition of a new PCK component – knowledge and beliefs of assessment of scientific literacy. The second

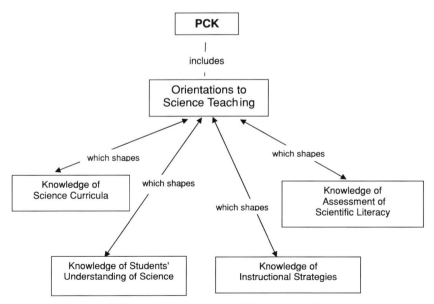

FIGURE 8.1   PCK model for science teaching (simplified version) (from Magnusson et al., 1999, p. 99; adapted with permission)

was to change the label of Grossman's "conceptions of purposes for teaching subject matter" component of PCK.

The second change appears on the surface to be cosmetic; yet on closer scrutiny, it is problematic. Magnusson and colleagues (1999) substituted the term "orientations toward teaching science" for Grossman's "conceptions of purposes for teaching subject matter" (p. 99). As in Grossman's (1990) diagram, this component remains at the top of the PCK model, shown as an overarching element for the other PCK components. Magnusson et al. defined orientations toward teaching science as "knowledge and beliefs about the purposes and goals for teaching science at a particular grade level" (p. 97), which is consistent with Grossman's definition of conceptions of purposes for teaching subject matter. In the same paragraph, however, the authors added to their definition that an orientation is "a general way of viewing or conceptualizing science teaching" (p. 97). This definition was closer to Anderson and Smith's (1987) definition of orientations but omitted their focus on teacher behavior. Magnusson and colleagues indicated they preferred the term "orientations toward teaching science" because it was used in the science education literature. Thus they equated Grossman's "conceptions" to Anderson and Smith's "teachers' orientations" to their own "orientations toward teaching science". However, the name change is problematic because of real differences in how each construct was defined. Magnusson et al. (1999) proposed nine different orientations to science teaching, including the four originally identified by Anderson and Smith (1987): process, academic rigor, didactic, conceptual change, activity-driven, discovery, project-based science, inquiry, and guided inquiry. In the next section, we summarize each orientation as described by Magnusson and colleagues and analyze the origins of each orientation.

Nine Orientations to Teaching Science

Magnusson et al. (1999) defined each orientation by providing the goal of teaching science and the characteristics of instruction for that orientation. They cautioned that a particular teaching strategy (e.g., use of laboratory investigations) may be characteristic of more than one science teaching orientation: "this similarity indicates that it is not the use of a particular strategy but the *purpose* of employing it that distinguishes a teacher's orientation to teaching science" (p. 97). Friedrichsen (2002) reviewed this list of science teaching orientations and grouped the orientations in two main categories: (a) teacher-centered orientations (didactic and academic rigor) and (b) orientations based on reform efforts and associated curriculum projects. She subdivided the latter category into orientations based on the reform efforts of the 1960s (process, activity-driven, and discovery) and orientations based on contemporary reform efforts and curriculum projects (conceptual change, project-based science, inquiry, and guided inquiry). We use this classification scheme to describe the orientations as we attempt to understand the empirical basis for each.

Teacher-Centered Orientations

Didactic and academic rigor orientations are both teacher-centered orientations (Friedrichsen, 2002). A teacher with a *didactic* orientation has the goal to "transmit the facts of science" (Magnusson et al., 1999, p. 100). Instruction for this orientation is characterized as "The teacher presents information, generally through lecture or discussion, and questions directed to students are to hold them accountable for knowing the facts produced by science" (p. 101). Magnusson et al. provided no references for the didactic orientation; one assumes the authors drew on the work of Anderson and Smith (1987). To support a didactic orientation, Anderson and Smith (1987) referenced studies by Slinger, Anderson, and Smith (1983) and Eaton, Anderson, and Smith (1984). Both of these studies reported on a single case of an elementary teacher. However, neither study focused on the teachers' orientations. The didactic label is not used in these papers but appears in the final project report (Smith and Anderson, 1984a). In a later paper, Anderson and Smith stated, "We have encountered this [didactic] orientation toward teaching far more often than any other among teachers at all levels" (Anderson & Smith, 1987, p. 100). We agree that this statement has a ring of truth, yet is problematic in that is supported by two case studies, neither of which focused on examining the teachers' thinking in regard to their goals.

Academic rigor is the second type of teacher-centered orientation to science teaching. A teacher holding an academic rigor orientation has the goal to "represent a particular body of knowledge" (Magnusson et al., 1999, p. 100) and uses instruction characterized as "Students are challenged with difficult problems and activities. Laboratory work and demonstrations are used to verify science concepts by demonstrating the relationship between particular concepts and phenomena" (p. 101). Magnusson et al. referenced Lantz and Kass (1987), who used the term "academic rigor" in a study of high school chemistry teachers' implementation of a new curriculum. Lantz and Kass framed their study using the construct of a "functional paradigm", which included teachers' perceptions of high school chemistry, teaching, students, and the school setting. They defined "perception of teaching" as the teacher's view of requirements for effective teaching, as well as the overall aims of teaching. Among the teachers in the study, three perceptions of teaching emerged. One perception placed a high value on pedagogical efficiency, another view valued academic rigor, whereas a third value emphasized student motivation. These varying perceptions of teaching were related to how the teachers taught a new chemistry curriculum. Several issues arise related to Magnusson's and colleagues' use of Lantz and Kass's study to empirically support academic rigor as a science teaching orientation. First, Lantz and Kass conceptualized "functional paradigms" as consisting of a set of beliefs and values related not only to teaching but also to high school chemistry, students, and the school setting. Second, Lantz and Kass identified three perceptions of teaching in their study. Thus, identifying only academic rigor as a science teaching orientation reduces the complexity of the original construct of functional paradigms and of the three teaching perceptions found. Overall, it is not clear how functional paradigms and perceptions of teaching, as defined by Lantz and Kass, relate to Magnusson's orientations to science teaching.

Orientations Based on the Reform Efforts of the 1960s

Process, activity-driven, and discovery orientations are student-centered orientations that we place in a subcategory of reform efforts of the 1960s (Friedrichsen, 2002). Magnusson et al. (1999) identified a *process orientation* as having the following goal: "Help students develop the 'process skills'" (p. 100). They list SAPA (Science – A Process Approach) as an example of a curriculum using a process orientation. SAPA, a U.S. National Science Foundation (NSF) sponsored elementary science curriculum of the 1960s, was based on Robert Gagne's view of science as process (Millar & Driver, 1987). "The course [SAPA] utilized a highly structured approach to teaching specific processes of science, such as observing, classifying, measuring, and predicting, while it de-emphasized the mastery of specific science facts" (DeBoer, 1991, p. 158). The process orientation label is problematic because it lacks a reference to an empirical study of teachers holding the process orientation.

An *activity-driven orientation* is defined by the following goal: "Have students be active with materials, 'hands-on' experiences" (Magnusson et al., 1999, p. 100). Anderson and Smith (1987) are cited as a reference for the activity-driven orientation. In describing this orientation, Anderson and Smith stated,

> We have observed this orientation primarily among elementary school teachers who are uncomfortable teaching science. These teachers focus primarily on the activities to be carried out in the classroom: textbook reading, demonstrations, experiments, answering questions, and the like. (pp. 99–100)

Anderson and Smith cited Smith and Sendelbach (1982) and Olson (1983) as references for an activity-driven orientation. The Smith and Sendelbach (1982) study described the practice of one elementary teacher, Ms. Ross, using a single unit in the SCIS and examined the differences among the curriculum's intentions, the teacher's intentions, and the actual instruction using the SCIS material. This study may better be described as examining one teacher's use of SCIS, rather than a study exploring a teacher's goals and purposes for teaching science. Olson (1983) sought to understand Mr. Swift, a sixth- to eighth-grade science teacher, and his views of the nature of his teaching. In the study, Mr. Swift is not described as a teacher with an activity-driven orientation, but rather as a teacher who closely followed the Ministry's syllabus with a focus on content and vocabulary. Thus the empirical basis for the activity-driven orientation is lacking.

Magnusson et al. (1999) defined the goal of the *discovery orientation* as to "provide opportunities for students on their own to discover targeted science concepts" (p. 100) and described the nature of the instruction associated with the orientation as "Students explore the natural world following their own interests and discover patterns of how the world works during their explorations" (p. 101). Magnusson and colleagues cited only Karplus and Thier (1967) in their description of the discovery orientation. In A *New Look at Elementary Science,* Karplus and Thier offered a description of the history and design of the SCIS program with advice for implementation. This reference is not a description of a discovery orientation held by teachers, but a description of the orientation of the SCIS curriculum. We returned to Smith and Anderson's (1984a) work in which the term *discovery teaching* was initially introduced. The authors reported on a group of 14 elementary teachers using two different commercial science curricula. They identified three teaching approaches among the 14 teachers: activity-driven teaching, didactic teaching, and discovery teaching. No explicit information is given about the teachers' goals and purposes; however, the authors stated the group of teachers having a discovery approach misinterpreted parts of the teacher's guide and perceived the curriculum as being "strictly a discovery program" (p. 9). From this group of teachers having a discovery approach, we found a single published case study of one, fifth-grade teacher Mrs. Howe (Smith & Anderson, 1984b). Mrs. Howe's discovery approach is attributed to her logical positivist view of the nature of science; she believed students could infer the role of light in photosynthesis from their observations of growing plants in light and dark conditions. The authors offer an alternative explanation that the teacher's guide "failed to adequately communicate the nature of the learning and the suggested instructional strategies to Mrs. Howe" (p. 693). It is difficult to discern from this case study if Mrs. Howe held a discovery orientation prior to using the new curriculum or is she simply failed to understand the orientation of the curriculum she was implementing. In the absence of inductive studies focusing on teachers' orientations and involving larger numbers of teachers, it is not possible to ascertain whether the discovery orientation is empirically sound.

Orientations Based on Contemporary Reform Efforts and Curriculum Projects

Conceptual change, project-based science, inquiry, and guided inquiry are student-centered orientations that represent contemporary reform efforts and curriculum projects (Friedrichsen, 2002). Magnusson et al. (1999) defined the *conceptual change orientation* with the goal to "facilitate the development of scientific knowledge by confronting students with contexts to explain that challenge their naïve conceptions" (p. 100). Roth, Anderson, and Smith (1987) are cited as a reference for this orientation. Roth et al. observed fifth-grade teachers teaching lessons on light and photosynthesis. Some teachers used a popular science textbook, some used SCIS materials, whereas other teachers used conceptual-change based instructional materials designed by the researchers. The paper illustrates how the teacher's choice of curriculum and its use shaped the classroom talk. Ms. Ramsey and Ms. Kain were able to effectively use the conceptual change-based curricular materials to improve their students' learning. Although the authors indicated that the larger study focused on the "mental lives of teachers and students", this paper did not include information about the teachers' goals or purposes. Instead, the paper focused on the teachers' practice and the type of teacher-student interactions based on the curriculum materials in use. As in the discovery and process orientations, grounding for the conceptual change orientation appears to come from analysis of curriculum implementation rather than studies of teachers' views.

Project-based science was defined with the goal to "involve students in investigating solutions to authentic problems" (p. 100) when instruction "centers around a 'driving question'" (p. 101). Marx et al. (1994) are referenced for this orientation. Marx and his colleagues studied four middle school teachers as they enacted project-based science in their classrooms. In their paper, they described the teachers' concerns about enacting the curriculum, their implementation of the curriculum, as well as the challenges they encountered. In some cases, the teachers' beliefs conflicted with the project-based curriculum. Rather than documenting that teachers have a project-based orientation, the study might be better categorized as an example of implementation of a project-based science curriculum. Thus the empirical foundation for the project-based science orientation is weak.

According to Magnusson et al. (1999), an *inquiry orientation* has the goal to "represent science as inquiry" and the nature of instruction is characterized as being "investigation centered" (pp. 100–101). Tamir (1983) is cited as a reference. In his study, Tamir compared preservice and practicing biology teachers' conceptions of inquiry. Data collection consisted of asking participants to write three associations that came to mind about the concept inquiry and to write a definition of inquiry. Tamir found that "experienced teachers are more inclined to associate inquiry with scientific research, while the student teachers associate inquiry more with learning and teaching" (p. 661). Tamir discussed the desirability of representing science as inquiry and offered suggestions for helping preservice teachers acquire the view of science as inquiry. Tamir examined preservice and practicing teachers conceptions of inquiry but did not examine teachers' inquiry orientation to teaching science, in terms of their views about goals and purposes of teaching science.

Guided inquiry is the ninth proposed orientation. Magnusson et al. (1999) described the goal of guided inquiry as to "constitute a community of learners whose members share responsibility for understanding the physical world, particularly aspects with respect to using the tools of science" (p. 100). Magnusson and Palinscar (1995), who were referenced for this orientation, described guided inquiry in the following way:

> Guided inquiry attempts to blend the emphases of several science education reform efforts of the past. First, it assumes an inquiry-based approach similar to curricula developed in the 1960s, which were focused on discovery learning .... Second, guided inquiry emphasizes the development of conceptual understandings of science, an essential feature of the conceptual change approaches first developed in the 1980s and still in development today. (p. 44)

Magnusson and Palinscar (1995) described the guided inquiry heuristic and highlighted one elementary teacher's implementation of the heuristic over the course of a school year. In their study, guided inquiry was used a curriculum orientation rather than a view of science teaching held by teachers.

Summary of Orientations to Teaching Science. In summary, if Magnusson and her colleagues (1999) intended to illustrate a variety of orientations identified in the science education literature, they accomplished their goal. However, upon closer analysis of the references for the nine different orientations to teaching science, we identified several concerns. First, the few empirical studies cited that included teachers' beliefs related to their planning and teaching science were based on a small number of cases, primarily of elementary teachers; middle and secondary science teachers were underrepresented in the studies cited. We think it is problematic to assume that these categories developed from studies of elementary teachers will apply to secondary science teachers. Second, many of the orientations to teaching science were based on curriculum orientations instead of empirical studies of the goals of teachers. Moreover, in some cases, the underlying theoretical background for even the curriculum orientations was not explicit. After analyzing the origins of the Magnusson et al. proposed orientations, we saw the need to examine the subsequent published research on orientations to teaching science to understand how the construct of orientations has been applied. In the next section of this paper, we discuss how PCK researchers have used, and sometimes misinterpreted or even misused, this list of science teaching orientations.

Issues in Studies of Orientations to Teaching Science

We have used the Magnusson et al. PCK model in our own research for several years. At research conferences, we have engaged in many discussions with other researchers as we have noted the variety of ways the model and orientations have been applied in research studies. After rereading the original chapter that introduced the model, and studying the references cited as sources for the model, several issues emerged. *First,* as pointed out above, there are different definitions of orientations toward teaching science: one focusing on the purposes and goals of teaching science (cf. Grossman, 1990) and one that describes orientations as a general way of viewing teaching science and connects views with teachers' actions (cf. Anderson & Smith, 1987). *Second,* from a rereading of the original chapter, it became apparent the relations between the components within the model are either not explicit or even absent. The orientations component is connected to the other components by two-way arrows; however, the connection is merely described as "shaping". There is no explanation for what "shaping" means. *Third,* as explained above, the nine different science teaching orientations that are identified by Magnusson et al. seem to come from different sources; their theoretical and empirical backgrounds are either weak or nonexistent.

To test this initial list of issues in light of published research, we conducted library searches using The Web of Science and SCOPUS, using the key words "pedagogical content knowledge and/or PCK" and "Magnusson, Krajcik and Borko". In combining results from these two searches, we compiled a list of 63 published papers citing Magnusson et al. (1999). We read each of these

63 papers to determine how the authors used the Magnusson et al. model and the orientations construct in their study. It turned out that about 60% of these papers only referred to the Magnusson et al. paper, sometimes not even mentioning the model. Roughly, the remaining papers used the model as (one of) the central framework(s) to the study. Obviously, we have focused on those papers that drew considerably on the Magnusson et al. model and on the use of the orientations construct in particular. By doing this, we aimed to elaborate on our initial list of issues within the published literature. It is not our intent to publish a list of "offenders", but rather to explore the set of issues in an attempt to move the field forward. As PCK researchers, we have grappled with these issues ourselves, and thus we will place our own published studies among those illustrating concerns.

Below, we discuss each of the above-mentioned issues in more detail, including one additional issue that emerged from our review of 24 published PCK studies that used the Magnusson et al. model to frame their study. It is not our aim to give a comprehensive review of the use of the orientations construct in all of these 24 papers. Instead, we have chosen to describe examples taken from these papers to illustrate the respective issues.

Issue 1: Using Orientations in Different or Unclear Ways

Orientations toward teaching science have been *used in different or unclear ways,* either focusing on purposes and goals of teaching science or on general views about teaching science, often in connection with typical patterns of teaching behavior. In some studies, the meaning of orientations is not made explicit. This may not seem surprising, since, as noted above, the Magnusson et al. (1999) chapter itself contains different definitions.

Our review of the literature showed that many researchers have used the idea of orientations toward science teaching focusing on the nine categories described by Magnusson et al. (e.g., Friedrichsen et al., 2009; Park & Oliver, 2008a, 2008b; Schwarz & Gwekwerere, 2007; Volkmann, Abell, & Zgagacz, 2005). These researchers interpreted orientations in terms of general views of science in relation to typical patterns of teaching actions, that is, consistent with the Anderson and Smith (1987) definition of orientations. In several studies, Appleton (2003, 2008) investigated how beginning primary science teachers developed PCK using the PCK framework adopted from Shulman (1986), Grossman (1990), and Magnusson et al. (1999). In one paper, Appleton (2003) concluded that primary teachers sometimes relied exclusively on "activities that work". He considers this a "distortion of discovery learning, and is an orientation to science" (p. 17), referring to Magnusson et al. In another study (Appleton, 2008), he concluded that primary teachers' interaction with children had changed "toward a more inquiry-based constructivist orientation" (p. 539). In both studies, Appleton did not define the meaning of orientation, nor were other possible orientations addressed. Although Park and Oliver (2008a, 2008b) used the nine orientations from Magnusson et al. (1999) as part of their instrument, they also presented a PCK model in which orientations to teaching science are made up of *beliefs about purposes of learning science, decision making in teaching,* and *beliefs about the nature of science.* The authors did not explain this part of the model.

Other scholars, staying closer to Grossman's definition, have focused on the goals and purposes of teaching science in their interpretation of orientations toward science teaching. Ball, Thames, and Phelps (2008) used the term orientations to content (e.g., literature), referring to Grossman, but without explaining what an orientation is, and not mentioning goals or purposes of teaching content. Similarly, Roehrig and Luft (2004, 2006) and Buaraphan et al. (2007) used orientations in an implicit, undefined way. Cohen and Yarden (2009) used the Magnusson et al. definition, emphasizing knowledge of purposes and goals for learning science, in a study of junior high teachers' PCK for teaching the cell. A questionnaire was used to probe teachers' orientations toward teaching the topic of cells. However, the results were framed in general terms such as "teachers had positive orientations toward the cell topic" (p. 141) and were explained in terms of the importance the teachers attached to the topic, or their affection or interest for it. None of the nine orientations as described by Magnusson et al. were mentioned in this paper. Lee and Luft (2008) use the term "orientation", distinguishing domain-specific and topic-specific orientations *toward* PCK. This, again, is a different use of the term orientation than Magnusson et al. (1999). Veal and MaKinster (1999) used orientations as general PCK strategies, for science, in contrast to subject-specific PCK strategies. By viewing orientations as strategies, these authors deviate from both original sources that were used by Magnusson et al. (1999; i.e., purposes or general views). In summary, the term "orientations" has been used extensively in the literature; however, the construct is defined in substantially different ways, if it is defined at all.

Issue 2: Unclear or Absent Relationship between Orientations and Other Model Components

In most research using the Magnusson et al. PCK model, the *relation of orientations with the other PCK components remains unclear* and/or is not empirically investigated. In particular, the role of orientations as "shaping" other PCK components is rarely made explicit or supported by empirical evidence. This seems related to the fact that in the Magnusson et al. chapter, the meaning of "shaping" is not elaborated, and that relations among components are not discussed.

Our review of the literature showed that many studies attempt to capture the PCK of science teachers at one moment in time. In such studies, typically the content of various components of PCK, including teachers' orientations toward teaching science, are investigated, but oftentimes not in relation to each other. To give an example, Avraamidou and Zembal-Saul (2005) investigated one first-year elementary teacher's specialized practice and knowledge, using the PCK model of Magnusson et al. to frame their study. They conducted an orientation interview to understand the teacher's "orientation to teaching and learning science" (p. 971). It is not made clear, however, how this orientation is related to other components of teacher knowledge. Although the authors found, among others, that the teacher frequently engaged students in collecting evidence, they did not draw a conclusion in terms of the teacher having a specific orientation toward science, nor did they use one of the nine orientations from the Magnusson et al. paper. Instead the authors focused on the relation between the teacher's knowledge and her practice.

In other studies, the development of PCK over time was investigated. In some of these studies, researchers investigated how one component of PCK impacts upon the development of another or how orientations shaped the other components. For instance, Nilsson (2008) provided examples of how orientations are related to other emerging components of preservice elementary teachers' PCK. However, most published papers are not clear about the relationships between orientations and other PCK components, or simply omit (most of) these components. For example, Volkmann and Zgagacz (2004) show how science teacher orientations may conflict between a teacher educator and a graduate teaching assistant, and how the interaction between these two actors, over time, results in shifts in both their orientations. However, other PCK components are not investigated. In summary, although orientations to teaching science are defined in the model of Magnusson et al. as shaping the various components of PCK, very few studies have addressed the relationship between orientations and the other PCK components.

Issue 3: Assigning Science Teachers to One of the Nine Orientations
For some studies, researchers *assign science teachers to one of the nine orientations* described by Magnusson et al., despite the fact that most of these orientations have a weak empirical basis. Moreover, although the Magnusson et al. chapter indicates that teachers can hold multiple orientations, for instance, depending on the topic or the grade level they teach, this has been overlooked by assigning teachers a single label. Magnusson and colleagues may not have intended for their list of nine orientations to become *the list of science teaching orientations;* however, once published, many researchers have interpreted the categories in this way.

The list of nine orientations is an attractive and quick "fix" to the thorny problem of characterizing teachers' complex beliefs systems, related to the purpose and goals for teaching their subject matter (Friedrichsen & Dana, 2005). However, our review of the literature revealed studies in which teachers were simplistically labeled as holding just one of the nine science teaching orientations. Schwarz and Gwekwerere (2007) noted that their prospective teachers held elements of multiple orientations as evidenced by their lesson plans, but the researchers chose to report only the orientation they thought was dominant. In our own work, we have also used the categories as a quick fix. We used the didactic label to describe the science teaching orientations of four beginning teachers entering an alternative certification program (Friedrichsen et al., 2009), even though some elements of the teachers' beliefs did not match this label. Kapyla, Heikkinen, and Asunta (2009) preferred to use only two orientations (i.e., constructivist and conceptual; derived from Adams and Krockover, 1997, and Hashweh, 1996) instead of Magnusson et al.'s list of nine orientations. These authors explained how these two orientations relate to (combinations of) the various orientations of Magnusson et al. They also labeled student teachers as having just one orientation. Similarly, Roehrig and Luft (2004, 2006), referring to Magnusson et al.'s orientations, assigned beginning science teachers to just one out of three (or four) possible orientations, thus reducing the range of orientations considerably. Other researchers, however, have applied multiple labels to identify the science teaching orientations held by a single individual. For example, Volkmann, in a self-study, described himself as holding three competing orientations: didactic, inquiry, and discovery (Volkmann et al., 2005; cf. Volkmann & Zgagacz, 2004).

These two strategies, reporting only the dominant orientation and identifying multiple orientations for an individual, cause us to question the usefulness of Magnusson et al.'s categories of nine orientations. As researchers, how do we sort through complex belief sets and distill these beliefs, for practical reasons and ease of comparison, to report only critical differences among groups of teachers? There is certainly a need for categories that distinguish among different sets of teacher beliefs. We conclude that Magnusson et al.'s list of nine categories is problematic for this purpose.

Issue 4: Ignoring the Overarching Orientations Component

Whereas the three previous issues are directly related to our analysis of the Magnusson et al. chapter, we found an additional issue when we reviewed the published PCK literature. Within the Magnusson et al. PCK model, orientations toward teaching science is an overarching component that shapes, and is shaped by, the other four components: knowledge and beliefs about curricula, students' understanding of science, instructional strategies, and assessment of scientific literacy. Some researchers have used the model but *ignored the overarching orientations component,* focusing on just one or two other PCK components. For example, some studies focused on one component of the model such as knowledge of student understanding of science, ignoring all the other components, including orientations (e.g., Gullberg, Kellner, Attorps, Thoren, & Tarneberg, 2008). Davis (2004) mentioned the Magnusson et al. PCK model as one of others that include various knowledge components. Without mentioning all the various components explicitly, she stated that her case study of a prospective elementary teacher's developing knowledge "focuses on instructional representations", because this aspect of PCK can be developed "even without much teaching experience" (p. 24).

Other studies compare and relate two components of the model such as students' understandings and instructional strategies while omitting the orientations component (Brown, Friedrichsen, & Abell, 2009; De Jong et al., 2005). Henze et al. (2008), although using the Magnusson et al. model to frame their study, ignored orientations toward science teaching. Instead, they included knowledge of goals and purposes in the PCK component "knowledge about goals and objectives in the curriculum". Brown (2008) originally planned to study beginning teachers' PCK development within two categories: knowledge of instructional strategies and knowledge of learners. He found that he was unable to explain the relationship between these two components without examining the mediating effect of the individuals' science teaching orientations (Brown, personal communication, Fall 2008). Although he added the orientations component to his dissertation study (Brown, 2008), it was omitted from some publications to meet journal page limit requirements (e.g., Brown et al., 2009). This may explain why in some studies only some PCK aspects are included, either with or without a connection to science teaching orientations. In summary, the overarching role of science teaching orientations in the PCK model is often neglected in empirical studies.

Discussion

In this section, we discuss possible reasons for the four issues described above and explore a set of teacher beliefs that appear to have consensus among some researchers. First, owing to their very nature, teacher beliefs are difficult to define; this difficulty has led to the "messiness" of the science teaching orientations construct in the literature (Friedrichsen & Dana, 2005). When we looked critically at the origins of the concept of science teaching orientations, we found a dual conceptualization (i.e., orientations are seen either as purposes for science teaching, or as general views about teaching science). As we have illustrated, the focus on purposes and goals is sometimes lost, and scholars have used orientations in a variety of ways, or used different constructs instead (Issue 1). Second, one avoids the messiness by simply ignoring the science teaching orientation component of the PCK model (Issue 4). We suspect this is a common rationale and, in part, this prompted us to write this paper. Also, researchers may choose to omit the orientations component due to the implicit or tacit nature of teacher beliefs (Eraut, 1994). Whereas it is fairly straightforward to observe a teacher's practice and then elicit and describe the teacher's knowledge of instructional strategies, beliefs about purposes, and goals for teaching science are often implicit, unobservable, and difficult to elicit. Third, as an alternative to omitting orientations, one may also choose to use the list of nine orientations as a "quick fix", pigeonholing teachers rather than doing justice to the complex nature of their orientations (Issue 3). Finally, the complexity of the orientations construct and the PCK model as a whole may lead scholars to limit themselves to investigating only certain aspects of it (Issue 4) or ignore the relationships between orientations and other PCK components (Issue 2). Multiple definitions and unclear use of science teaching orientations construct (Issue 1) likely contribute to the difficulty in examining relationships between teaching orientations and other PCK components (Issue 2). From a practical point of view, these issues could also be due to journal page limit constraints, which results in large qualitative studies being divided into multiple publications (Henze et al., 2007, 2008; Brown et al., 2009).

As a result of these issues, the research literature on PCK and science teaching orientations has become conceptually diverse and vague, which has hindered practical applications of this research in the context of in-service and preservice science teacher education. We would argue that this messiness, and the confusion that results from it, has also led to some researchers losing interest in studying the construct of science teaching orientations (Friedrichsen & Dana, 2005).

To move the field forward, we suggest that science teaching orientations, as a construct, needs a better theoretical basis. There is evidence (e.g., Brown et al., 2009; Nilsson, 2008) to support Magnusson et al.'s placement of science teaching orientations as filtering or shaping the content and development of the other PCK components. The question then becomes, what sorts of views, or beliefs, or conceptions, play a shaping or determining role in this respect? The research literature has focused on many different aspects of teachers' beliefs. To name the most important:
- Conceptions of science teaching and learning, including beliefs about the role of the teacher, the learner, how students learn science, and how to teach

it in ways that make science attractive and comprehensible. Some researchers have focused on these types of beliefs (e.g., Luft & Roehrig, 2007, using a teacher belief interview, or Veal & Makinster, 1999, who used the term "general PCK").
– Conceptions about the nature of science (e.g., Ledermann, 1992), sometimes divided into ontological beliefs, that is, beliefs about the status of reality or the existence of scientific objects (Kwak, 2001) and epistemological beliefs, about issues such as "what counts as knowledge, how this is produced and warranted or justified" (Phillips, 1997, p. 162).
– Conceptions about the goals or functions of science education in general, for example, divided into learning science, learning to do science, and learning about science (Hodson, 1992), or teaching science for intellectual development, or for individual fulfillment, or for socioeconomic benefit (Schulz, 2009).

Several authors have proposed models for the beliefs that – explicitly or implicitly – shape science teachers' knowledge and practice. These models consist of several dimensions, more or less similar to the ones described above. For instance, long before the introduction of the Magnusson et al. model, Roberts (1982) introduced the notion of *curriculum emphases* as

> a coherent set of messages to the student about science (rather than within science). Such messages constitute objectives which go beyond learning the facts, principles, laws and theories of the subject matter itself – objectives which provide an answer to the student question: "Why am I learning this?" (p. 245)

These messages can be conveyed through textbooks as well science teachers. Roberts identified seven distinct curriculum emphases; each one being portrayed in terms of underlying views of science, the learner, the teacher and society. The seven curriculum emphases are *everyday coping; structure of science; science, technology, decisions; scientific skill development; correct explanations; self as explainer,* and *solid foundation* (Roberts, 1988). To give just one example, the curriculum emphasis *correct explanations* is based on a view of science as "the best meaning system ever developed for getting at the truth about natural objects and events", a view of the learner as "someone whose preconceptions need to be replaced and corrected", a view of the teacher as "one responsible for identifying and correcting the errors in student thinking", and a view of society that needs "true believers in the meaning system most appropriate for natural objects and events" (1988, p. 45). One can see that this description includes elements of the nature of science, goals of science education, and views of teaching and learning.

In a later study, Smith and Neale (1989) proposed dimensions similar to Roberts' (1988) curriculum emphases. The authors built on Anderson and Smith's (1987) orientation categories and conceptualized four dimensions for each orientation by providing descriptions to the following prompts: Science is, School science is, Learning science is, and Teaching science is. For example, for the *processes* orientation, science is viewed as the "scientific method, processes of science", whereas school science is defined as "learning scientific method, process approaches" (p. 11). Learning science (the student's role) is characterized in this orientation as "learning steps in scientific methods and practicing them: observing, drawing conclusions, collecting data, testing hypotheses, inferring, observing teacher model correct steps" (p. 11). With a *processes* orientation, teaching science (the teacher's role) is characterized as "demonstrating and teaching steps in scientific method, providing opportunities to practice, maintaining children's correct use of method, managing activities" (p. 11). Although the language is slightly different, Smith and Neale (1989) used dimensions similar to Roberts' curriculum emphases: nature of science, goals of science education, and views of science teaching and learning.

As another example, Lotter, Harwood, and Bonner (2007), who did not use Magnusson et al.'s PCK model, proposed a model for the critical dimensions of teacher beliefs. They identified four types of core conceptions, not very different from the ones mentioned above: conceptions of science, conceptions of overarching purposes of education, conceptions of students, and conceptions of effective teaching. For each of the core beliefs, these authors offer a continuum of dimensions. The core conception of science was represented on a continuum from facts to process. The core conception of purpose of education was represented on a continuum from amass information to develop problem-solving skills. The core conception of students' abilities was represented on a continuum from limited ability to expanding ability. The core conception of effective teaching was represented on a continuum of transmission of information to encouraging independent thought. On the basis of our review of the literature and these studies in particular, we make recommendations for defining the construct of science teaching orientations in the next section.

Conclusions and Further Research

Given the importance of beliefs in the development of teachers' PCK and practice and given the current attention to the Magnusson et al. model in this respect, there is a need for conceptual and methodological clarity concerning the role of science teaching orientations.

What Are Science Teaching Orientations?

The examples described above share the idea that science teachers' knowledge and practice are shaped by multiple beliefs, or that teachers' belief systems consist of various dimensions. There appears to be some consensus in the literature that these dimensions include beliefs about the goals or purposes of science teaching, (the nature of) science, and science teaching and learning. By looking for relationships between, and patterns in these beliefs, one can construct profiles of science teachers' interrelated beliefs (cf. Volkmann et al., 2005). These profiles allow for a more nuanced way to portray science teachers' ideas than simply labeling or pigeonholing teachers, using a predetermined list of categories. We see this as a promising way to sort through complex belief sets to allow comparisons that distinguish among different sets of teacher beliefs. Therefore, we propose that orientations toward science teaching be reconceptualized as consisting of interrelated sets of beliefs that teachers hold in regard to the dimensions listed above. Consequently, the list of nine categories has to be critically reexamined.

How Can Science Teaching Orientations Be Investigated?

The above recommendation has implications for research on science teaching orientations. Based on a sound theoretical framework, empirical studies are needed to determine which distinctive different science teaching orientations exist in practice. For this purpose, a specific instrument needs to be designed. Obviously, researchers can draw upon existing instruments for this purpose (e.g., teacher belief interview, Luft & Roehrig, 2007; metaphors, as used by Henze et al., 2007) and instruments that are used to investigate teachers' views on the nature of science (e.g., Chen, 2006). The instrument should enable a systematic investigation of the various dimensions that make up science teaching orientations. Typical patterns or profiles of these dimensions need to be identified, in terms of interrelated beliefs about purposes of science teaching, views about science, and beliefs about learning and teaching science. Patterns or profiles that are found empirically should be interpreted from a theoretical point of view, leading to the identification of labels or categories of distinctly different science teaching orientations.

Implications for Future Research

We recommend researchers investigate science teaching orientations from the multiangle perspective outlined above, instead of categorizing teachers into one of the nine categories of Magnusson et al., or any other list of categories (Issue 3). In addition, we recommend researchers investigate the interaction between science teaching orientations and the other PCK components (Issue 4). Studies that focus on how science teaching orientations impact science teachers' emerging or developing PCK, and whether, and how, the development of PCK affects science teacher orientations are needed (Issue 2). Alternatively, the relationship between science teaching orientations and teachers' classroom practice is a relevant focus of future research, in particular, in the context of initial teacher education programs or during curriculum innovation. In any case, researchers using science teaching orientations should be explicit about their definition of the construct, situating their definition within the research literature (Issue 1).

In conclusion, our purpose was to illuminate issues that have arisen in PCK studies related to science teaching orientations used in the context of the Magnusson et al. (1999) PCK model for science teaching. We reviewed the historical context of the model and examined the relatively weak empirical basis of the nine categories of science teaching orientations. From a review of published studies, we identified a set of issues related to the use of the orientations construct. We identified these issues, in part, to serve as a cautionary note to PCK researchers. We acknowledge that these issues arise from problems inherent in the messiness of teacher beliefs, which are complex and implicitly held. Next, we reviewed the literature searching for consensus on the dimensions of teachers' beliefs that influence practice. We propose the following three dimensions for science teaching orientations: beliefs about the goals or purposes of science teaching, beliefs about the nature of science, and beliefs about science teaching and learning. In making the above recommendations, we see this as the first step toward developing conceptual and methodological clarity.

Acknowledgement

Contract grant sponsor: National Science Foundation Teacher Professional Continuum (TPC) program. Contract grant number: 0202847.

Any opinions, findings, and conclusions or recommendations expressed in this material are those of the author(s) and do not necessarily reflect the views of the National Science Foundation.

This article is dedicated in memory of Sandra K. Abell, who co-wrote this article and passed away on August 24, 2010, after a courageous battle with cancer.

Note

1 Originally published as Friedrichsen, P., Van Driel, J. H., & Abell, S.K. (2011). Taking a closer look at science teaching orientations. *Science Education, 95*(2), 358–376. Reprinted, with minor edits, with permission from the publisher.

References

Abell, S. K. (2007). Research on science teacher learning. In S. K. Abell & N. G. Lederman (Eds.), *Handbook of research on science education* (pp. 1105–1149). Erlbaum.

Adams, P. E., & Krockover, G. H. (1997). Beginning science teacher cognition and its origin in the preservice secondary science teacher program. *Journal of Research in Science Teaching, 34*, 633–653.

Anderson, C. W., & Smith, E. L. (1987). Teaching science. In V. Richardson-Koehler (Ed.), *Educators' handbook: A research perspective* (pp. 84–111). Longman.

Appleton, K. (2003). How do beginning primary teachers cope with science? Toward an understanding of science teaching practice. *Research in Science Education, 33*, 1–25.

Appleton, K. (2008). Developing science pedagogical content knowledge through mentoring elementary teachers. *Journal of Science Teacher Education, 19*, 523–545.

Avraamidou, L., & Zembal-Saul, C. (2005). Giving priority to evidence in science teaching: A first-year elementary teacher's specialized practices and knowledge. *Journal of Research in Science Teaching, 42*, 965–986.

Ball, D. L., Thames, M. H., & Phelps, G. (2008). Content knowledge for teaching. *Journal of Teacher Education, 59*, 389–407.

Berry, A., Loughran, J. J., & Van Driel, J. H. (2008). Revisiting the roots of pedagogical content knowledge. *International Journal of Science Education, 30*, 1271–1279.

Berry, A., Friedrichsen, P., & Loughran, J. (2015). *Re-examining pedagogical content knowledge in science education*. Routledge Press.

Blecha, M. K., Gega, P. C., & Green, M. (1979). *Exploring science – Green book* (Teacher's ed.). Laidlaw Brothers.

Brophy, J. E., & Good, T. C. (1986). Teacherbehaviorand student achievement. In M. C. Wittrock (Ed.), *Handbook of research on teaching* (3rd ed., pp. 328–375). Macmillan.

Brown, P. (2008). *Investigating teacher knowledge of learners and learning and sequence of science instruction in an alternative certification program* [Unpublished doctoral dissertation]. University of Missouri, Columbia.

Brown, P., Friedrichsen, P., & Abell, S. (2009, April). *Teachers' knowledgeoflearners andinstrnctionalsequencing in an alternative certification program* [Paper presentation]. The annual meeting of the American Educational Research Association, San Diego, CA.

Buaraphan, K., Roadrangka, V., Srisukvatananan, P., Singh, P., Forret, M., & Taylor, I. (2007). The development and exploration of preservice physics teachers' pedagogical content knowledge: From a methods course to teaching practice. *Kasetsart Journal, 28*, 276–287.

Carlson, J., Daehler, K. R., Alonzo, A. C., Barendsen, E., Berry, A., Borowski, A., Carpendale, J., Chan, K. K. H., Cooper, R., Friedrichsen, P., Gess-Newsome, J., Henze-Rietveld, I., Hume, A., Kirschner, S., Liepertz, S., Loughran, J., Mavhunga, E., Neumann, K., Nilsson, P., Park, S., Rollnick, M., Sickel, A., Schneider, R. M., Suh, J. K., Van Driel, J., & Wilson, C. D. (2019). The refined consensus model of pedagogical content knowledge in science education. In A. Hume, R. Cooper, & A. Borowski (Eds.), *Repositioning pedagogical content knowledge in teachers' knowledge for teaching science* (pp. 77–92). Springer.

Carlson, J., Stokes, L., Helms, J., Gess-Newsome, J., & Gardner, A. (2015). The PCK Summit. In A. Berry, P. Friedrichsen, & J. Loughran (Eds.), *Re-examining pedagogical content knowledge in science education* (pp. 14–27). Routledge Press.

Chen, S. (2006). Development of an instrument to assess views on nature of science and attitudes toward teaching science. *Science Education, 90*, 803–819.

Cohen, R., & Yarden, A. (2009). Experienced junior-high-school teachers' PCK in light of a curriculum change: "The cell is to be studied longitudinally". *Research in Science Education, 39*, 131–155.

Cooper, R., & Van Driel, J. H. (2019). Developing research on PCK as a community. In A. Hume, R. Cooper, & A. Borowski (Eds.), *Repositioning pedagogical content knowledge in teachers' knowledge for teaching science* (pp. 301–313). Springer.

Davis, E. (2004). Knowledge integration in science teaching: Analysing teachers' knowledge development. *Research in Science Education, 34*, 21–53.

Davis, E. A., Petish, D., & Smithey, J. (2006). Challenges new science teachers face. *Review of Educational Research, 76*, 607–651.

DeBoer, G. (1991). *The history of ideas in science education: Implications for practice.* Teachers College Press.

De Jong, O., Van Driel, J. H., & Verloop, N. (2005). Preservice teachers' pedagogical content knowledge of using particle models in teaching chemistry. *Journal of Research in Science Teaching, 42*, 947–964.

Eaton, J. F., Anderson, C. W., & Smith, E. L. (1984). Students' misconceptions interfere with science learning: Case studies of fifth-grade students. *The Elementary School Journal, 84*, 365–379.

Eraut, M. (1994). *Developing professional knowledge and competence.* Falmer Press.

Friedrichsen, P. (2002). *A substantive-level theory of highly-regarded secondary biology teachers' science teaching orientations* [Unpublished doctoral dissertation]. The Pennsylvania State University, University Park.

Friedrichsen, P. (2015). My PCK research trajectory. A purple book prompts new questions. In A. Berry, P. Friedrichsen, & J. Loughran (Eds.), *Re-examining pedagogical content knowledge in science education* (pp. 147–161). Routledge Press.

Friedrichsen, P., Abell, S., Pareja, E., Brown, P., Lankford, D., & Volkmann, M. (2009). Does teaching experience matter? Examining biology teachers' prior knowledge for teaching in an alternative certification program. *Journal of Research in Science Teaching, 46,* 357–383.

Friedrichsen, P., & Dana, T. (2005). A substantive-level theory of highly-regarded secondary biology teachers' science teaching orientations. *Journal of Research in Science Teaching, 42,* 218–244.

Friedrichsen, P., Van Driel, J. H., & Abell, S. K. (2011). Taking a closer look at science teaching orientations. *Science Education, 95,* 358–376.

Gess-Newsome, J. (1999). Secondary teachers' knowledge and beliefs about subject matter and their impact on instruction. In J. Gess-Newsome & N. G. Lederman (Eds.), *Examining pedagogical content knowledge* (pp. 51–94). Kluwer.

Gess-Newsome, J. (2015). A model of teacher professional knowledge and skill including PCK. In A. Berry, P. Friedrichsen, & J. Loughran (Eds.), *Re-examining pedagogical content knowledge in science education* (pp. 28–42). Routledge Press.

Gess-Newsome, J., & Lederman, N. G. (Eds.). (1999). *Examining pedagogical content knowledge.* Kluwer.

Grossman, P. L. (1990). *The making of a teacher: Teacher knowledge and teacher education.* Teachers College Press.

Gullberg, A., Kellner, E., Attorps, I., Thoren, I., & Tarneberg, R. (2008). Prospective teachers' initial conceptions about pupils' understanding of science and mathematics. *European Journal of Teacher Education, 31,* 257–278.

Hashweh, M. (1996). Effects of science teachers' epistemological beliefs in teaching. *Journal of Research in Science Teaching, 33,* 47–63.

Henze, I., Van Driel, J. H., & Verloop, N. (2007). Science teachers' knowledge about teaching models and modelling in the context of a new syllabus on public understanding of science. *Research in Science Education, 37,* 99–122.

Henze, I., Van Driel, J. H., & Verloop, N. (2008). The development of experienced science teachers' pedagogical content knowledge of models of the solar system and the universe. *International Journal of Science Education, 30,* 1321–1342.

Hodson, D. (1992). In search of a meaningful relationship: An exploration of some issues relating to integration in science and science education. *International Journal of Science Education, 14,* 541–562.

Jones, M. G., & Carter, G. (2007). Science teacher attitudes and beliefs. In S. K. Abell & N. G. Lederman (Eds.), *Handbook of research on science education* (pp. 1067–1104). Erlbaum.

Kapyla, M., Heikkinen, J., & Asunta, T. (2009). Influence of content knowledge on pedagogical content knowledge: The case of teaching photosynthesis and plant growth. *International Journal of Science Education, 31*, 1395–1415.

Karplus, R., & Thier, H. D. (1967). *A new look at elementary school science.* Rand McNally & Co.

Kwak, Y. (2001). *Profile change in preservice science teacher's epistemological and ontological beliefs about constructivist learning: Implications for science teaching and learning* [Unpublished doctoral dissertation]. The Ohio State University, Columbus.

Lantz, O., & Kass, H. (1987). Chemistry teachers' functional paradigms. *Science Education, 71*(1), 117–134.

Lederman, N. G. (1992). Students' and teachers' conceptions of the nature of science: A review of the research. *Journal of Research in Science Teaching, 29*, 331–359.

Lee, E., & Luft, J. (2008). Experienced secondary science teachers' representation of pedagogical content knowledge. *International Journal of Science Education, 30*, 1343–1363.

Little, J. W. (2003). Inside teacher community: Representations of classroom practice. *Teachers College Record, 105*, 913–945.

Lotter, C., Harwood, W. S., & Bonner, J. J. (2007). The influence of core teaching conceptions on teachers' use of inquiry teaching practices. *Journal of Research in Science Teaching, 44*, 1318–1347.

Loughran, J., Milroy, P., Berry, A., Gunstone, R., & Mulhall, P. (2001). Documenting science teachers' pedagogical content knowledge through PaP-eRs. *Research in Science Education, 31*, 289–307.

Loughran, J., Mulhall, P., & Berry, A. (2008). Exploring pedagogical content knowledge in science teacher education. *International Journal of Science Education, 30*, 1301–1320.

Louws, M. L., Meirink, J. A., Van Veen, K., & Van Driel, J. H. (2017). Teachers' self-directed learning and teaching experience: What, how, and why teachers want to learn. *Teaching and Teacher Education, 66*, 171–183.

Luft, J., & Roehrig, G. (2007). Capturing science teachers' epistemological beliefs: The development of a teacher beliefs interview. *Electronic Journal of Science Education, 11*(2), 38–63.

Magnusson, S., Krajcik, J., & Borko, H. (1999). Nature, sources and development of pedagogical content knowledge for science teaching. In J. Gess-Newsome & N. G. Lederman (Eds.), *Examining pedagogical content knowledge* (pp. 95–132). Kluwer.

Magnusson, S. J., & Palinscar, A. S. (1995). The learning environment as a site of science education reform. *Theory into Practice, 34*, 43–50.

Marx, R. W., Blumenfeld, P. C., Krajcik, J. S., Blunk, M., Crawford, B., Kelly, B., et al. (1994). Enacting project-based science: Experiences of four middle grade teachers. *The Elementary School Journal, 94*, 517–538.

Millar, R., & Driver, R. (1987). Beyond processes. *Studies in Science Education, 14*, 33–62.

Nilsson, P. (2008). Teaching for understanding: The complex nature of pedagogical content knowledge in preservice education. *International Journal of Science Education, 30*, 1281–1299.

Olson, J. K. (1983, April). *Mr. Swift and the clock: Understanding teacher influence in the science classroom* [Paper presentation]. The American Educational Research Association Meeting, Montreal, Canada. ERIC Document Reproduction Services No. ED2280064.

Pajares, M. F. (1992). Teachers' beliefs and educational research. Cleaning up a messy construct. *Review of Educational Research, 62*, 307–332.

Park, S., & Oliver, J. S. (2008a). Revisiting the conceptualization of Pedagogical Content Knowledge (PCK): PCK as a conceptual tool to understand teachers as professionals. *Research in Science Education, 38*, 261–284.

Park, S., & Oliver, J. S. (2008b). National Board Certification (NBC) as a catalyst for teachers' learning about teaching: The effects of the NBC process on candidate teachers' PCK development. *Journal of Research in Science Teaching, 45*, 812–834.

Phillips, D. C. (1997). How, why, what, when and where: Perspectives on constructivism in psychology and education. *Issues in Education: Contributions from Educational Psychology, 3*(2), 151–194.

Richardson-Koehler, V. (Ed.). (1987). *Educators' handbook: A research perspective*. Longman.

Roberts, D. A. (1982). Developing the concept of "curriculum emphases" in science education. *Science Education, 66*, 243–260.

Roberts, D. A. (1988). What counts as science education? In P. J. Fensham (Ed.), *Development and dilemmas in science education* (pp. 27–54). Falmer Press.

Roehrig, G. H., & Luft, J. (2004). Constraints experienced by beginning secondary science teachers implementing scientific inquiry lessons. *International Journal of Science Education, 26*, 3–24.

Roehrig, G. H., & Luft, J. (2006). Does one size fit all? The induction experience of beginning science teachers from different teacher-preparation programs. *Journal of Research in Science Education, 43*, 963–985.

Rosenshine, B., & Stevens, R. (1986). Teaching functions. In M. C. Wittrock (Ed.), *Handbook of research on teaching* (3rd ed., pp. 376–391). Macmillan.

Roth, K. J., Anderson, C. W., & Smith, E. L. (1987). Curriculum materials, teacher talk and student learning: Case studies in fifth grade science teaching. *Journal of Curriculum Studies, 19*, 527–548.

Schulz, R. M. (2009). Reforming science education, Part I: The search for a philosophy of science education. *Science & Education, 18*, 225–249.

Schwartz, C. V., & Gwekwerere, Y. (2007). Using a guided inquiry and modeling instructional framework (EIMA) to support preservice K-8 science teaching. *Science Education, 91*, 158–186.

SCIS (Science Curriculum Improvement Study). (1971). *Communities teacher's guide.* Rand McNally.

Shulman, L. S. (1986). Those who understand: Knowledge growth in teaching. *Educational Researcher, 15*(2), 4–14.

Shulman, L. S. (1987). Knowledge and teaching: Foundations of the new reform. *Harvard Educational Review, 57*(1), 1–21.

Slinger, L. A., Anderson, C. W., & Smith, E. L. (1983). *Studying lightinthe fifth-grade: A case study of text-based science teaching* (Research Series No. 129). The Institute for Research on Teaching, Michigan State University.

Smith, D. C., & Neale, D. C. (1989). The construction of subject matter knowledge in primary science teaching. *Teaching & Teacher Education, 5*, 1–20.

Smith, E. L., & Anderson, C. W. (1984a). *The planning and teaching intermediate science study: Final report* (Research Series No. 147). The Institute for Research on Teaching, Michigan State University.

Smith, E. L., & Anderson, C. W. (1984b). Plants as producers: A case study of elementary science teaching. *Journal of Research in Science Teaching, 2*, 685–698.

Smith, E. L., & Sendelbach, N. B. (1982). The programme, the plans and the activities of the classroom: The demands of activity-based science. In J. Olson (Ed.), *Innovation in the science curriculum: Classroom knowledge and curriculum change* (pp. 72–106). Croom Helm.

Tamir, P. (1983). Inquiry and the science teacher. *Science Education, 67*, 657–672.

Van Driel, J. H., & Abell, S. K. (2010). Science teacher education. In B. McGraw, P. L. Peterson, & E. Baker (Eds.), *International encyclopedia of education* (3rd ed., Vol. 7, pp. 712–718). Elsevier.

Van Driel, J. H., De Jong, O., & Verloop, N. (2002). The development of preservice chemistry teachers' PCK. *Science Education, 86*(4), 572–590.

Van Driel, J., Verloop, N., & de Vos, W. (1998). Developing science teachers' pedagogical knowledge. *Journal of Research in Science Teaching, 35*, 763–695.

Veal, W. R., & MaKinster, J. (1999). Pedagogical content knowledge taxonomies. *Electronic Journal for Research in Science & Mathematics Education, 3*(4).

Volkmann, M., Abell, S., & Zgagacz, M. (2005). The challenges of teaching physics to preservice elementary teachers: Orientations of the professor, teaching assistant, and students. *Science Education, 89*, 847–869.

Volkmann, M., & Zgagacz, M. (2004). Learning to teach physics through inquiry: The lived experiences of a graduate teaching assistant. *Journal of Research in Science Teaching, 41*, 584–602.

CHAPTER 9

Professional Learning of Science Teachers

1   How the Chapter Came About

In 2011, I was invited by the organisation committee of the 9th ESERA conference in Lyon, France to give one of the plenary keynote lectures. I was honoured and happily accepted the invitation. It provided me with an opportunity to give an overview talk about the professional learning of science teachers, including pre-service teachers in the context of initial teacher education and in-service teachers, related to educational reform or innovation.

I started the talk with an overview of the main problems in science education internationally, such as overloaded curricula and problematic attitudes towards science, to highlight the central role of science teachers and, referring to our 2001 article in JRST (Van Driel et al., 2011; see Chapter 2), the importance of their practical knowledge as underlying and informing teacher practice. This was followed by a brief historical overview of research on teachers and teaching, culminating in two main questions for the presentation: 1) How to prepare high quality science teachers and how to foster their ongoing professional development? and 2) How can we understand science teachers' development in relation to personal variables and their professional context? With 'we' in the latter question, I referred to the audience as an international community of researchers in science education.

To address these questions, I divided the talk in two parts, the first focusing on pre-service teachers and the second on in-service teachers of science. In both parts, I presented examples from PhD (Pernilla Nilsson, Ineke Henze, Dirk Wongsopawiro) and postdoc (Rosária Justi) projects that I had supervised in recent years. I decided to use the Interconnected Model of Teacher Professional Growth (IMTPG; Clarke & Hollingsworth, 2002) as a framework to connect the two parts of the talk. According to this model, teachers' professional learning can be represented by four domains – the personal domain, the external domain, the domain of practice and the domain of consequence – which are connected through the mediating processes of reflection and enactment. The model had been applied in the project with Rosária (see Chapter 6) as well as in the recently completed PhD study of Dirk Wongsopawiro on PCK development of in-service science teachers in a professional development context. Showcasing the studies of Rosária (pre-service) and Dirk (in-service) and presenting some of their findings enabled me to demonstrate how the IMTPG can be used to both design and analyse teachers' professional learning in a way that recognises that teacher learning is a non-linear and idiosyncratic process which is to a large extent determined by teachers' personal and professional experiences. I concluded the talk by arguing that teachers, as professionals, have a responsibility to keep learning and developing, however, teacher learning is hard to plan and control, and the outcomes of teacher development programs are hard to predict.

The ESERA conference resulted in a book of 35 papers, selected and edited by members of the local organising committee and published by Springer in a series entitled 'Contributions from Science Education Research'. I was asked to contribute a chapter based on my keynote. The chapter, more or less, followed the structure of the talk, however, it provided more space to elaborate on the methodological aspects of the studies with Rosária and Dirk, such as the context, the design and the procedures related to data collection and analysis. This enabled me to explain how in both projects teachers had conducted an action research project and how this had contributed to forge connections between the four domains of the IMTPG. For instance, in Rosária's study, the pre-service teachers used input from the workshops (External Domain) in their classroom experimentation (Domain of Practice) and, as part of their research project, documented and analysed the outcomes of their teaching (Domain of Consequences), leading to changes in their practical knowledge (Personal Domain). Also, I could demonstrate how data analysis with the IMTPG had made it possible to characterise similarities and differences in the knowledge development processes of different teachers.

In Dirk Wongsopawiro's project, the IMTPG was applied to identify pathways that lead to changes in science teachers' pedagogical content knowledge in a professional development program that he had facilitated in the USA. The analysis of the data of in-service science teachers (n = 12) demonstrated how their action research had contributed to PCK development. In particular, conducting a literature review, interacting with peers and reflecting on classroom outcomes appeared to be crucial. At the time of my ESERA talk, Dirk had just completed his PhD thesis. While I was working on the chapter, I was also writing an article with Dirk and Rosanne Zwart on the basis of his thesis (this explains the use of 'we' in this part of the chapter; see pp. 152–154). In this article, which was eventually published in 2016, we proposed to refine the IMTPG by distinguishing between simple and complex growth networks (Wongsopawiro et al., 2016). Teachers whose development was characterised by a simple growth network did not demonstrate whether they learned from their classroom actions, whereas teachers whose development was indicative of a complex growth network, reflected on their students' learning and were able to specify what they learned from their students. I explained this distinction between simple and complex growth networks in my chapter and concluded it with the following comment: "The IMTPG appears to help to make the often tacit and implicit change pathways explicit, and, furthermore, it makes it possible to indicate powerful elements within professional learning programmes" (Van Driel, 2014, p. 155).

The chapter was included in a volume called *Topics and trends in current science education* which was published in 2014. It has only been cited 18 times to date, however, I selected it for this volume because of its emphasis on models of teacher professional learning and how one of these models (i.e., the IMTPG) can be used to design and analyse teacher learning, or growth. The scope of the chapter is relevant beyond the domain of science education and it could potentially speak to an audience with an interest in teacher education and learning more broadly. Note that articles with Rosária and Dirk were published in journals with a focus on teaching and teacher education, one (Justi & Van Driel, 2006) in *Teaching & Teacher Education*, the same journal that had published the Clarke and Hollingsworth article in 2002, and one (Wongsopawiro, Zwart, & Van Driel, 2016) in *Teachers and Teaching: Theory & Practice*.

2   Follow Up

The ESERA lecture took place in a large auditorium and was attended by about 600 delegates. It was concluded with a couple of questions from the audience, after which most of the crowd left the room for a coffee break. A few people walked up to the stage to engage in further discussion with me. One man introduced himself as David Clarke. I had not met him before but realised immediately that he was the first author of the model that had played an important role in my talk. I felt a slight panic coming up and said something like "I hope I did justice to your work". He responded in a friendly tone: "Yes, it was very interesting" and thanked me for the talk. We continued our conversation for a short while, however, I cannot recall the details of that. I could not suspect that this short meeting would be the beginning of a new chapter in my career!

Some time after the ESERA conference, I was contacted by Jim Ryder, editor of the journal *Studies in Science Education*. This journal exclusively publishes review articles of research in science education. Referring to my keynote, Jim invited me to write a review of research on professional learning of in-service science teachers, which I was happy to accept. At that time, my institute hosted a national expertise centre on teacher learning, funded by the Dutch government. They had just published a report which synthesised the research literature on effective teacher professional development (PD). We decided to join forces, the author team thus consisting of Jacobiene Meirink, Rosanne Zwart, Klaas van Veen and myself. We selected 44 articles and analysed these in terms of the goals of the study, the focus, the design of the PD program and the outcomes. We paid specific attention to the congruence of goals, design features and outcome measures. The IMTPG was used to categorise the goals of each study in terms of the domains of the IMTPG that were included. This led us to distribute the studies in four categories: (1) studies focusing on the impact of the PD program (i.e., the External Domain) on either classroom practice (Domain of Practice), or (2) on teacher knowledge (Personal Domain), (3) studies that investigated how the PD had led to changes in both domains, and (4) studies that also included student outcomes (Domain of Consequence). It turned out that the latter two categories carried the large majority of all articles (22 and 15, respectively).

The design of the PD programs was assessed in terms of six core features of what makes PD effective. These features had been identified in the review of Jacobiene, Rosanne and Klaas on the basis of a number of recent studies, mostly from the USA, by scholars such as Borko, Desimone and Yoon. We summarised these design features as follows: (1) focus, (2) active and inquiry-based learning, (3) collaborative learning, (4) duration and sustainability, (5) coherence and (6) school organisational conditions. Our analysis showed that almost all the selected studies had incorporated most of these six features. Every PD program had a focus on specific science content, was related to classroom activities and involved teachers in an active or inquiry-based way. Many were collective in nature. Most programs appeared to be coherent and had a long enough duration. The only features missing in most studies were sustainability and school organisational aspects, which led us to suggest that "PD developers and researchers may not take the daily school reality of science teachers participating in their PD into account, or at least fail to report on it" (Van Driel et al., 2012, p. 154). We also noted that the articles were silent about the expertise of PD providers and typically did not investigate the relation between effectiveness of PD and success of the reform of science education the program was associated with. As for the IMTPG, we concluded that the model was helpful to identify outcomes of PD in different domains and in relation to each other. We recommended to use the IMTPG for the design of powerful professional learning programs. The article was published in 2012, exactly a year after my ESERA keynote (Van Driel, Meirink, Van Veen, & Zwart, 2012). It started to get cited quickly and has accumulated more than 190 citations in Google Scholar to date.

I would meet David Clarke again at the annual conference of the Australasian Science Education Research Association (ASERA) in Melbourne, 2014.

Although most of his research was related to mathematics education, David was one of the few academics in that domain who also attended conferences in science and STEM education, such as ESERA and ASERA. If he hadn't, we might never have met. By this time, I was starting to think of continuing my career in Australia. When I found out that both of us were going to be at the annual meeting of the American Education Research Association (AERA) in Chicago in 2015, I wrote an email to David: "I am exploring job opportunities in Australia. Would you be available for an informal chat?" We met over coffee and at the end David said, "Let me talk to my dean". Things moved quickly after that, and in September 2016 I commenced in the Melbourne Graduate School of Education (MGSE) of the University of Melbourne as a professor of science education.

The opportunity to work with David was a major attraction to move to MGSE. We were both very interested in teacher professional learning and met regularly to discuss possible projects. We started supervising PhD candidates together. David introduced me to Hilary Hollingsworth, co-author of the IMTPG article, and I learned about the origins and context in which the model had been developed. We discussed how the model, which is focused on the growth of individual teachers, could account for the influence of peers and colleagues and whether it could be amended to cover collaborative teacher learning. The impact of peers on teacher learning was a major theme in the study of Dirk Wongsopawiro and also emerged as an important factor in our review of studies for the article in *Studies in Science Education*. We began to plan the writing of a paper on a revised IMTPG, however, around that time David became ill. Tragically, he passed away early 2020. Hilary and I are still keen to do further work on the model and we are currently working with colleagues in Germany to review how the model has been used in the research literature. The aim is to publish this review to celebrate the 20th anniversary of the IMTPG.

Professional Learning of Science Teachers[1]

Jan H. van Driel

Introduction

Professional learning of teachers, both pre-service and in-service, is a complex process. Only recently research has begun to demonstrate that what and how teachers learn from teacher education and professional development programmes has an impact on whether and how they change their knowledge and practice (Desimone et al., 2002; Fishman et al., 2003). Studies on teachers' professional learning have shown that high-quality professional development programmes must entail a form of inquiry (Little, 2001; Lotter et al., 2006) that enables (pre-service and in-service) teachers to actively construct knowledge through practice and reflection (Guskey, 1986, 2002; Schön, 1983). Moreover, it has become clear that multiple strategies are necessary to effectively promote teacher learning. Several review studies revealed that for strategies aimed at promoting professional learning of teachers to be successful, the following elements are important: (a) an explicit focus on teachers' initial knowledge, beliefs and concerns, (b) opportunities for teachers to experiment in their own practice, (c) collegial co-operation or exchange among teachers and (d) sufficient time for changes to occur (e.g. Bell & Gilbert, 1996; Garet et al., 2001; Hawley & Valli, 1999; Hewson, 2007; Van Veen et al., 2010).

Many professional development programmes, however, have been found lacking with respect to stimulating teacher learning (Ball & Cohen, 1999; Little, 2001), since they neglect the knowledge, beliefs and attitudes that these teachers bring into the programme (Van Driel et al., 2001) and also ignore the context in which teachers work (Kennedy, 2010). Furthermore, many professional learning programmes also fail to take into account existing knowledge about how teachers learn (cf. Ball & Cohen, 1999; Borko, 2004).

In this chapter, I will first discuss models of professional learning from the literature, selecting one that will serve as a framework for the following sections. Using this framework, I will then concentrate on the learning of pre-service science teachers, in the context of initial science teacher education, in particular by discussing a case study from my own work. Next, I will use the same framework to focus on professional learning of in-service science teachers, in the context of programmes of continuing professional development, discussing another case study from my own research.

Models for Teacher Professional Learning

There is a general agreement in the educational research community about the importance of teachers' professional learning as one of the ways to improve education. However, there is no consensus about how such a process occurs and how it can be analysed and promoted. This may be because it was only in the last decades that the nature and development of teachers' knowledge started to be understood by educational researchers (Munby et al., 2001).

A major question in teacher learning literature relates to the issue of whether and how changes in knowledge, beliefs and attitudes relate to changes in teacher practice (Wubbels, 1992; Richardson & Placier, 2001). For a long time, it has been widely assumed that when teachers change their knowledge, beliefs and attitudes on, for example, new instructional methods, their teaching practice will improve and accordingly result in better student outcomes. Since the middle of the 1980s, ideas about teacher change have been more focused on learning through reflection on one's own practice (Guskey, 1986, 2002; Korthagen et al., 2001). Guskey (1986), for example, proposed a linear model of teacher change, assuming that a professional development programme causes changes in teachers' practice, which in turn lead to changes in students' learning and therefore result in changes in teachers' knowledge, beliefs and attitudes (see Figure 9.1).

The facilitating process here is reflection. Other researchers, however, cautioned that teacher learning is not a linear process, but covers a complex system of processes in which teachers are engaged in active and meaningful learning (Borko, 2004, Clarke & Hollingsworth, 2002; Desimone et al., 2002). In a review study, Borko (2004) proposed a non-linear model in which the programme, the teachers, the facilitators and the context in which the professional development occurs are key elements in a professional development system. Borko states that the relations between these elements have been investigated in various studies. These studies focused on explaining factors found in each element, but were not explicit about what the precise relations are between

FIGURE 9.1 A model of teacher change (Guskey, 1986)

these elements or how exactly the elements are related, thus leaving the nature of actual teacher growth processes vague.

According to Sprinthall et al. (1996), there are three main types of models for explaining teachers' development: the craft, the expert and the interactive models. The first model advocates the view that teachers develop as a result of becoming experienced teachers. In this case, knowledge emerges from classroom experiences. However, the model does not make clear how teachers produce new meanings from their experiences nor why some teachers only reproduce the same experience many times without learning from it. The expert model is focused on teachers being taught what and how to do by experts. As discussed by Clarke and Hollingsworth (2002), for a long time, changes in teachers' knowledge have been assumed to be the results of 'training', that is, of something that is done to teachers and in which they are relatively passive participants. Typically, the outcomes of such changes are generally 'measured' at the end of the training. In order to be effective, however, many researchers have recognised that such programmes should involve meaningful learning activities. This is the basis of what Sprinthall et al. (1996) characterised as the interactive model. Although programmes which are characterised as interactive present particularities concerned with how teachers' learning is both analysed and supported, they assume the occurrence of a process of changing prior knowledge with some help from experts. Within this perspective, one of the models proposed for teachers' professional growth is the Interconnected Model of Teacher Professional Growth (IMTPG; Clarke & Hollingsworth, 2002). Using empirical data on which to base their findings, this model is made up of four different domains: (1) the personal domain (PD), which is concerned with teachers' knowledge, beliefs and attitudes; (2) the external domain (ED), which is associated with external sources of information or stimuli; (3) the domain of practice (DP) which involves professional experimentation; and (4) the domain of consequence (DC), which is comprised of salient outcomes related to classroom practice (see Figure 9.2).

According to this model, teachers' professional learning is represented by changes in these four domains, through the mediating processes of 'reflection' and 'enactment' (represented as arrows linking the domains). The authors explain:

> The term 'enactment' was chosen to distinguish the translation of a belief or a pedagogical model into action from simply 'acting', on the grounds that acting occurs in the domain of practice and each action represents the enactment of something a teacher knows, believes or has experienced. (Clarke & Hollingsworth, 2002, p. 951)

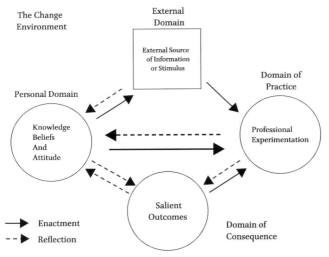

FIGURE 9.2   The interconnected model of teacher professional growth
            (Clarke & Hollingsworth, 2002, p. 951)

The term 'reflection' refers to 'a set of mental activities to construct or reconstruct experiences, problems, knowledge or insights' (Zwart et al., 2007, p. 169), for example, when a science teacher realises that an analogy to explain the model of an atom enables the students to visualise the model so that they understand the differences between the protons and the electrons. Within their model, Clarke and Hollingsworth distinguish different types of pathways for teacher learning, that is, a 'change sequence' or a 'growth network'. Change sequences occur when a change in one domain leads to a change in another, supported by enactive or reflective links; a growth network refers to a more complex and ongoing change process in more than one domain. The multiplicity of possible pathways between the domains reflects the non-linearity and the complexity of teachers' professional development. In terms of the development of teachers' professional knowledge, the authors assert that

> teacher growth becomes a process of the construction of a variety of knowledge types (content knowledge, pedagogical knowledge and pedagogical content knowledge) by individual teachers in response to their participation in the experiences provided by the professional development programme and through their participation in the classroom. (Clarke & Hollingsworth, 2002, p. 955)

In the next section, the Interconnected Model of Teacher Professional Growth will be used as a framework to study the professional learning of pre-service science teachers.

Pre-service Science Teachers' Learning

The Curriculum for Science Teacher Education
Most programmes for science teacher preparation around the world recognise the importance of subject matter knowledge, general pedagogical knowledge and pedagogical content knowledge in preparing high-quality science teachers (Van Driel & Abell, 2010). Thus, these programmes include recognisable and common components to build these knowledge bases: liberal arts courses, science content courses, general pedagogy courses (e.g., educational psychology, classroom management, educational history and philosophy) and subject-specific teaching and learning courses (called 'methods courses' in the USA and an equivalent of 'subject matter for teaching' in Europe, e.g., 'Fachdidaktik' in Germany or 'didactique disciplinaire' in France). Most programmes also value the authority of learning from experience (Russell & Martin, 2007) and thus include significant supervised field experiences in school classrooms. Programmes vary widely in terms of the relative emphasis placed on these components, on programme length and on academic level. As an example, in the Netherlands, a 4-year programme at college level ('Hogeschool', or University of Applied Sciences) prepares science teachers for the lower grades of secondary education (students aged 11–14), whereas science teacher preparation for upper secondary education (students aged 15–18) is a 1-year programme either within or after a 5-year master's programme at university. Recently, countries suffering from science teacher shortages, such as the USA, the UK and the Netherlands, have seen the advent of relatively short post-baccalaureate alternative certification programmes that attract mid-career individuals into the teaching profession.

The enactment of these components is influenced by the philosophical orientation of the teacher preparation programme. Researchers have proposed different ways to categorise the purposes and goals for science education. For example, Roberts (1988) defined various curriculum emphases in science education, including providing a solid foundation in science, preparing students for the next grade level, science skills development and helping students generate everyday explanations. Such classification schemes can help us think about the curriculum of science teacher education as well. For example, science teacher preparation programmes of the past focused on preparing teachers as technicians capable of implementing specific strategies (e.g., wait time, cooperative groups). Recent views of science teacher education recognise the importance of challenging future teachers' prior knowledge and beliefs and helping them see viable alternatives to transmission-oriented science teaching. Russell and Martin (2007) called this orientation to science teacher education 'teaching for conceptual change'. Science teacher education curricula that follow a conceptual change orientation are aimed at helping future teachers reflect on practice and make decisions grounded in student learning.

An Empirical Study on Pre-service Teachers' Learning

Whereas the 'technical' approach to science teacher education referred to above often resulted in teachers strictly following their textbooks and focusing on 'teaching for the test', recent programmes for science teacher education often aim at preparing science teachers to design and test curricular materials. An example of a study in the context of such a programme was conducted in the Netherlands (Justi & Van Driel, 2006). In this study, the Interconnected Model of Teacher Professional Growth (IMTPG) was chosen as the framework for the design of a part of the teacher education programme, which was aimed at the development of pre-service teachers' knowledge and practice about models and modelling in science. In this context, the pre-service teachers conducted a project during which they developed and tested curricular materials focusing on models and modelling, in particular, about states of matter and phase transitions and about the particulate nature of matter. In this study, the IMTPG was also used as a framework for analysing the data. The study was guided by the following questions:

1. How does the 'external domain' contribute to the development of pre-service teachers' content knowledge, curricular knowledge and pedagogical content knowledge (PCK) on models and modelling?
2. How do specific aspects of pre-service teachers' content knowledge, curricular knowledge and PCK on models and modelling change when they participate in the project?
3. How do pre-service teachers' changes manifest themselves in their classes?

Method

Five science teachers, who were following the 1-year postgraduate teacher education programme at Leiden University, the Netherlands, voluntarily participated in this research. Three were male and two were female. Before entering this programme, the participants had obtained master's degrees in chemistry or physics. The programme prepared them to teach at the level of upper secondary education (students aged 15–18). Below, the teachers are identified by the use of codes (T1, T2, etc.).

In order to characterise teachers' initial knowledge on models and modelling, they answered the written questionnaire VOMM C (Views on Models and Modelling, version C; Justi & Gilbert, 2003) and were interviewed. They then took part in four meetings of 3 h each that were held over a period of 6 weeks.

During these meetings, they were involved in learning activities concerned with all the main aspects that might be part of their knowledge on models and modelling (e.g., the nature and uses of models in science, the production and use of various sorts of teaching models [two-dimensional, three-dimensional and computerised models], the nature and importance of the modelling process in science and in science education). These activities were explicitly related to teachers' practice (for instance, by analysing pictures – two-dimensional models – provided by textbooks), to involve them in thinking about new aspects from their existing knowledge, to consider them as learners during the discussion and, simultaneously, to ask them to reflect on their teaching practices. This approach aimed to contribute to making their learning more meaningful (Borko & Putnam, 1996).

Next, the teachers chose one of the aspects of models and modelling that was discussed in the meetings as the basis of a research and development project that they conducted in their own classes. For this purpose, they designed a lesson series that they conducted in a particular class. To support their project, an extra meeting focusing on methodological aspects was organised. Before the teachers actually conducted their project, they were interviewed for a second time. As part of their projects, the teachers collected data in their own classes (for instance, threedimensional or written material produced by their students, video recordings of classroom discussions) that they analysed before writing reflective research reports about their projects. A third and final interview occurred after the presentation of their research reports during a final group meeting.

After everything that was said or written by each of the teachers during their participation in this project was transcribed or copied, the process of analysis occurred in distinct phases:

1. The categorisation of all the data collected for each teacher. This meant that their knowledge expressed in each of the data sources was identified for each of the various knowledge aspects mentioned in the research questions.
2. The analysis of each teacher's personal development, part A. This meant the reorganisation of all the data previously categorised in order to show the content knowledge, the curricular knowledge and the PCK expressed by each teacher in each of the four domains of the IMTPG.
3. The analysis of each teacher's personal development, part B. For each category of teachers' knowledge, this meant the characterisation of the relationships between the four domains of the IMTPG.
4. The representation of the relationships according to the pictorial representation of the IMTPG. For each teacher, the relationships established

between the four domains in relation to each of the knowledge aspects were represented in a summarised picture of the IMTPG, which was then classified in terms of either a change sequence or a growth network (see below).

In order to assure the internal validity of the data analysis, some of the phases were conducted independently by the two researchers (Cohen et al., 2000). The results obtained by each of them were compared. Whenever there was a difference in the initial categorisation, it was discussed in order to reach agreement.

Results

In analysing the pictorial representations of the IMTPG, the complexity of these representations was assessed. A change sequence was characterised by the establishment of one or two relationships between different domains for a given aspect of teachers' knowledge, what we interpreted as a superficial change in teachers' knowledge. On the other hand, when the pictorial representation of the IMTPG of a given aspect consisted of more than two relationships between different domains, thus meaning more complex changes in teachers' knowledge, it was identified as a growth network. The classification as change sequences or growth networks is presented in Table 9.1.

TABLE 9.1 Identification of the types of teachers' change for each of the aspects (CS change sequence, GN growth network)

Aspect		T1	T2	T3	T4	T5
Content knowledge	Models	GN	GN	GN	GN	GN
	Modelling process	GN	GN	CS	GN	GN
Curricular knowledge	Curricular models	–	CS	CS	CS	–
	Introduction of modelling activities	GN	GN	GN	GN	CS
PCK	Teaching models – purpose of their use	GN	CS	CS	CS	CS
	Teaching models – production	GN	GN	GN	GN	CS
	Teaching models – use	GN	GN	GN	GN	CS
	Conducting of modelling activities	GN	GN	GN	GN	GN
	Students' ideas about models and modelling	GN	GN	GN	GN	GN

Table 9.1 shows that only 11 (24%) of the representations can be identified as change sequences. Most were concerned with teachers' ideas about curricular models or with teachers' PCK on the purposes of using teaching models. Nearly all other representations (32 out of 45, that is, 71%) were identified as growth networks, with several levels of complexity. For instance, the development of T4's content knowledge about models did not include any relationship with the domain of consequences, while the development of the same knowledge by T2 included relationships originating from all the domains, making evident the improvement of her personal domain.

In addition, the pictorial representations of the IMTPG were analysed in terms of the types of relationships established between different domains. Sometimes, reflective relationships dominated a teacher's growth network – as occurred in the development of T1's PCK about the production of teaching models (Figure 9.3).

T1 commented on the production of teaching models in her classes and reflected on this experience at different levels, e.g., by emphasising aspects that she had never paid attention to before and by considering students' current outcomes. However, as the focus of her research project was on the building of models by students, it was not possible to make other enactment relationships evident. In other cases, the teacher's growth networks were mainly built from enactment relationships – as occurred in the development of T3's PCK about

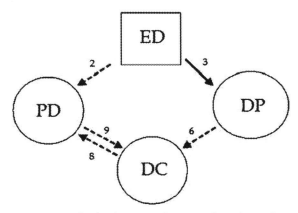

FIGURE 9.3   The development of T1's PCK about the production of teaching models. Meaning of the numbers at the *arrows*: 2: Reflection on activities in the external domain, leading to changes in a teacher's knowledge. 3: Enactment of input from the external domain in a teacher's practice. 6: Activities of students and teacher in practice leading to certain outcomes. 8: Reflection of outcomes, leading to changes in a teacher's knowledge. 9: Using a teacher's knowledge to reflect on certain outcomes of teaching.

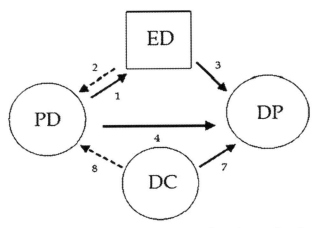

FIGURE 9.4   The development of T3's PCK about the use of teaching models. Meaning of the numbers at the arrows: 1: Using a teacher's knowledge to react on input given in the external domain. 2: Reflection on activities in the external domain, leading to changes in a teacher's knowledge. 3: Enactment of input from the external domain in teachers' practice. 4: Enactment of a teacher's knowledge in his or her practice. 7: Enacting on certain outcomes to make modifications in a teachers' practice. 8: Reflection of outcomes, leading to changes in a teacher's knowledge.

the use of teaching models (Figure 9.4). From the ideas expressed by T3 at different times, it became clear that this occurred because, in his research project, he analysed how students understood different teaching models for a given phenomenon, and from his results, he was able to both propose how he would change the activity for the following academic year and think about similar activities that could be developed for the teaching of other scientific ideas.

Conclusion and Discussion

On the basis of the findings, it was concluded that the use of the IMTPG was fruitful and productive. As for the design of the professional learning project, the meetings (the external domain) were carefully organised in such a way that these were connected both with the teachers' initial ideas (the personal domain) and with their teaching practice (domain of practice). In particular, the IMTPG informed the decision to organise the activities in the domain of practice in the form of an action research project, which stimulated pre-service teachers to experiment, in their practices, with some of the ideas that were discussed during the meetings. Asking the teachers to write a report about their action research project and to discuss their reports helped to establish connections between the domain of practice and their personal domains. As for the analysis of the teachers' knowledge growth, the use of the IMTPG was crucial. Without the IMTPG, all aspects of teachers' knowledge could have been categorised, but a framework would have been lacking to monitor and understand the development of these knowledge aspects. By identifying relationships between the four domains, the IMTPG made it possible to understand each teacher's development in a detailed way. Moreover, data analysis with the IMTPG was essential in order to support the characterisation of differences in the development of the knowledge across different teachers. It also supported the emergence of differences in the development of distinct aspects of the knowledge of a given teacher. In other words, this made possible the characterisation of the teachers' knowledge development as an idiosyncratic process. Overall, it was concluded that in the present project, the IMTPG helped to organise and to discuss data in a way that favoured the discussion of the research questions.

In the following section, I will seek to demonstrate how the IMTPG can also be useful to frame the professional learning of in-service science teachers.

In-Service Science Teachers' Learning and Curriculum Reform

Professional learning of in-service teachers is often, although not always, related to educational reform or innovation. Often, the question is how to involve teachers in these reform efforts so that the chances of a successful innovation are enhanced. For science education, in particular, 'ever since the birth of the science curricular reform movement in the late 1950s, a large portion of science teacher education has been connected in some way to attempts to introduce curricular change' (Anderson & Mitchener, 1994, p. 36). Traditionally, this process consisted, roughly, of the following steps (Van Driel et al., 2001):

1. The core elements of the innovation were defined by curriculum developers or policymakers.
2. A description was made of the teaching behaviour expected of teachers who would loyally implement the innovation or of the skills teachers should acquire.
3. A series of training sessions or supervision activities were designed, aimed at developing the desired teaching behaviour (cf. Joyce & Showers, 1980). In particular, 'single shot interventions', like in-service workshops, were used to achieve this aim.
4. Usually, the implementation was not adopted by the teachers in the manner intended, or initially observed changes in the teachers' behaviour did not persist.

Of course, not every reform effort in the past followed this scheme. There have been many attempts to improve on this outline (cf. Loucks-Horsley et al., 2003), but on the whole, it can be concluded that the role of teachers in the context of curriculum change usually has been perceived as 'executing' the innovative ideas of others (policymakers, curriculum designers, researchers and the like). Ball and Cohen (1999) have argued that the role of the government should be limited to establishing a framework for reforms (e.g., by setting standards and providing useful tools, like curricular materials). The reform of actual practice, however, should be in the hands of the professional sector.

In the research literature, there is a growing consensus that educational reform efforts are doomed to fail if the emphasis is on developing specific teaching skills, unless the teachers' cognitions, including their beliefs, intentions and attitudes, are taken into account (Haney et al., 1996). Reforms call for radical changes in teachers' knowledge and beliefs about subject matter, teaching, children and learning. The implementation of reforms can therefore be seen as essentially a matter of teacher learning (Ball & Cohen, 1999). However, many authors have pointed out that teachers' ideas about subject matter, teaching and learning do not change easily or rapidly. There are various reasons why teachers' cognitions are usually stable and why innovative ideas are not easily applied in their teaching practice. First, teachers do not tend to risk changing their own practice, which is rooted in practical knowledge built up over the course of their careers. Over the years, this knowledge has proven workable in a satisfying way. Rather, teachers tend to change their practice in a tinkering manner, picking up new materials and techniques here and there and incorporating these in their existing practice (Thompson & Zeuli, 1999). Others, such as Kennedy (2010), have explained how reform efforts tend to ignore the practicalities of working in schools and classrooms and therefore often lack ecological validity (Doyle & Ponder, 1977). Finally, although experience contributes to an increase in a teacher's practical knowledge, at the same time, the variety within this knowledge tends to decrease. This phenomenon is known as knowledge concentration: Professionals gradually feel more at home in an area that becomes smaller (Bereiter & Scardamalia, 1993). Consequently, it becomes more and more difficult for someone to move into an area with which he or she is not familiar. For these reasons, innovators often tend to consider teachers' practical knowledge conservative (cf. Tom & Valli, 1990). However, as it is the expression of what teachers really know and do, teachers' practical knowledge is a relevant source for innovators when preparing educational reform, in particular when designing professional development programmes aimed at implementing such reform.

An Empirical Study of In-Service Teachers' Learning

Although numerous studies have focused on the development of teachers' knowledge (Beijaard et al., 2000), teachers' individual professional learning processes have not been studied extensively (Zwart et al., 2007; Hashweh, 2003; Wilson & Berne, 1999).

In a recent study (Wongsopawiro, 2012), the aim was to understand what and how individual teachers learn from taking part in a professional development action research programme, specifically with respect to the development of their pedagogical content knowledge (PCK). Regarding PCK, Kind (2009) argued that studies on professional development programmes are needed in order to gain a deeper understanding of whether and how such programmes affect individual PCK development. Wongsopawiro (2012) studies this development using Clarke and Hollingsworth's IMTPG model. The research focused on identifying possible pathways of change that indicate the development of science teachers' pedagogical content knowledge, in the context of participating in a professional development programme that incorporated conducting an action research project in their classrooms. The following research question was central to the study: What are the possible pathways that lead to changes in science teachers' pedagogical content knowledge in a professional development programme?

To answer the research question, the following sub-questions were formulated:

1. What pathways of change can be identified among the participants of a professional development programme using the IMTPG model?
2. Which of the identified pathways are related to the development of science teachers' pedagogical content knowledge?
3. Which specific elements of the professional development programme contribute to development in the teachers' pedagogical content knowledge?

Method

The study was conducted in the context of a 1-year professional development programme called the Mathematics and Science Partnership (MSP) programme, which aimed at increasing teachers' professional knowledge. In this programme, teachers were encouraged to use action research as part of a professional development tool by which to improve their classroom performance. The MSP programme started with a 2-week summer session in which teachers were introduced to action research. In the first week, the teachers created an action research plan in which they selected a topic from their curriculum and considered materials and strategies to teach this topic. They attended presentations from university staff on various science and mathematics topics and best practices in education. In the second week, the teachers continued working on their plan, doing literature research in order to deepen their understanding of the subject and to find successful instructional strategies on the topic in question. The teachers were asked to reflect upon their earlier teaching of this topic and to provide reasons why they now intended to use different instructional methods. They developed research questions and identified methods by which to assess their projects. After creating lesson plans and teaching materials, they conducted their action research programme in the following school year. During that year, they had four meetings with the university staff. The academic staff acted as facilitators and peers (i.e., school colleagues) as critical friends in this professional development programme (Ponte et al., 2004).

Twelve in-service science teachers from middle and high schools in the Midwest region of the USA volunteered to participate in this study. Their schools were located in small rural communities (Table 9.2). All participating teachers were present at the 2-week summer programme and the four follow-up sessions during the school year 2005–2006. Three teachers were male, nine were female. The subjects that they taught were biology (e.g. cell structure, human body) and earth science (e.g. volcanoes, earthquakes), and in order to understand the complex pathways between the domains for each PCK component (Magnusson

TABLE 9.2   Demographics of the in-service teachers participating in the study

Teacher	Name (fictitious)	Years of experience	Subject taught	Grade level
1	Betsy	12	Deserts	8th
2	Josh	7	Atomic theory	5th
3	Carlene	8	Rocks and minerals	8th
4	Dana	17	The human body	4th
5	Diane	22	Cell structure	7th/8th
6	Donna	21	Volcanoes	7th
7	Matt	28	Photosynthesis and respiration	7th
8	Norma	3	Cell structure	7th
9	Rhonda	26	Bats	7th
10	Shania	21	Cell structure	6th
11	Stephanie	10	The human body systems	7th
12	Trisha	2	Earthquakes	4th

PROFESSIONAL LEARNING OF SCIENCE TEACHERS 279

et al., 1999), three data sources were used: (1) the teachers' action research reports, (2) the teachers' reflective journals about their professional learning processes and (3) a semi-structured interview. During the MSP programme, the teachers worked on their action research reports. As the programme continued, the teachers were able to build upon this document and make revisions. In this way, they gradually compiled their report, which also included an overview of their lesson plans and of products made by students that they collected during the year. During the entire programme, all teachers kept a personal electronic journal in which they reflected on their personal progress. Teachers were asked to reflect on the presentations by the university staff and the workshop activities during the summer course, as well as on their findings in the classroom and their action research project. At the end of the year, the teachers submitted this journal together with their action research report, as part of the evaluation process. Finally, they were interviewed about these documents, in particular about what they had learned from their action research project.

Data analysis followed a procedure similar to that used by Justi and van Driel (2006) (see Section 3.2.1). First, the data sources were explored looking for statements that were considered indicators of change in PCK. Next, these changes were examined to determine relationships between the different domains of the IMTPG. Then, pictorial representations (pictograms) were constructed for the development of each PCK component, showing relationships between the domains of the IMTPG. One pictogram for each PCK component per teacher was thus constructed, resulting in 48 pictograms. In accordance with the work of Zwart et al. (2007), the 48 pictograms were studied in order to identify particular pathways on the basis of the common entry points (starts), the sequences of changes and the end points.

Results

We found three different pathways of change for each PCK component. In this section, we discuss an example of each pathway by explaining how they were constructed and how they differed from each other. For this purpose, we focus on the PCK component *knowledge of instructional strategies*. Where necessary, we will use statements from the teachers' journals to explain the typical enactments and reflections associated with each of the pathways.

Data analyses for the PCK component *knowledge of instructional strategies* show pictograms with similar entry points but with three different pathways leading to three distinctly different learning outcomes (see Figure 9.5).

All entry points are in the external domain, where teachers reviewed the literature. The participants used the literature extensively to search for appropriate instructional strategies for their lessons. Some teachers discussed their

280　　　　　　　　　　　　　　　　　　　　　　　　　　　　　　　　CHAPTER 9

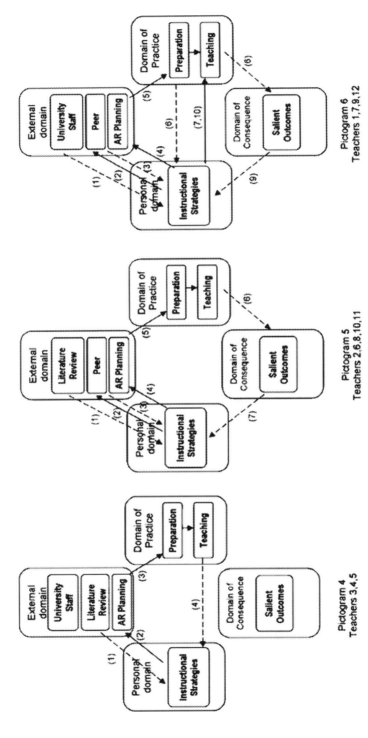

FIGURE 9.5　Pictorial representations of development of knowledge of instructional strategies

instructional strategies with their peers (pictograms 5 and 6), and others did not (pictogram 4). After planning (arrow 2), preparing (arrow 3) and conducting their lessons, pictogram 4 teachers reflected on their lessons (arrow 4). An example from Dana (teacher 4):

> I used experiments while studying the human body because I wanted my students to have as many experiences as possible. I think that they do learn better by providing different evidence themselves, not just out of a book. (pictogram 4, arrow 4; source: teacher interview)

Pictogram 5 teachers reflected on their classroom practice (arrow 6) and their classroom outcomes (arrow 7). An example of arrows 6 and 7 is as follows: After Shania (teacher 10) taught her sixth grade class about volcanoes, she told us that her students did not learn that much when they were taught in the traditional way. Now, she was convinced that her students did learn something:

> Now they remembered something ... throughout their school life, anything that has to do with cells will come back to them and I think that alone makes a lot of difference. (pictogram 5, arrows 6 and 7; source: teacher interview)

Pictogram 6 teachers continuously reflected on their instructional strategies: after presentations from the university staff (arrow 1), after consulting peers (arrow 3), after preparing lesson plans (arrow 6), and after teaching (arrow 8). Furthermore, after these teachers reflected on their classroom outcomes (arrow 9), they acted on it in order to change their classroom teaching (arrow 10). Matt's (teacher 7) example of arrows 9 and 10:

> Through using them [micro-based computer labs], I was forced to reflect on how these types of labs work with seventh graders. I saw how they impacted the learning in my room as we reviewed video tapes of students doing microcomputer-based labs (arrow 10; source: action research report) .... We also did a study last year on our pond. And it had all kinds of little spin-offs, where we wanted to go with it. So the second time I did it [the micro-based computer labs], it was actually better than the first. (arrow 11; source: teacher interview)

Conclusion and Discussion

Although we found different pathways for each teacher, we were able to categorise these pathways, based on similar entry points, similar domains and similar ending points. We found two distinct pathways that lead to changes in PCK:

pathways that include the domain of consequence (DC; see pictograms 5 and 6) and pathways without the domain of consequence (pathways in pictogram 4). We consider pathways *without* the DC to reflect 'simple growth networks', whereas pathways *including* the DC can be seen as more 'complex growth networks'. When closely examining those pathways showing a 'simple growth network', we did find changes in the different domains; however, the teachers did not demonstrate whether they learned from their classroom actions. For example, Dana (teacher 4) reflected on her knowledge of instructional strategies after preparing lesson plans, but failed to reflect on how her students perceived this new way of teaching (see pictogram 4). In the pathways with a 'complex growth network', the teachers reflected on their students' learning (a change in the domain of consequence) and were able to specify what they learned from their students. For example, Matt (teacher 7) reflected on the teaching strategy used in his classroom on the basis of student feedback and was able to argue whether the instructional strategy was effective or not (see pictogram 6). In our study, we found that teachers with a more 'complex growth network' indicated obvious changes in their pedagogical content knowledge. Teachers with a 'simple growth network' did show change, for example, in cognition, but it is doubtful whether this change affected their teaching. These findings show that reflections on classroom outcomes were important for the PCK development of these in-service teachers.

Investigation of the different entry points led us to conclude that changes in the external domain often induced major changes in the PCK found in the personal domain. 41 of the 48 entry points were located in the external domain. Fourteen entry points were linked to the university staff, 17 entry points were found when teachers used their literature review and ten were prompted by teachers participating in peer discussions. Furthermore, we noted that the university staff contributed most in helping participants define science curricula and in constructing knowledge of student understanding. The literature review and peer discussions were used extensively in the search for instructional strategies and assessment methods. It should also be noted that teachers valued the use of the educational and science literature reviews to improve their teaching. When teachers studied the literature, they were able to adapt their instructions more to current recommendations from this literature (e.g., pictograms 4 and 6). This tallies with the findings of Rhine (1998), who asserted that resources on educational research can be crucial for inservice teachers as a 'lifelong resource' for lesson planning. Teachers in this study used the literature to find information on science subjects and to learn about effective ways to teach these subjects. Then when they discussed their findings from the literature with peers, this helped them reflect on this new-found knowledge, providing a deeper understanding of their PCK (e.g., pictogram 6). In general, we found that teachers who conducted a literature review and participated in peer discussions acquired a better understanding of the use of instructional strategies and assessment methods, such as the use of micro-based computer labs to increase students' science skills and the use of students' journals to assess their students' knowledge. In the planning of professional development programmes, therefore, teachers' reading of educational research literature should not be underestimated, since it creates opportunities to construct new knowledge.

Final Remarks

Reviewing the findings of the studies in the previous sections, it may be concluded that science teachers' professional learning PCK may effectively be supported by providing opportunities to experiment with new teaching approaches in their classroom and to reflect on their experiences, both individually and collectively. This approach acknowledges that teachers, as professionals, working individually at different schools, hold the key to improving the effectiveness of science education (Bell & Gilbert, 1996). In particular, working with the IMTPG as an analytical tool proved to be helpful, giving more insight into the processes involved in professional learning. The IMTPG appears to help to make the often tacit and implicit change pathways explicit, and, furthermore, it makes it possible to indicate powerful elements within professional learning programmes. However, it should be noted that more research evidence is needed to support the claims made above. Ultimately, we need research that demonstrates how professional development programmes contribute to changes in teachers' professional knowledge and their practice, in a way that enhances student learning and appreciation of science (cf. Yoon et al., 2007; Desimone, 2009).

Acknowledgments

The author wishes to thank Dr. Rosaria Justi and Dr. Dirk Wongsopawiro for allowing me to use the results of their studies and Dr. Amanda Berry for her help with the preparation of my plenary lecture and this chapter.

Note

1 Originally published as Van Driel, J. H. (2014). Professional learning of science teachers. In C. Bruguiere, A. Tiberghien, & P. Clement (Eds.), *Topics and trends in current science education* (pp. 139–156). Reprinted, with minor edits, with permission from the publisher.

References

Anderson, R. D., & Mitchener, C. P. (1994). Research on science teacher education. In D. Gabel (Ed.), *Handbook of research on science teaching and learning* (pp. 3–44). National Association for Research in Science Teaching and National Science Teachers Association/Macmillan Publisher.

Ball, D. M., & Cohen, D. (1999). Developing practice, developing practitioners: Toward a practice-based theory of professional development. In L. Darling-Hammond & G. Sykes (Eds.), *Teaching as the learning profession: Handbook of policy and practice* (pp. 3–32). Jossey-Bass.

Beijaard, D., Verloop, N., Wubbels, T., & Feiman-Nemser, S. (2000). The professional development of teachers. In R. J. Simons, J. van de Linden, & T. Duffy (Eds.), *New learning*. Kluwer Academic.

Bell, B., & Gilbert, J. K. (1996). *Teacher development: A model from science education*. Falmer Press.

Bereiter, C., & Scardamalia, M. (1993). *Surpassing ourselves: An inquiry into the nature and implications of expertise*. Open Court.

Borko, H. (2004). Professional development and teacher learning: Mapping the terrain. *Educational Researcher, 33*(8), 3–15.

Borko, H., & Putnam, R. (1996). Learning to teach. In D. C. Berliner & R. C. Calfee (Eds.), *Handbook of educational psychology* (pp. 673–708). Macmillan.

Clarke, D., & Hollingsworth, H. (2002). Elaborating a model of teacher professional growth. *Teaching and Teacher Education, 18,* 947–967.

Cohen, L., Manion, L., & Morrison, K. (2000). *Research methods in education* (5th ed.). Routledge Falmer.

Desimone, L. M. (2009). Improving impact studies of teachers' professional development: Toward better conceptualizations and measures. *Educational Researcher, 38,* 181–199.

Desimone, L. M., Porter, A. C., Garet, M., Yoon, K. S., & Birman, B. (2002). Does professional development change teachers' instruction? Results from a three-year study. *Educational Evaluation and Policy Analysis, 24,* 81–112.

Doyle, W., & Ponder, G. A. (1977). The practicality ethic in teacher decision-making. *Interchange, 3,* 1–25.

Fishman, B. J., Marx, R. W., Best, S., & Tal, R. T. (2003). Linking teacher and student learning to improve professional development in systemic reform. *Teaching and Teacher Education, 19,* 643–658.

Garet, M., Porter, A., Desimone, L., Birman, B., & Yoon, K. S. (2001). What makes professional development effective? Results from a national sample of teachers. *American Education Research Journal, 38,* 915–945.

Guskey, T. R. (1986). Staff development and the process of teacher change. *Educational Researcher, 15*(5), 5–12.

Guskey, T. R. (2002). Professional development and teacher change. *Teachers and Teaching: Theory and Practice, 8,* 381–391.

Haney, J. J., Czerniak, C. M., & Lumpe, A. T. (1996). Teacher beliefs and intentions regarding the implementation of science education reform strands. *Journal of Research in Science Teaching, 33,* 971–993.

Hashweh, M. Z. (2003). Teacher accommodative change. *Teaching and Teacher Education, 19,* 421–434.

Hawley, W., & Valli, L. (1999). The essentials of effective professional development: A new consensus. In L. Darling-Hammond & G. Sykes (Eds.), *Teaching as the learning profession. Handbook of policy and practice* (pp. 127–150). Jossey-Bass.

Hewson, P. W. (2007). Teacher professional development in science. In S. Abell & N. Lederman (Eds.), *Handbook of research on science education* (pp. 1179–1203). Lawrence Erlbaum Associates.

Joyce, B., & Showers, B. (1980). Improving in-service training: The message of research. *Educational Leadership, 37,* 379–385.

Justi, R., & Gilbert, J. K. (2003, August 19–23). *Investigating teachers' ideas about models and modelling: Some issues of authenticity* [Paper presentation]. The fourth international conference of the European Science Education Research Association, Noordwijkerhout.

Justi, R., & Van Driel, J. H. (2006). The use of the IMTPG as a framework for understanding the development of science teachers' knowledge on models and modelling. *Teaching and Teacher Education, 22,* 437–450.

Kennedy, M. M. (2010). Attribution error and the quest for teacher quality. *Educational Researcher, 39,* 591–598.

Kind, V. (2009). Pedagogical content knowledge in science education: Perspectives and potential for progress. *Studies in Science Education, 45*(2), 169–204.

Korthagen, F. A. J., Kessels, J., Koster, B., Lagerwerf, B., & Wubbels, T. (2001). *Linking practice and theory: The pedagogy of realistic teacher education.* Lawrence Erlbaum Associates.

Little, J. W. (2001). Professional development in pursuit of school reform. In A. Lieberman & L. Miller (Eds.), *Teachers caught in the action: Professional development that matters* (pp. 28–44). Teachers College Press.

Lotter, C., Harwood, W. S., & Bonner, J. J. (2006). Overcoming a learning bottleneck: Inquiry professional development for secondary science teachers. *Journal of Science Teacher Education, 17,* 185–216.

Loucks-Horsley, S., Love, N., Stiles, K. E., Mundry, S., & Hewson, P. W. (2003). *Designing professional development for teachers of science and mathematics* (2nd ed.). Corwin.

Magnusson, S., Krajcik, J., & Borko, H. (1999). Nature, sources and development of pedagogical content knowledge. In J. Gess-Newsome & N. G. Lederman (Eds.), *Examining pedagogical content knowledge* (pp. 95–132). Kluwer Academic Publishers.

Munby, H., Russell, T., & Martin, A. K. (2001). Teachers' knowledge and how it develops. In V. Richardson (Ed.), *Handbook of research on teaching* (4th ed., pp. 877–904). American Educational Research Association.

Ponte, P., Ax, J., Beijaard, D., & Wubbels, T. (2004). Teachers' development of professional knowledge through action research and the facilitation of this by teacher educators. *Teaching and Teacher Education, 20,* 571–588.

Rhine, S. (1998). The role of research and teachers' knowledge base in professional development. *Educational Researcher, 27*(5), 27–31.

Richardson, V., & Placier, P. (2001). Teacher change. In V. Richardson (Ed.), *Handbook of research on teaching* (4th ed., pp. 905–947). American Educational Research Association.

Roberts, D. A. (1988). What counts as science education? In P. J. Fensham (Ed.), *Development and dilemmas in science education* (pp. 27–54). Palmer Press.

Russell, T., & Martin, A. K. (2007). Learning to teach science. In S. Abell & N. Lederman (Eds.), *Handbook of research on science education* (pp. 1151–1176). Lawrence Erlbaum Associates.

Schön, D. (1983). *The reflective practitioner: How professionals think.* Basic Books.

Sprinthall, N. A., Reiman, A. J., & Thies-Sprinthall, L. (1996). Teacher professional development. In J. Sikula, T. J. Buttery, & E. Guyton (Eds.), *Handbook of research on teacher education* (2nd ed., pp. 666–703). Macmillan.

Thompson, C. L., & Zeuli, J. S. (1999). The frame and the tapestry: Standards-based reform and professional development. In L. Darling-Hammond & G. Sykes (Eds.), *Teaching as the learning profession. Handbook of policy and practice* (pp. 341–375). Jossey-Bass.

Tom, A. R., & Valli, L. (1990). Professional knowledge for teachers. In W. R. Houston (Ed.), *Handbook of research on teacher education* (pp. 372–392). Macmillan.

Van Driel, J. H. (2014). Professional learning of science teachers. In C. Bruguiere, A. Tiberghien, & P. Clement (Eds.), *Topics and trends in current science education* (pp. 139–156). Springer.

Van Driel, J. H., & Abell, S. K. (2010). Science teacher education. In B. McGraw, P. L. Peterson, & E. Baker (Eds.), *Third international encyclopedia of education* (pp. 712–718). Elsevier.

Van Driel, J. H., Beijaard, D., & Verloop, N. (2001). Professional development and reform in science education: The role of teachers' practical knowledge. *Journal of Research in Science Teaching, 38,* 137–158.

Van Driel, J. H., Meirink, J. A., Van Veen, K., & Zwart, R. C. (2012). Current trends and missing links in studies on teacher professional development in science education:

A review of design features and quality of research. *Studies in Science Education, 48*(2), 129–160.

Van Veen, K., Zwart, R., Meirink, J., & Verloop, N. (2010). *Professional development of teachers: A review study on the effective characteristics of professional interventions of teachers* [Professionele ontwikkeling van leraren: een reviewstudie naar effectieve kenmerken van professionaliseringsinterventies van leraren]. ICLON/Expertisecentrum: Leren van Docenten.

Wilson, S. M., & Berne, J. (1999). Teacher learning and the acquisition of professional knowledge: A review of research on contemporary professional development. *Review of Research in Education, 24*, 173–209.

Wongsopawiro, D. (2012). *Examining science teachers' pedagogical content knowledge in the context of a professional development programme* [Doctoral dissertation]. Leiden University.

Wongsopawiro, D., Zwart, R. C., & Van Driel, J. H. (2016). Identifying pathways of teachers' PCK development. *Teachers and Teaching: Theory & Practice, 23*(2), 191–210.

Wubbels, T. (1992). Taking account of student teachers' preconceptions. *Teaching and Teacher Education, 8*(2), 137–150.

Yoon, K. S., Duncan, T., Lee, S. W. Y., Scarloss, B., & Shapley, K. (2007). *Reviewing the evidence on how teacher professional development affects student achievement* (Issues and answers report, REL 2007, Vol. 033). US Department of Education.

Zwart, R. C., Wubbels, T., Bergen, T. C. M., & Bolhuis, S. (2007). Experienced teacher learning within the context of reciprocal peer coaching. *Teachers and Teaching: Theory and Practice, 13*(2), 165–187.

CHAPTER 10

Attention to Intentions

How to Stimulate Strong Intentions to Change

1   How the Article Came About

As evident from the selection of articles in this volume, a lot of my research was conducted in the context of supporting teachers to teach science in ways that make it more interesting, enjoyable and accessible to students. All projects were based on the notion that it is essential to understand teachers and their contexts: What do they know, what matters to them, and what are they capable of? Aiming for teacher change or educational reform without knowing where teachers are and what drives them, is bound to be fruitless. It's like trying to reach a destination without knowing one's point of departure.

In previous chapters, I have documented the collaborations with a number of colleagues and students who shared an interest in these issues. For this last chapter, I selected an article that resulted from a long standing and ongoing collaboration with a colleague at Leiden University, Fred Janssen. Fred did his PhD in Utrecht University, in the same institute where I did mine a decade earlier. He joined Leiden University Graduate School of Teaching in 1999. As a biologist with an engineering degree, Fred brings a design perspective to his teaching and research. In addition, he has a strong interest in philosophical and psychological theories and applies these in his work (Janssen & Van Berkel, 2015). Over a period of many years, he has consistently worked towards developing a framework that supports pre-service and in-service teachers to develop, build and expand their professional repertoire to teach science in ways that engage students and foster understanding.

Over the years, Fred and I attracted six competitive research grants (totalling around € 850,000), we co-authored 20 papers and co-supervised one postdoc and five PhD students. In an article that was published in *Teachers College Record*, we introduced a bridging methodology that aims

> to connect a particular teacher's practice to a particular instructional innovation in a way that takes both the teacher and the innovation seriously, i.e., in a way that builds on the teacher's goals, knowledge, beliefs and way of working, and yet preserves the core ideas of the innovation. (Janssen, Westbroek, Doyle, & Van Driel, 2013, pp. 17–18)

By making innovations practical for teachers the likelihood of successful implementation will be increased. This article built on the seminal work of Walter Doyle (University of Arizona) on classroom ecology and teacher practicality. Walter stayed as a visiting professor at Leiden University on a number of occasions and worked closely with us on this paper. Working with Fred and Walter has broadened my horizon from a focus on teacher knowledge and beliefs to include the goals teachers have within their specific contexts, and the practical issues that enable or hinder them in achieving these goals.

Among the research funding Fred and I obtained were three scholarships for biology teachers to conduct research in biology education. These scholarships came out of a competitive scheme funded by the Dutch government to strengthen connections between educational research and practice. The scholarships enable practicing teachers to engage in research, in particular, research that is related or relevant to their teaching practice, and that can serve as input to reform their own teaching as well as that of others. The scholarship implies that teachers are released from teaching for three days per week for a period of four years. Their schools receive funding to hire a substitute teacher for this time. Universities provide supervision and an academic environment for these teacher-researchers, and work with them to disseminate the research findings. Preferably, the projects are concluded with a PhD thesis. This ongoing scheme was initiated in 2007 for a cohort of 20 science teachers and has been expanded to accommodate more and other teachers and teacher educators. It is quite a unique example of government investment in the quality of teachers and education; apart from a similar scheme in Sweden I am not aware of other countries where this kind of research funding exist.

Fred and I successfully applied in the first two rounds of the scheme and organised a selection process which led to two teachers embarking on a PhD project: Nienke Wieringa started hers in 2007 and Michiel Dam in 2008. Both Nienke and Michiel had completed their teacher education recently at Leiden University and had been teaching biology at secondary schools since then. Both their projects focused on supporting biology teachers to implement a new curriculum for grades 7–12 with an emphasis on context-based teaching and increasing student self-regulated learning. This nationwide curriculum reform was rather similar to the one in chemistry described in Chapter 7. The third scholarship was awarded in 2014 to Eveline de Boer for a project on preservice biology teachers. This will be discussed below.

Central in Nienke Wieringa's project was the design and implementation of context-based biology lessons by in-service teachers. Building on the practical knowledge framework outlined in Chapters 2 and 3, Nienke investigated how the use of personal rules-of-thumb informed the design of the context-based lessons of six biology teachers, with teaching experience ranging from 1 to 22 years. The study showed how these rules-of-thumb were often strongly associated with intended lesson outcomes and broader teaching goals. The rules-of-thumb appeared to be powerful in determining the lesson design although they sometimes conflicted with the goals and design principles related to the context-based innovation. Some teachers, for instance, opposed the use of authentic contexts to motivate their students and used other rules-of-thumb instead. In an article about this study, we related rules-of-thumb to teachers' practical knowledge. In particular, we demonstrated how these rules-of-thumb served to "integrate parts of teachers' pedagogical content knowledge that are relevant for that specific moment, those specific students, that specific topic, that specific context in which they design their lesson" (Wieringa, Janssen, & Van Driel, 2011, p. 2456).

In a later study, Nienke investigated teachers' goal systems and showed how this can help to understand teachers' interpretation and implementation of the curriculum reform. Twelve biology teachers who participated in a professional development program related to this reform took part in a so-called laddering interview to explore their personal goal system. It appeared that the central goals in each teacher's system strongly influenced the manner in which the teachers integrated the innovation in their teaching practice. Therefore, it was concluded that mapping teachers' goal systems, as a valid representation of their cognitive structure, provides information that can be used to design educational reform and professional development that takes into account teachers' ambitions and needs (Wieringa, Janssen, & Van Driel, 2013). Nienke's study was innovative through the use of frameworks and methodologies (i.e., the laddering interview) that helped me to expand my view of teachers' practical knowledge and how to study it. She completed her PhD thesis in 2018 and is currently working as a teacher educator in the Leiden University Graduate School of Teaching.

Michiel Dam's project focused on making the reform of the biology curriculum practical for teachers. In his study, Michiel drew on Walter Doyle's ideas on teacher practicality and classroom ecology. He also built on previous research that I had done on teachers' practical knowledge and beliefs in the context of innovations, in particular, the studies presented in Chapters 2 and 7 of this volume. In addition, he used the research on effective teacher professional development (see Chapter 9) to inform his approach to working with in-service biology teachers. This way, he nicely brought together, and benefitted from, a variety of sources provided by his academic environment.

2   What Is the Article About

The article describes an empirical study which applied the bridging methodology mentioned above. Bridging the gap between the rather abstract reform proposal (i.e., a revised curriculum for biology for grades 7–12) and the actual enactment in classrooms was an important motive for this study. The bridging methodology addresses the tension signalled in Chapter 2, where we advocated to respect teachers' professional expertise and existing beliefs but also cautioned to consider teachers' existing practical knowledge as 'the norm per se'. Using the Theory of Planned Behaviour (Fishbein & Ajzen, 2010) as a theoretical framework, Michiel developed an intervention which concentrates on teachers' intentions. The Theory of Planned Behaviour states that people's behaviour is based on intentions, which in turn are determined by three types of beliefs (behavioural beliefs, normative beliefs and control beliefs). According to the theory, the strength of intentions predicts the occurrence of specific behaviour.

In the paper, we argue that existing approaches to teacher professional development in the context of educational reforms tend to focus on the development of knowledge and skills but fail to pay attention to teachers' intentions to change. Therefore, we propose to target teachers' willingness rather than their ability to change: "The question should not be why teachers are not motivated for a reform but for what part of the reform they are motivated. We therefore propose a shift away from what teachers *should be* motivated for to what teachers *are* motivated for" (p. 384). Michiel developed an intervention based on the idea that implementing an innovation becomes easier and more attractive for teachers if they understand what it implies in terms of lesson design and specific teaching behaviour and if teachers can build on success experiences with aspects of the desired behaviour.

The intervention took the form of a two-hour conversation between a teacher and a facilitator (i.e., Michiel) and was called MECI: Motivating for Educational Change Interview. During the conversation, the idea of lesson segments was introduced to represent and rearrange lesson structures. Lesson segments are phases of single lessons such as explaining, reflecting, or presenting a context with a central question. Teachers' intentions to change were addressed with an open question ('What could take your regular teaching practice one step towards the goal situation?'), and teachers were asked to rate the strength of each of their intentions on a Likert scale (cf. Fishbein & Ajzen, 2010). Finally, teachers' beliefs related to their intentions were discussed to explore their attitudes and self-efficacy regarding the intended changes.

Michiel conducted a MECI with nine experienced biology teachers around the time when the new curriculum was introduced. It appeared that teachers were able to represent their current teaching practice in a sequence of lesson segments. Seeing the reform represented in lesson segments enabled them to compare their current practice with a context-based approach. When asked to recall successful teaching situations that included elements of context-based teaching, all teachers expressed benefits for their students and envisioned ways in which they could change their practice towards this approach. For instance, teachers moved the lesson segment 'application questions' from the end to the start of their lesson plans, thus making an important step towards the essence of the context-based reform. Comparing the intentions that were collected during the MECI with those that teachers had expressed in a baseline test, it was found that teachers formulated stronger and more intentions. The intentions were also more specific in their description of how to enact the context-based curriculum. We concluded that the intervention had helped teachers to understand the reform in terms of classroom practice and how it connected with their existing expertise thus guiding them towards implementation of the reform.

3 Follow Up

In the following phase of his PhD project, Michiel delivered a professional development program based on both the modular (i.e., lesson segment) and the success-oriented approach that were applied in the MECI. He supported a small group of biology teachers (n = 8) according to their individual needs, finding that they were able to change their regular teaching practice in a rather independent and step-by-step way towards the educational reform while preserving the essence of the reform. In his PhD thesis (2014), Michiel concluded that this approach had helped teachers to experience the benefits of the proposed reform in a relatively short time. The approach met Walter Doyle's practicality criteria, that is, it was *congruent* with teachers' current practice, had classroom validity enabling teachers to make sense of it (*instrumental*) and efficient for them to implement (*low cost*).

Working with Fred Janssen and co-supervising PhD students like Michiel and Nienke has led me to broaden my vision on developing teachers' expertise in the context of educational innovation. It has made clear how teachers' goal systems and the practical issues of their daily work determine to a large part what drives their behaviour and what they can be expected to change. Michiel Dam's study helped me to appreciate the Theory of Planned Behaviour as a powerful framework that connects teachers' beliefs with their actual classroom practice. Our collaboration has extended to include a project with Betsy

Davis (University of Michigan) on the use of science curriculum materials by teachers. This resulted in a jointly written article in *Studies in Science Education* that combined a review of the research literature on science curriculum materials with a self-regulation perspective to propose a mechanism to understand how science teachers interact with these materials. Ideas from previous projects (goal systems; lesson segments) were included in a framework which aims to develop targeted support for science teachers resulting in the uptake, adaptation and enactment of curriculum materials in ways that are intended, and that teachers themselves experience as an improvement of their teaching (Davis, Janssen, & Van Driel, 2016).

Although this chapter concentrates on in-service science teachers and educational reform, another strand of our collaborative work is focused on pre-service teachers. As a teacher educator who teaches biology method courses, Fred has developed a generative toolkit aimed at supporting pre-service biology teachers to develop a repertoire of adaptive teaching strategies. As in the bridging methodology, teachers' goal systems play a central role in this toolkit. The approach is described in a book chapter we wrote together (Janssen & Van Driel, 2017) and inspired the PhD project of Eveline De Boer. Eveline started her project in 2014, supported with a grant that enables teachers to do a PhD on a part-time basis. In her study, she applied some of the ideas discussed above (e.g., goal systems, building on success experiences, using lesson segments as building blocks for lesson design) to build and test an ecological professional learning model that enables pre-service biology teachers to direct their own development. In a number of studies, Eveline addressed specific aspects of the model and investigated the use of tools that support pre-service teachers' efficacy related to those aspects (e.g., their ability to generate questions about biological topics using a range of perspectives; De Boer et al., 2019).

I hope this chapter illustrates how Fred Janssen has developed a coherent and productive research program focused on understanding and supporting the self-directed development of expertise among pre-service and in-service science teachers. This program, at least in part, builds on the practical knowledge research program, initiated by Nico Verloop, that I have contributed to, but also complements and extends it with theories and concepts from a variety of source. Having contributed to and benefitted from working with Fred, I was happy that he was appointed as a full professor of science education at Leiden University in 2016, just before I left the university. Our collaboration has continued since then with a focus on joint supervision of PhD students.

Attention to Intentions – How to Stimulate Strong Intentions to Change[1]

M. Dam, F. J. J. M. Janssen and J. H. van Driel

Abstract

The implementation of educational reforms requires behavioral changes from the teachers involved. Theories on successful behavioral change prescribe the following conditions: teachers need to possess the necessary knowledge and skills, form strong positive intentions to perform the new behavior, and have a supporting environment for change. However, existing approaches to teacher professional development in the context of educational reforms are predominantly aimed at the development of knowledge and skills and at creating a supporting environment, but lack attention to teachers' intentions to change. In the study described in this article, we performed "motivating-for-educational-change" interviews (MECI) and explored the influence on teachers' intentions to change in the direction of the proposed national biology education reform, that is, the introduction of a context-based curriculum. The MECI comprised two tools: building on earlier successful experiences and using lesson segments to rearrange instructional approaches. We explored the influence of the MECI technique on the strength and specificity of participating teachers' intentions. When conducting the MECI, many participants expressed that they now realized how they had already implemented aspects of the reform in their regular instructional approaches. Furthermore, all the participants formulated stronger and more specific intentions to change their regular instructional approach towards that of the proposed reform while taking their regular instructional approach as a starting point.

Introduction

In recent years, there has been much debate on educational reforms and their implementation in secondary education. Many educational reforms have been found to cause implementation problems, and the teachers involved have questioned the value of the proposed reform for their daily practice (Fullan, 2007). Research about the implementation of educational reforms shows that teachers play a crucial role in achieving the goals of a reform (Fullan, 2007; Van Driel et al., 2001). A reform proposal can therefore only succeed if teachers expand and change their behavioral repertoire in line with the reform. However, changing teachers' regular practices and routines has proven to be very difficult. For a successful behavioral change, it is not enough to simply offer teachers new knowledge and skills; they also need to be motivated to change. Literature on behavioral change shows that people need both the ability and the willingness to change their behavior successfully (Fishbein & Ajzen, 2010). However, in current approaches to teacher professional development, there seems to be an emphasis on supporting teachers in their ability to change, whereas teachers' willingness to change receives too little attention (Borko et al., 2010).

In the study described in this article, we therefore explored teachers' willingness to change by focusing on intentions to change. We performed "motivating-for-educational-change" interviews (MECI) and explored the resulting developments in the strength and specificity of teachers' intentions to change in the direction of a context-based reform proposal. If successful in achieving strong intentions, the MECI could be a useful tool to administer at moments such as the start of a professional development program or when motivation to continue professionalization is lacking. The MECI technique was based on two approaches: (1) analysis and redesign of teaching practices by using lesson segments and (2) the use of teachers' earlier successful experiences with parts of the proposed reform. Both approaches are further elaborated in the theoretical framework. We explicitly focused on the strength and specificity of intentions, as these are found to be the closest determinants for the occurrence of new behavior (Fishbein & Ajzen, 2010). The research took place in the Netherlands, where the National Reform Committee for Biology Education proposed a context-based reform program (Boersma et al., 2007) in secondary biology education. The research question was the following: To what extent do the strength and specificity of biology teachers' intentions to implement a context-based educational reform change when teachers are subjected to a MECI and how do the two approaches in a MECI affect the outcomes?

Theoretical Framework

One of the most important factors in the success rate of any educational reform is the way in which it is implemented. Often, the goals and vision of an educational reform are formulated by a reform committee at a rather abstract level and need to find their way into day-to-day teaching practices. However, such goals and visions of educational reforms such as increased student outcomes or higher student motivation are often watered down in the process of implementation (Van den Akker, 2003). In the process of implementing a reform proposal, there are many actors. There is a vast amount of literature concerning the change of classroom practices that places teachers as "key agents" in attempts to change classroom practice (Ball & Forzani, 2009; Borko et al., 2010; Wilson, 2013). As Fullan (2007) stated: "Educational change depends on what teachers do and think-it's as simple and as complex as that" (p. 129).

In the implementation of any educational reform, it is therefore important that teachers expand their behavioral repertoire on the basis of the reform requirements. In the field of social psychology, there is a wide consensus on the conditions for effective behavioral change. Three major conditions are considered to be necessary for any new behavior to occur (Fishbein & Ajzen, 2010):

1. An individual has to have the knowledge and skills necessary to perform the new behavior.
2. The environment must support the occurrence of the behavior.
3. An individual has formed a strong positive intention to perform the new behavior.

In many of the current approaches to teacher professional development in the context of implementing educational reform, there is a strong emphasis on the first condition (Loucks-Horsley et al., 2010; Wilson, 2013). In such an approach, there is attention to the development of knowledge that teachers need to implement a reform (Borko et al., 2010). Also, in recent years, the notion has sprung up that teachers need to develop the skills necessary to be capable of implementing the change proposal (Ball & Forzani, 2009; Grossman et al., 2009). In regard to the second condition, some of the existing approaches also pay attention to the limited availability of time, possibilities, and resources that teachers have for changing their behavior (Doyle, 2006; Kennedy, 2010). However, the third condition, the formation of a strong intention to change, is explicitly lacking in many attempts to implement a reform proposal. This formation of strong intentions to change behavior, however, may well be a crucial step in the process of implementing a reform proposal into corresponding classroom behavior.

In their influential work on understanding intentions, Fishbein and Ajzen (2010) state that intentions can be defined as the readiness to perform a certain behavior or an indicator of how hard people are willing to try to perform the behavior. The stronger the intention, the more likely it is that the goal behavior will be carried out. In their theory of planned behavior, Fishbein and Ajzen (2010) state that three kinds of beliefs serve to determine the strength of an intention:

a. Behavioral beliefs: positive or negative consequences people might experience if they performed the goal behavior. Together, these beliefs are responsible for a positive or negative attitude.

b. Normative beliefs: beliefs about the approval or disapproval of important groups or persons on the execution of the goal behavior. These beliefs are responsible for the perceived social pressure to engage or not to engage in the behavior.
c. Control beliefs: factors that help or hinder the attempt to carry out the goal behavior. These beliefs constitute the perceived behavioral control and are thought to be closely related to Bandura's (1977, 1997) well-known concept of self-efficacy.

What follows from the above is that if there are many factors that hinder attempts to carry out the behavior (control beliefs), many expected disadvantages of the outcomes (behavioral beliefs), and low social support (normative beliefs), the strength of an intention will be lowered, and vice versa. Beliefs about certain goal behavior have been studied extensively in educational research (see Pajares, 1992). Such belief studies are, however, mainly focused on general educational beliefs about, e.g., teaching and learning, or teachers' epistemology (Boulton-Lewis et al., 2001; Schommer, 1990). In recent years, there has been a call for more domain-specific beliefs, belief studies that are as teachers' orientations towards specific topics (Van Driel, Bulte, & Verloop, 2007). But even in such more domain-specific belief studies, a straightforward relationship between the beliefs and the actual practice of teaching seems to be lacking (Ajzen & Fishbein, 2005; Richardson, 1996; Stipek, 2001). In the present research we propose that this gap between teachers' beliefs and concrete teaching practices can be bridged by using intentions as proposed by Fishbein and Ajzen (2010). These intentions are underpinned by beliefs (see Figure 10.1), but are also closely related to the actual behavior. In fact, the strength of intentions is known to predict the occurrence of specific behavior (Fishbein & Ajzen, 2010).

It is, however, not solely the strength of an intention that determines the likelihood of new behavior occurring. People can have strong intentions but not act on upon them (Orbell & Sheeran, 2000). In his work analyzing this discrepancy between intentions and behavior, Gollwitzer (1999) tried to narrow the gap between intentions and behavior. He found that goals formulated in intentions are more easily attained when intentions are more specific about the how, when, and where. This measure of specificity could well be the complementing factor needed to fully understand how intentions influence behavior.

The theory of planned behavior has been used extensively to predict behavior in many fields of society, such as health care (donating blood) and political behavior (voting choice) (Fishbein & Ajzen, 2010). In such research, interviews are performed that serve as a basis for questionnaires in which participants

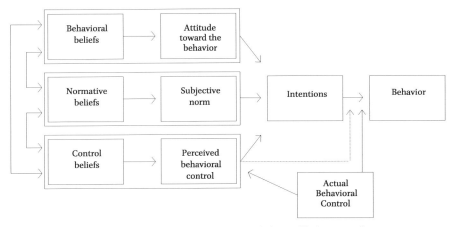

FIGURE 10.1 Graphical representation of the theory of planned behavior. Behavior is influenced by intentions, which in turn are underpinned by three categories of beliefs (Fishbein & Ajzen, 2010)

report on their beliefs to engage in specific behavior (e.g., running, attending classes, losing weight), which together predict the strength of the intention to actually perform that behavior (Fishbein & Ajzen, 2010). Although we make use of interviews and the theory of planned behavior, the purposes of interviews in this article are rather different. The interviews presented in this article are not primarily designed to collect data or report on change but to stimulate strong and specific intentions for change. A conventional interview technique that includes interview questions regarding participants' thoughts about a certain change proposal and/or questions about the extent to which a participant intends to perform a proposed change (intentions) is not suitable for a number of reasons. Primarily, it may be hard for participants to estimate how a change proposal works out in their specific situations. Next, it may also be difficult for them to estimate how their current situation relates to the proposed change. What follows from such difficulties is that for participants, it can be hard to estimate how a change proposal affects their existing beliefs, current behavior, and, in this specific study, students' behavior alike. Finally, not knowing how a change proposal works out in one's specific situation and not knowing the effects of implementing change on one's beliefs, current behavior, and student behavior are not likely to result in strong and specific intentions.

With that in mind, we can formulate certain conditions for an interview technique that motivates for change by stimulating the formation of strong and specific intentions. The first condition is that participants should be enabled to understand the proposed change, which in this study involves introducing a context-based reform, in such a manner that they understand how this works out in their specific situation, which in this study is the classroom level. If the reform is represented in the same terminology and level of abstraction of their regular classroom practice, both understanding and comparison of the proposed change and the existing situation are made possible. For this, we present the concept of lesson segments, which are phases of single lessons such as explaining, reflecting, or presenting a context. The second condition is that participants are enabled to understand the consequences of changing their existing classroom practice. For this, we ask participants to explicate previous experiences with aspects of the goal behavior. More specifically, we ask participants to think back to earlier successful experiences with the goal behavior or parts of the goal behavior. If teachers can be made aware that they already executed parts of the desired behavior successfully in earlier settings, we hypothesize that they will be able to see the positive consequences of this behavior in new settings, which in turn might affect their beliefs, leading to the formulation of strong intentions. In the next sections, we will further elaborate these conditions into two approaches used in a MECI.

Using Lesson Segments to Rearrange Instructional Approaches

From the literature, it is known that the strength of an intention to perform acertain new behavior depends for a large part on how much the individual in question values the goal situation as an improvement (Pollock, 2006). In order to judge whether a proposed goal situation is an improvement, one has to be able to compare the existing and goal situations (Simon, 1978). However, this is often not possible due to different terminology or levels of abstraction of the two situations. In educational settings, the change proposal (goal behavior) is usually formulated as a vision or rationale instead of a program for practice. Such visions conflict with the practices of many teachers, which are very specific and concrete about how to act. This situation asks for a tool in which both existing teaching practices and the proposed reform can be represented at the same level of abstraction and in the same terminology. To construct such a tool, we made use of the work of Holland (2000), who states that most, if not all, innovations can be understood as the rearrangement of the smaller parts or building blocks that make up a certain structure. Holland (2000) argues that in order to propose an innovation, one first needs to find the essential building blocks within a certain environment and, next, arrange them differently to propose innovation. Translated to education, this implies that educational innovation can be reached by rearranging the main building blocks of educational settings (Janssen et al., 2015). These building blocks should be focused on the most effective elements of education that directly influence student learning. Research by Merrill (2001) and Merrill et al. (2008) showed that these most effective parts of classroom education are the main teaching-learning activities such as presenting, practice, or giving demonstrations. In our research, we therefore determined the building blocks to be segments of lessons that constitute lessons, as teachers teach many every day. Put in specific orders, such lesson segments can then represent a variety of instructional approaches. In our research, we made use of lesson segments in the setting where teachers have to learn to shift their practices towards the reform requirements. Lesson segments could serve as a tool to (1) represent teachers' regular practices, (2) represent the change proposal at classroom level, (3) make comparison possible, and (4) facilitate teachers to recombination or adaption of the lesson segments of their regular teaching practice to change in the direction of the change proposal. This concept of lesson segments has been used in previous research by the authors and others (Dam et al., 2013; Janssen et al., 2015). Elaboration of the actual lesson segments for the present study is described in the Methods section.

Building on Earlier Successful Experiences

The second approach in the MECI is structured around the use of teachers' earlier successful experiences with the goal behavior or parts of the goal behavior. If teachers think back to successful experiences, they can see that they have already performed the goal behavior, or parts of it, successfully in the past. This implies that the use of earlier successful experiences could also help teachers to think back to the benefits of their execution of that behavior in the past, which in turn could positively influence the strength and/or specificity of their intentions and their behavioral beliefs for future behavior.

The idea of working with successful experiences is derived from the field of psychology, where Seligman and Csikszentmihalyi (2000) emphasized that "treatment is not just fixing what is broken; it is nurturing what is best" (p. 7). Central to this positive approach is helping people to use their positive qualities and strengths of character for personal growth and change. On the basis of the same idea, psychotherapists in the early 1980s worked on a new method for helping patients to tackle problems (De Shazer, 1985; Miller et al., 1996). Their approach focused directly on patients' skills and goals instead of an in-depth analysis of patients' problems. Patients first stated what goals they wished to achieve, followed by a check whether they had ever actually realized these goals in previous settings (i.e., finding positive exceptions in the past in which the desired behavior was already present). These sometimes small, positive exceptions were rephrased into solutions for the patients to solve their problems and achieve their goals. In short, this approach focuses on solutions instead of problems and aims to build on earlier successful experiences with the goal behavior, or sometimes parts thereof. Translating this approach to the field of education, Janssen, De Hullu, and Tigelaar (2008) found that preservice teachers' reflection on successful experiences led to stronger intentions and more positive beliefs than when they reflected on problematic experiences. In this study, teachers were explicitly asked to think back to earlier successful experiences with parts of the goal behavior, that is, teaching according to the context-based curriculum proposal. For this, we made use of standard solution-focused questions like: Did you ever have positive experiences with context-based education or parts of context-based education? and When you compare your regular teaching practice to context-based education, can you think of anything that could take your regular behavior one step towards context-based education?

The MECI technique thus comprised two approaches, i.e., building on successful experiences with aspects of the goal behavior and using lesson segments to rearrange lesson structures and make sense of a specific innovation. Combining these tools was hypothesized to positively influence both the strength and specificity of biology teachers' intentions to make a change towards the proposed context-based reform. Interviews in general mainly serve as a source of information and questions that are intended to be unbiased. The MECI in this study is, however, developed to affect teachers' thinking and is therefore biased.

The Introduction of a Context-Based Curriculum

This research took place in the setting of introducing a context-based curriculum proposal in secondary biology education in the Netherlands. A National Reform Committee for Biology Education (CVBO) proposed a context-based curriculum (Boersma et al., 2007) that was designed to increase the relevance and coherence of the curriculum and reduce the curriculum overload. The aim was to achieve appealing curricula in which the subject matter is taught and organized through contexts. Context-based education is characterized by the use of a context that is relevant to students so that they can feel relate to. Students are encouraged to direct their own learning process and work around a central question or problem that arises from the context, and then reflect on the outcomes and the learning process (Bennett et al., 2005, 2007; Boersma, 2011; Bulte et al., 2006). The underlying idea of this context-based curriculum is that students will learn to direct their own learning and come to see the important role of biology in society and further education. The use of a context in education is thought to increase relevance, coherence, and meaning for students (Gilbert, 2006). As the aim for contexts in the proposed reform is to be culturally defined and realistic, the reform committee has proposed three categories for these contexts: professional, academic, and the public sphere (Boersma et al., 2007). In the Netherlands, government policy states that educational policy makers can prescribe certain content and final requirements, but not specific teaching methods. Teachers in secondary education thus have a great deal of autonomy. The reform committee therefore focused on updating the biological subject matter of the curriculum and on the formulation of new objectives and final requirements. However, meeting these new objectives and requirements will inevitably have pedagogical implications for biology teachers. Bridging the gap between the rather abstract reform proposal and the actual enactment in classrooms was an important motive for this study. The MECI technique in this study was administered at the moment of the nationwide introduction of the context-based curriculum.

Methods

Selection of Participants

The introduction of a context-based curriculum with subsequent didactical implications is meant for all biology teachers at the secondary level in the Netherlands. Therefore, participants needed to be selected to vary in terms of characteristics such as teaching experience, experience with context-based education, gender, and grade level. We consulted two experts with a wide network of biology teachers, and after invitations to specific teachers were sent, six biology teachers from six different secondary schools in the west of the Netherlands enlisted for this research, which had a qualitative design using case studies. Three of these teachers had colleagues who also wanted to participate in this research, so they were also included as participants. The final nine participating teachers (five female, four male) had a wide range of teaching experience and taught upper- and/or lower-level classes in general secondary or pre-university education, and only Ryan and Howard had experience with context-based education (see Table 10.1).

Lesson Segments

The lesson segments in this study were designed as a tool to bridge the perceived gap between a teacher's regular practice and the change proposal for

TABLE 10.1   Details of participants

Participant	Age	Teaching experience (years)	Experience with context-based education (years)	Grade level	Upper/lower secondary level
Walter	40	10	0	PUE	Higher
Anne	52	4	0	GSE	Lower
Ryan	34	5	4	PUE	Higher
Kathryn	49	12	0	PUE	Higher
Howard	49	11	3	PUE	Higher
Becky	46	10	0	GSE	Lower
Mark	28	3	0	GSE	Higher
Julia	47	10	0	GSE	Higher
Ivy	42	10	0	PUE	Higher

PUE pre-university education, GSE general secondary education

biology education, that is, the introduction of a context-based curriculum. By rearranging and/or adapting one or more lesson segments, teachers were given a tool to propose a change in the direction of the proposed reform. We chose to base the lesson segments on the work of Merrill (2001), who proposed four lesson segments to design different forms of direct instruction (tell, show, ask, and do). However, we also needed to add lesson segments that enabled the design of context-based teaching practices. For this, we looked into the characteristics of context-based education, e.g., starting with a context with a central question.

The teachers' regular practice served as a starting point for change (e.g., explain-type questions to recall and/or apply-type questions). Next, the teachers were asked to propose an intention stating how they wanted to change their regular practice in the direction of the reform. For this, the lesson segments that constituted context-based education were presented to them and they were asked in what way they could rearrange or adapt the lesson segments that constitute their regular practice to approach context-based education. For the complete set of lesson segments used in this research, see Table 10.2.

Procedure
When constructing the MECI protocol, we first trialled the interviews with four secondary school biology teachers (pre-university education n = 3, general secondary education n = 1) and asked them to provide feedback on issues such

TABLE 10.2 Survey of lesson segments used in this research

Lesson segment	Definition
Orienting	Introducing the subject, formulating goals, activating prior knowledge, and planning time and activities
Testing	Assessing to what extent the learning outcomes and/or processes match the pre-set goals
Reflecting	Looking back on results or processes, finding explanations for success or failure, finding improvements
Explaining	Explaining or presenting the content
Introducing context with a central question	Introducing the context with an attendant central question or problem
Recalling and/or applying	Recalling: assigning questions or tasks for which knowledge or skills learned earlier have to be literally repeated Applying: assigning questions or tasks in which knowledge acquired earlier has to be applied in new settings
Answering questions	Answering the question or questions

as language use, practicality of the lesson segments, and utility of the MECI. Based on this, we adapted the interview protocol with regards to the order and phrasing of the questions.

Before administering the MECI, we first conducted a baseline test (t = 0) in which we introduced the participating teachers to the reform using official reports published by the reform committee. These reports are the main source of information related to this education reform for any biology teacher in the Netherlands. In this baseline test, the teachers were asked how they would naturally implement context-based education in their own teaching practice based on reading the official reports. Next, this was formulated as an intention to change. The teachers then indicated the strength of the intention on a Likert scale (1 = weak to 7 = very strong).

After this, we conducted the MECI. In the following, we will briefly explain the main steps of the protocol (for precise questioning and order, please see the Appendix). The interviewer first asked participants to describe their regular teaching practices. We then asked participants to represent the same regular teaching practice in the given lesson segments. When the meaning of a lesson segment was unclear from the list (see Table 10.2), the interviewer gave additional explanation. After this, the interviewer presented the following two representations of context-based lesson structures to the participants:

(1) context with a central question answering questions-explain and (2) context with a central question-explain-answering questions. Next, the interviewer asked questions to elicit earlier successful experiences with parts of context-based education, for example, Have you ever had positive experiences with either form of the presented sequence of context-based education or aspects of context-based education, and if so, why was this successful?

The intention to change was calculated from the answers to the following open question in the MECI: What could take your regular teaching practice one step towards the goal situation? After collecting the intentions, teachers were asked to indicate the strength of their new intentions on a Likert scale (1 = weak to 7 = very strong). This method of rating intentions was previously described by Fishbein and Ajzen (2010). The final step was to elicit specific beliefs about the new intention or intentions. We therefore posed questions on behavioral beliefs (advantages and disadvantages), normative beliefs (people that approve or disapprove), and control beliefs (enabling and hindering factors). Each MECI lasted between 1.75 and 2 hours and were recorded using voice recording technology.

Data Gathering and Analysis

To determine the development of the strength and specificity of biology teachers' intentions, we gathered several data. First, we gathered all the intentions and their strengths, both from the baseline test and those expressed during the MECI. We also listened to the recorded interviews to transcribe the exact phrasing of the intentions in order to determine the specificity of an intention. This specificity of intentions was then determined by analyzing to what extent an intention is specific about the how, when, and where (Gollwitzer, 1999). There was a clear goal for the participants, i.e., the two sequences of lesson segments that represent context-based education. This restricted the formulation of intentions, so that in fact all intentions were aimed at the goals of the context-based reform. However, as shown in the MECI protocol (Appendix, Questions 3 and 4), the questions gave the participants the possibility to individually determine the aspect or aspects of context-based education they were most motivated for.

To understand how the two approaches in a MECI affect the outcomes, we analyzed their specific roles during the interview and looked into the underlying beliefs of the intentions. We expected that earlier successful experiences helped the teachers to think back to situations where they were able to execute the required behavior and see the benefits of the goal behavior. We expected the set of lesson segments to assist the teachers in recombining and adapting their regular teaching practice in order to propose a change towards the goal situation, in this study being context-based education. On the basis of these hypothesized outcomes, we specifically looked into data from the interview recordings where the teachers spoke about (a) earlier successful experiences, (b) their regular practice and the sequence of lesson segments that represents it, (c) the rearrangement or adaptation of the sequence or content of lesson segments, and (d) beliefs about intentions. For each participant, we made a document with an overview of these data, which was then sent back to the participant for a member check to ensure internal validity (Miles & Huberman, 1994). After all the teachers had approved the documents as good representations of the interview, the first and second authors further analyzed the data. We first checked whether intentions were formulated in terms of rearranging and/or adapting lesson segments. Also, did teachers refer to specific successful experiences when formulating intentions to change? If so, were these successful experiences helpful in predicting hindering and enabling factors, advantages and disadvantages, and/or people that approve or disapprove due to the fact that they already executed the required behavior?

Results

There were several distinctive outcomes in this study. Regarding the changes in the strength and specificity of teachers' intentions, the first thing to note is that, compared to the baseline test, all the teachers scored the strength of their intentions higher when subjected to the MECI (see Table 10.3). Important here is that intentions formulated in the baseline test ($t = 0$) are often qualitatively different from those formulated within the MECI. Comparison of the intentions also showed that the teachers formulated more intentions compared to the baseline test.

A second result of the MECI technique is that it indeed resulted in intentions that are more specific than those found in the baseline test. Mark, for example, first formulated an intention in which he wanted to connect student activities to the topic within a context. During the MECI, however, he formulated an intention in which he wanted to start the lesson using a context and work from examples and movies he had already used in previous classes. Another participant, Anne, formulated the following intention in the baseline test: "I want to do something with pupils' prior knowledge by constructing something together". During the MECI, she was able to be more specific in the how: "I want to start the lessons by using a context" and "I want the pupils to be actively searching for information to answer the central question".

As to the roles of the two approaches in the MECI, i.e., building on successful experiences and using lesson segments, it seems that each functioned to

TABLE 10.3 Survey of intentions in the baseline test and the MECI

Name	Baseline test (t = 0)		Formulated in the MECI	
	Intentions	Strength	Intentions	Strength
Walter	I want to choose a subject that is spread over several chapters of the textbook and teach this in a more coherent way.	3.5	I want to start the lesson with an example or situation, which I normally plan at the end of the lesson. From this example, I will formulate central questions for the pupils. After that, I will explain the topic and give notes. With this explanation and the textbook, pupils will have to answer the central questions.	6.5
Anne	I want to do something with the pupils' prior knowledge by constructing something together.	5	I want pupils to be actively searching for information to answer the central question.	7
			I want to start the lessons by using a context.	7
Ryan	I want to be able to help students to learn specific contents.	5.5	I want the pupils to look for and find the required specific knowledge themselves on the basis of specific questions.	6
			I want to start the lesson with a context more often.	6
			I want to use more student-centered activities.	6
Kathryn	I want to start the lesson by presenting a context.	6	I want to start the lesson by presenting a context followed by a central question.	7
			I want to give pupils a more prominent role in reflecting on the lesson.	7
			I want to demonstrate first how to answer questions.	7
Howard	I want to focus the lesson on the concepts to be learned.	6	I want to use a context to motivate students for practical work in the next week.	6
			I want students to be involved in designing contexts.	6.5

(cont.)

TABLE 10.3 Survey of intentions in the baseline test and the MECI. (*cont.*)

Name	Baseline test (t = 0)		Formulated in the MECI	
	Intentions	Strength	Intentions	Strength
Becky	I want to start the lesson by presenting a context.	6	I want to construct contexts from the questions that pupils asked in earlier lessons. After that, I want the pupils to answer the questions themselves.	7
Mark	I want to connect student activities to the subject within a context.	4	I want to start the lesson with a context, working from the examples and movies I normally show separately.	6
			I want to pose a central question that follows from the context and have students find the answers.	4
			I want students to work in small groups on solving the central questions.	4
Julia	None	–	I would like to start the lesson with a context, for which I will use application exercises that I normally hand out later in the lesson.	5.5
			I want to start the lesson by presenting a context, for which I will use adapted assignments that I would normally hand out after the explanation phase.	6.5
Ivy	I want to have pupils work together on a certain problem within a context.	6.5	I want the pupils to look up and find the required information themselves.	6.5

Note: Rated on a Likert scale (1 = low and 7 = high)

assist teachers in specific ways. First, teachers were indeed able to represent their regular teaching practice in a specific sequence of lesson segments, which made comparison with the sequences of context-based education possible. Such an instrumental comparison enabled the participants to realize that sometimes they had already implemented a certain part of context-based education in their regular practices. For example, the participants recognized that they already used larger examples or application exercises in which the students had to find an answer to certain problems by themselves. However, they would normally assign such exercises or tasks later on in their lessons. In this study, they arranged lesson segments differently and shifted the lesson segment "context with central question" to the start of a lesson. In Julia's own words: "I would like to start the lesson with a context, for which I will use application exercises that I normally hand out later in the lesson" (Table 10.3) or Mark's words: "I want to start the lesson with a context, working from the examples and movies I normally show separately" (Table 10.3). Knowing how to design and introduce a context, even in a small variant, stimulated feelings of ability (control beliefs), as further illustrated in the case studies below. Second, teachers were also able to use the terminology of the lesson segments in formulating intentions, which implies that seeing the reform represented in lesson segments helped them to devise ways in which they could change towards the reform. Third, when asked about earlier successful experiences, all the participants were able to think back to relevant successful experiences with parts of the proposed reform. Doing so, they envisioned situations in which they had already successfully implemented parts of the reform from which they were able to predict the specific advantages and disadvantages (behavioral beliefs) of how this had worked in those situations. This also seemed to lead to high feelings of control (control beliefs), as these experiences were successful. In the remainder of this section, we will describe two cases of participating teachers in which we try to visualize the process and outcomes of the MECI technique and the way in which the teachers' intentions interrelate to certain beliefs. We selected Walter because of his interesting attitude of not seeing the benefits of the reform and Mark because he is a younger teacher who is willing but has little experience that he can draw on. Both of these participants were not previously trained or educated in introducing a context-based reform such as the one reported in this article.

The Case of Walter

Walter is a 40-year-old biology teacher with 10 years of teaching experience. He is an enthusiastic biologist with a huge private collection of bird skeletons who likes to convey his passion for biology to the students. His reasons for participation in our research were his curiosity about what the context-based reform proposal would mean for his everyday practice and the opportunity to expand his teaching repertoire in a broader sense. His most common approach to instruction is to present biological topics in a traditional classroom setting. He really feels that he has to emphasize the most important terms from the textbook and show the students how these relate together. In his lessons

(50 minutes) he regularly lectures most of the time and has the students do recall (sometimes application) exercises for the last 10 minutes of the lesson. He is not very enthusiastic about the reform proposal. In the baseline test, Walter mentioned that he had read the official reports published by the National Reform Committee and that he recognized the notion about little curricular coherence in his own teaching practice. Because of this, he formulated the following intention in the baseline test: "I want to choose a subject that is spread over several chapters of the textbook and teach this in a more coherent way". He rated the strength of this intention 3.5 [I think this scale has been sufficiently introduced previously.] In the subsequent interview, he represented his regular teaching practice in the following lesson segments: orientation-explain-reflect-recall and/or apply-answering questions.

During the MECI, the interviewer showed the context-based lesson sequences (goal situation), represented by the same set of lesson segments (see Methods section). We then asked Walter whether he had ever had a successful experience related to the goal behavior. He stated that he had already tried to engage pupils by using examples from pupils' everyday lives, for examples by presenting the ADH hormone in relation to the maximum amount of alcoholic drinks on a night out. He also had had some experience with teaching thematic units and at that time had found pupils to be active learners. However, pupils had also said to him that he could explain subjects really well and that his notes were excellent and helpful. He stressed the importance of giving notes and the central role of the textbook in his lessons. However, he also admitted that students were more engaged and concentrated more when he asked them an interesting question, for instance, about the role of the liver in the breakdown of alcohol. After reflecting on such examples, he exclaimed: "So if the reform program proposes a context to engage and motivate students to find information themselves, this means that I sometimes already apply part of the reform within my regular lessons?" On the basis of his successful experiences, he formulated the following intention to change his lesson sequence in line with context-based education: "I want to start the lesson with an example or situation, which I normally plan at the end of the lesson. From this example I will formulate central questions for the pupils. After that, I will explain the topic and give notes. With this explanation and the textbook pupils will have to answer the central questions". The strength of this intention was 6.5.

Next, we asked questions concerning his beliefs about this intention. As behavioral beliefs (advantages and disadvantages), he mentioned that he saw advantages in creating increased relevance for the students by connecting to the students' experiences in the context, in the idea that he could still explain the topic at hand before the phase of finding answers, and in the idea of being able to use students' questions in his explanation. As disadvantages, he expected a slower pace throughout the lessons and students' negative reactions to their changing roles. As normative beliefs (people that approve or disapprove), he mentioned no persons or groups in particular that he thought would approve or disapprove. As control beliefs (enabling and hindering factors), he mentioned the limiting aspects of not having enough time to let students find the necessary information themselves, the fact that not all information needed to solve a task can be found in the students' textbooks, and the fact that not all topics are suitable for starting with a context because sometimes the necessary pre-existing knowledge is lacking. Finally, he considered an enabling factor to be the fact that he already had some experience within a thematic unit in which he started the lesson series with an example from everyday life.

The Case of Mark

Mark is a 28-year-old teacher with only three years of experience who loves the interaction with students but feels that he has a lot to learn as a teacher. He was educated at the bachelor level and was teaching upper secondary level for the first year at the time of the MECI. He is very creative in finding the interesting and funny sides of biological subjects in media and books. He formulated the following intention in the baseline test: "I want to connect student activities to the subject within a context". He rated the strength of this intention 4. In the following interview, he represented his regular teaching practice in the following lesson segments: explain-test and/or reflect-recall-context with central questions-answering questions. When comparing this regular teaching practice to the sequences of context-based education, he mentioned that he sometimes used a short video or news article to let the students calm down after entering his classroom or at the end of his lessons to fill up some time. However, he did not connect these to the learning goals or the subject at hand. He also had good experiences in solving problems together with the students.

Based on these successful experiences, he formulated several intentions for the long and short term. Here, we only mention the short-term intention: "I want to start the lesson with a context, working from the examples and movies I normally show separately". He rated the strength of this intention 6. As advantages, he mentioned that he expected students to be positively surprised by starting with a context. Also, he expected students to be more motivated and actively involved in finding answers for the attendant problems and questions. Disadvantages would be his idleness – he liked the idea of being listened to – and his desire to please students in what they want. People that agree would be the school board members and his colleagues. His concerns for people who disagree relate to the parents who cannot control what is learned when he starts to teach topics outside the textbook. As an enabling factor, he mentioned that he already showed examples and movies, which means that connecting these to the subject is only a small step. Further enabling factors are his talent in designing contexts with attendant questions that are relevant to the students and his progressiveness in using ICT in the classroom. As factors that might hinder, Mark mentioned extra preparation time, the textbook with its focus on exercises to recall information, and the school climate, where in most lessons, the majority of the students are used to sitting back and listening to their teachers.

Conclusions and Implications

Professional development aimed at the implementation of an educational change proposal often focuses on the skills and knowledge that teachers need to improve and/or changes in the environment in which they work. However, formulating strong intentions to change is often not included in professional development programs (Fishbein & Ajzen, 2010). In this article, we reported on our research into the changes of teachers' intentions to change in the direction of context-based biology education when using a "motivating-for-educational-change" interview (MECI). The results show that intentions to change were positively influenced by the MECI technique. When subjected to a MECI, all participating teachers formulated intentions that were stronger than those in the baseline test (see Table 10.3). The intentions were also found to be more specific in their description of how to enact the reform, and eight out of nine teachers also formulated more intentions to change. The ninth teacher (Julia) could not think of any intention to change her teaching behavior in the baseline test, but was able to formulate in what way she wanted to change when subjected to the MECI.

Both MECI tools seem to have contributed to the results, with a partial overlap. The first tool was explicitly intended for teachers to look back on past successful teaching experiences. From the literature, we expected that successful experiences would positively influence both control and behavioral beliefs. Unfortunately, comparing beliefs with those in the baseline test was not possible, as we did not measure beliefs in the baseline test. Measuring beliefs in both phases is a recommendation for future research. However, data show that thinking back to earlier successful experiences resulted in positive beliefs about the new behavior in several ways. For example, the participants thought back to earlier successful experiences, such as working around stories from cancer patients (Ivy), to understand in what way the reform would affect both their teaching practice and their materials. The teachers also discovered personal strengths, such as talent to design relevant contexts (Mark), that they used to formulate intentions to change. Interestingly, data from the case studies also imply that this process of thinking back to earlier successful experiences for future use does not require extensive teaching experience, as not only Walter but also Mark showed his ability to do so. Thinking back to situations in which the participants already successfully enacted parts of the reform, they generally saw the direct benefits for their students (positive control beliefs) and possible ways to implement the reform (control beliefs). However, they also mentioned limiting factors (control beliefs) of the proposed reform such as extra preparation time, a lack of creativity in designing contexts, or problems with directing students towards the scheduled topic. The second tool in the MECI technique was the use of lesson segments to rearrange lesson structures. Our expectation for this tool was that it would enable teachers to better compare their regular practices with context-based education and understand how to reach that reform by rearranging and adapting their regular practices. The results show that the teachers were able to formulate an intention to change towards the reform proposal in terms of rearranging or adapting lesson segments. This is illustrated in the following intention, formulated by Anne: "I want pupils to be actively searching for information to answer the central question", whereas in the baseline test she had stated that she "wanted to do something with the pupils' prior knowledge". When asked to describe their regular practice, all participating teachers reported that they normally design a lesson with questions to recall or apply information at the end. When subjected to the MECI, eight of the nine participants in our sample extended such exercises into a context and moved that lesson segment to the start of the lesson. In this way, the participants made an important step towards the essence of the proposed reform, i.e., increasing the appeal of biology by teaching and organizing subject matter through contexts.

True and meaningful change, however, can be hard to accomplish. This is especially true for educational settings, where teachers have so many targets, responsibilities, and students and so little time, income, and mandate. As Hargreaves and Fink (2006) wrote: "Change in education is easy to propose, hard to implement, and extraordinarily difficult to sustain" (p. 6). We are aware of the limitations of this study, such as the limits to generalizability given the small sample. Also, we do not know how intentions will translate into drivers for change in practice. We focused on the formulation of strong and specific intentions because these are thought to be the closest determinants for the occurrence of new behavior (Fishbein & Ajzen, 2010). On the one hand, we think that we narrowed the gap between intentions and actual behavior by emphasizing the participants' unique and personal factors, such us thinking back to personal earlier successful experiences and understanding how a reform might work out in the participants' personal classrooms by representing the reform in the same terminology and level of abstraction as their regular practice. On the other hand, we are aware that a gap between intentions and actual behavior may occur. The participants expressed their intentions and specific behavioral, normative, and control beliefs in an interview setting where they were asked to picture their everyday classroom situations. We do not know if and how these intentions and beliefs will remain in place after the specific setting of the interview and how the participants will act upon their intentions in classroom practice. We also want to emphasize the importance of distinguishing perceived behavioral control beliefs from actual behavioral control (see Figure 10.1). The participants of this research stated their perceptions of behavioral control, but the occurrence of the actual behavior depends at least to some degree on opportunities and availability of other factors that determine the actual control, such as time, money, and cooperation with others (Fishbein & Ajzen, 2010).

Coming back to literature on educational change processes, we can now see how this study relates to what is already known about educational change processes and what it can add. In educational change processes, people who design a change proposal are often different from the ones who enact it (the teachers or practitioners). It therefore follows that, there can be rather distinct perspectives on educational change processes depending on one's position on the implementation continuum, ranging from the reformers' perspective to the teachers' perspective (Doyle & Rosemartin, 2012). On the one end of the continuum, the reformers' perspective mostly emphasizes the use of innovative procedures, new curriculum standards, or advanced instructional approaches and implies that professional development should increase teachers' capacity to use these. Research in regard to this perspective focuses on how teachers can best be trained to use the procedures and approaches associated with the reform according to their design and often sees teachers as obstacles to successful implementation (Davis & Krajcik, 2005; Remillard, 2008). The teachers' perspective of the implementation continuum, on the other hand, emphasizes teachers' professional expertise and autonomy, which may lead to creative adaptation of a reform with the risk of losing the essence. Existing approaches to reform implementation that aim to combine these two perspectives and take a mutual approach start by setting standards for the reform, followed by a check for knowledge and skills already present. Next, those that are not yet in place are offered in workshops or other training settings (Borko et al., 2010). In this study, however, we argue that such an approach needs elaboration. First, we have shown that strong intentions to implement change can be elicited by focusing not on missing knowledge or skills but on the personal strengths and successful earlier practices. The question should not be why teachers are not motivated for a reform but for what part of the reform they are motivated. We therefore propose a shift away from what teachers *should be* motivated for to what teachers *are* motivated for. Second, we propose that the concept of practicality needs more attention. Teachers have many goals and responsibilities and work in complex classroom settings where change will only be considered an improvement when it can be related to their daily teaching practices and earlier experiences. Within the MECI, we have shown that the concept of lesson segments can assist teachers in doing so.

By combining a set of lesson segments with a focus on earlier successful experiences, administering a MECI can be successful in stimulating strong and specific intentions to change in the direction of an educational change proposal. We recommend that the MECI be tested in other settings, for other reforms, and for other school subjects. Future research should also more explicitly focus on the developments of teachers' beliefs about a reform proposal. The results of this study, however, could inform both reform committees wanting to find ways in which teachers can be motivated to change and to find ways in which they can meet the new objectives and requirements. MECI can then be administered at key moments, such as the start of professional development programs, to determine for what part of a change proposal teachers are motivated. Next, teachers could start their development in the direction of the proposed reform on the basis of their specific intentions and beliefs gained through the MECI. In this way, teachers are guided by strong and specific intentions to change in the direction of a change proposal, which prevents failure of a reform's implementation (Fullan 2007).

Funding was received from the Dutch Ministry of Education, Culture and Science.

Note

1 Originally published as Dam, M., Janssen, F.J.J.M., & Van Driel, J. H. (2018). Attention to intentions – How to stimulate strong intentions to change. *Research in Science Education, 48,* 369–387. Reprinted, with minor edits, with permission from the publisher.

References

Ajzen, I., & Fishbein, M. (2005). The influence of attitudes on behavior. In D. Albarracin, B. T. Johnson, & M. P. Zanna (Eds.), *The handbook of attitudes* (pp. 173–221). Lawrence Erlbaum.

Ball, D. L., & Forzani, F. M. (2009). The work of teaching and the challenge for teacher education. *Journal of Teacher Education, 60*(5), 497–511.

Bandura, A. (1977). Self-efficacy: Toward a unifying theory of behavioural change. *Psychological Review, 84,* 191–215.

Bandura, A. (1997). *Self-efficacy: The exercise of control.* Freeman.

Bennett, J., Grasel, C., Parchmann, I., & Waddington, D. (2005). Context-based and conventional approaches to teaching chemistry: Comparing teachers. *International Journal of Science Education, 27*(13), 1521–1547.

Bennett, J., Lubben, F., & Hogarth, S. (2007). Bringing science to life: A synthesis of the research evidence on the effects of context-based and STS approaches to science teaching. *Science Education, 91*(3), 347–370.

Boersma, K. T. (2011). *Ontwerpen van op de concept-contextbenadering gebaseerd biologieonderwijs* [Designing instruction based on the concept-context approach]. NIBI.

Boersma, K. T., van Graft, M., Harteveld, A. L., de Hullu, E., Knecht-van Eekelen, A., Mazereeuw, M., et al. (2007). *Leerlijn biologie van 4 tot 18 jaar. Uitwerking van de concept-contextbenadering tot doelstellingen voor het biologieonderwijs.* CVBO.

Borko, H., Jacobs, J., & Koellner, K. (2010). Contemporary approaches to teacher professional development. In E. Bekaer, B. McGaw, & P. Peterson (Eds.), *International Encyclopedia of Education* (3 ed., pp. 548–555). Elsevier Scientific Publishers.

Boulton-Lewis, G. M., Smith, D. J. H., McCrindle, A. R., Burnett, P. C., & Campbell, K. J. (2001). Secondary teachers' conceptions of teaching and learning. *Learning and Instruction, 11*(1), 35–51.

Bulte, A. M. W., Westbroek, H. B., de Jong, O., & Pilot, A. (2006). A research approach to designing chemistry education using authentic practices as contexts. *International Journal of Science Education, 29*(9), 1063–1086.

Dam, M., Janssen, F. J. J. M., & Van Driel, J. H. (2013). Concept-context onderwijs leren ontwerpen en uitvoeren – een onderwijsvernieuwing praktisch bruikbaar maken voor docenten [Learning to design and enact context-based biology education – making an educational reform practical for teachers]. *Pedagogische Studien, 90*(2), 63–77.

Davis, E. A., Janssen, F. J. J. M., & Van Driel, J. H. (2016). Teachers and science curriculum materials: Where we are and where we need to go. *Studies in Science Education, 52*(2), 127–160.

Davis, E. A., & Krajcik, J. S. (2005). Designing educative curriculum materials to promote teacher learning. *Educational Researcher, 34*(3), 3–14.

De Boer, E., Dam, M., Janssen, F. J. J. M., & Van Driel, J. H. (2019). Perspective-based generic questions as a tool to promote student biology teacher questioning. *Research in Science Education.* doi:10.1007/s11165-019-9853-9

De Shazer, S. (1985). *Keys to solution in brief therapy.* Norton.

Doyle, W. (2006). Ecological approaches to classroom management. In C. Evertson & C. Weinstein (Eds.), *Handbook of classroom management: Research, practice and contemporary issues* (pp. 97–125). Lawrence Erlbaum.

Doyle, W., & Rosemartin, D. (2012). The ecology of curriculum enactment: Frame and tasks narratives. *Interpersonal Relationships in Education, 3*, 137–147.

Fishbein, M., & Ajzen, I. (2010). *Predicting and changing behavior: The reasoned action approach.* Psychology Press (Taylor & Francis).

Fullan, M. (2007). *The new meaning of educational change* (4th ed.). Teachers College Press.

Gilbert, J. (2006). On the nature of 'context' in chemical education. *International Journal of Science Education, 28*(9), 957–976.

Gollwitzer, P. M. (1999). Implementation intentions: Strong effects of simple plans. *American Psychologist, 54*(7), 493–503.

Grossman, P., Compton, C., Igra, D., Ronfeldt, M., Shahan, E., & Williamson, P. W. (2009). Teaching practice: A cross-professional perspective. *Teachers College Record, 111*(9), 2055–2100.

Hargreaves, A., & Fink, D. (2006). *Sustainable leadership.* Jossey-Bass.

Holland, J. H. (2000). *Emergence: From chaos to order.* Oxford University Press.

Janssen, F. J. J. M., De Hullu, E., & Tigelaar, D. (2008). Positive experiences as input for reflection by student teachers. *Teachers and Teaching: Theory and Practice, 14*(2), 115–127.

Janssen, F. J. J. M., & Van Berkel, B. (2015). Making philosophy of science education practical for science teachers. *Science & Education, 24*, 229–258.

Janssen, F. J. J. M., & Van Driel, J. H. (2017). Developing a repertoire for teaching biology. In A. Sickel & S. Witzig (Eds.), *Designing and teaching the secondary science methods course: An international perspective* (pp. 91–107). Sense Publishers.

Janssen, F. J. J. M., Grossman, P., & Westbroek, H. B. (2015). Facilitating decomposition and recomposition in practice-based teacher education: The power of modularity. *Teaching and Teacher Education, 51*, 137–146.

Janssen, F. J. J. M., Westbroek, H., Doyle, W., & Van Driel, J. H. (2013). How to make innovations practical? *Teachers College Record, 115*(7), 1–42.

Kennedy, M. M. (2010). Attribution error and the quest for teacher quality. *Educational Researcher, 39*(8), 591–598.

Loucks-Horsley, S., Stiles, K. E., Mundry, S., Love, N., & Hewson, P. W. (2010). *Designing professional development for teachers of science and mathematics* (3rd ed.). Sage.

Merrill, M. D. (2001). Components of instruction. Toward a theoretical tool for instructional design. *Instructional Science, 29*, 291–310.

Merrill, M. D., Barclay, M., & van Schaak, A. (2008). Prescriptive principles for instructional design. In J. M. Spector, M. D. Merrill, J. J. G. Van Merrienboer, & M. F. Driscoll

(Eds.), *Handbook of research on educational communications and technology* (3rd ed., pp. 173–184). Lawrence Erlbaum.

Miles, M., & Huberman, A. (1994). *Qualitative data analysis: An expanded sourcebook.* Sage.

Miller, S., Hubble, M., & Duncan, B. (Eds.). (1996). *Handbook of solution-focused brief therapy.* Josey-Bass.

Orbell, S., & Sheeran, P. (2000). Motivational and volitional processes in action initiation: A field study of the role of implementation intentions. *Journal of Applied Social Psychology, 30*(4), 780–797.

Pajares, M. F. (1992). Teachers beliefs and educational research: Cleaning up a messy construct. *Review of Educational Research, 62*(3), 307–332.

Pollock, J. L. (2006). *Thinking about acting. Logical foundations for rational decision making.* Oxford University Press.

Remillard, J. T. (2008). Considering what we know about the relationship between teachers and curriculum materials. In J. T. Remillard, B. A. Herbel-Eisenmann, & G. M. Lloyd (Eds.), *Mathematics teachers at work: Connecting curriculum materials and classroom instruction* (pp. 85–92). Routledge.

Richardson, V. (1996). The role of attitudes and beliefs in learning to teach. In J. Sikula, T. Buttery, & E. Guyton (Eds.), *Handbook of research on teacher education* (pp. 102–119). Simon & Schuster Macmillan.

Schommer, M. (1990). Effects of beliefs about the nature of knowledge on comprehension. *Journal of Educational Psychology, 82,* 498–504.

Seligman, M. E. P., & Csikszentmihalyi, M. (2000). Positive psychology: An introduction. *American Psychologist, 55*(1), 5–14.

Simon, H. A. (1978). Information processing theory of human problem solving. In W. K. Estes (Ed.), *Handbook of learning and cognitive processes* (Vol. V, pp. 271–295). Lawrence Erlbaum.

Stipek, D. J., Givvin, K. B., Salmon, J. M., & MacGyvers, V. L. (2001). Teachers' beliefs and practices related to mathematics instruction. *Teaching and Teacher Education, 17*(2), 213–226.

Van den Akker, J. (2003). Curriculum perspectives: An introduction. In J. van den Akker, W. Kuiper, & U. Hameyer (Eds.), *Curriculum landscape and trends.* Kluwer Academic Publishers.

Van Driel, J. H., Beijaard, D., & Verloop, N. (2001). Professional development and reform in science education: The role of teachers' practical knowledge. *Journal of Research in Science Teaching, 38*(2), 137–158.

Van Driel, J. H., Bulte, A. M. W., & Verloop, N. (2007). The relationships between teachers' general beliefs about teaching and learning and their domain specific curricular beliefs. *Learning and Instruction, 17*(2), 156–171.

Wieringa, N., Janssen, F. J. J. M., & Van Driel, J. H. (2011). Biology teachers designing context-based lessons for their classroom practice – The importance of rules-of-thumb. *International Journal of Science Education, 33*(17), 2437–2462.

Wieringa, N., Janssen, F. J. J. M., & Van Driel, J. H. (2013). Het gebruik van doelsystemen om de interpretatie en implementatie van concept-contextonderwijs door biologiedocenten te begrijpen [Using goal systems to understand teachers' implementation of innovations]. *Pedagogische Studiën, 90*(3), 37–55.

Wilson, S. M. (2013). Professional development for science teachers. *Science, 340*(6130), 310–313.

Appendix: The MECI protocol

Questions

1. How would you describe your regular instructional approach of a single lesson?
2. How would you represent this regular approach using the given set of lesson segments?[a]
3. How you ever had positive experiences with either form of the presented sequence of context-based Education[b] or aspects of context-based education, and if so, why was this successful?
4. When you compare your regular lesson sequence to that used in context-based education, can you think of anything that could take your own regular lesson sequence (Question 1) a step towards context-based education?
5. How would you phrase the answer to Question 4 as an intention to perform certain teaching behavior in the upcoming weeks?
6. How strong is your intention on a scale from 1 to 7? (1 = weak and 7 = strong)
7. What are the advantages of performing the intended behavior?
8. What are the disadvantages of performing the intended behavior?
9. Are there any individuals or groups that approve of performing the intended behavior?
10. Are there any individuals or groups that disapprove of performing the intended behavior?
11. What factors or circumstances would enable you to perform the intended behavior?
12. What factors or circumstances would make it difficult for you to perform the intended behavior?

a See Table 10.2
b Version A: context with attendant questions-answering questions-explain; version B: context with attendant questions-explain-answering questions

Reflection

My first experiences with educational research were in the early 1980s, almost 40 years ago. I hope that the commentaries provided in the previous chapters have illuminated my journey and clarified some of the decisions I made in terms of the topics of my studies, the theories that underpinned them and the methodologies that were applied. I am confident that I made clear how much my research trajectory has been shaped by and benefitted from working with other scholars, both senior and beginning. Two events have influenced my career path more than any other. First, a meeting with Wobbe De Vos in 1982, which resulted in my decision to conduct a study on student learning of chemical concepts as part of my Master's degree in chemistry. Wobbe's ideas about teaching and learning of chemistry were an incredible source of inspiration for this study and motivated my decision to embark on a PhD a couple of years later. If I hadn't met him, I might have become a chemistry teacher, or maybe I'd have done a PhD in chemistry, but I would have had a very different career. Second, my decision to apply for a job as assistant professor in Leiden University in 1995, and to accept Nico Verloop's offer, implied a radical shift in my research from student learning towards teacher knowledge. The fact that Nico is co-author of seven of the 10 papers that I selected for this volume, says enough. I cannot thank Nico enough for his support and mentoring over a long period of time.

Having established myself as a researcher in the area of science teacher knowledge, it became rather easy to connect with other scholars. As evidenced in this volume, meetings at international conferences often formed the starting point or catalyst of such connections. These connections have led to collaborations each of which enriched my knowledge of theoretical perspectives and extended my repertoire of methodological approaches. The same can be said of working together with colleagues such as Onno De Jong and Fred Janssen. Also, my experiences as a supervisor of PhD candidates and post-doc researchers have broadened my horizon and contributed to my own professional development as a researcher. The previous chapters contain examples of what I learned from these collaborations, and how they influenced my studies. In short, I think my research has shifted from describing and documenting aspects of teacher knowledge and beliefs, towards trying to understand how teacher knowledge and beliefs evolves and develops over time and how this development can be supported. As explained in Chapter 3, the basic idea about studying teacher practical knowledge is that it will lead to understanding what teachers do in their classrooms, and why. Recent research experiences have made me more aware of how to incorporate other factors that feed into teacher behaviour, such as their goals, values and their environment (colleagues, school context). This is where I find theories about classroom ecology, practicality and planned behaviour (see Chapter 10) to be helpful.

Ultimately, I am keen to better understand the complex interactions between what science teachers know and believe, what they do in their classrooms and how their interactions with students impact students' understanding and appreciation of science. In this context I am inspired by models that consider teacher development and student learning in relation to each other, such as the consensus models produced by the two PCK summits in 2012 and 2016 (see Chapter 8), and the Interconnected Model of Teacher Professional Growth (IMTPG; Clarke & Hollingsworth, 2002; see Chapter 9). These models have more explanatory power than older models of teacher knowledge, such as those of Shulman (1986) and Magnusson et al. (1999).

The gist of PCK research, to me, is that it helps us to understand a crucial aspect of teachers' expertise, that is, teachers' ability to recognise the ideas, motivation and learning difficulties of individual students and respond to these, both planned and on the spot, flexibly, in ways that are helpful to those students. This ability is strongly related to teachers' knowledge of the content they teach, and the various ways that this content can be understood and learned by their students. In recent years, my research in PCK has led me to develop an interest in the constructs of teacher noticing and adaptive expertise. Teacher noticing has emerged as a construct to capture the dynamic and situational aspects of teaching expertise that underlies teachers' in-the-moment teaching decisions and actions. In mathematics education research, teacher noticing has been studied to understand how teachers attend to, and make sense of, students' mathematical thinking and reasoning (Sherin, Jacobs, & Philipp, 2011). This construct has recently found its way into the science education literature. The refined consensus model of teachers' PCK (Carlson & Daehler et al., 2019) introduced the notion of 'enacted PCK' (ePCK), which represents the PCK that teachers draw on to perform teaching tasks in moments of action which require more than static, declarative knowledge. Both conceptually and methodologically, teacher noticing and enacted PCK are related, and research in these domains may benefit from each other to improve our understanding of how and why teachers make certain pedagogical decisions when they interact with students about particular subject matter. To explore the use of teacher noticing in science education research, I conducted a review study with a group of colleagues, most of whom participated in the second PCK summit. This was recently published in *Studies in Science Education* (Chan, Xu, Cooper, Berry, & Van Driel, 2021).

Adaptive expertise is a construct that emerged from studies on how experts quickly adapt to new situations and regain high-level performance. Some characteristics of adaptive expertise include highly developed meta-cognitive skills, flexibility, ability to innovate, continuous learning, risk taking and creativity (Carbonell et al., 2014). As it is essential for teachers to innovate their teaching to enhance student learning and interest, adaptive expertise has been identified as a critical component of quality teaching. In my view, it is related to teachers' ability to enact their PCK flexibly and adapt or extend it, for instance, in the context of curriculum reform. To date, however, little is known about how adaptive expertise develops among teachers. To address this gap, I worked with a group of Australian colleagues on a grant application for a project that aims to investigate the development of primary teachers' adaptive expertise in interdisciplinary mathematics and science. Specifically, we wish to explore how adaptive expertise can be fostered through classroom innovations purposefully co-constructed by teachers and researchers. This proposal has been granted an amount of nearly AUD 300,000 by the Australian Research Council, providing an exciting opportunity to conduct a study on primary teachers' adaptive expertise with a team consisting of scholars in mathematics and science education.

In the longer term, and following up on the abovementioned studies, I would love to break new ground by investigating connections between teacher learning and student learning of science. As teacher learning and student learning are typically investigated in isolation of each other, there is still little understanding of how science teachers' expertise impacts the development of student understanding and attitudes towards science, and vice versa, what and how teachers learn from the responses of their students to their teaching of science content. Specifically, I would like to study the relationships between co-occurring processes of teachers' knowledge development and student learning. A proposal for a prestigious and highly competitive scheme funded by the Australian Research Council that I submitted late 2020 was based on the assumption that incorporating student voice in the teaching and learning of science will boost the development of teachers' PCK and simultaneously empower students, thus increasing the likelihood of providing a compelling science learning experience for all students. This idea underpinned a design-based research program in which groups of science teachers, supported by a coach, plan, deliver and evaluate science units *for and with* consecutive cohorts of students (Year 7). As the start of secondary education is crucial to enhance student interest and uptake of science in later years, the project has the potential to result in improved science engagement and achievement among students and increased confidence and competence in science teachers. Although the proposal was unsuccessful in the 2020 round, I will continue to look for opportunities to do research in this area. Also, I am keen to diversify my research interest through collaborative studies on informal science learning, interdisciplinary science learning and/or STEM education, and science and gender.

Reflecting on nearly 40 years in educational research, I'd like to conclude this volume with some general remarks. Working as an academic in schools of (teacher) education, opportunities for research are not always evident. Most academics, especially early and mid-career academics, are faced with high teaching loads, which significantly reduce the time available for research. Also, funding for educational research in most countries is very hard to obtain and even if one attracts or wins it, it doesn't necessarily lead to having more time for research. I have been extremely fortunate that in the first decade that I worked at Leiden University Graduate School of Teaching (1995–2005), I was provided with a substantial amount of time to conduct research and work on my publications. Also, I was encouraged to work from home 1 or 2 days per week, which boosted my research productivity (I expect that many academics would have had a similar experience during the COVID-19 pandemic). However, there is never enough time to do as much research as you'd like to. To address this issue, I have experienced the following 'rules-of-thumb' to be very beneficial:

a. Organising research projects in a collaborative manner. Working together implies pooling time and expertise and sharing responsibilities to keep the project going and producing outputs. You can work with colleagues in your own institute, or anywhere on the planet. It's crucial to be very explicit about expectations, such as, who does what and when, and who leads the writing of particular publications?

b. Seeing PhD candidates and other research students as partners in research. Avoid seeing them just as beginners who need supervising and respect them for the knowledge and experiences they bring to their project. In education research, most PhD candidates have teaching experience which typically forms a source of expertise and motivation for their studies. For me, working with PhD candidates, and with their other supervisor(s), is one of the most exciting and rewarding aspects of academic work. Of course, PhD candidates are working towards their own thesis which – by definition – constitutes a proof of their academic abilities, but you can work with them, without taking over from them.

c. Doing research in your own (educational) practice. Most academics in education teach in programs for pre-service and in-service teachers. If you are interested, like me, in teacher knowledge and teacher learning, it makes a lot of sense to conduct studies in the cohorts that you are teaching. Obviously, you need to meet the ethical standards in your institution, and you depend on the willingness and consent of your students to participate, but this has never created barriers in my research. Not only is it efficient to research in your own practice, but also the outcomes of the research can often be used directly and immediately to improve this practice.

This volume is centred around 10 publications that I co-authored in the past 20+ years. When I was working on my PhD, there were voices saying that we should be writing a thesis based on articles for international journals, just like our colleagues in science did, rather than a monograph in Dutch. However, in those days, the late 1980s, no one did this. When I started working in Leiden University in 1995, the pressure to produce articles in international journals of good standing (i.e., indexed in the Web of Science) had increased substantially. Nico Verloop made it very clear to me from my first day in Leiden that this is what I was expected to do. At the same time, he generously offered his time and expertise and worked with me on those articles, naturally becoming a co-author in the process.

The PhD candidates in Leiden University were always clearly instructed upfront that they would work on a thesis by publications. Their articles were a core element of their research plans and formed a major part of my supervision activities. In my experience it is crucial to work this way from the start. Deciding halfway the process that maybe a thesis by publications could be a good idea, is likely to be problematic. All the PhD projects I supervised have resulted in at least one and up to five articles in international journals. Each of these articles names the PhD candidate as the first author and their supervisors as co-authors, ranked according to their specific contributions. The articles were included as chapters in their theses, typically with minor amendments or edits, accompanied with a note explaining that the chapter had been published in a particular journal, or was currently under review. Each thesis was assessed by an independent panel of examiners, regardless of the number of articles that was published at the time of submission. Acknowledging the tension between the thesis being the candidate's unique and individual work and the fact that the articles were jointly produced with supervisors, I am convinced of the benefits of this approach to PhD studies in education. The candidate graduates with a set of articles that will actually be read by colleagues in the field (who ever reads a traditional thesis, apart from the examiners?) and positions them well for an academic career, if that is what they aspire to. At the same time, the supervisors and their institutes benefit from these outputs, which contribute to their productivity and status.

These days, the importance of international journal articles for individual academics (promotion, tenure, grant applications) and institutions (research assessment, international rankings) is well established across all domains of academic work. This is not the place to discuss the pros and cons of this situation, however, I would like to argue that despite the emphasis on these articles, other ways to disseminate educational research continue to be essential. In some of the commentaries in this chapter, I have highlighted how conference presentations have been instrumental to set up (international) connections, sometimes leading to joint projects and outputs. A conference presentation is also a great way to see how some of your research, even if it is in progress, resonates with colleagues and receive feedback that can be incorporated in a manuscript based on the presentation. Book chapters, although typically much less competitive than articles in high ranked journals and therefore less valued, can provide opportunities to disseminate different aspects of your research, for instance, exploring theoretical ideas or explaining the design of an innovative course. This volume contains one book chapter which I wrote to show how different studies, which were published in journal articles, could be related through the use of a particular model (IMTPG; see Chapter 9). Finally, I think it is crucial for educational researchers to publish articles in journals for teachers and policy makers, in their first language. My first article for *NVOX*, the journal of the Dutch association for science teachers, was published in 1987 and I published two papers for its Australian equivalent, *Teaching Science*, in 2020 and 2021.

This leads me to a final remark, that is, about impact of research in education. In this volume, I have often referred to numbers of citations of specific articles as an indication of impact. Of course, papers can be cited in many different ways, and may include very critical appraisals of the cited work (e.g., "we totally disagree with Van Driel et al. (1998) who asserted that PCK ..."). Unfortunately, in educational research papers, a citation is often limited to including a reference to a paper without discussing its content, which undermines the meaning of counting citations. However, the fact that a paper is cited indicates that others find it relevant enough to mention it. In referring to my own publications, I have chosen to refer to Google Scholar rather than more selective platforms, such as Web of Science. Not because higher numbers are more impressive, but because Web of Science only counts citations in selected academic outlets, whereas Google Scholar includes citations from any public source. I would argue that it is important for an article to be cited not only by fellow academics, but also in policy reports and journals for professionals. Obviously, we need to consider other measures than citations to assess the impact of educational research on the practice and policy of education.

Communicating with professionals through publications in professional journals, presentations and workshops and messages on social media helps to disseminate research, however, ultimately, the real impact of educational research should be established in the classroom. To me, that means building relationships with teachers and schools and continuing to do research *with* rather than *on* science teachers, *and* with students for that matter, to explore ways that make science teaching and learning a fascinating experience for all.

References

Carbonell, K. B., Stalmeijer, R. E., Könings, K. D., Segers, M., & Van Merriënboer, J. J. (2014). How experts deal with novel situations: A review of adaptive expertise. *Educational Research Review*, *12*, 14–29.

Carlson, J., Daehler, K. R., Alonzo, A. C., Barendsen, E., Berry, A., Borowski, A., Carpendale, J., Chan, K. K. H., Cooper, R., Friedrichsen, P., Gess-Newsome, J., Henze-Rietveld, I., Hume, A., Kirschner, S., Liepertz, S., Loughran, J., Mavhunga, E., Neumann, K., Nilsson, P., Park, S., Rollnick, M., Sickel, A., Schneider, R. M., Suh, J. K., Van Driel, J., & Wilson, C. D. (2019). The Refined Consensus Model of pedagogical content knowledge in science education. In A. Hume, R. Cooper, & A. Borowski (Eds.), *Repositioning pedagogical content knowledge in teachers' knowledge for teaching science* (pp. 77–92). Springer.

Chan, K. K. H., Xu, L., Cooper, R., Berry, A., & Van Driel, J. H. (2021). Teacher noticing in science education: Do you see what I see? *Studies in Science Education*, *57*(1), 1–44.

Clark, C. M., & Peterson, P. L. (1986). Teachers' thought processes. In M. C. Wittrock (Ed.), *Handbook of research on teaching* (3rd ed., pp. 255–296). Macmillan.

Magnusson, S., Krajcik, J., & Borko, H. (1999). Nature, sources and development of pedagogical content knowledge for science teaching. In J. Gess-Newsome & N. G. Lederman (Eds.), *Examining pedagogical content knowledge* (pp. 95–132). Kluwer.

Sherin, M. G., Jacobs, V. R., & Philipp, R. A. (2011). *Mathematics teacher noticing: Seeing through teachers' eyes*. Routledge.

Shulman, L. S. (1986). Those who understand: Knowledge growth in teaching. *Educational Researcher*, *15*, 4–14.

Index

ANW (Algemene Natuurwetenschappen; General Science)   40–42, 76, 77, 103–105, 107, 125–129, 131, 134, 192, 227

chemistry education   3, 23, 88, 157, 158, 170, 190, 194, 197
context-based
    curriculum   195, 197, 220, 292, 294, 301–303
    teaching   198, 289, 292, 303

De Jong, Onno   XI, 6, 107, 108, 157, 163, 165, 197, 320
De Vos, Wobbe   XI, 1, 2, 4, 7, 102, 105, 107, 192, 193, 320

education reform/innovation   20, 38, 39, 41, 42, 57, 62, 74, 80, 92, 126, 133, 192–201, 242, 288–296, 299, 304

Henze, Ineke   XI, 6, 42, 76, 126, 130, 132, 227, 230

in-service teachers   X, 12, 14–32, 48–58, 74, 88, 113, 114, 167, 168, 193, 197, 206, 227, 249, 260, 265, 275, 277, 278, 282, 288, 289, 323

Janssen, Fred   XI, 198, 288, 292–294, 320
Justi, Rosária   XI, 6, 76, 107, 162, 260

models and modelling in science   IX, 76, 77, 102–107, 109, 110, 112–117, 120–123, 126–128, 135–137, 153, 157–164, 192, 270–272

Pedagogical Content Knowledge (PCK)   IX, X, 1, 3–7, 9–13, 15–23, 26–33, 38, 51–53, 55, 58, 59, 62, 63, 73, 74, 76, 87–89, 108, 127–134, 136–140, 143–145, 148, 150–153, 157–174, 176–180, 182–186, 227–237, 243–251, 253, 260, 261, 270–274, 277–279, 281–283, 321, 322, 325
practical knowledge   IX, 8, 38–45, 49–56, 59–61, 64, 65, 73–78, 81–84, 86, 87, 90, 91, 96, 97, 103–110, 112, 113, 121, 122, 126–131, 157, 164, 167, 185, 192, 198, 260, 261, 276, 289–291, 293, 320
pre-service teachers (PSTs)
    chemistry   108, 157, 166, 170, 184
    science   X, 6, 12–17, 31, 32, 73, 76, 136, 157–191, 242, 246, 249, 260–270, 288, 293, 301, 323
professional development   2–4, 38–41, 44, 46, 47, 60–65, 76, 78, 80, 103–105, 125, 128, 131, 152, 198, 221, 260, 261, 263, 265, 266, 268, 276–278, 283, 290–292, 294–296, 312, 314, 315, 320

teacher beliefs/belief structures   14, 193, 195, 196, 199, 206, 215, 217–219, 221, 226, 229, 247–253
teacher education   IX, 3, 8, 10, 12, 17–19, 29, 31, 32, 48, 53, 56, 74, 76, 78, 79, 81–83, 85, 92, 93, 95, 108, 157, 161–163, 165–167, 185, 190, 226, 227, 231, 233, 249, 253, 260, 269, 270, 323
teacher knowledge   3–5, 10, 19, 38, 73–97, 106, 127, 128, 132, 227, 231, 234, 246, 263, 289, 320, 321, 323

Verloop, Nico   XI, 3, 4, 7, 38, 44, 73, 78, 105–107, 109, 126, 130, 132, 162, 165, 199, 293, 320, 324

Printed in the United States
by Baker & Taylor Publisher Services